GREEN AND BLACK ARROW CANARY

BIG GAME

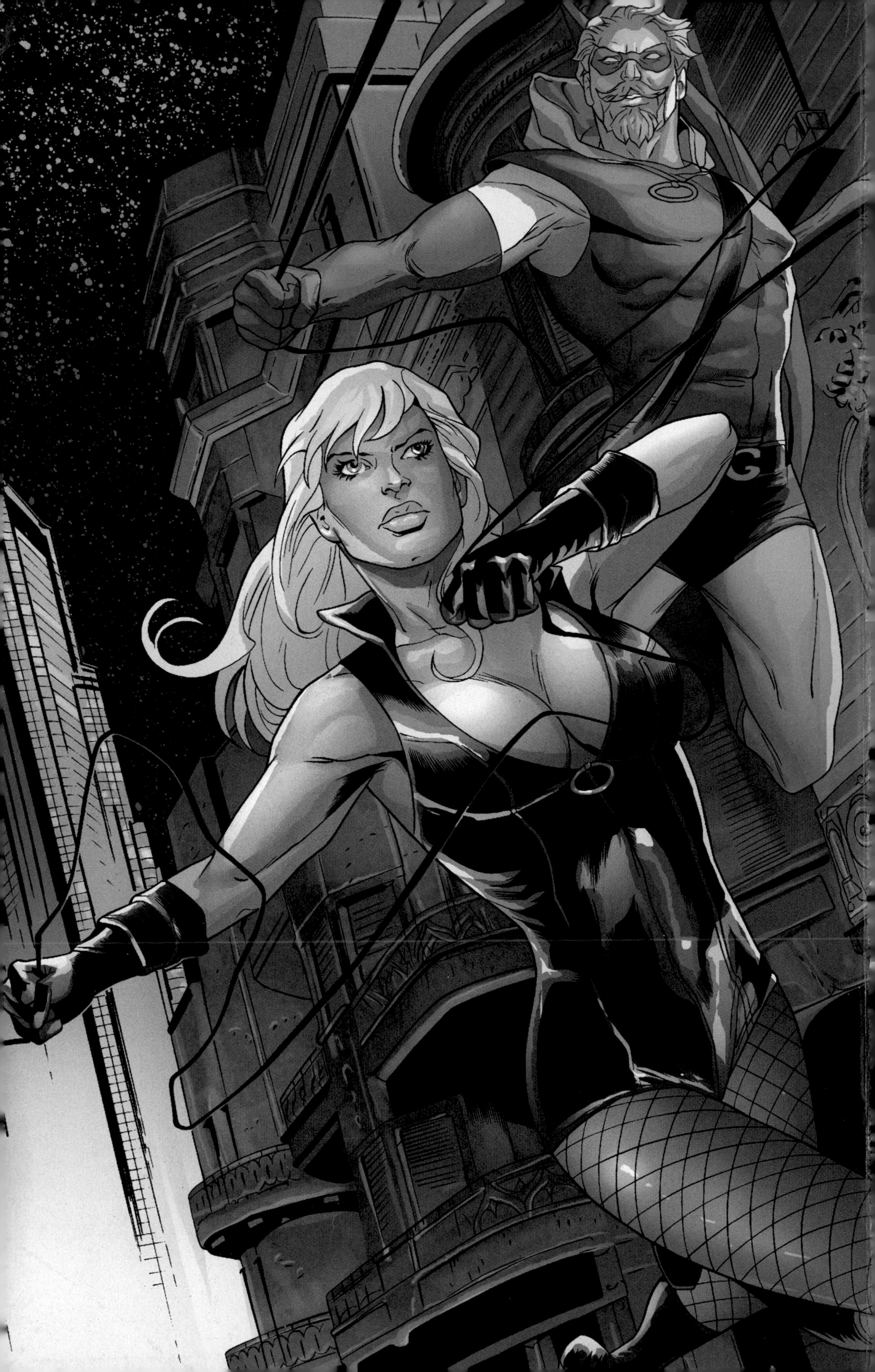

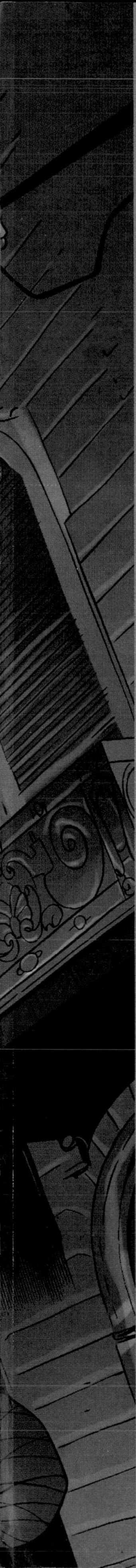

GREEN ARROW AND BLACK CANARY

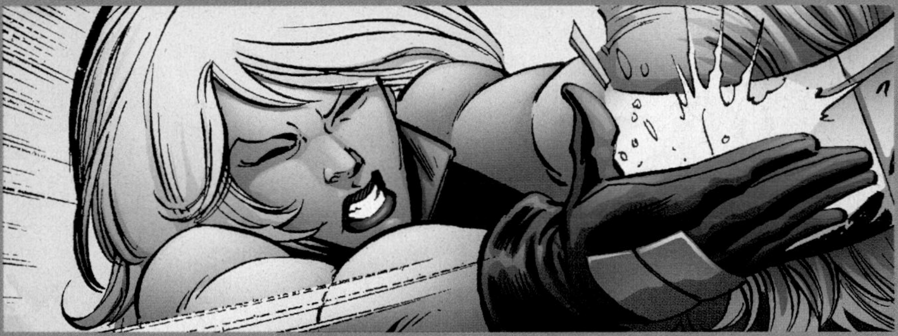

BIG GAME

Andrew Kreisberg Writer

Mike Norton / Renato Guedes Pencillers

Joe Rubinstein / Bill Sienkiewicz / José Wilson Magalhães Inkers

David Baron / David Curiel / Allen Passalaqua Colorists

Sal Cipriano / Pat Brosseau Letterers

Original series covers by **Ladrönn**

Mike Carlin Editor-original series
Rachel Gluckstern Associate Editor-original series
Bob Harras Group Editor-Collected Editions
Bob Joy Editor
Robbin Brosterman Design Director-Books

DC COMICS
Diane Nelson President
Dan DiDio and **Jim Lee** Co-Publishers
Geoff Johns Chief Creative Officer
Patrick Caldon EVP-Finance and Administration
John Rood EVP-Sales, Marketing and Business Development
Amy Genkins SVP-Business and Legal Affairs
Steve Rotterdam SVP-Sales and Marketing
John Cunningham VP-Marketing
Terri Cunningham VP-Managing Editor
Alison Gill VP-Manufacturing
David Hyde VP-Publicity
Sue Pohja VP-Book Trade Sales
Alysse Soll VP-Advertising and Custom Publishing
Bob Wayne VP-Sales
Mark Chiarello Art Director

Cover by Ladrönn

GREEN ARROW/BLACK CANARY: BIG GAME

DC Comics, 1700 Broadway, New York, NY 10019
A Warner Bros. Entertainment Company
Printed by World Color Press, Inc., Dubuque, IA USA. 5/10/10.
First printing. ISBN: 978-1-4012-2709-8

SUSTAINABLE FORESTRY INITIATIVE
Certified Chain of Custody
Promoting Sustainable Forest Management
www.sfiprogram.org

Fiber used in this product line meets the sourcing requirements of the SFI program.
www.sfiprogram.org NFS-SPICOC-C0001801

PREVIOUSLY...

Before newlyweds Green Arrow and Black Canary could go on their honeymoon, Oliver Queen's son Connor Hawke was kidnapped and almost murdered. The globe-spanning rescue mission profoundly affected Green Arrow and his sense of how far is too far.

Black Canary desperately fought to keep him from crossing a line, as the Emerald Archer began losing his grip when he nearly killed his rival archer, Merlyn.

The situation grew worse when the love-sick psychopath Cupid arrived on the scene. A young woman who was apparently saved from an abusive husband by Green Arrow, she became obsessed with the Emerald Archer and isn't keen on sharing him with anyone — even his wife. Killing several of his enemies as "gifts," her obsession with Ollie drove a wedge between Black Canary and her husband.

They desperately need to talk, but their own problems will have to wait, as all of Star City has mysteriously gone deaf. With no leads, Green Arrow and Black Canary are lost in silence as Star City is gripped in panic...

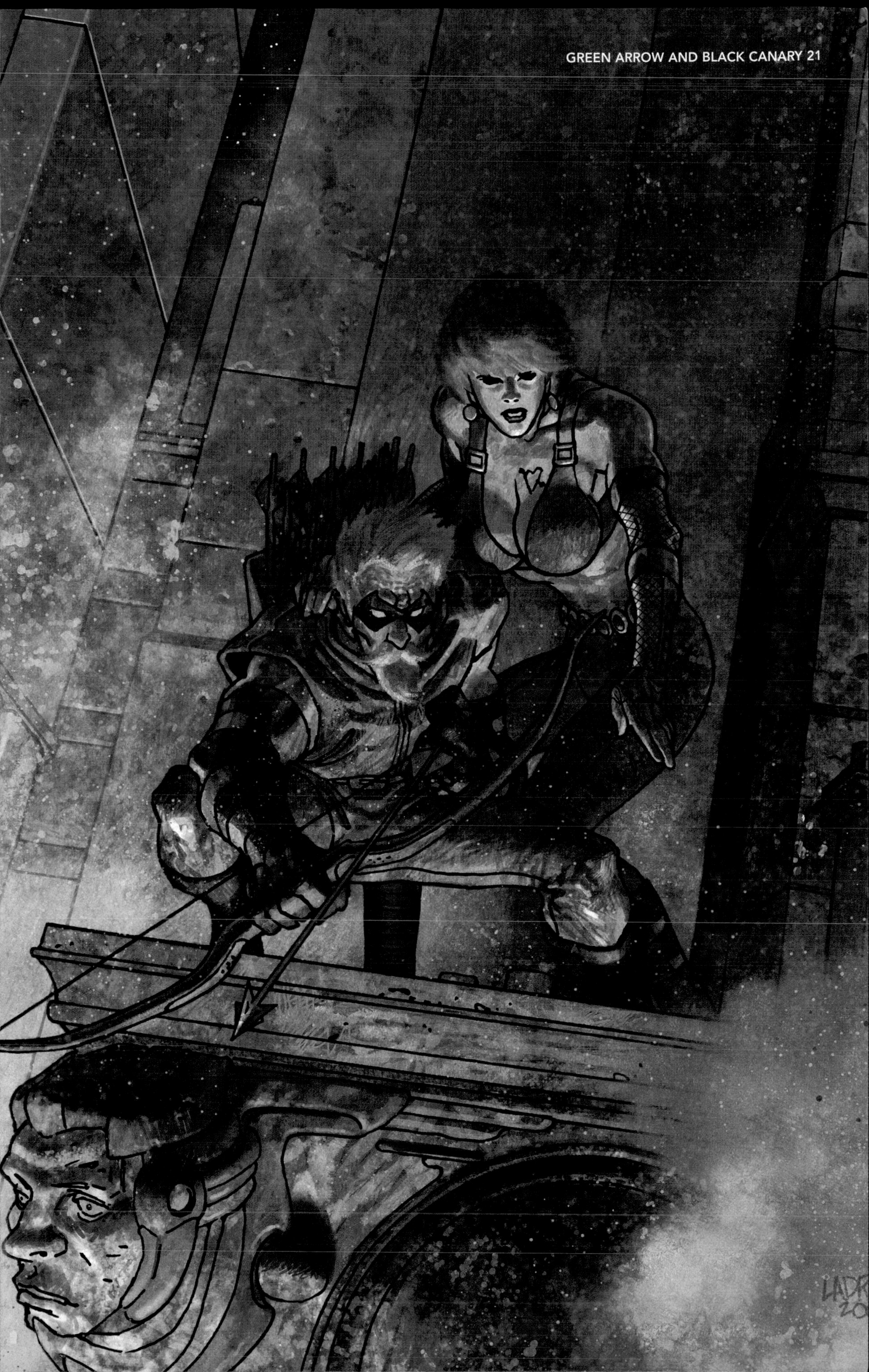

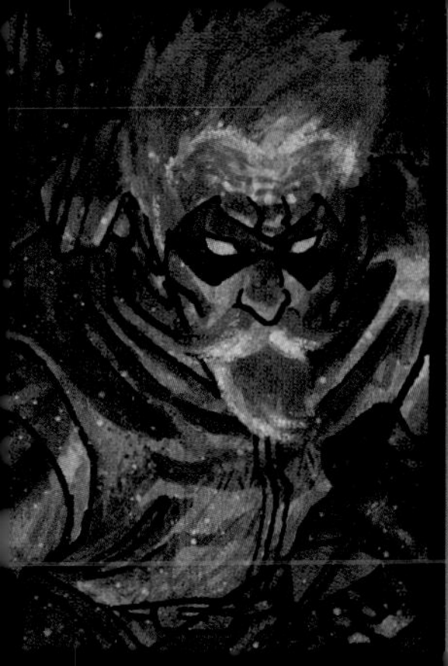

BACKGROUND NOISE

Mike Norton Penciller

Josef Rubinstein Inker

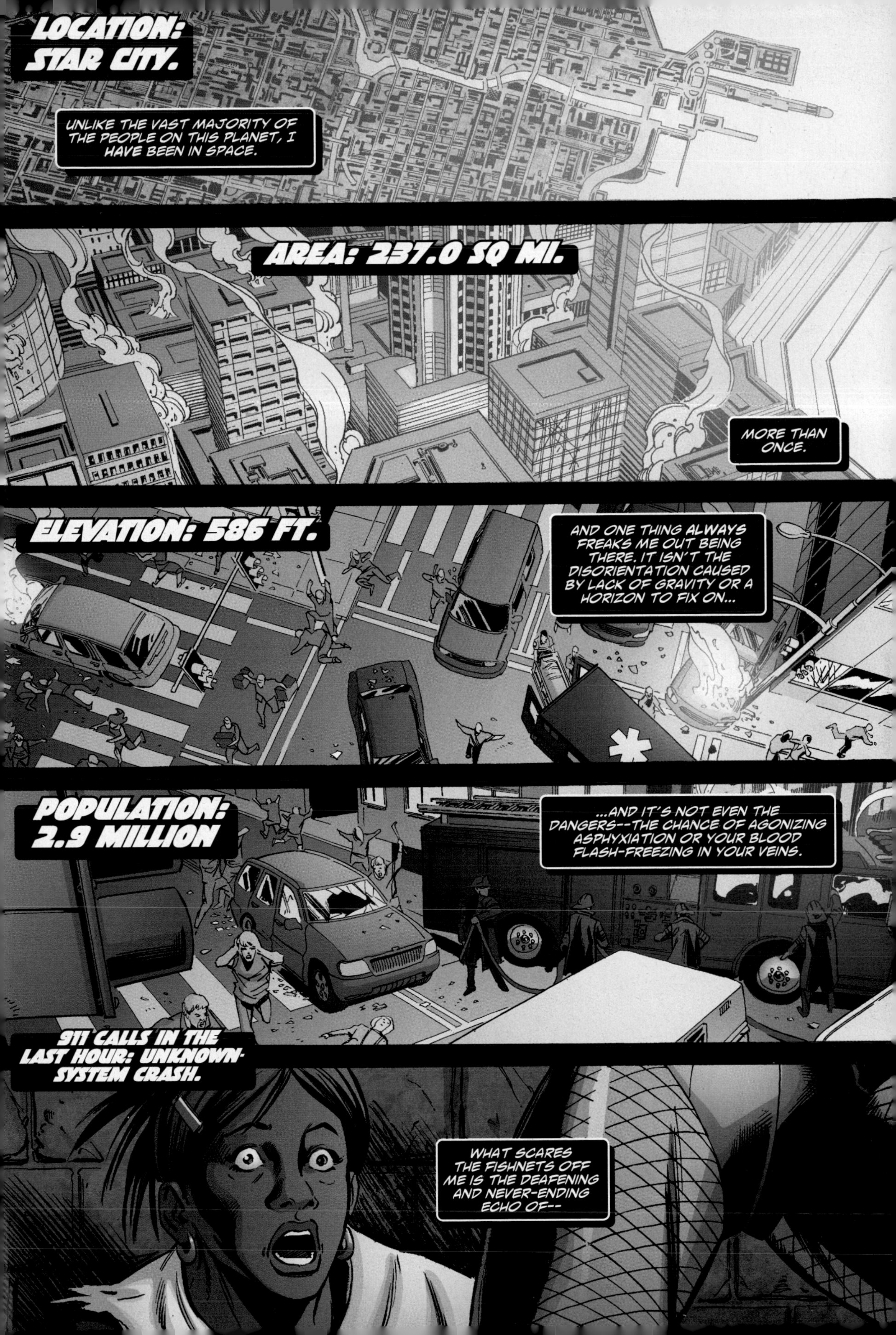
LOCATION: STAR CITY.
UNLIKE THE VAST MAJORITY OF THE PEOPLE ON THIS PLANET, I HAVE BEEN IN SPACE.
AREA: 237.0 SQ MI.
MORE THAN ONCE.
ELEVATION: 586 FT.
AND ONE THING ALWAYS FREAKS ME OUT BEING THERE. IT ISN'T THE DISORIENTATION CAUSED BY LACK OF GRAVITY OR A HORIZON TO FIX ON...
POPULATION: 2.9 MILLION
...AND IT'S NOT EVEN THE DANGERS--THE CHANCE OF AGONIZING ASPHYXIATION OR YOUR BLOOD FLASH-FREEZING IN YOUR VEINS.
911 CALLS IN THE LAST HOUR: UNKNOWN-SYSTEM CRASH.
WHAT SCARES THE FISHNETS OFF ME IS THE DEAFENING AND NEVER-ENDING ECHO OF--

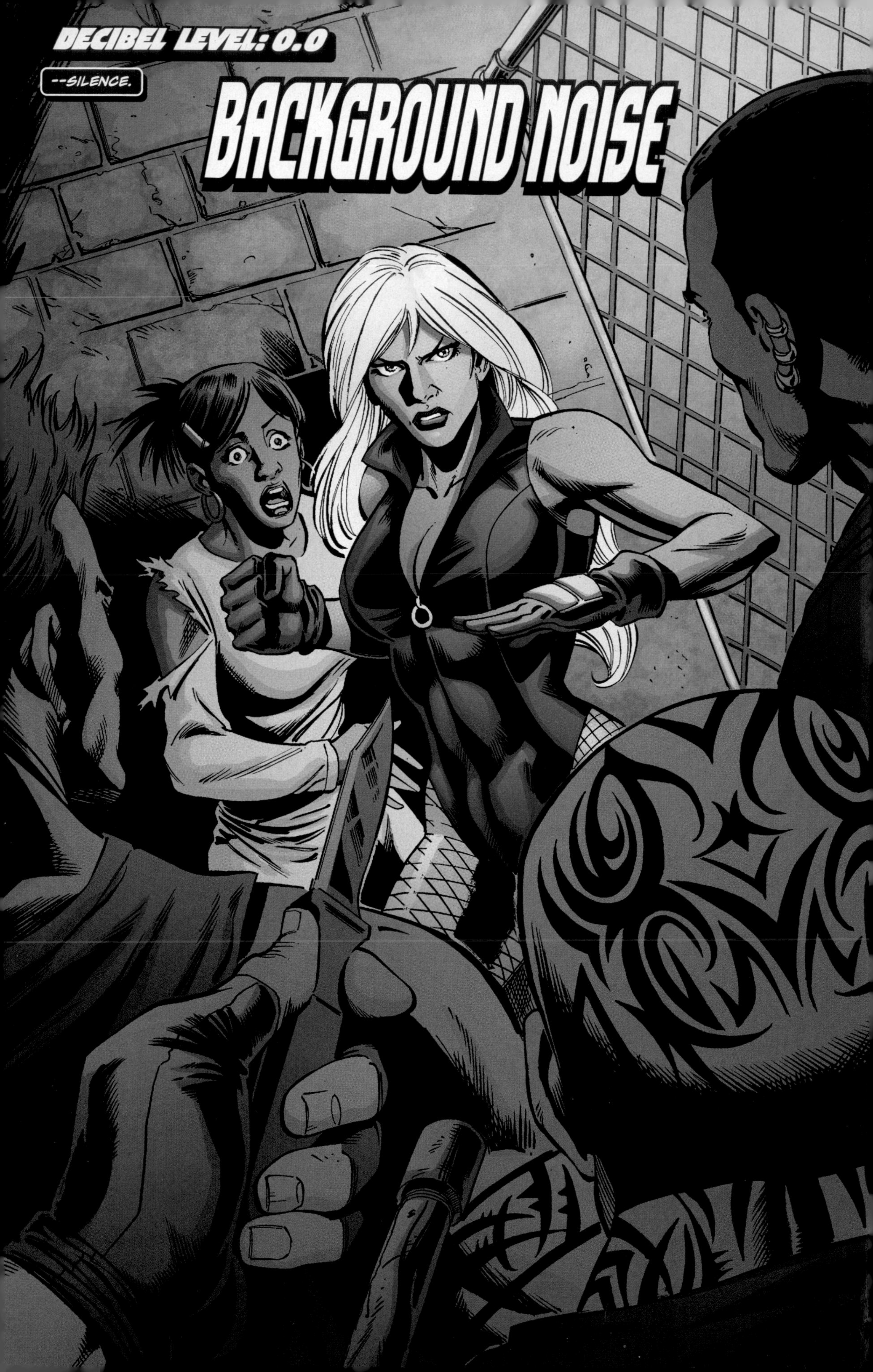
DECIBEL LEVEL: 0.0
--SILENCE.
BACKGROUND NOISE

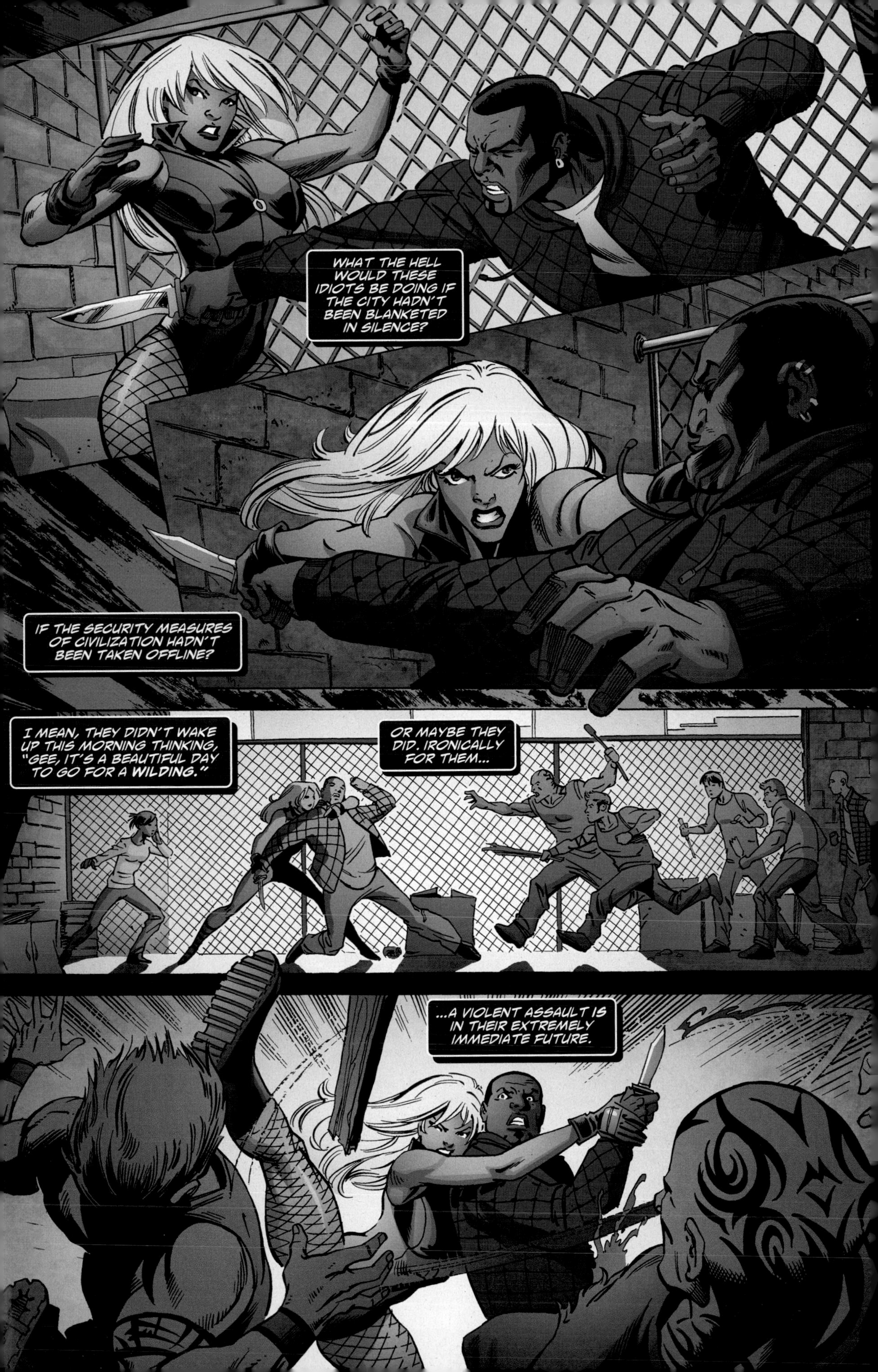
WHAT THE HELL WOULD THESE IDIOTS BE DOING IF THE CITY HADN'T BEEN BLANKETED IN SILENCE?
IF THE SECURITY MEASURES OF CIVILIZATION HADN'T BEEN TAKEN OFFLINE?
I MEAN, THEY DIDN'T WAKE UP THIS MORNING THINKING, "GEE, IT'S A BEAUTIFUL DAY TO GO FOR A WILDING."
OR MAYBE THEY DID. IRONICALLY FOR THEM...
...A VIOLENT ASSAULT IS IN THEIR EXTREMELY IMMEDIATE FUTURE.

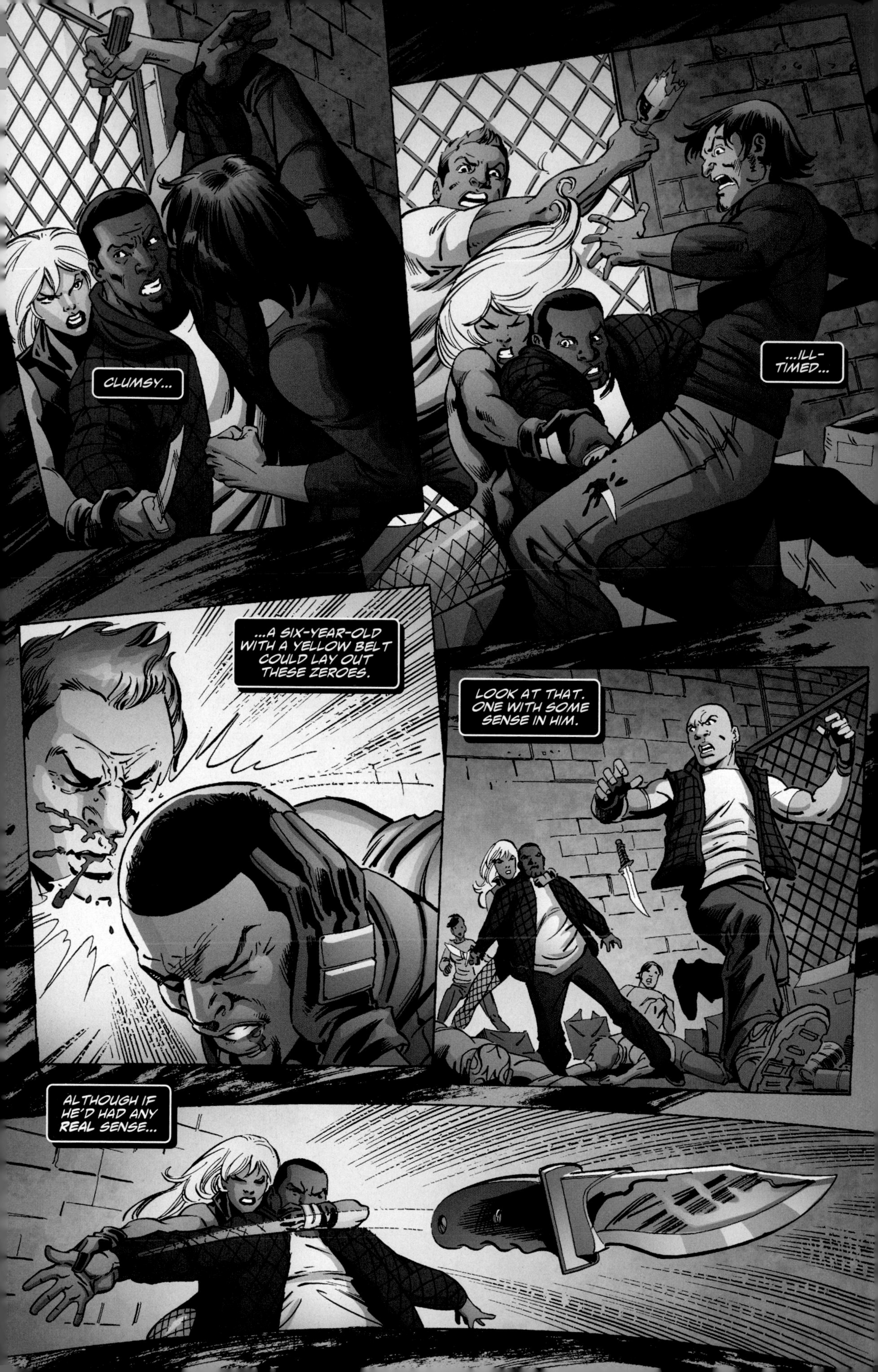
CLUMSY...
...ILL-TIMED...
...A SIX-YEAR-OLD WITH A YELLOW BELT COULD LAY OUT THESE ZEROES.
LOOK AT THAT. ONE WITH SOME SENSE IN HIM.
ALTHOUGH IF HE'D HAD ANY REAL SENSE...

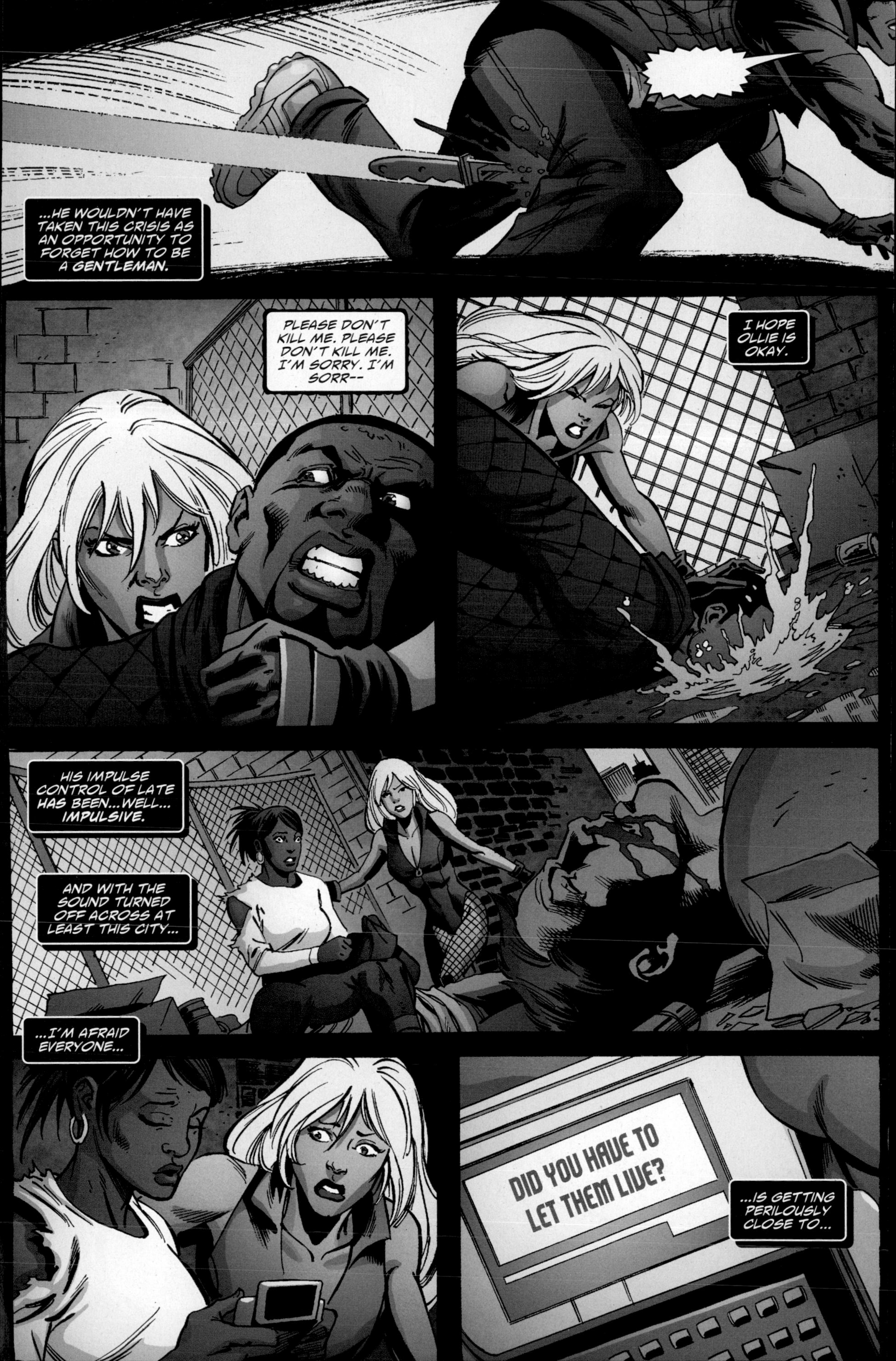
...HE WOULDN'T HAVE TAKEN THIS CRISIS AS AN OPPORTUNITY TO FORGET HOW TO BE A GENTLEMAN.
PLEASE DON'T KILL ME. PLEASE DON'T KILL ME. I'M SORRY. I'M SORR--
I HOPE OLLIE IS OKAY.
HIS IMPULSE CONTROL OF LATE HAS BEEN...WELL... IMPULSIVE.
AND WITH THE SOUND TURNED OFF ACROSS AT LEAST THIS CITY...
...I'M AFRAID EVERYONE...
DID YOU HAVE TO LET THEM LIVE?
...IS GETTING PERILOUSLY CLOSE TO...

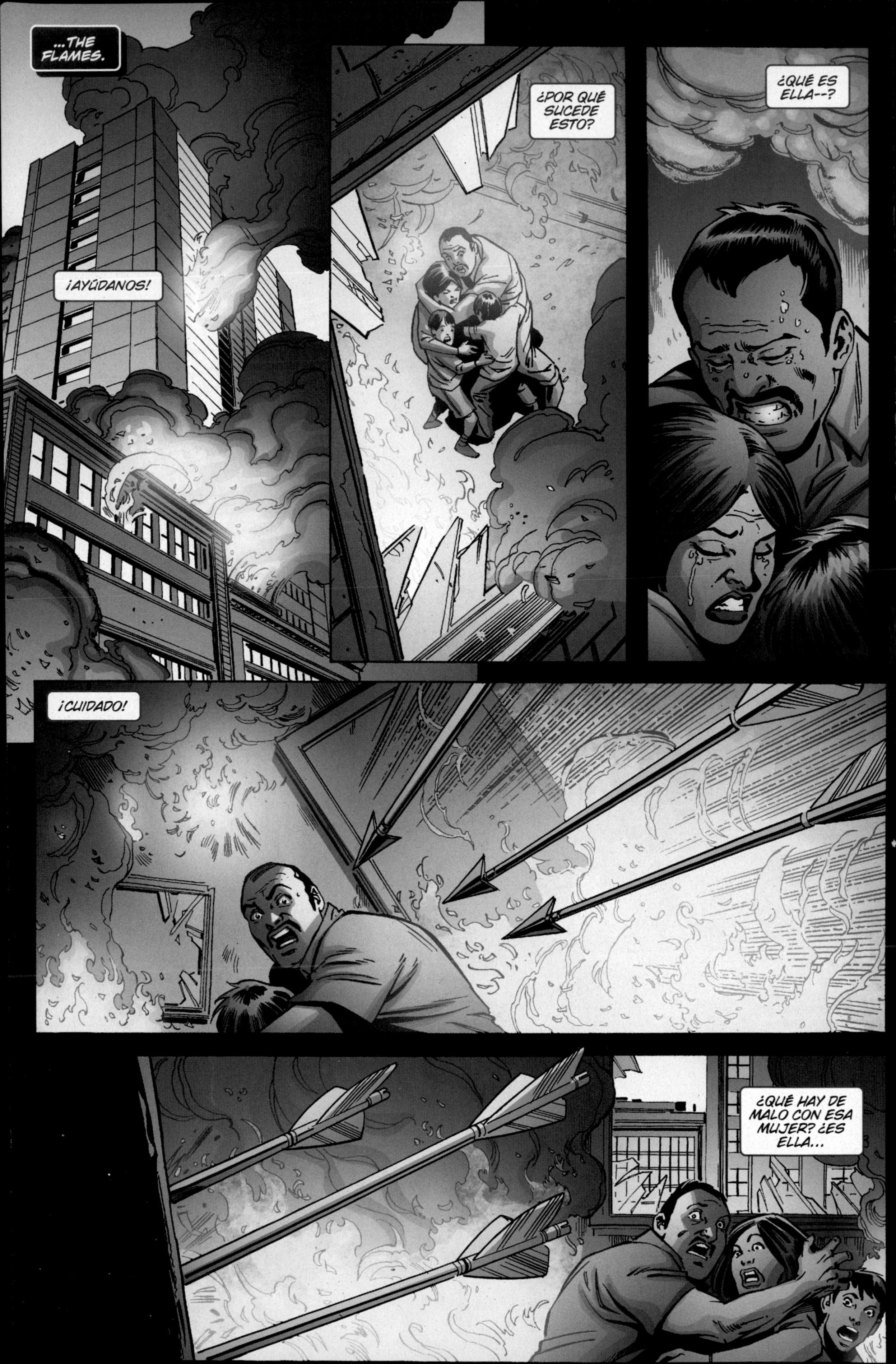
...THE FLAMES.
¡AYÚDANOS!
¿POR QUÉ SUCEDE ESTO?
¿QUÉ ES ELLA--?
¡CUIDADO!
¿QUÉ HAY DE MALO CON ESA MUJER? ¿ES ELLA...

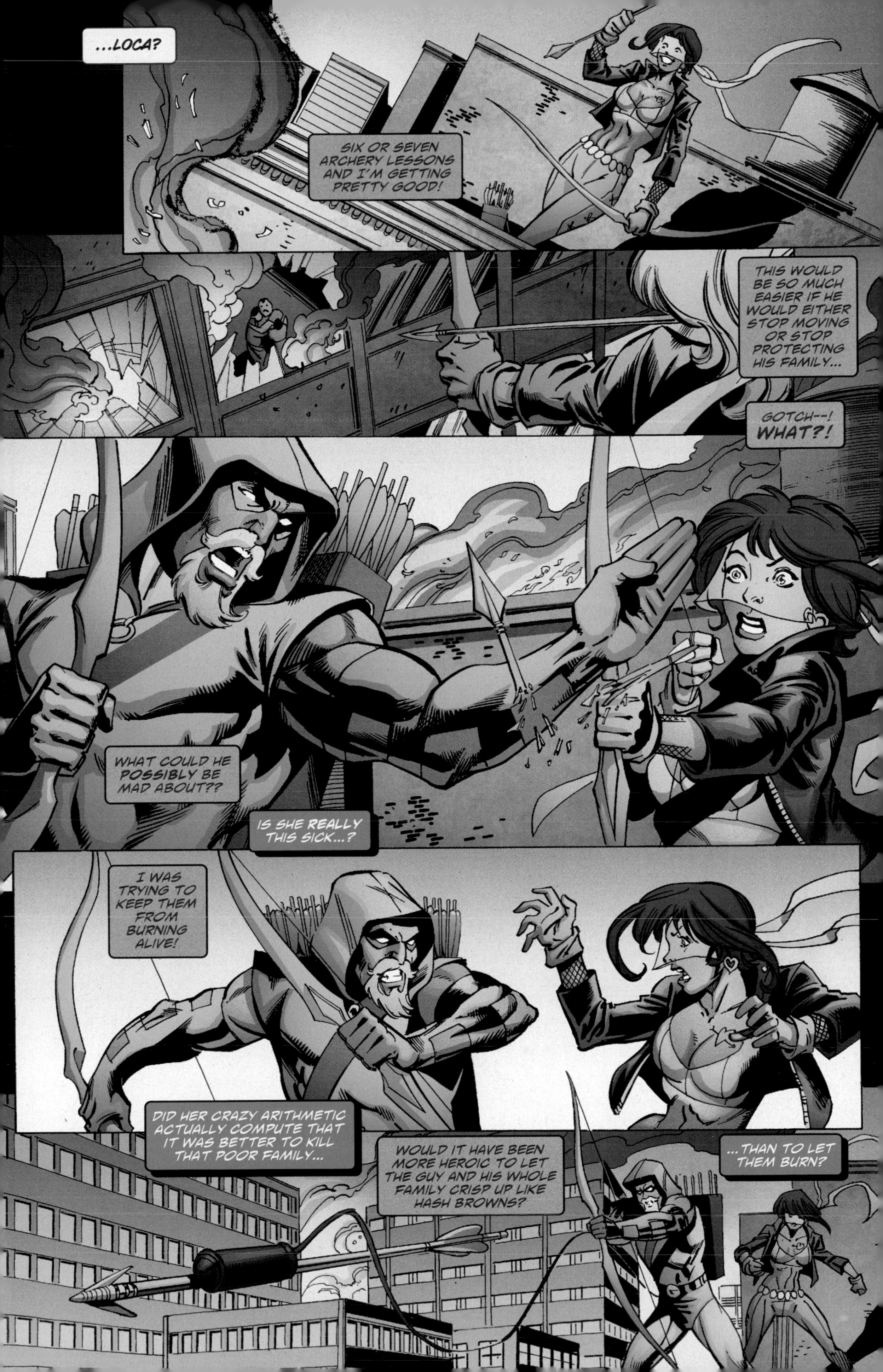
...LOCA?
SIX OR SEVEN ARCHERY LESSONS AND I'M GETTING PRETTY GOOD!
THIS WOULD BE SO MUCH EASIER IF HE WOULD EITHER STOP MOVING OR STOP PROTECTING HIS FAMILY...
GOTCH--! WHAT?!
WHAT COULD HE POSSIBLY BE MAD ABOUT??
IS SHE REALLY THIS SICK...?
I WAS TRYING TO KEEP THEM FROM BURNING ALIVE!
DID HER CRAZY ARITHMETIC ACTUALLY COMPUTE THAT IT WAS BETTER TO KILL THAT POOR FAMILY...
WOULD IT HAVE BEEN MORE HEROIC TO LET THE GUY AND HIS WHOLE FAMILY CRISP UP LIKE HASH BROWNS?
...THAN TO LET THEM BURN?

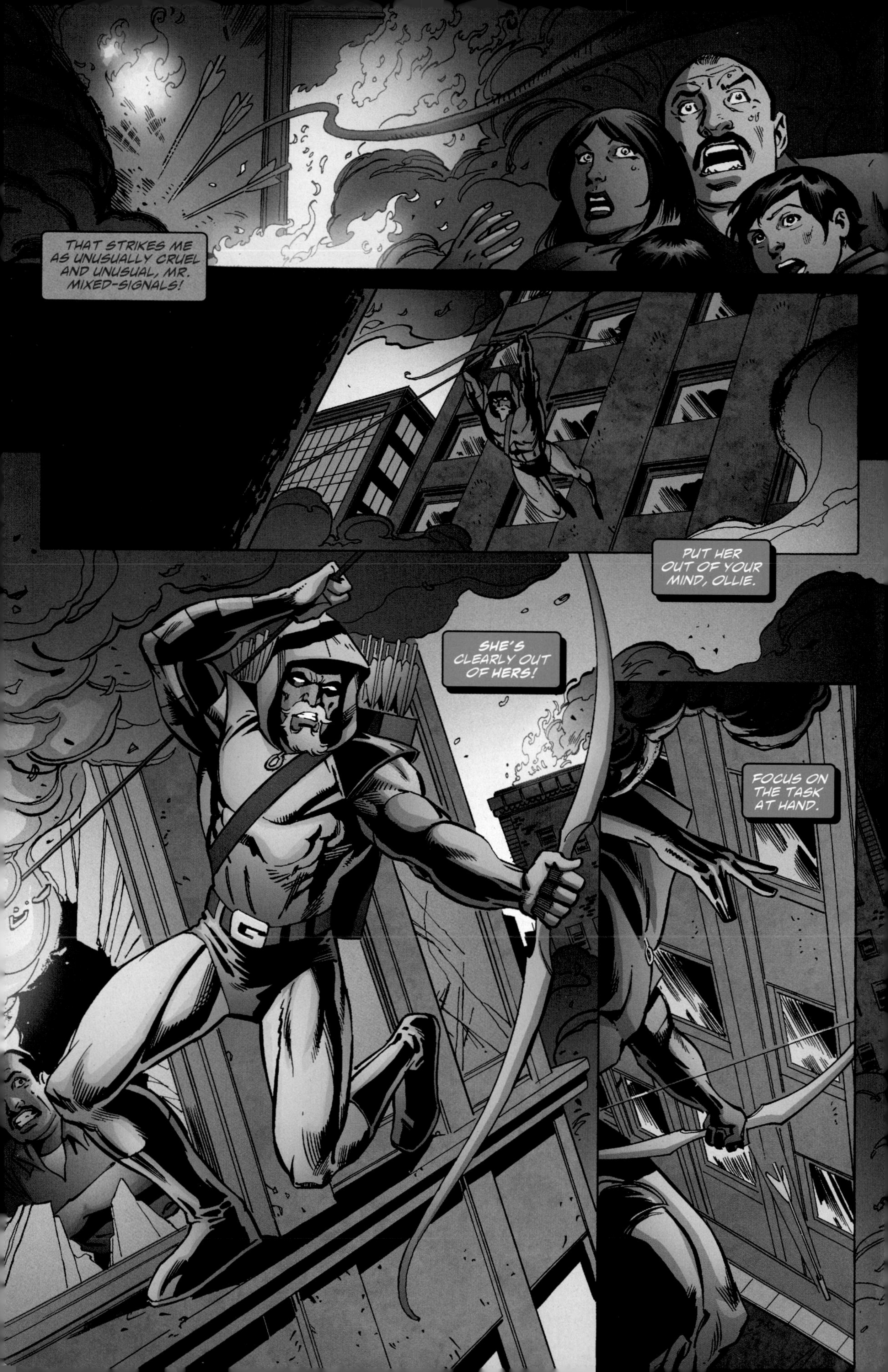
THAT STRIKES ME AS UNUSUALLY CRUEL AND UNUSUAL, MR. MIXED-SIGNALS!
PUT HER OUT OF YOUR MIND, OLLIE.
SHE'S CLEARLY OUT OF HERS!
FOCUS ON THE TASK AT HAND.

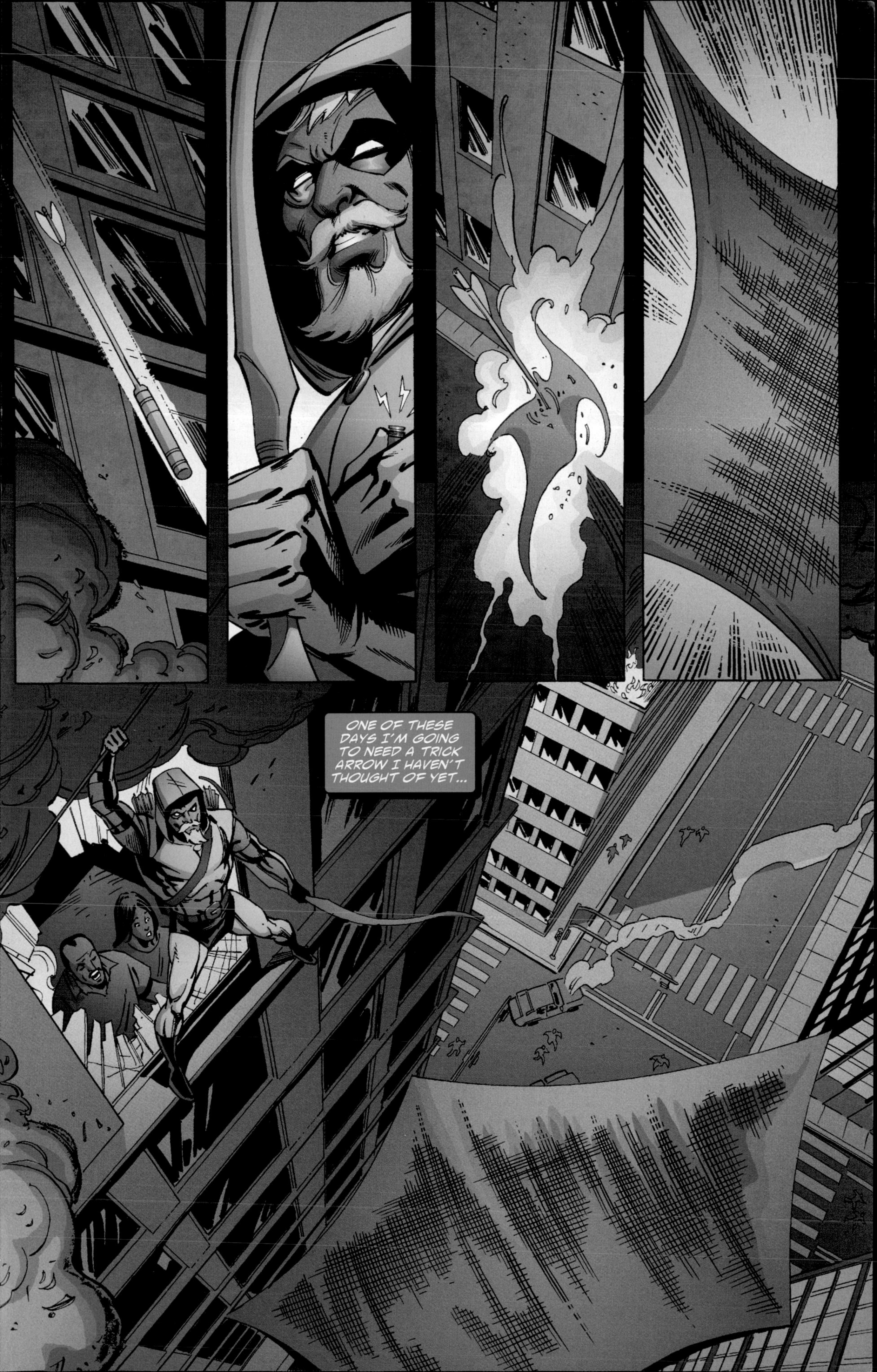
ONE OF THESE DAYS I'M GOING TO NEED A TRICK ARROW I HAVEN'T THOUGHT OF YET...

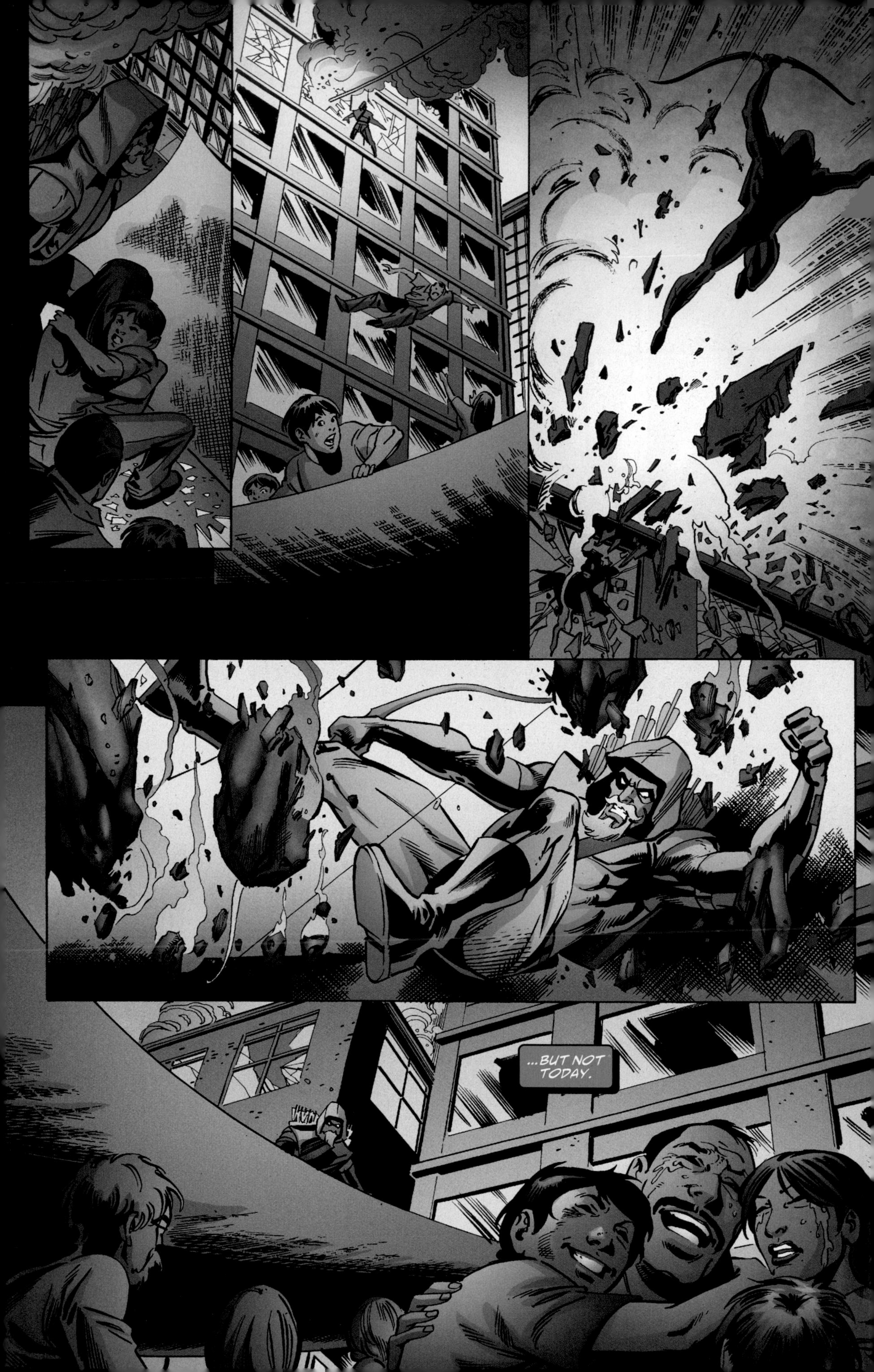
...BUT NOT TODAY.

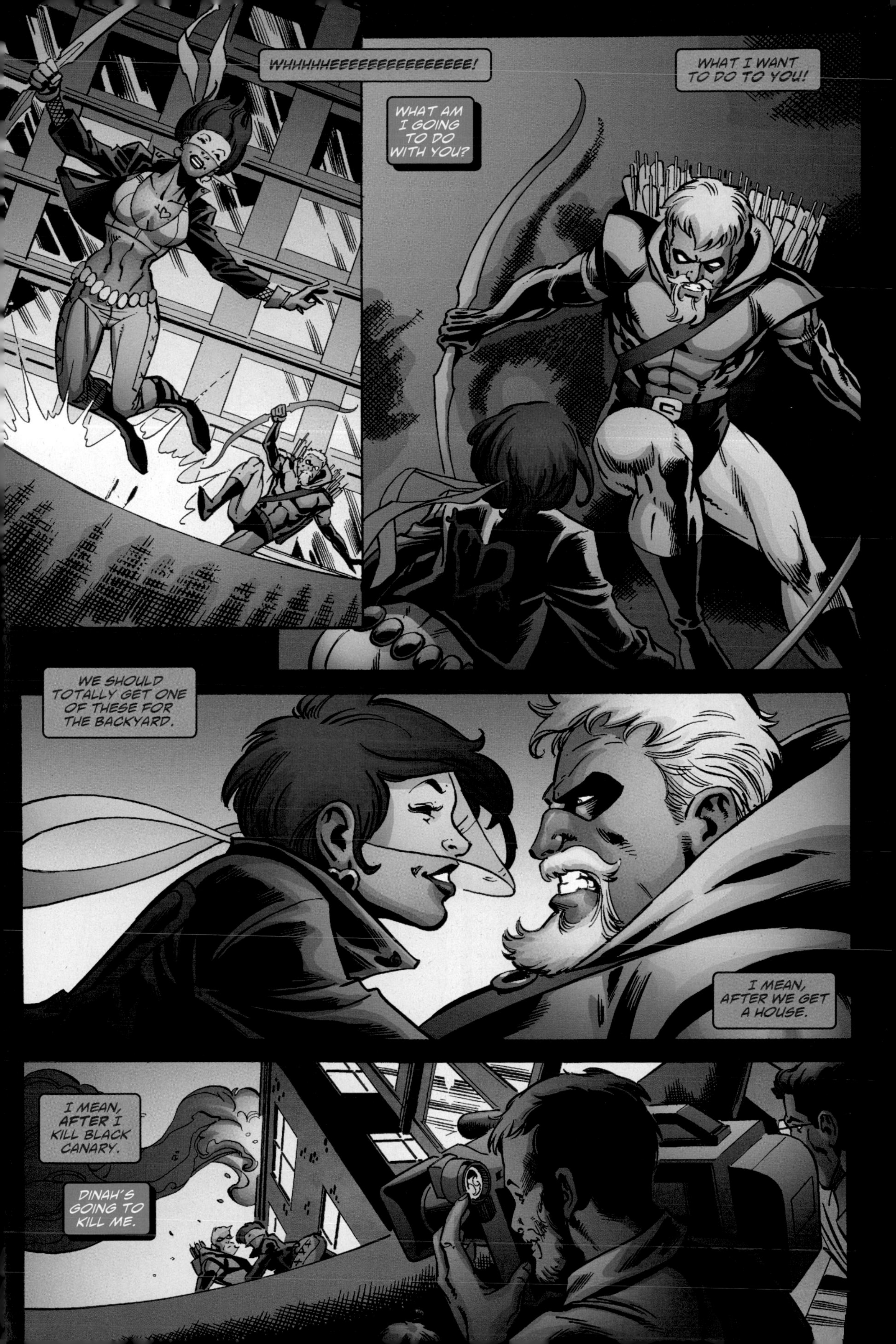
WHHHHHEEEEEEEEEEEEEEEE!
WHAT AM I GOING TO DO WITH YOU?
WHAT I WANT TO DO TO YOU!
WE SHOULD TOTALLY GET ONE OF THESE FOR THE BACKYARD.
I MEAN, AFTER WE GET A HOUSE.
I MEAN, AFTER I KILL BLACK CANARY.
DINAH'S GOING TO KILL ME.

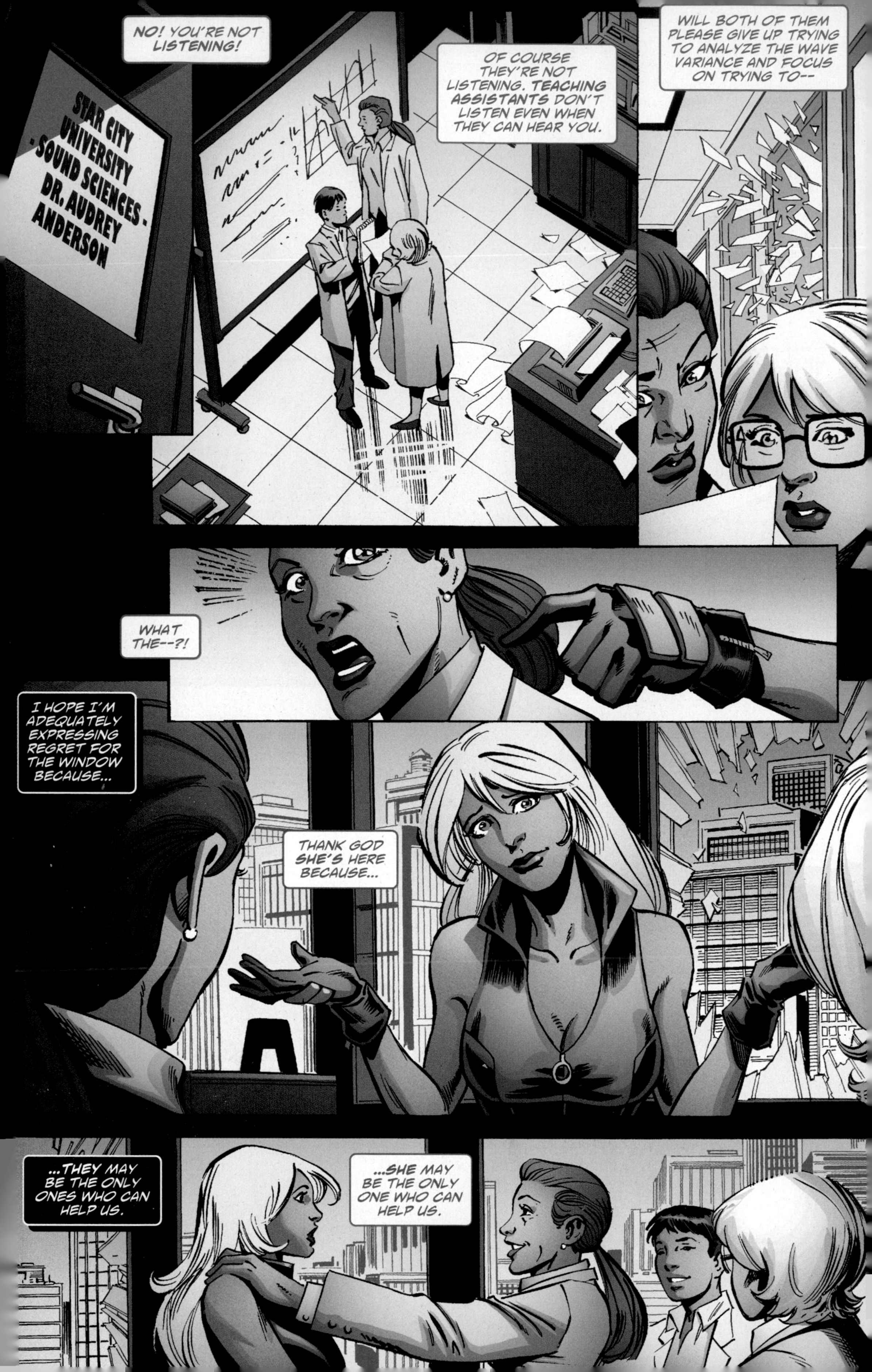
NO! YOU'RE NOT LISTENING!
STAR CITY UNIVERSITY - SOUND SCIENCES - DR. AUDREY ANDERSON
OF COURSE THEY'RE NOT LISTENING. TEACHING ASSISTANTS DON'T LISTEN EVEN WHEN THEY CAN HEAR YOU.
WILL BOTH OF THEM PLEASE GIVE UP TRYING TO ANALYZE THE WAVE VARIANCE AND FOCUS ON TRYING TO--
WHAT THE--?!
I HOPE I'M ADEQUATELY EXPRESSING REGRET FOR THE WINDOW BECAUSE...
THANK GOD SHE'S HERE BECAUSE...
...THEY MAY BE THE ONLY ONES WHO CAN HELP US.
...SHE MAY BE THE ONLY ONE WHO CAN HELP US.

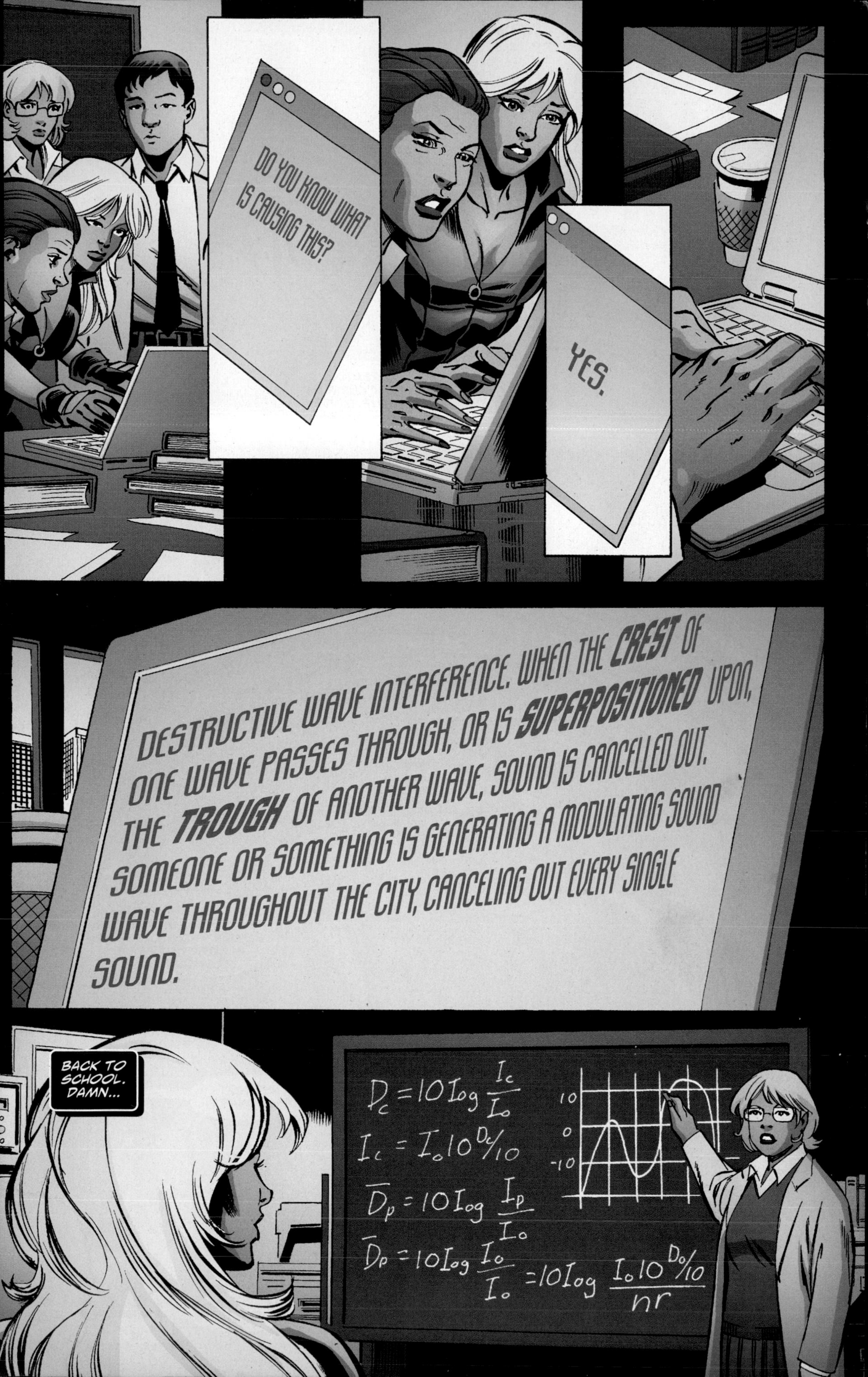
DO YOU KNOW WHAT IS CAUSING THIS?
YES.
DESTRUCTIVE WAVE INTERFERENCE. WHEN THE CREST OF ONE WAVE PASSES THROUGH, OR IS SUPERPOSITIONED UPON, THE TROUGH OF ANOTHER WAVE, SOUND IS CANCELLED OUT. SOMEONE OR SOMETHING IS GENERATING A MODULATING SOUND WAVE THROUGHOUT THE CITY, CANCELING OUT EVERY SINGLE SOUND.
BACK TO SCHOOL. DAMN...
$D_c = 10 \log \frac{I_c}{I_o}$
$I_c = I_o 10^{D_c/10}$
$\bar{D}_p = 10 \log \frac{I_p}{I_o}$
$\bar{D}_p = 10 \log \frac{I_o}{I_o} = 10 \log \frac{I_o 10^{D_o/10}}{nr}$
10
0
-10

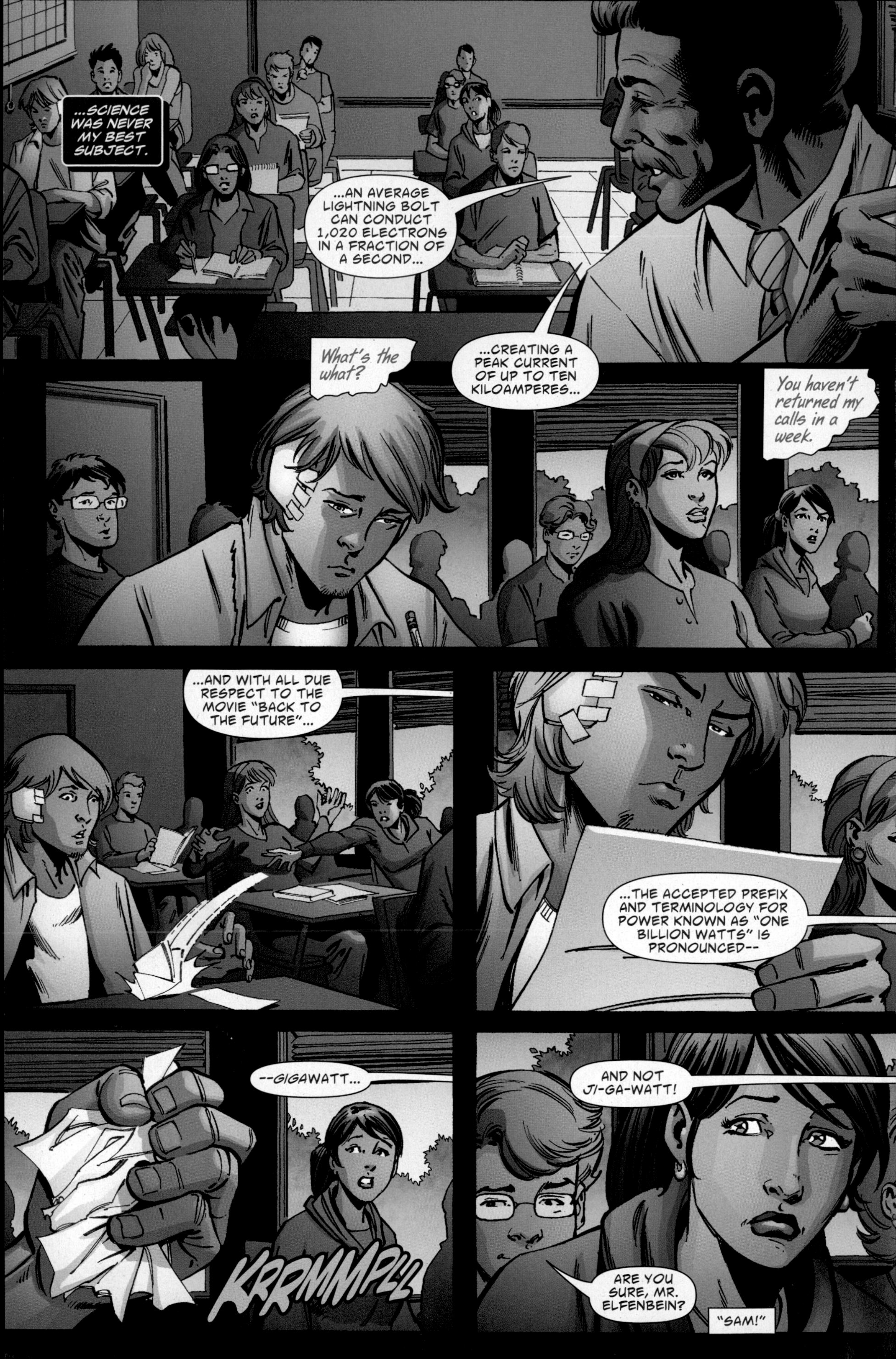
...SCIENCE WAS NEVER MY BEST SUBJECT.
...AN AVERAGE LIGHTNING BOLT CAN CONDUCT 1,020 ELECTRONS IN A FRACTION OF A SECOND...
What's the what?
...CREATING A PEAK CURRENT OF UP TO TEN KILOAMPERES...
You haven't returned my calls in a week.
...AND WITH ALL DUE RESPECT TO THE MOVIE "BACK TO THE FUTURE"...
...THE ACCEPTED PREFIX AND TERMINOLOGY FOR POWER KNOWN AS "ONE BILLION WATTS" IS PRONOUNCED--
--GIGAWATT...
KRRMMPLL
AND NOT JI-GA-WATT!
ARE YOU SURE, MR. ELFENBEIN?
"SAM!"

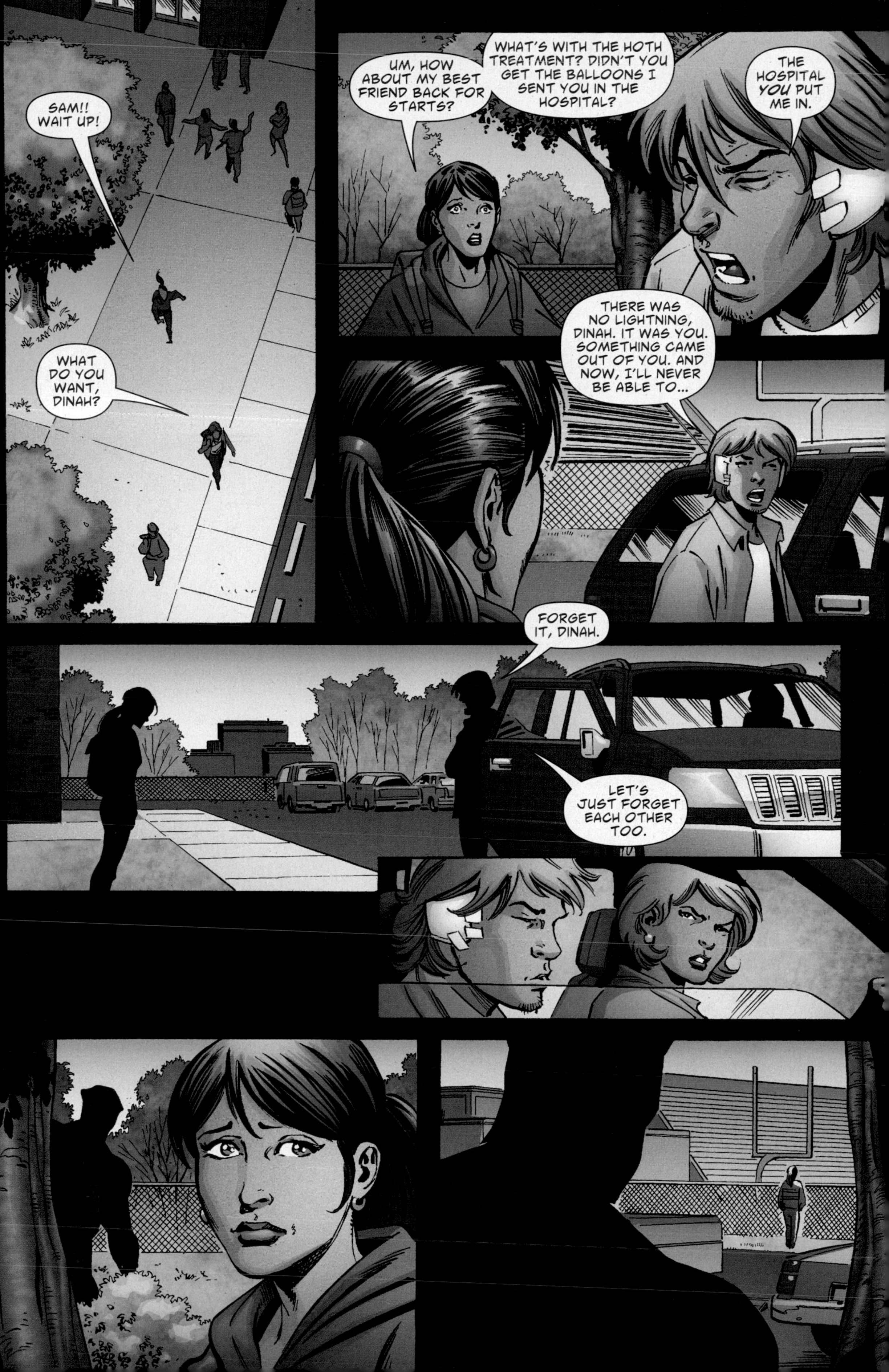
SAM!! WAIT UP!
WHAT DO YOU WANT, DINAH?
UM, HOW ABOUT MY BEST FRIEND BACK FOR STARTS?
WHAT'S WITH THE HOTH TREATMENT? DIDN'T YOU GET THE BALLOONS I SENT YOU IN THE HOSPITAL?
THE HOSPITAL YOU PUT ME IN.
THERE WAS NO LIGHTNING, DINAH. IT WAS YOU. SOMETHING CAME OUT OF YOU. AND NOW, I'LL NEVER BE ABLE TO...
FORGET IT, DINAH.
LET'S JUST FORGET EACH OTHER TOO.

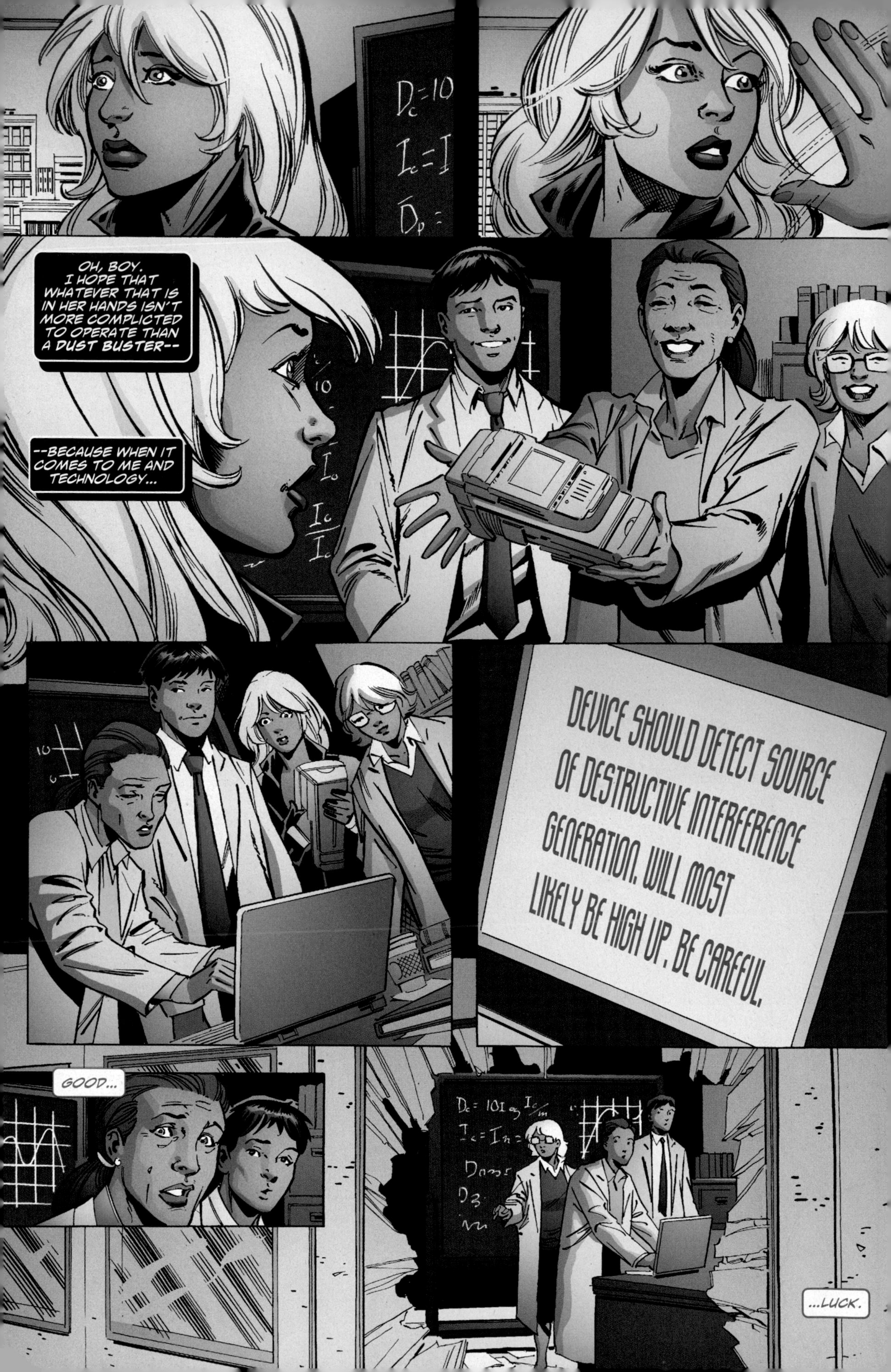
OH, BOY. I HOPE THAT WHATEVER THAT IS IN HER HANDS ISN'T MORE COMPLICTED TO OPERATE THAN A DUST BUSTER--
--BECAUSE WHEN IT COMES TO ME AND TECHNOLOGY...
DEVICE SHOULD DETECT SOURCE OF DESTRUCTIVE INTERFERENCE GENERATION. WILL MOST LIKELY BE HIGH UP. BE CAREFUL.
GOOD...
...LUCK.

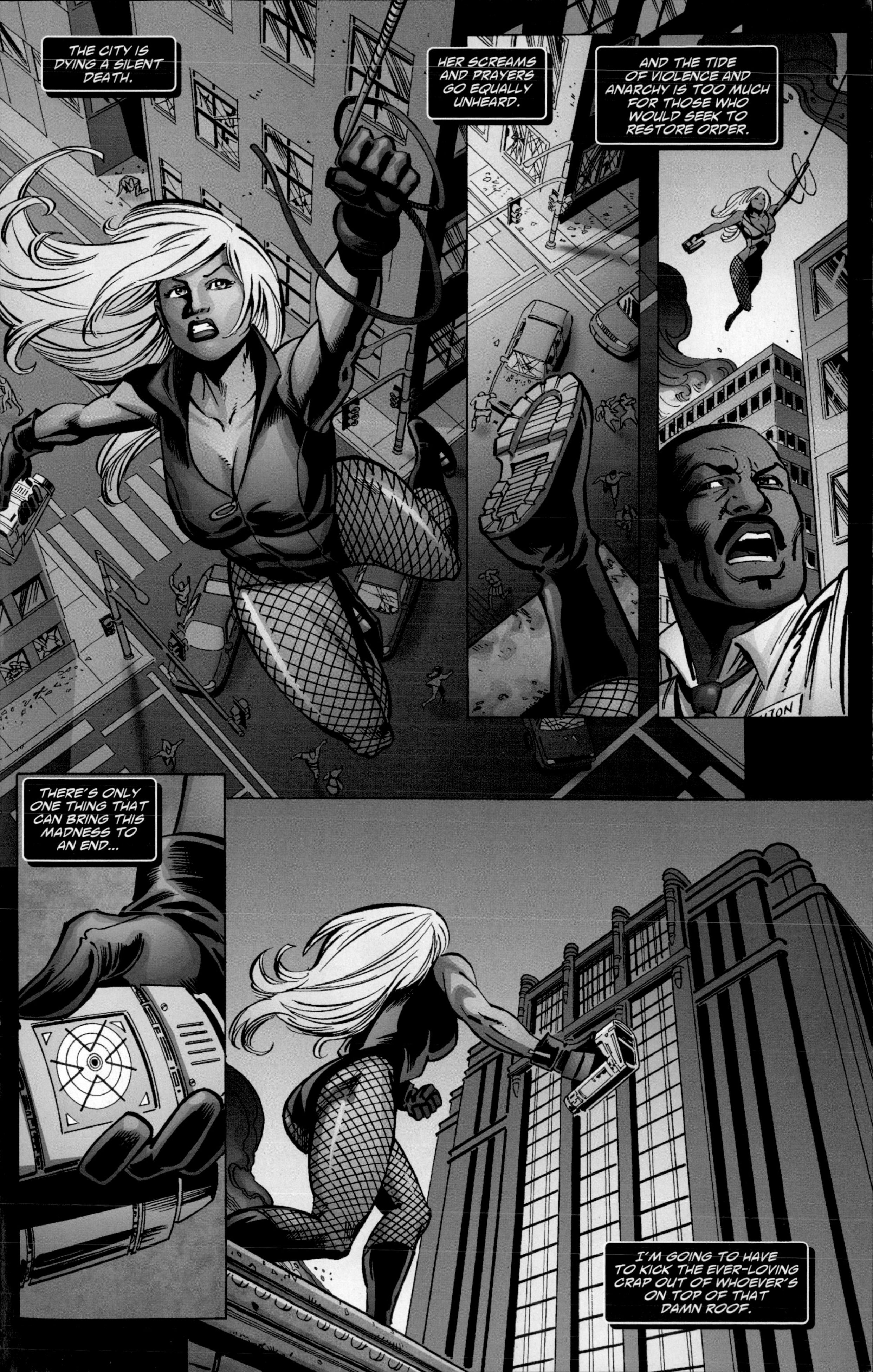
THE CITY IS DYING A SILENT DEATH.
HER SCREAMS AND PRAYERS GO EQUALLY UNHEARD.
AND THE TIDE OF VIOLENCE AND ANARCHY IS TOO MUCH FOR THOSE WHO WOULD SEEK TO RESTORE ORDER.
THERE'S ONLY ONE THING THAT CAN BRING THIS MADNESS TO AN END...
I'M GOING TO HAVE TO KICK THE EVER-LOVING CRAP OUT OF WHOEVER'S ON TOP OF THAT DAMN ROOF.

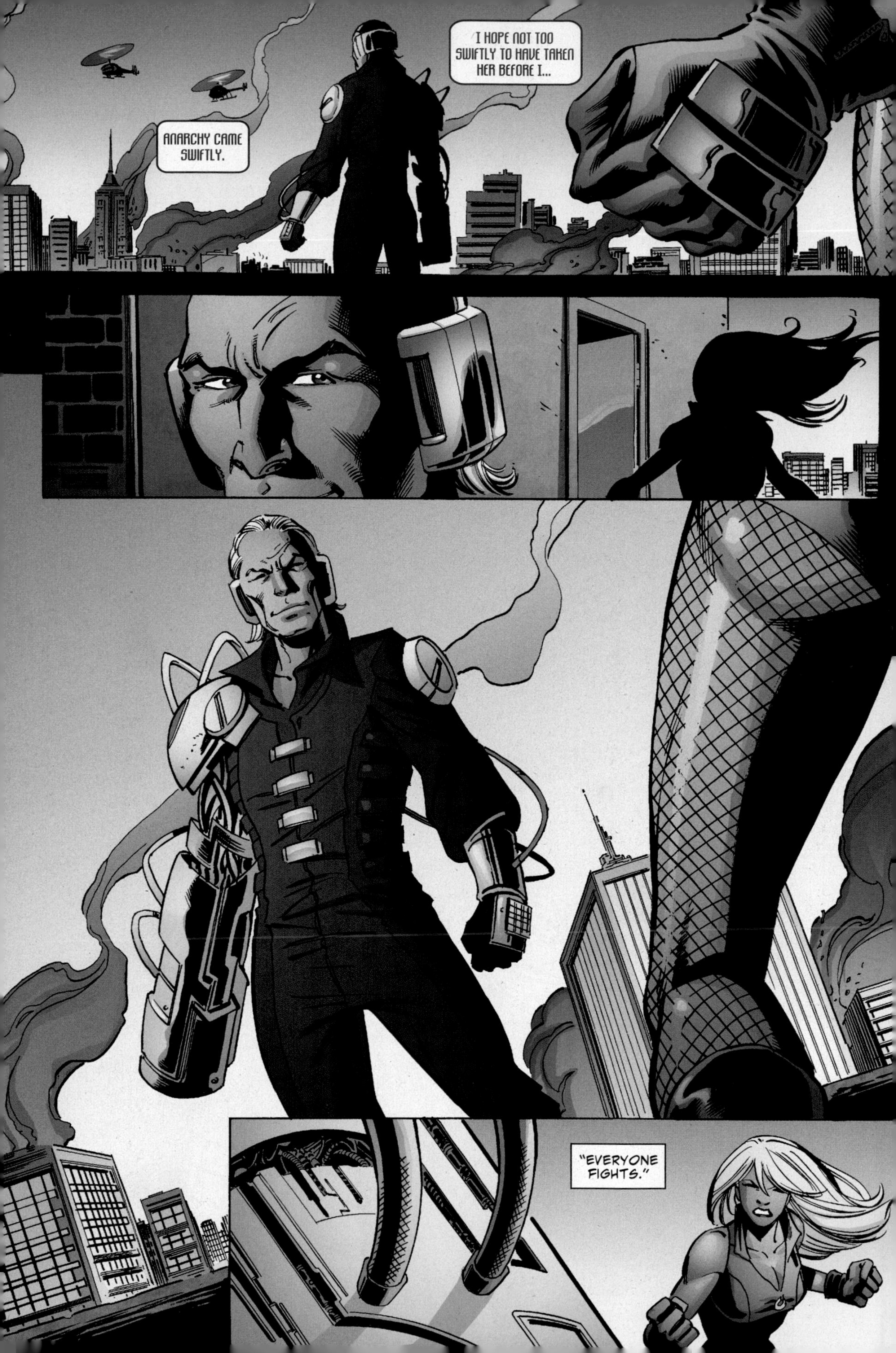
ANARCHY CAME SWIFTLY.
I HOPE NOT TOO SWIFTLY TO HAVE TAKEN HER BEFORE I...
"EVERYONE FIGHTS."

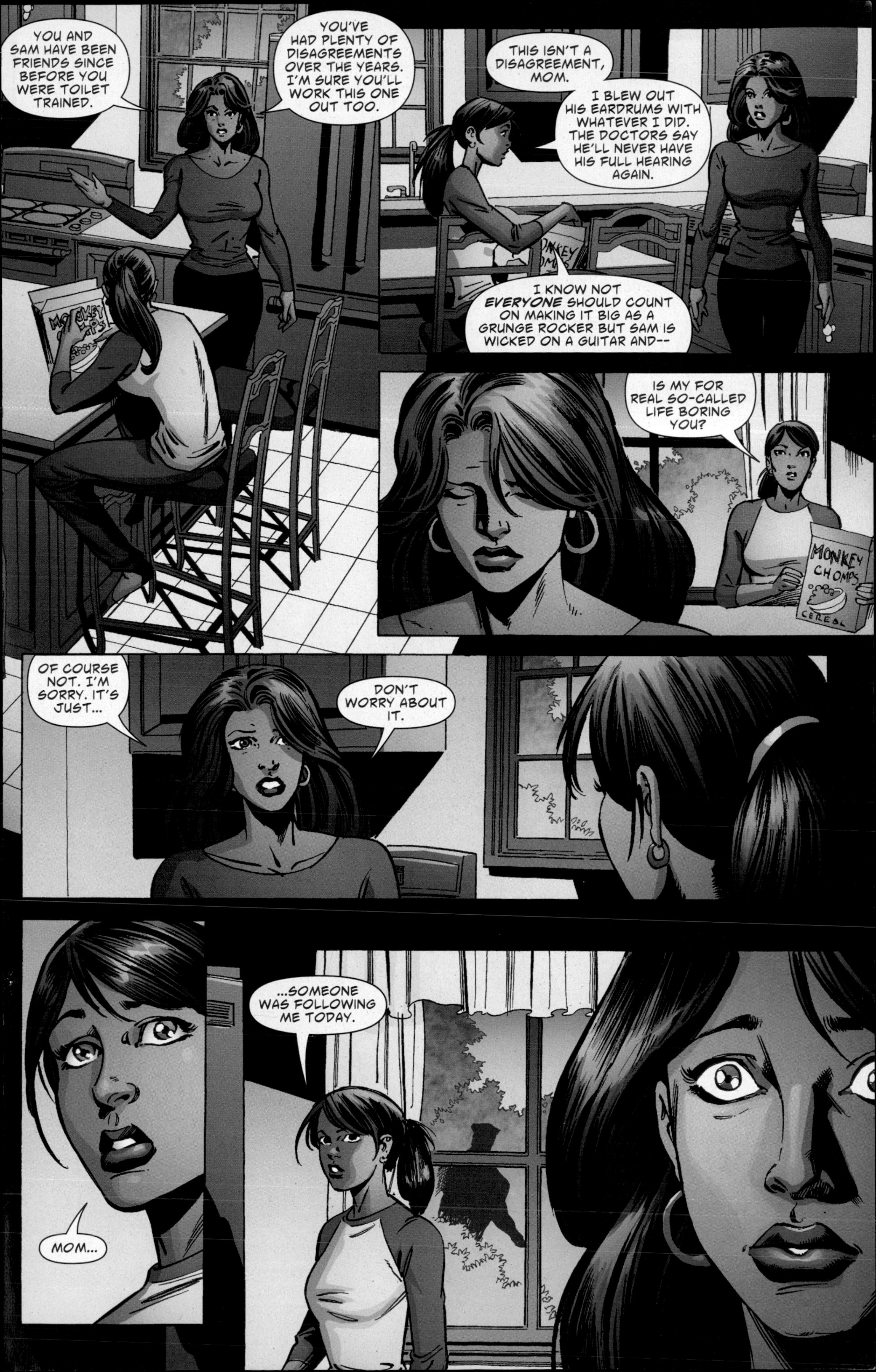
YOU AND SAM HAVE BEEN FRIENDS SINCE BEFORE YOU WERE TOILET TRAINED.
YOU'VE HAD PLENTY OF DISAGREEMENTS OVER THE YEARS. I'M SURE YOU'LL WORK THIS ONE OUT TOO.
MONKEY CHOMPS
THIS ISN'T A DISAGREEMENT, MOM.
I BLEW OUT HIS EARDRUMS WITH WHATEVER I DID. THE DOCTORS SAY HE'LL NEVER HAVE HIS FULL HEARING AGAIN.
I KNOW NOT EVERYONE SHOULD COUNT ON MAKING IT BIG AS A GRUNGE ROCKER BUT SAM IS WICKED ON A GUITAR AND--
IS MY FOR REAL SO-CALLED LIFE BORING YOU?
MONKEY CHOMPS CEREAL
OF COURSE NOT. I'M SORRY. IT'S JUST...
DON'T WORRY ABOUT IT.
MOM...
...SOMEONE WAS FOLLOWING ME TODAY.

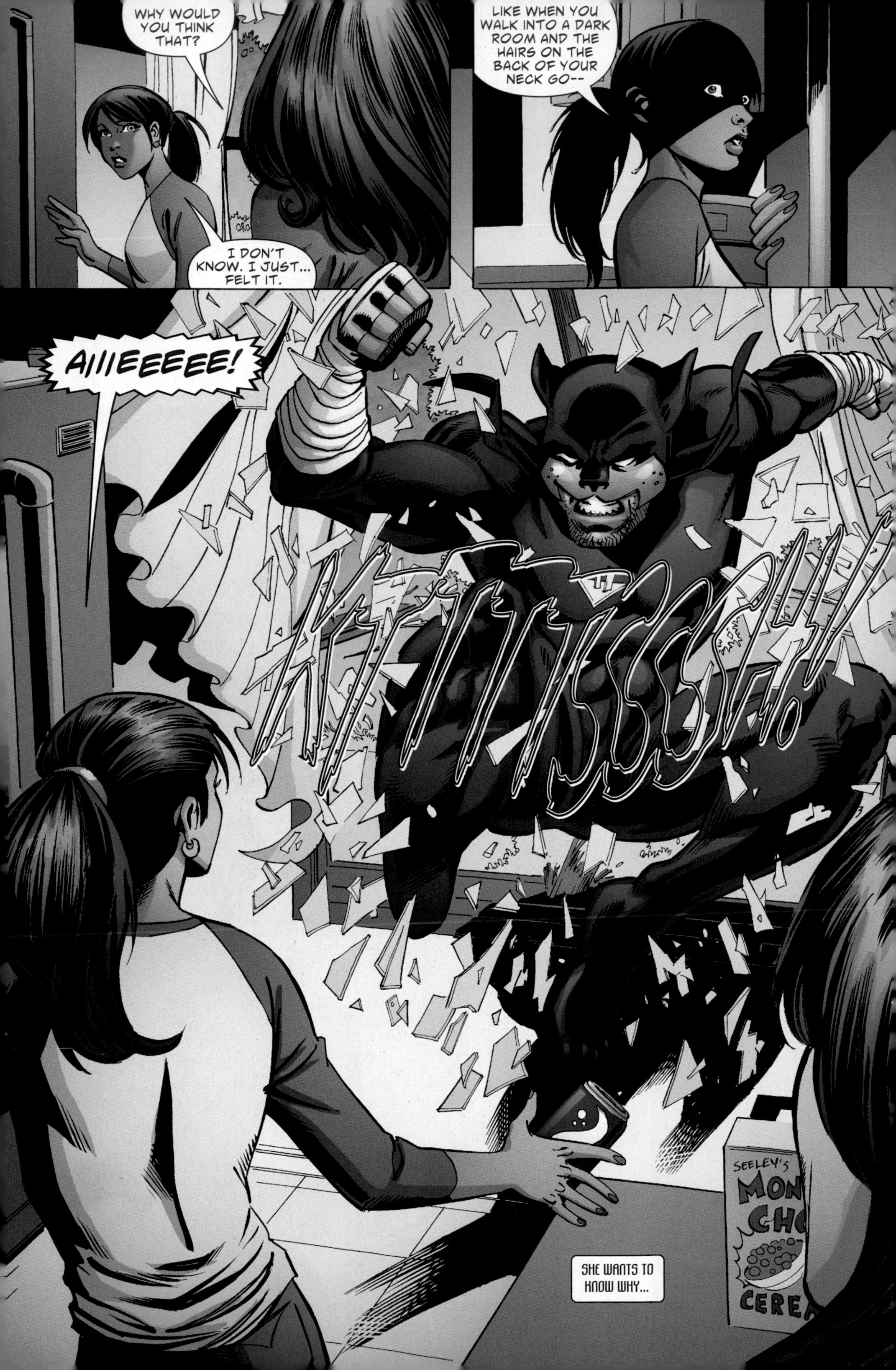
WHY WOULD YOU THINK THAT?
I DON'T KNOW. I JUST... FELT IT.
LIKE WHEN YOU WALK INTO A DARK ROOM AND THE HAIRS ON THE BACK OF YOUR NECK GO--
AIIIEEEEE!
SHE WANTS TO KNOW WHY...
SEELEY'S
CEREA

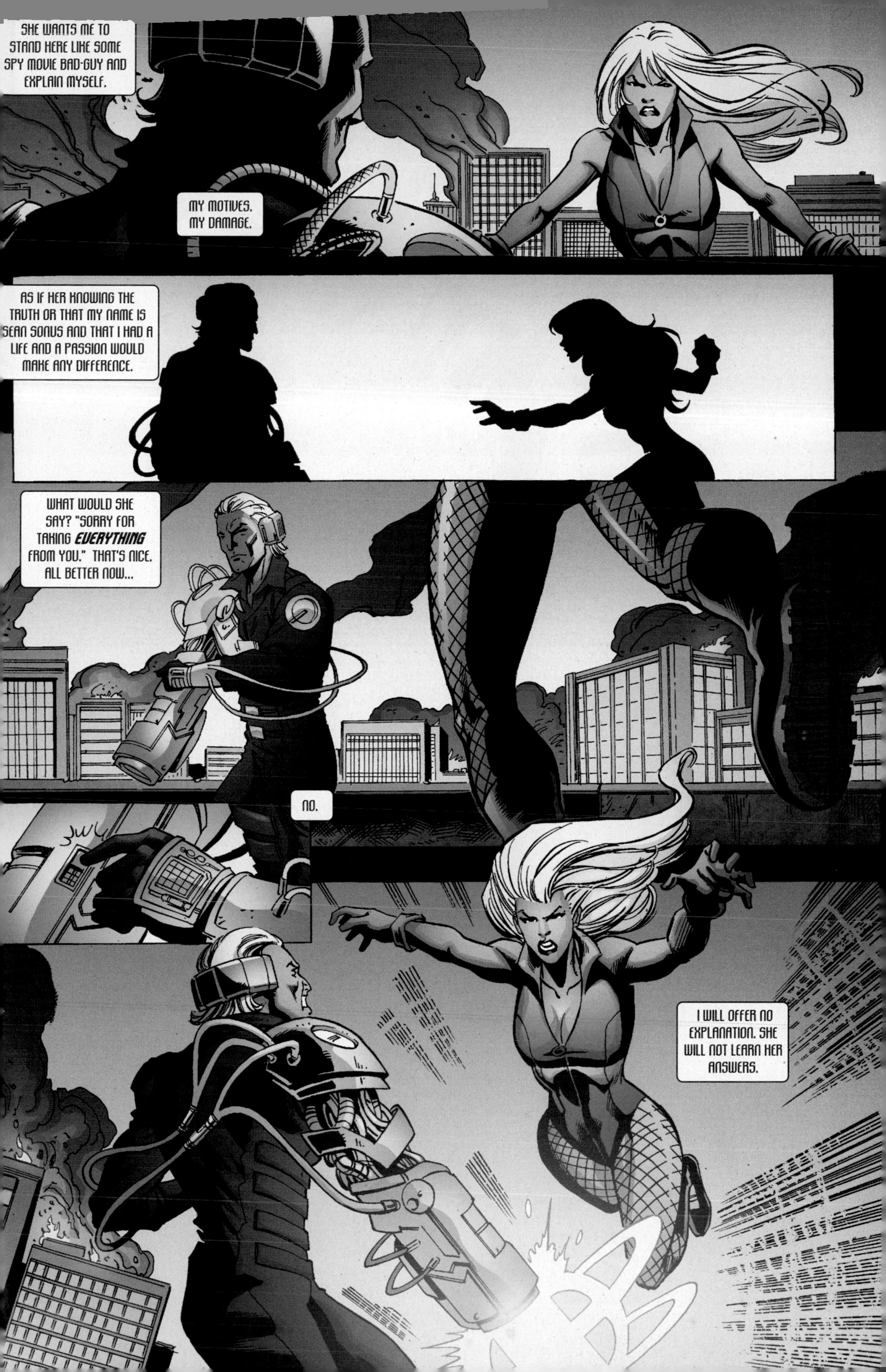
SHE WANTS ME TO STAND HERE LIKE SOME SPY MOVIE BAD-GUY AND EXPLAIN MYSELF.
MY MOTIVES. MY DAMAGE.
AS IF HER KNOWING THE TRUTH OR THAT MY NAME IS SEAN SONUS AND THAT I HAD A LIFE AND A PASSION WOULD MAKE ANY DIFFERENCE.
WHAT WOULD SHE SAY? "SORRY FOR TAKING *EVERYTHING* FROM YOU." THAT'S NICE. ALL BETTER NOW...
NO.
I WILL OFFER NO EXPLANATION. SHE WILL NOT LEARN HER ANSWERS.

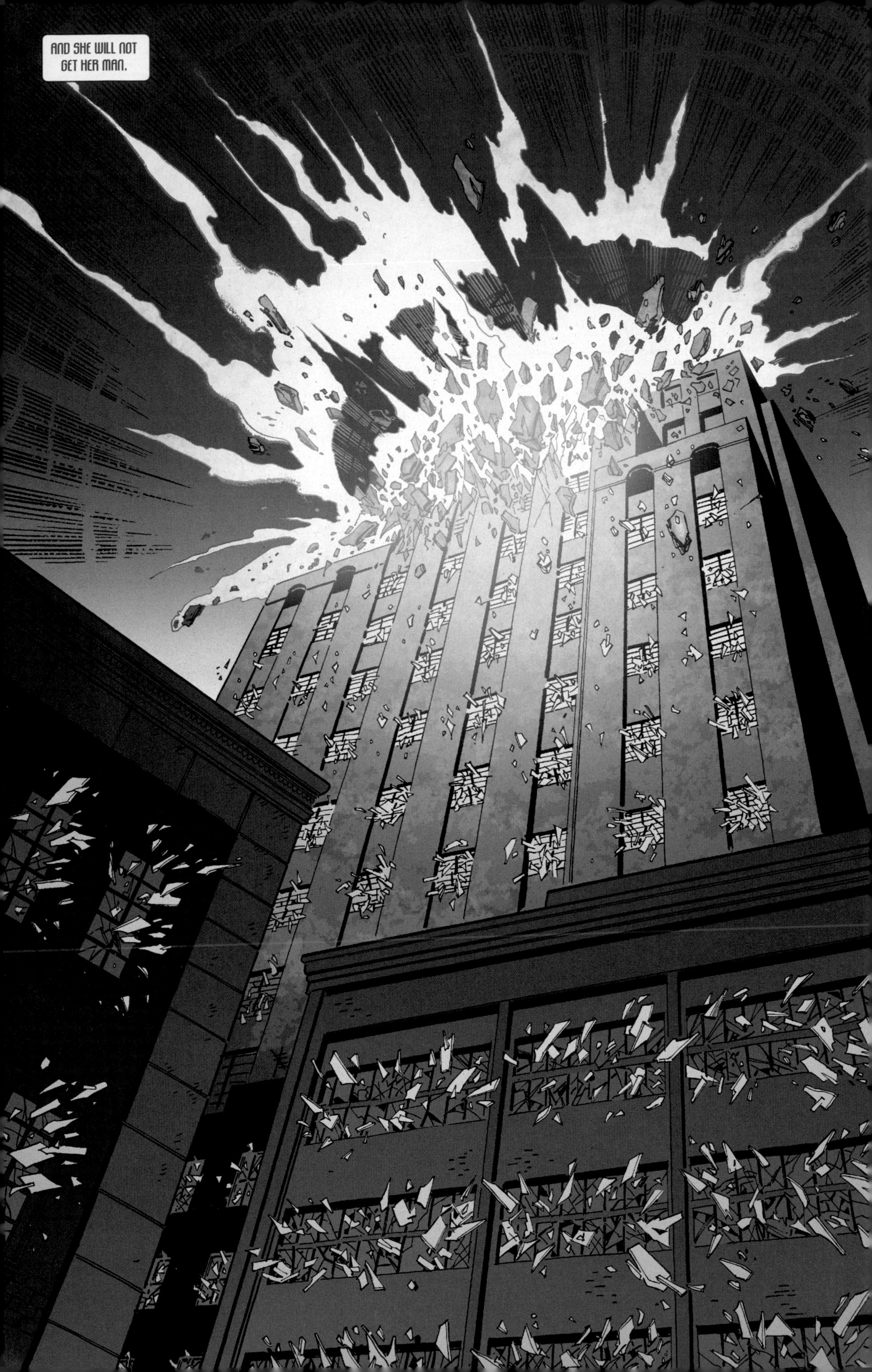
AND SHE WILL NOT GET HER MAN.

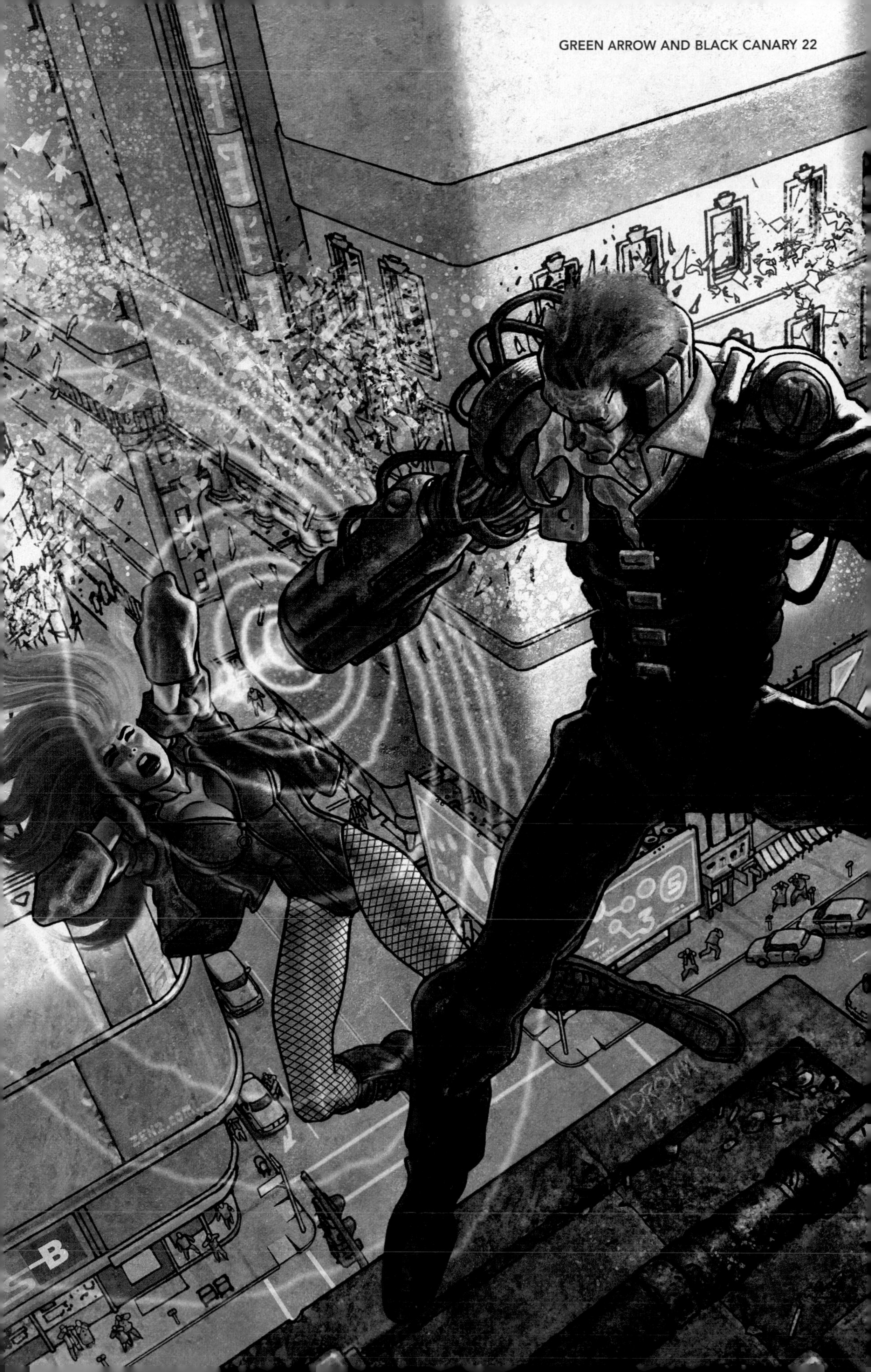

PEACE AND QUIET
Mike Norton Penciller
Josef Rubinstein Inker

OPENING NIGHT JITTERS
Mike Norton Layouts
Bill Sienkiewicz Finishes

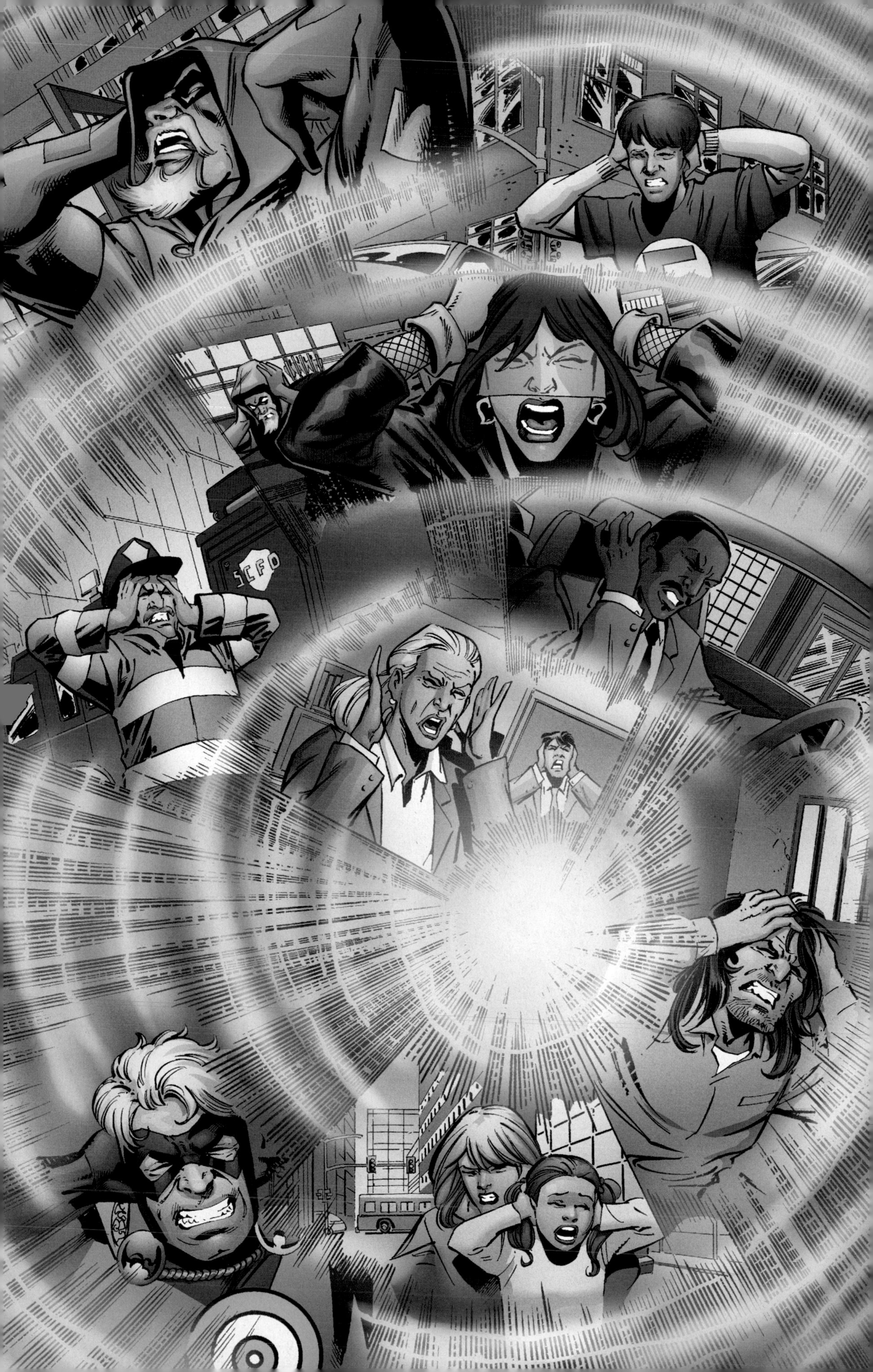

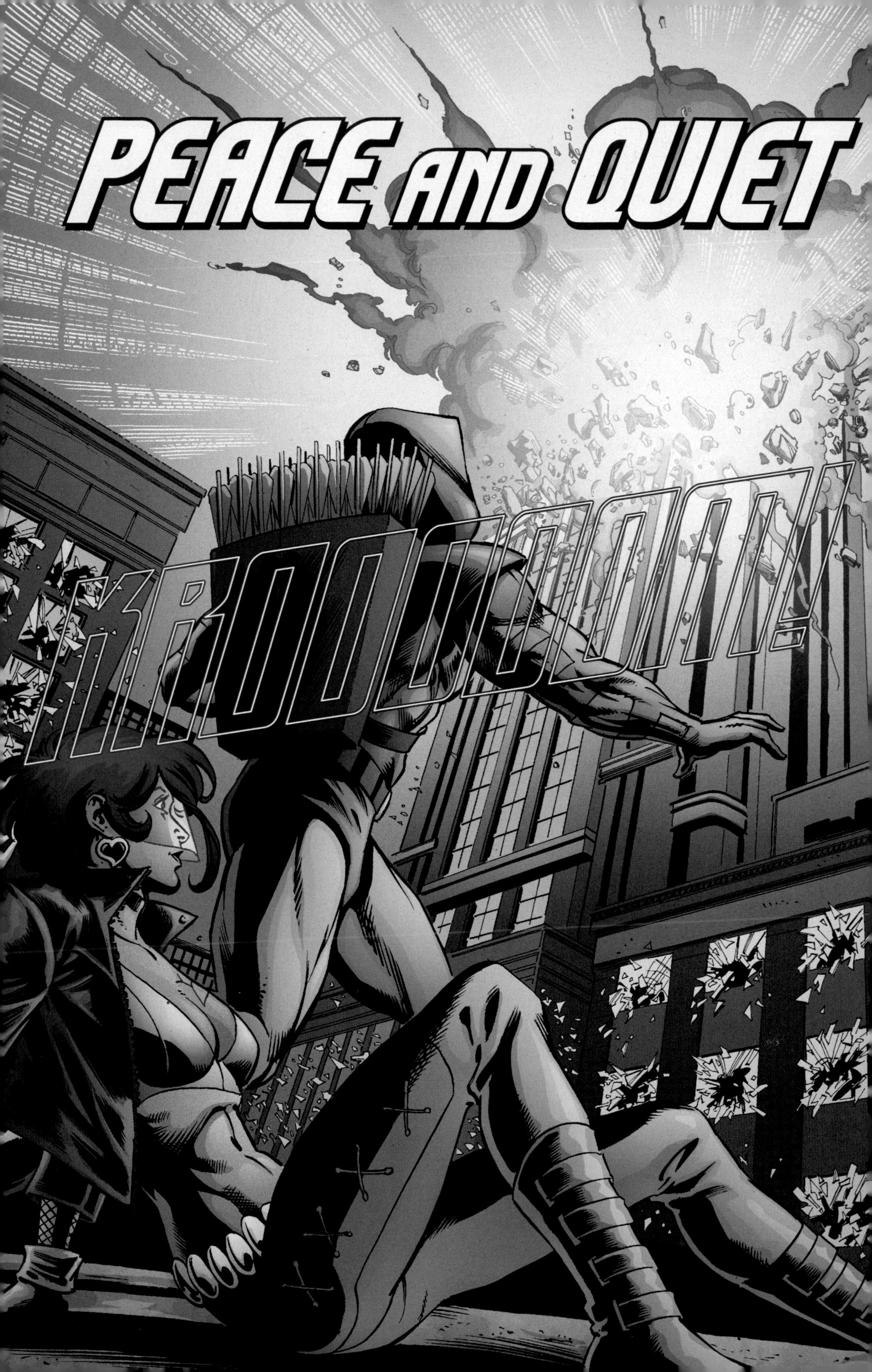
PEACE AND QUIET
KRBOOOOOM!

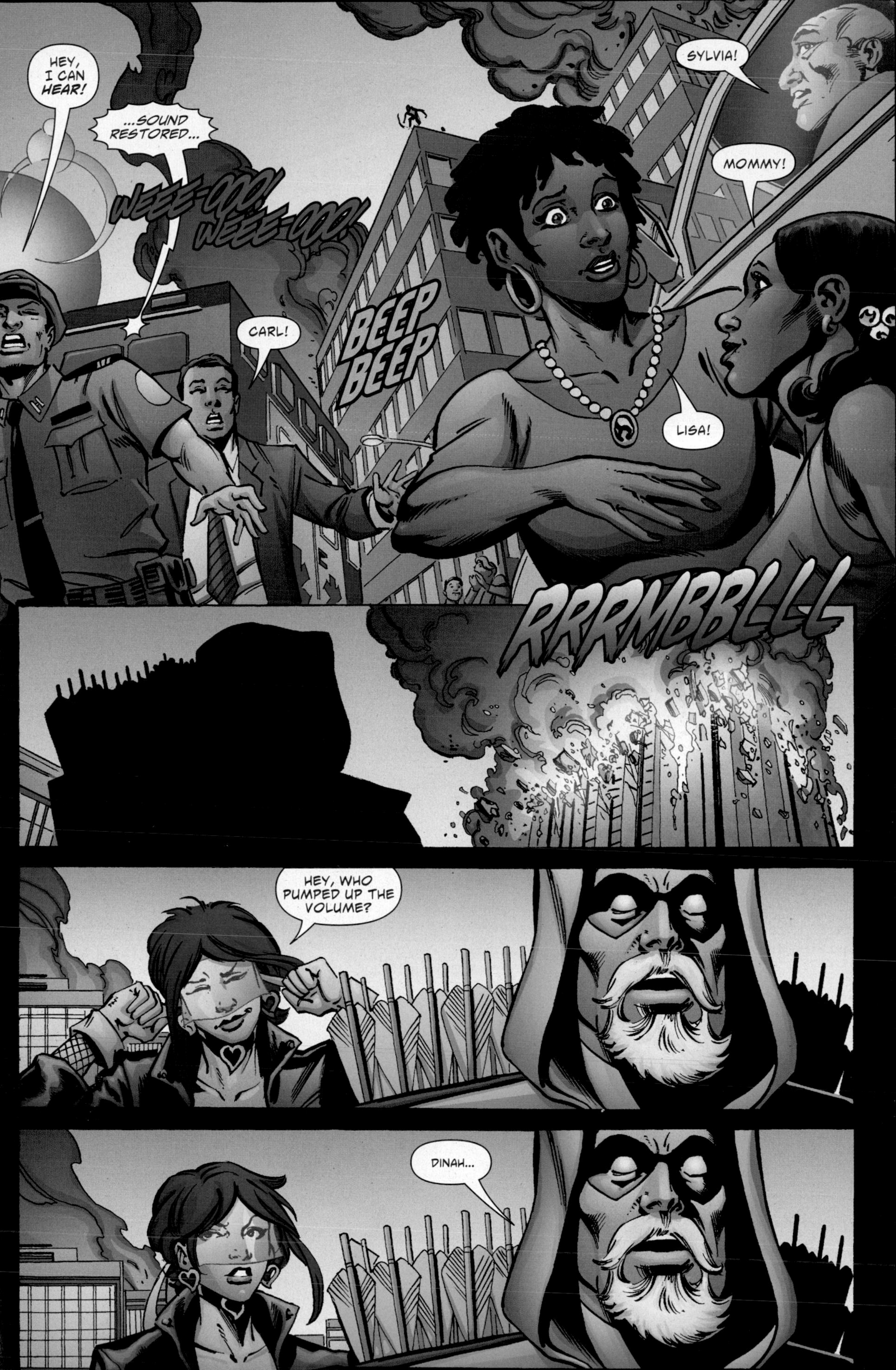
HEY, I CAN HEAR!
...SOUND RESTORED...
WEEE-OOO! WEEE-OOO!
SYLVIA!
MOMMY!
CARL!
BEEP BEEP
LISA!
RRRMBBLLL
HEY, WHO PUMPED UP THE VOLUME?
DINAH...

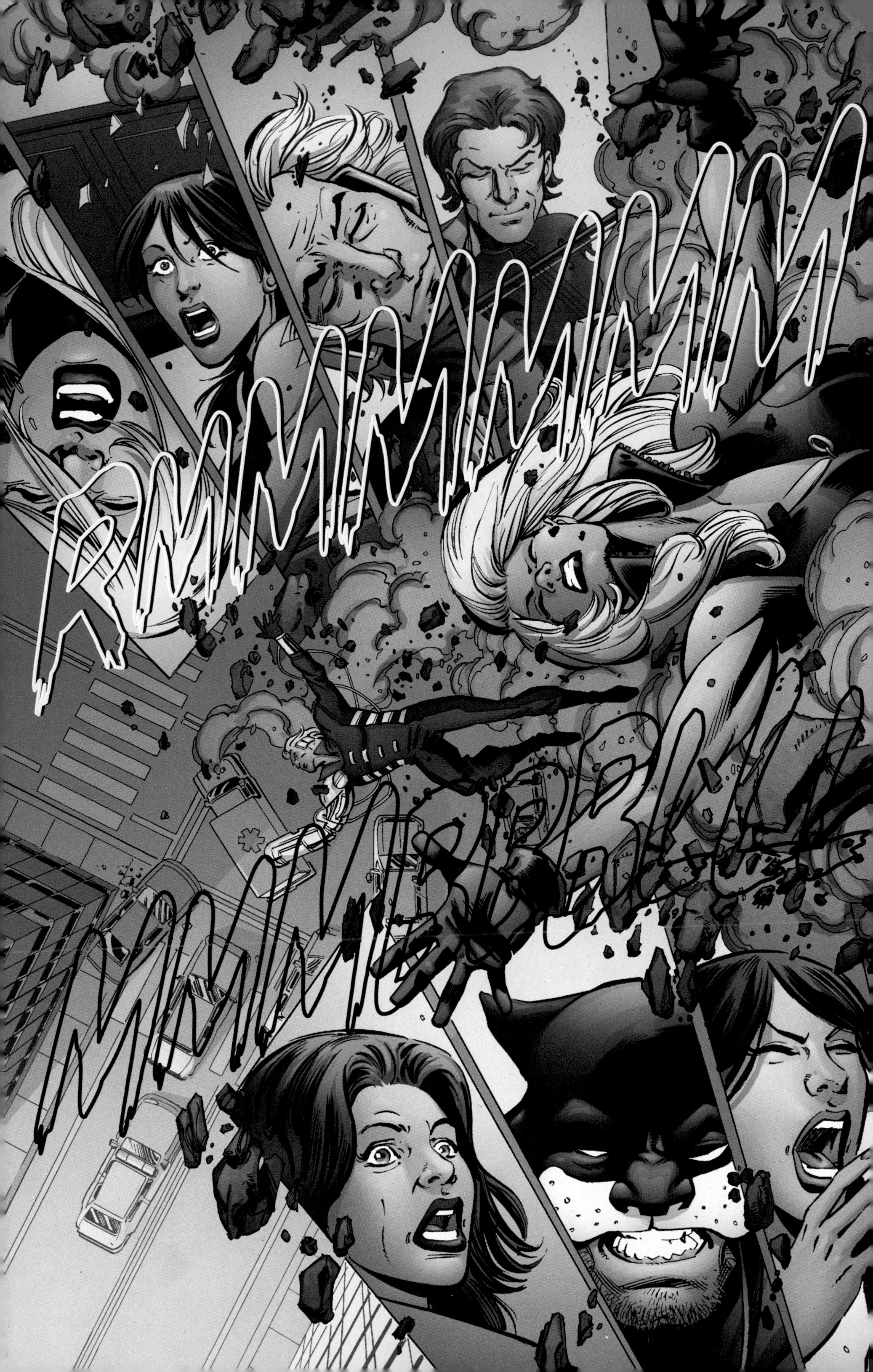

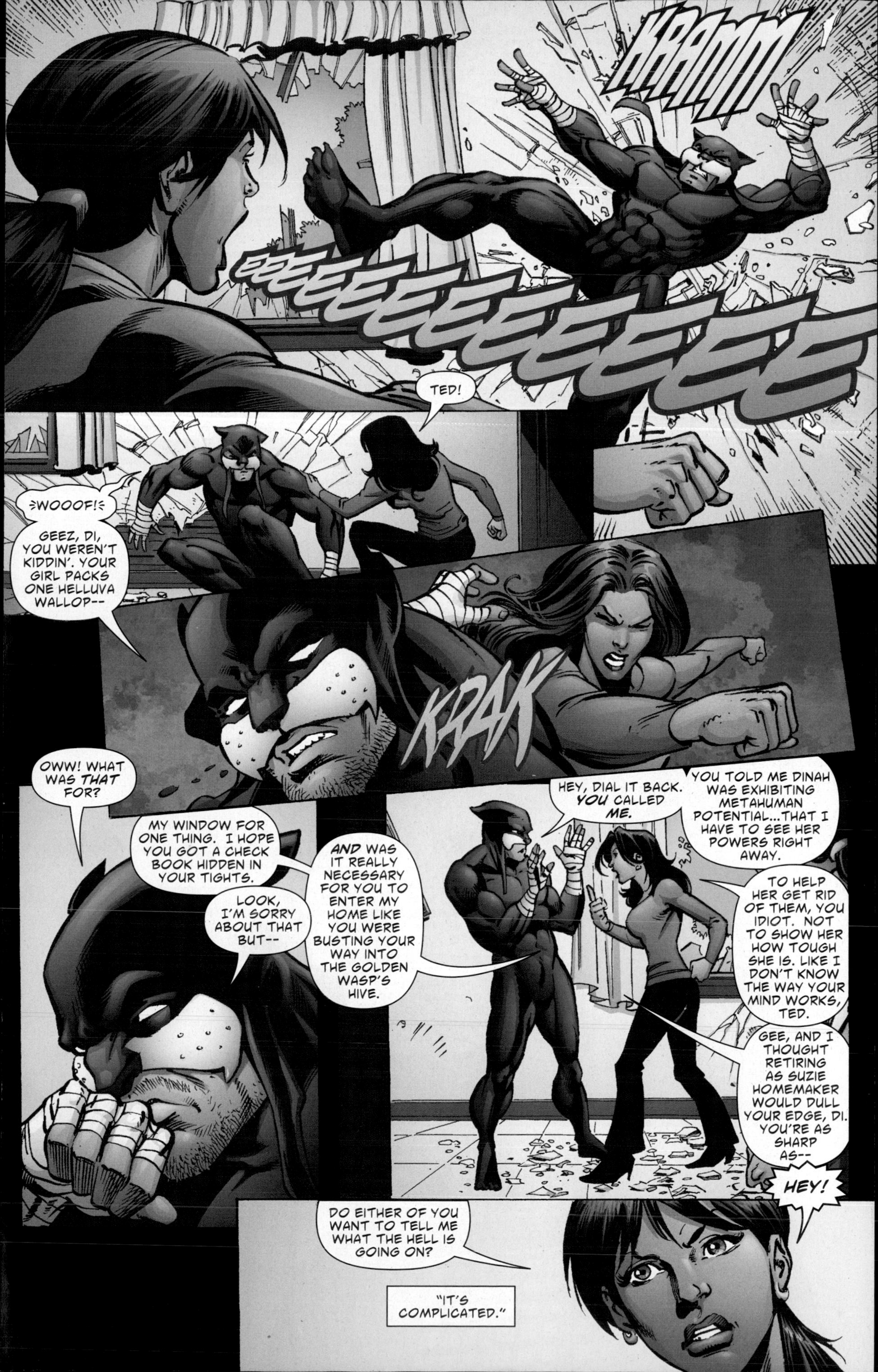
KRAMM
EEEEEEEEEEEEEEEE
TED!
WOOOF!
GEEZ, DI, YOU WEREN'T KIDDIN'. YOUR GIRL PACKS ONE HELLUVA WALLOP--
KRAK
OWW! WHAT WAS THAT FOR?
MY WINDOW FOR ONE THING. I HOPE YOU GOT A CHECK BOOK HIDDEN IN YOUR TIGHTS.
LOOK, I'M SORRY ABOUT THAT BUT--
AND WAS IT REALLY NECESSARY FOR YOU TO ENTER MY HOME LIKE YOU WERE BUSTING YOUR WAY INTO THE GOLDEN WASP'S HIVE.
HEY, DIAL IT BACK. YOU CALLED ME.
YOU TOLD ME DINAH WAS EXHIBITING METAHUMAN POTENTIAL...THAT I HAVE TO SEE HER POWERS RIGHT AWAY.
TO HELP HER GET RID OF THEM, YOU IDIOT. NOT TO SHOW HER HOW TOUGH SHE IS. LIKE I DON'T KNOW THE WAY YOUR MIND WORKS, TED.
GEE, AND I THOUGHT RETIRING AS SUZIE HOMEMAKER WOULD DULL YOUR EDGE, DI. YOU'RE AS SHARP AS--
HEY!
DO EITHER OF YOU WANT TO TELL ME WHAT THE HELL IS GOING ON?
"IT'S COMPLICATED."

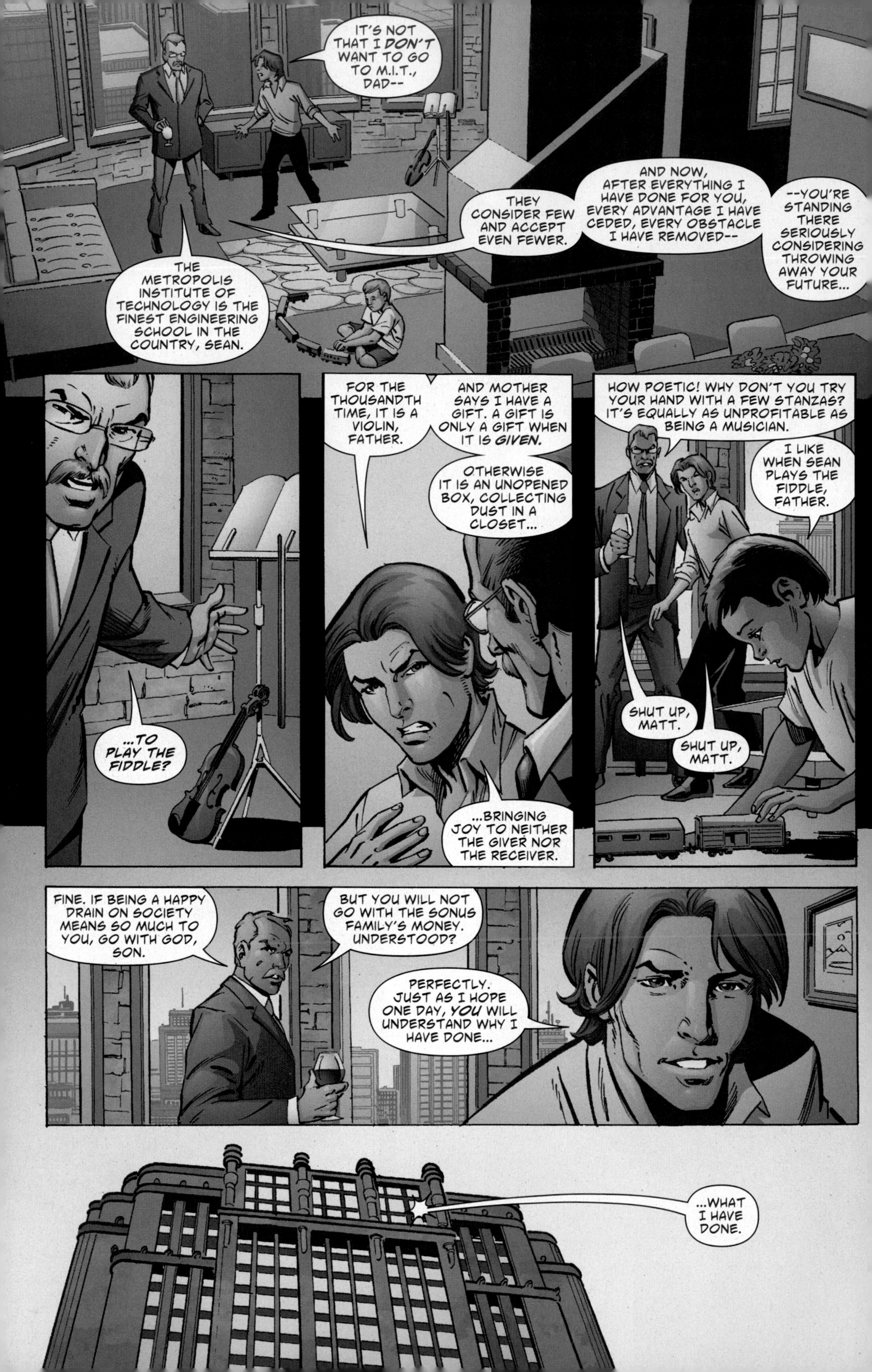
IT'S NOT THAT I DON'T WANT TO GO TO M.I.T., DAD--
THE METROPOLIS INSTITUTE OF TECHNOLOGY IS THE FINEST ENGINEERING SCHOOL IN THE COUNTRY, SEAN.
THEY CONSIDER FEW AND ACCEPT EVEN FEWER.
AND NOW, AFTER EVERYTHING I HAVE DONE FOR YOU, EVERY ADVANTAGE I HAVE CEDED, EVERY OBSTACLE I HAVE REMOVED--
--YOU'RE STANDING THERE SERIOUSLY CONSIDERING THROWING AWAY YOUR FUTURE...
...TO PLAY THE FIDDLE?
FOR THE THOUSANDTH TIME, IT IS A VIOLIN, FATHER.
AND MOTHER SAYS I HAVE A GIFT. A GIFT IS ONLY A GIFT WHEN IT IS GIVEN.
OTHERWISE IT IS AN UNOPENED BOX, COLLECTING DUST IN A CLOSET...
...BRINGING JOY TO NEITHER THE GIVER NOR THE RECEIVER.
HOW POETIC! WHY DON'T YOU TRY YOUR HAND WITH A FEW STANZAS? IT'S EQUALLY AS UNPROFITABLE AS BEING A MUSICIAN.
I LIKE WHEN SEAN PLAYS THE FIDDLE, FATHER.
SHUT UP, MATT.
SHUT UP, MATT.
FINE. IF BEING A HAPPY DRAIN ON SOCIETY MEANS SO MUCH TO YOU, GO WITH GOD, SON.
BUT YOU WILL NOT GO WITH THE SONUS FAMILY'S MONEY. UNDERSTOOD?
PERFECTLY. JUST AS I HOPE ONE DAY, YOU WILL UNDERSTAND WHY I HAVE DONE...
...WHAT I HAVE DONE.

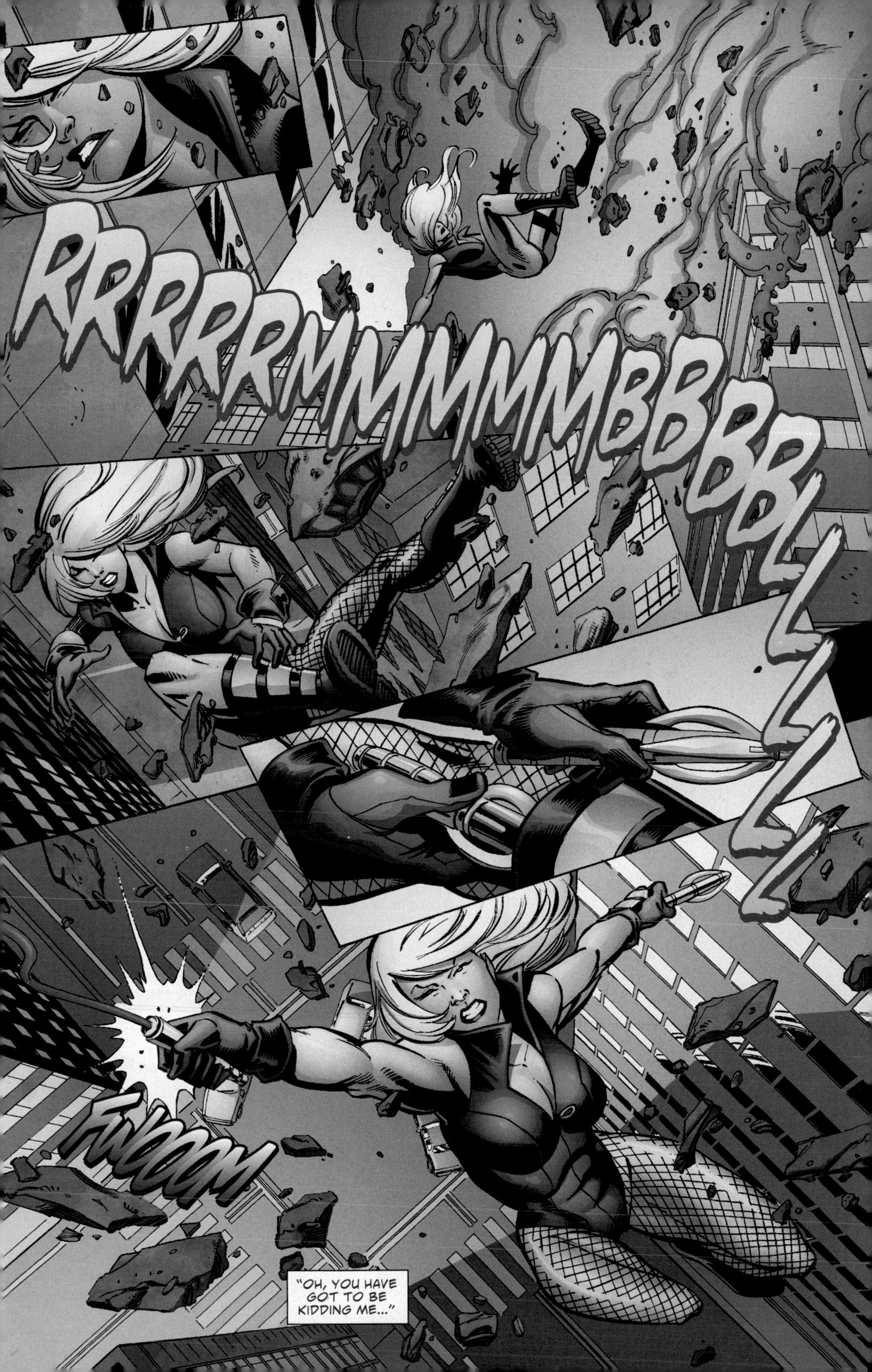
RRRRRMMMMMMBBBBLLLLL
FWOOOM
"OH, YOU HAVE GOT TO BE KIDDING ME..."

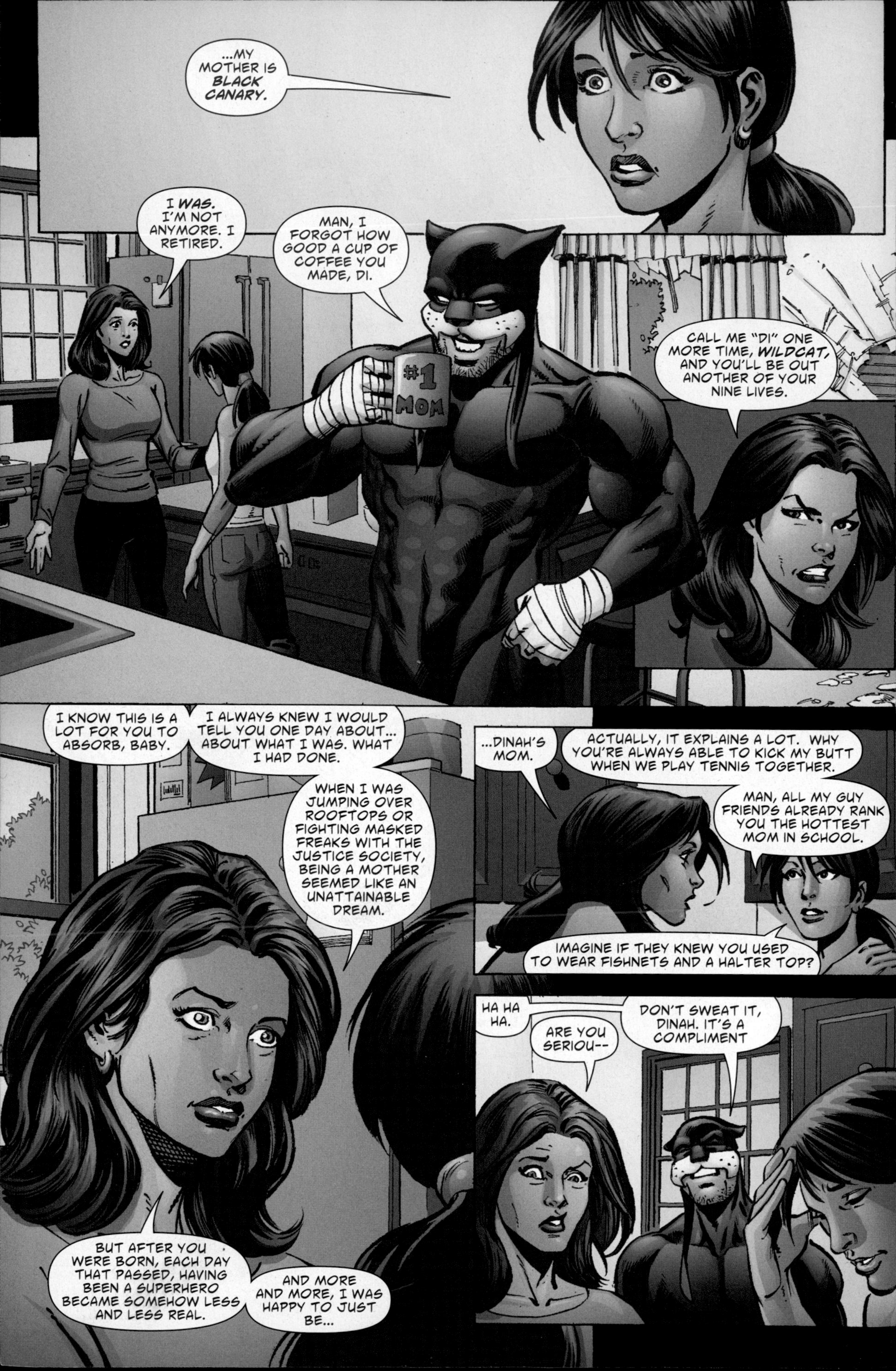
...MY MOTHER IS BLACK CANARY.
I WAS. I'M NOT ANYMORE. I RETIRED.
MAN, I FORGOT HOW GOOD A CUP OF COFFEE YOU MADE, DI.
#1 MOM
CALL ME "DI" ONE MORE TIME, WILDCAT, AND YOU'LL BE OUT ANOTHER OF YOUR NINE LIVES.
I KNOW THIS IS A LOT FOR YOU TO ABSORB, BABY.
I ALWAYS KNEW I WOULD TELL YOU ONE DAY ABOUT... ABOUT WHAT I WAS. WHAT I HAD DONE.
WHEN I WAS JUMPING OVER ROOFTOPS OR FIGHTING MASKED FREAKS WITH THE JUSTICE SOCIETY, BEING A MOTHER SEEMED LIKE AN UNATTAINABLE DREAM.
BUT AFTER YOU WERE BORN, EACH DAY THAT PASSED, HAVING BEEN A SUPERHERO BECAME SOMEHOW LESS AND LESS REAL.
AND MORE AND MORE, I WAS HAPPY TO JUST BE...
...DINAH'S MOM.
ACTUALLY, IT EXPLAINS A LOT. WHY YOU'RE ALWAYS ABLE TO KICK MY BUTT WHEN WE PLAY TENNIS TOGETHER.
MAN, ALL MY GUY FRIENDS ALREADY RANK YOU THE HOTTEST MOM IN SCHOOL.
IMAGINE IF THEY KNEW YOU USED TO WEAR FISHNETS AND A HALTER TOP?
HA HA HA.
ARE YOU SERIOU--
DON'T SWEAT IT, DINAH. IT'S A COMPLIMENT

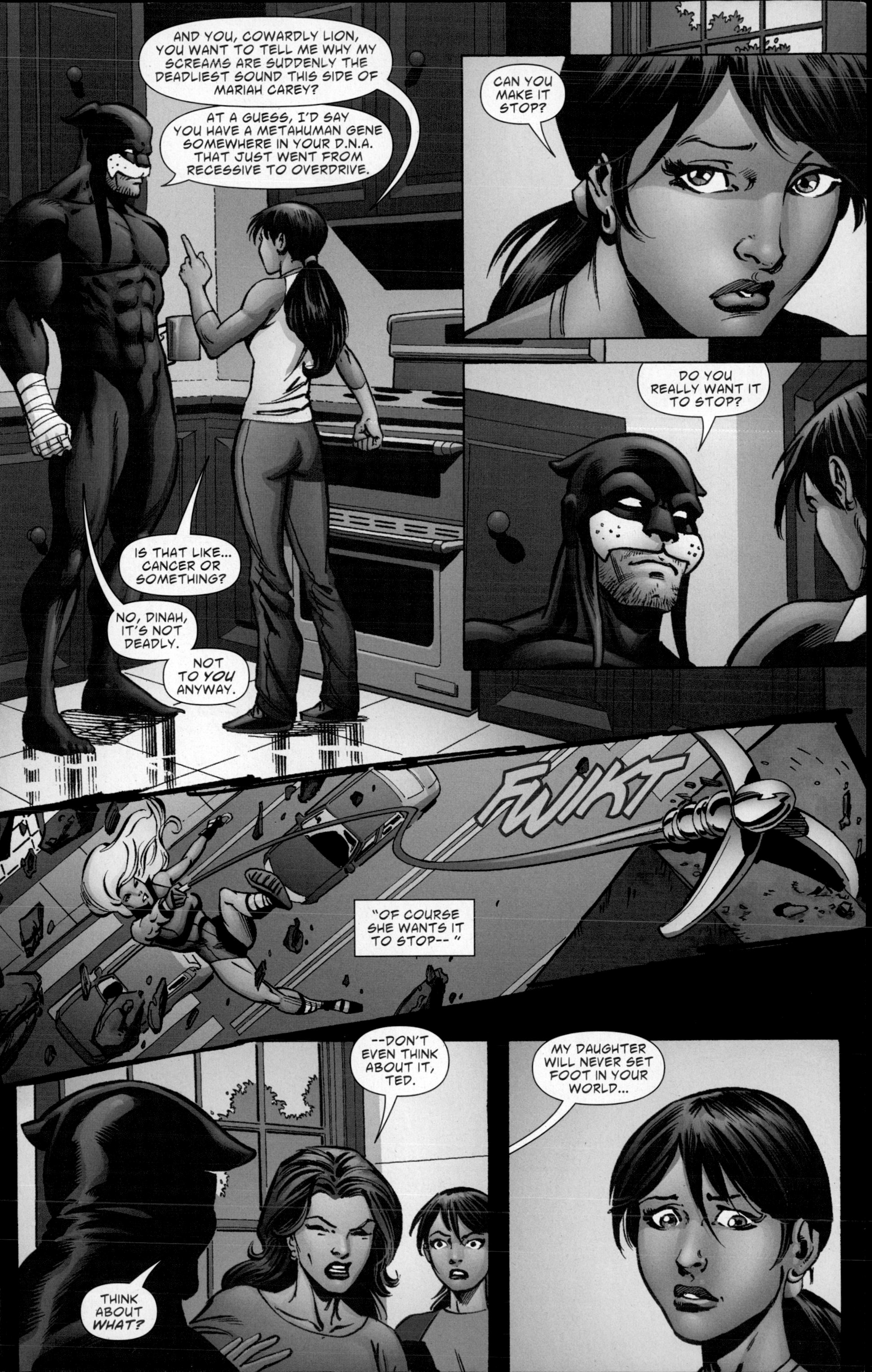
AND YOU, COWARDLY LION, YOU WANT TO TELL ME WHY MY SCREAMS ARE SUDDENLY THE DEADLIEST SOUND THIS SIDE OF MARIAH CAREY?
AT A GUESS, I'D SAY YOU HAVE A METAHUMAN GENE SOMEWHERE IN YOUR D.N.A. THAT JUST WENT FROM RECESSIVE TO OVERDRIVE.
IS THAT LIKE... CANCER OR SOMETHING?
NO, DINAH, IT'S NOT DEADLY.
NOT TO *YOU* ANYWAY.
CAN YOU MAKE IT STOP?
DO YOU REALLY WANT IT TO STOP?
FWIKT
"OF COURSE SHE WANTS IT TO STOP-- "
--DON'T EVEN THINK ABOUT IT, TED.
THINK ABOUT *WHAT?*
MY DAUGHTER WILL NEVER SET FOOT IN YOUR WORLD...

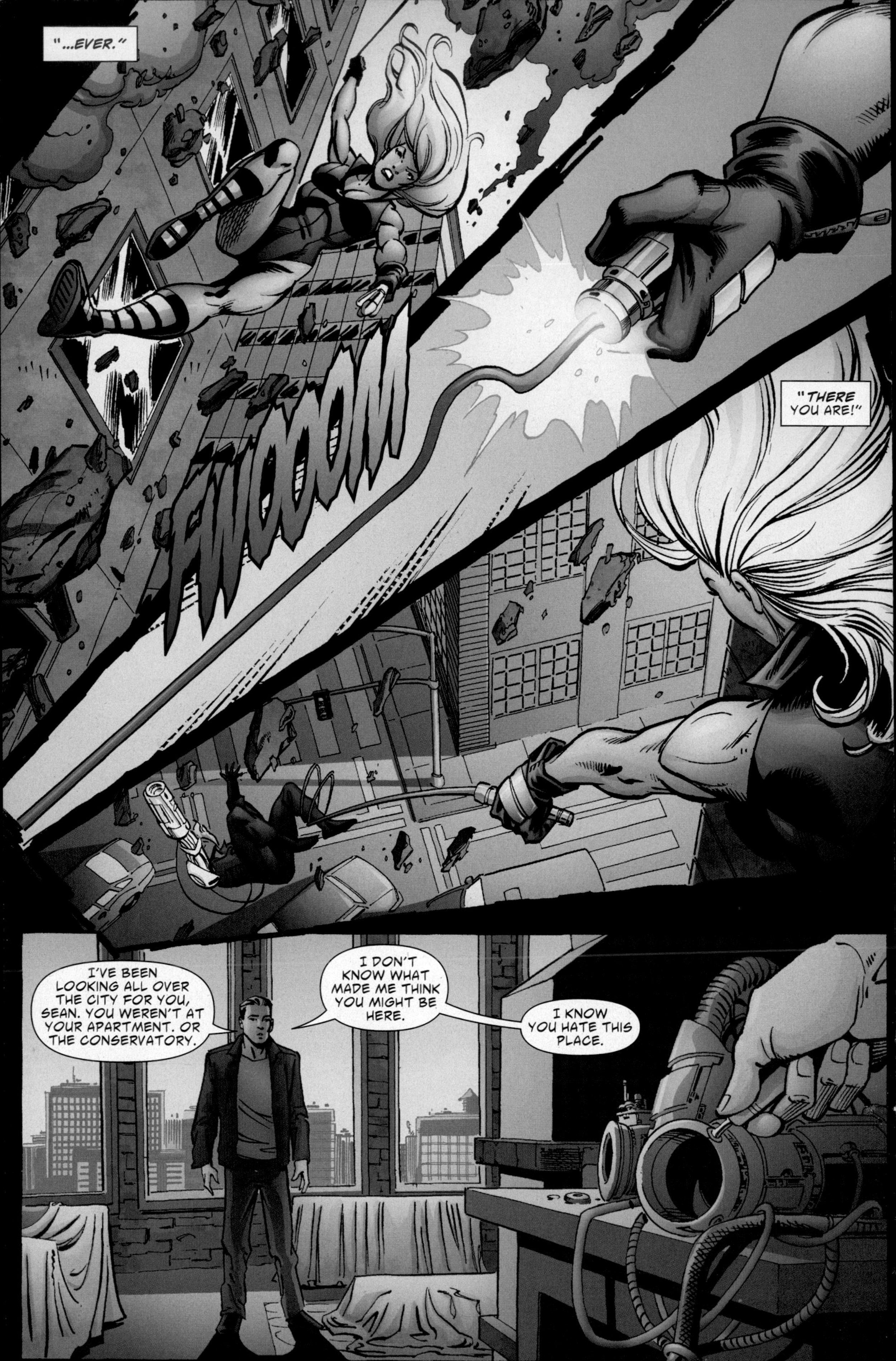
"...EVER."
FWOOOM
"THERE YOU ARE!"
I'VE BEEN LOOKING ALL OVER THE CITY FOR YOU, SEAN. YOU WEREN'T AT YOUR APARTMENT. OR THE CONSERVATORY.
I DON'T KNOW WHAT MADE ME THINK YOU MIGHT BE HERE.
I KNOW YOU HATE THIS PLACE.

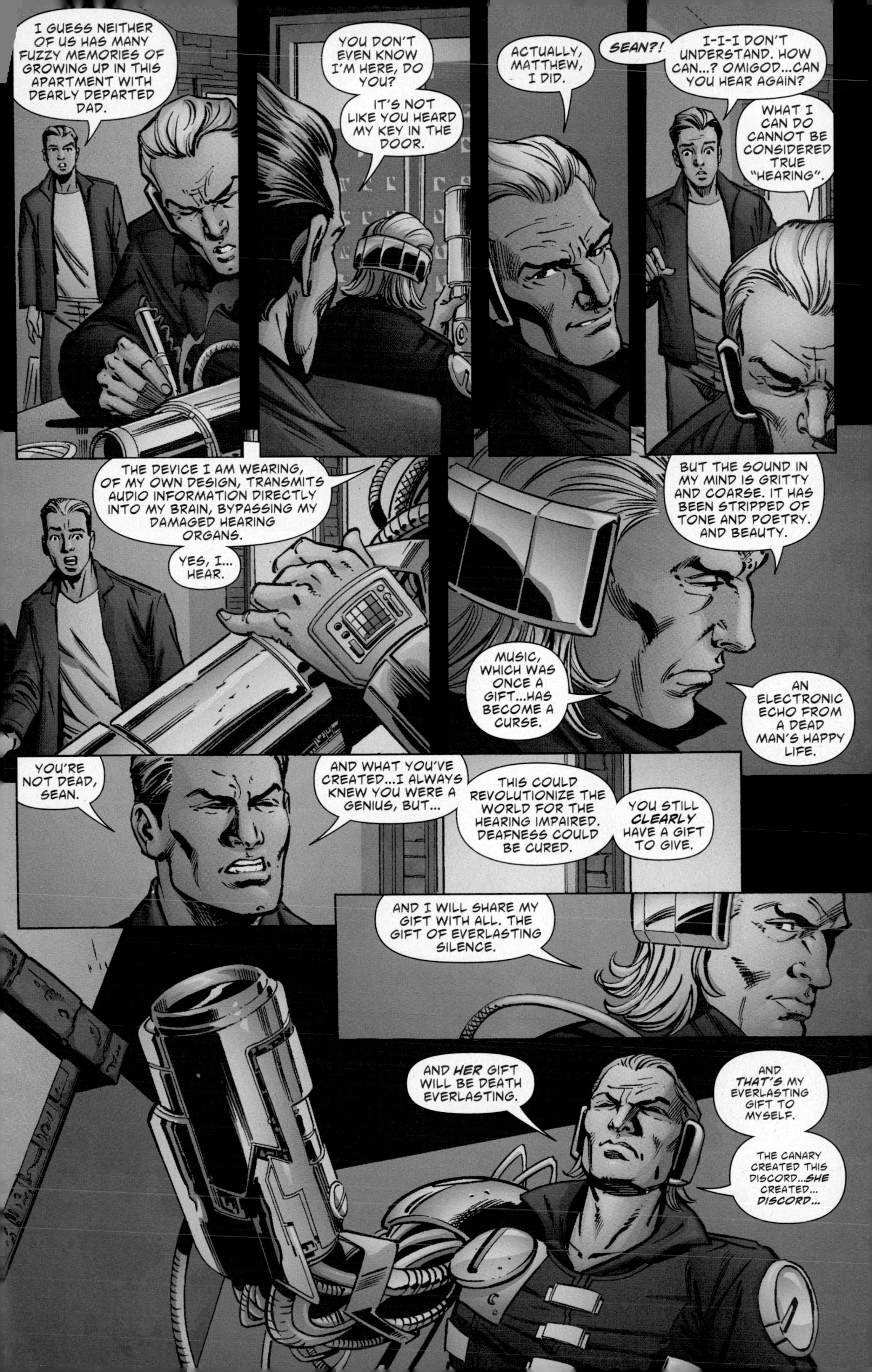
I GUESS NEITHER OF US HAS MANY FUZZY MEMORIES OF GROWING UP IN THIS APARTMENT WITH DEARLY DEPARTED DAD.
YOU DON'T EVEN KNOW I'M HERE, DO YOU?
IT'S NOT LIKE YOU HEARD MY KEY IN THE DOOR.
ACTUALLY, MATTHEW, I DID.
SEAN?!
I-I-I DON'T UNDERSTAND. HOW CAN...? OMIGOD...CAN YOU HEAR AGAIN?
WHAT I CAN DO CANNOT BE CONSIDERED TRUE "HEARING".
THE DEVICE I AM WEARING, OF MY OWN DESIGN, TRANSMITS AUDIO INFORMATION DIRECTLY INTO MY BRAIN, BYPASSING MY DAMAGED HEARING ORGANS.
YES, I... HEAR.
BUT THE SOUND IN MY MIND IS GRITTY AND COARSE. IT HAS BEEN STRIPPED OF TONE AND POETRY. AND BEAUTY.
MUSIC, WHICH WAS ONCE A GIFT...HAS BECOME A CURSE.
AN ELECTRONIC ECHO FROM A DEAD MAN'S HAPPY LIFE.
YOU'RE NOT DEAD, SEAN.
AND WHAT YOU'VE CREATED...I ALWAYS KNEW YOU WERE A GENIUS, BUT...
THIS COULD REVOLUTIONIZE THE WORLD FOR THE HEARING IMPAIRED. DEAFNESS COULD BE CURED.
YOU STILL CLEARLY HAVE A GIFT TO GIVE.
AND I WILL SHARE MY GIFT WITH ALL. THE GIFT OF EVERLASTING SILENCE.
AND HER GIFT WILL BE DEATH EVERLASTING.
AND THAT'S MY EVERLASTING GIFT TO MYSELF.
THE CANARY CREATED THIS DISCORD...SHE CREATED... DISCORD...

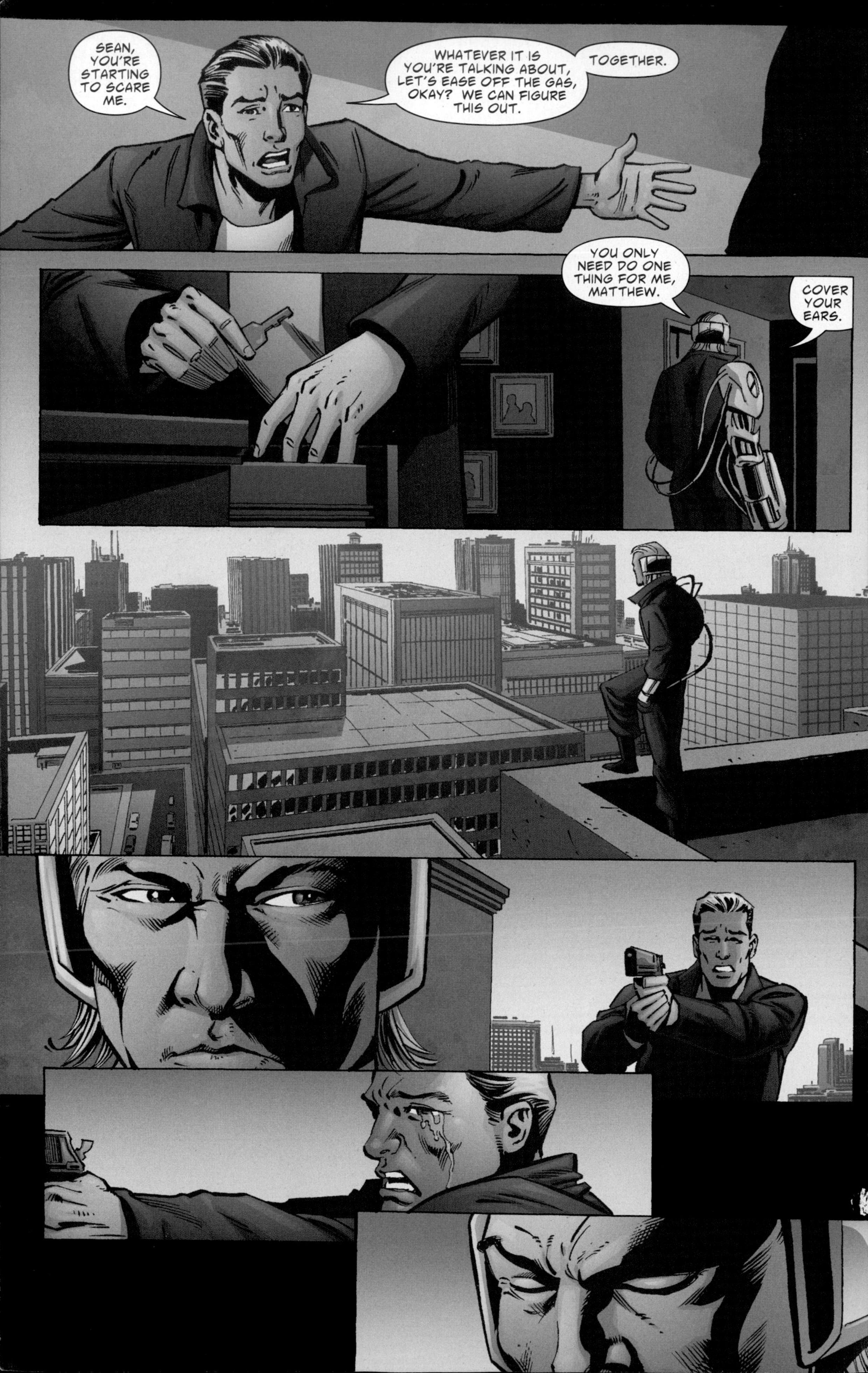
SEAN, YOU'RE STARTING TO SCARE ME.
WHATEVER IT IS YOU'RE TALKING ABOUT, LET'S EASE OFF THE GAS, OKAY? WE CAN FIGURE THIS OUT.
TOGETHER.
YOU ONLY NEED DO ONE THING FOR ME, MATTHEW.
COVER YOUR EARS.

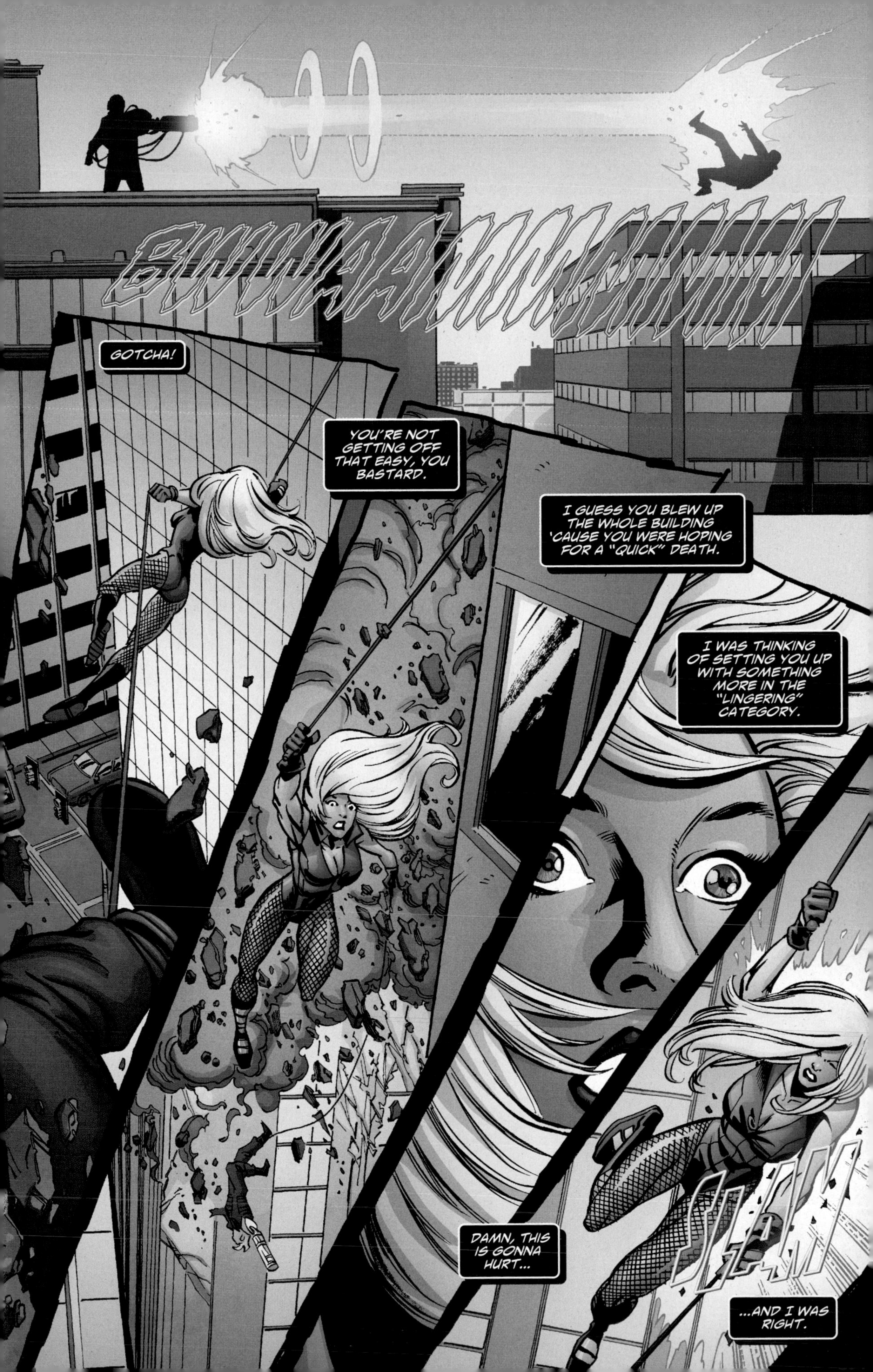
GOTCHA!
YOU'RE NOT GETTING OFF THAT EASY, YOU BASTARD.
I GUESS YOU BLEW UP THE WHOLE BUILDING 'CAUSE YOU WERE HOPING FOR A "QUICK" DEATH.
I WAS THINKING OF SETTING YOU UP WITH SOMETHING MORE IN THE "LINGERING" CATEGORY.
DAMN, THIS IS GONNA HURT...
SLAM
...AND I WAS RIGHT.

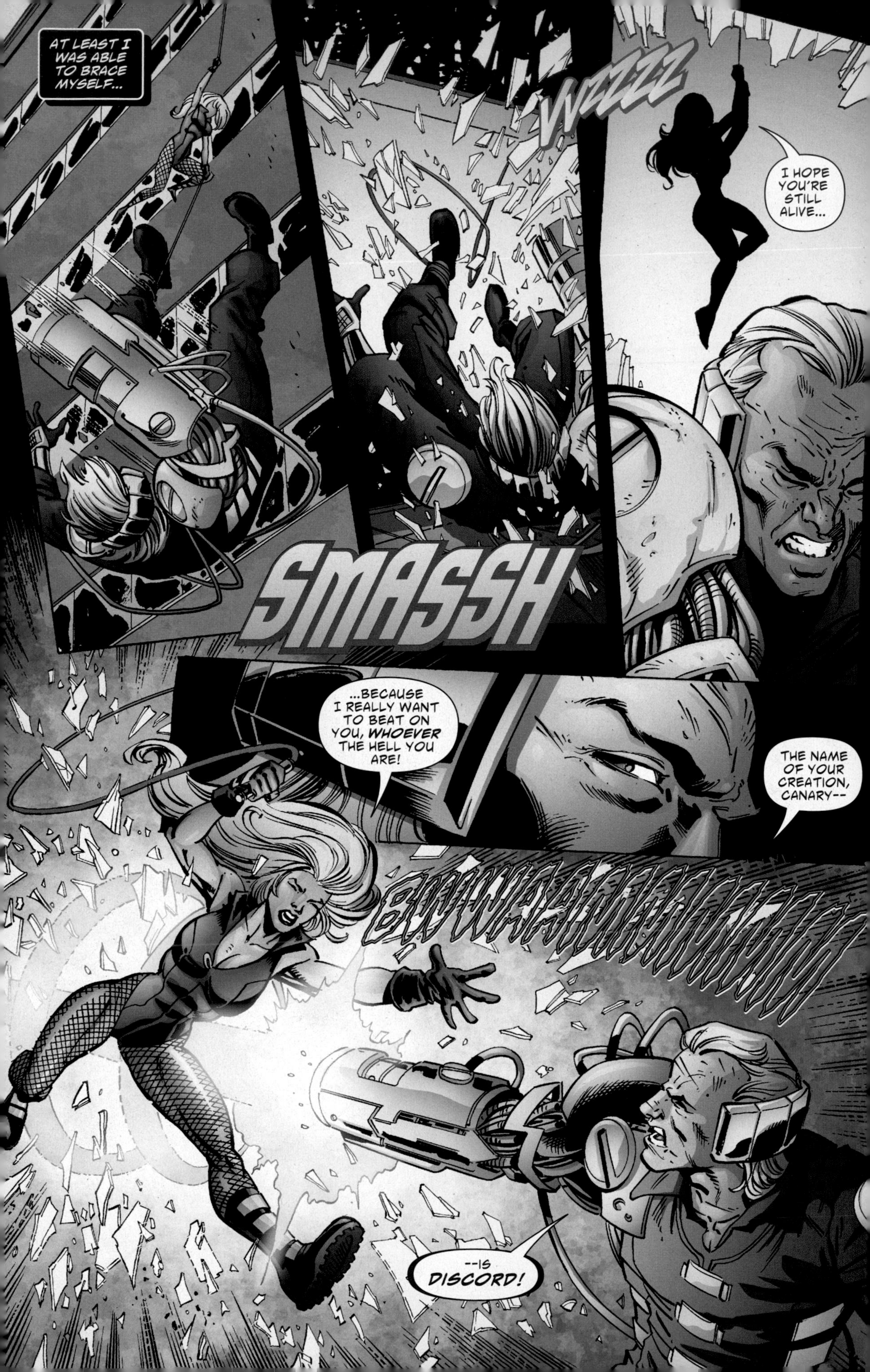
AT LEAST I WAS ABLE TO BRACE MYSELF...
VVZZZZ
I HOPE YOU'RE STILL ALIVE...
SMASSH
...BECAUSE I REALLY WANT TO BEAT ON YOU, WHOEVER THE HELL YOU ARE!
THE NAME OF YOUR CREATION, CANARY--
--IS DISCORD!

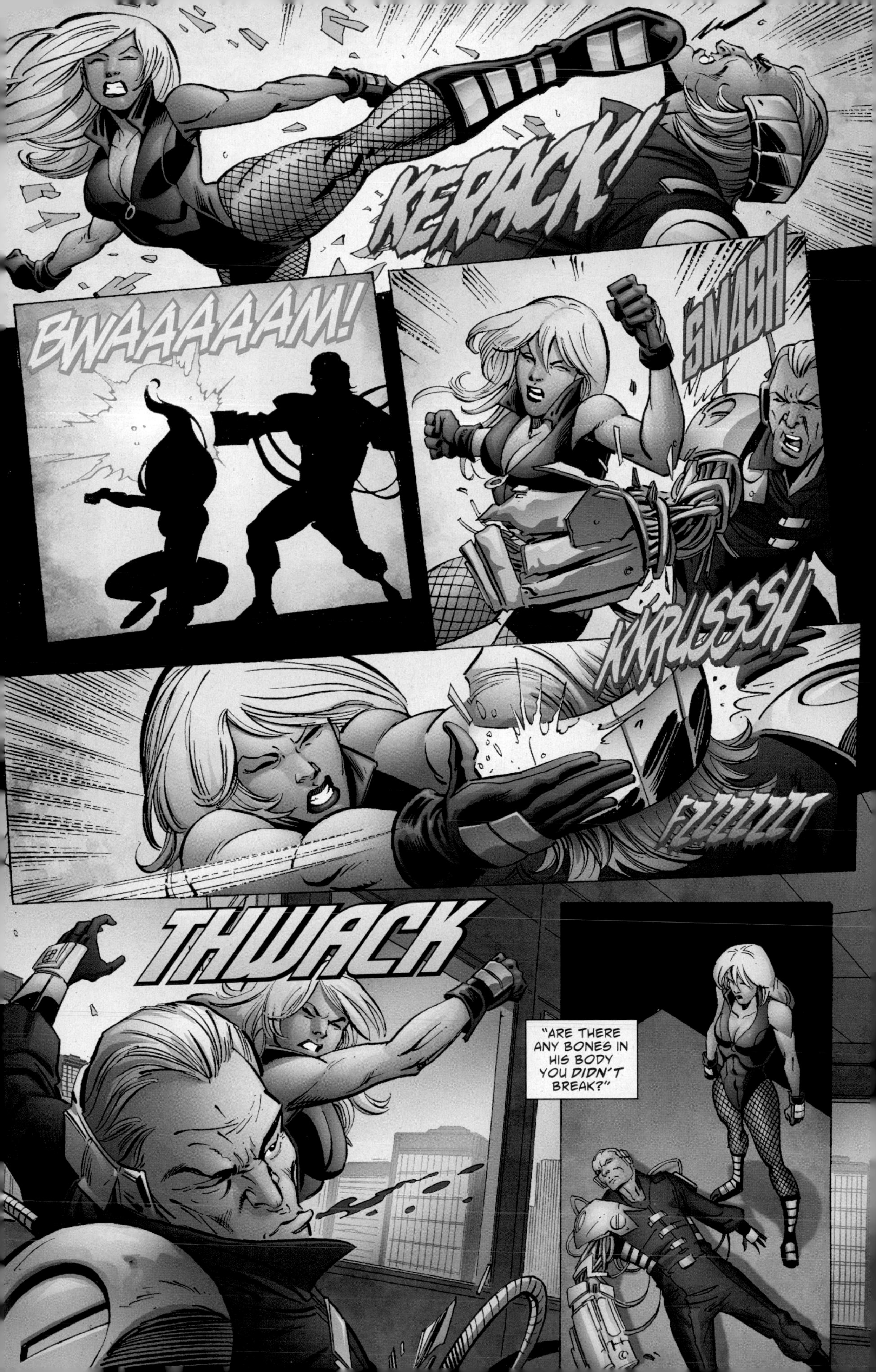
KERACK!
BWAAAAAM!
SMASH
KKRUSSSH
FZZZZZZT
THWACK
"ARE THERE ANY BONES IN HIS BODY YOU *DIDN'T* BREAK?"

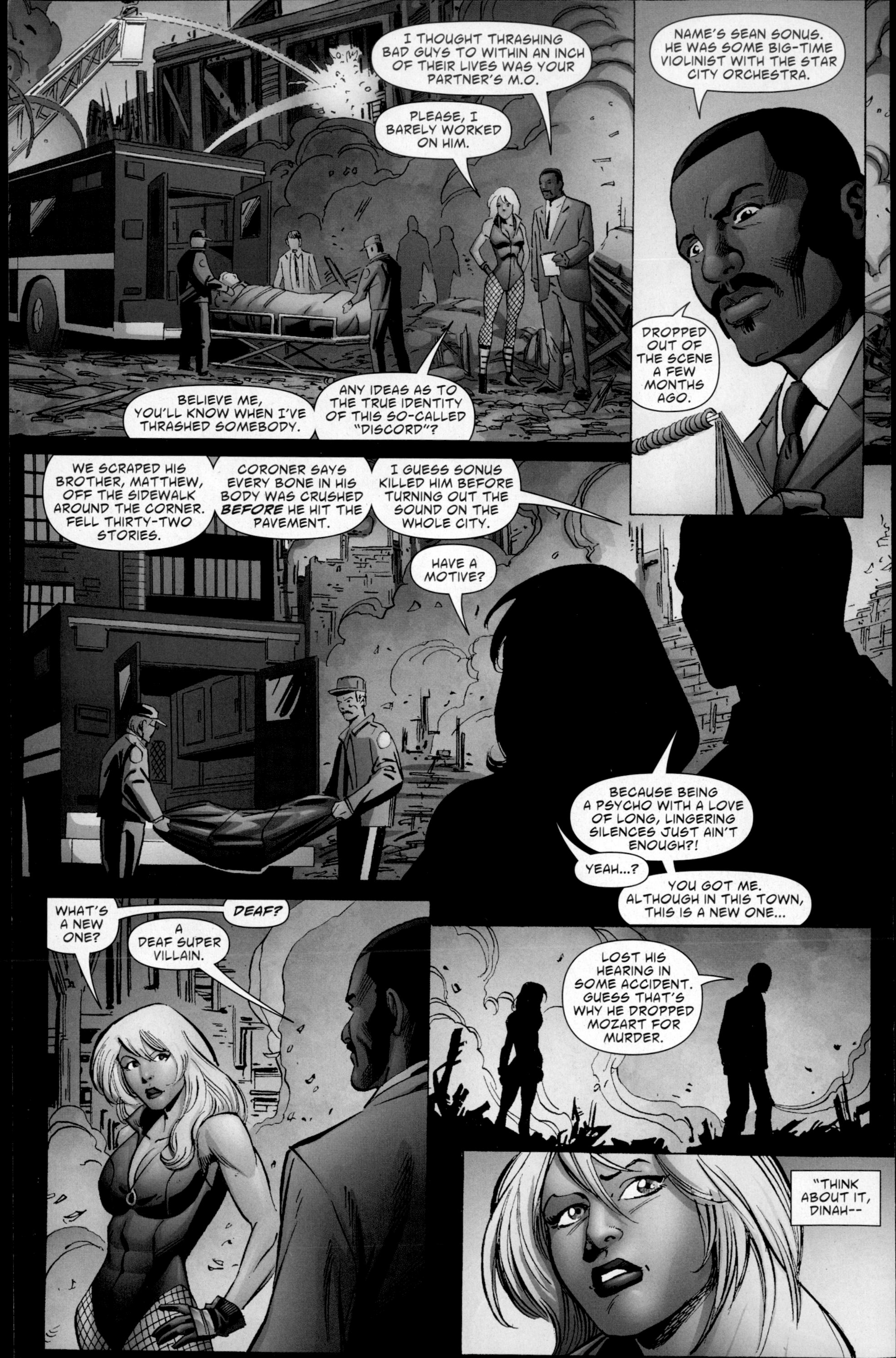
I THOUGHT THRASHING BAD GUYS TO WITHIN AN INCH OF THEIR LIVES WAS YOUR PARTNER'S M.O.
PLEASE, I BARELY WORKED ON HIM.
BELIEVE ME, YOU'LL KNOW WHEN I'VE THRASHED SOMEBODY.
ANY IDEAS AS TO THE TRUE IDENTITY OF THIS SO-CALLED "DISCORD"?
NAME'S SEAN SONUS. HE WAS SOME BIG-TIME VIOLINIST WITH THE STAR CITY ORCHESTRA.
DROPPED OUT OF THE SCENE A FEW MONTHS AGO.
WE SCRAPED HIS BROTHER, MATTHEW, OFF THE SIDEWALK AROUND THE CORNER. FELL THIRTY-TWO STORIES.
CORONER SAYS EVERY BONE IN HIS BODY WAS CRUSHED *BEFORE* HE HIT THE PAVEMENT.
I GUESS SONUS KILLED HIM BEFORE TURNING OUT THE SOUND ON THE WHOLE CITY.
HAVE A MOTIVE?
BECAUSE BEING A PSYCHO WITH A LOVE OF LONG, LINGERING SILENCES JUST AIN'T ENOUGH?!
YEAH...?
YOU GOT ME. ALTHOUGH IN THIS TOWN, THIS IS A NEW ONE...
WHAT'S A NEW ONE?
A DEAF SUPER VILLAIN.
DEAF?
LOST HIS HEARING IN SOME ACCIDENT. GUESS THAT'S WHY HE DROPPED MOZART FOR MURDER.
"THINK ABOUT IT, DINAH--

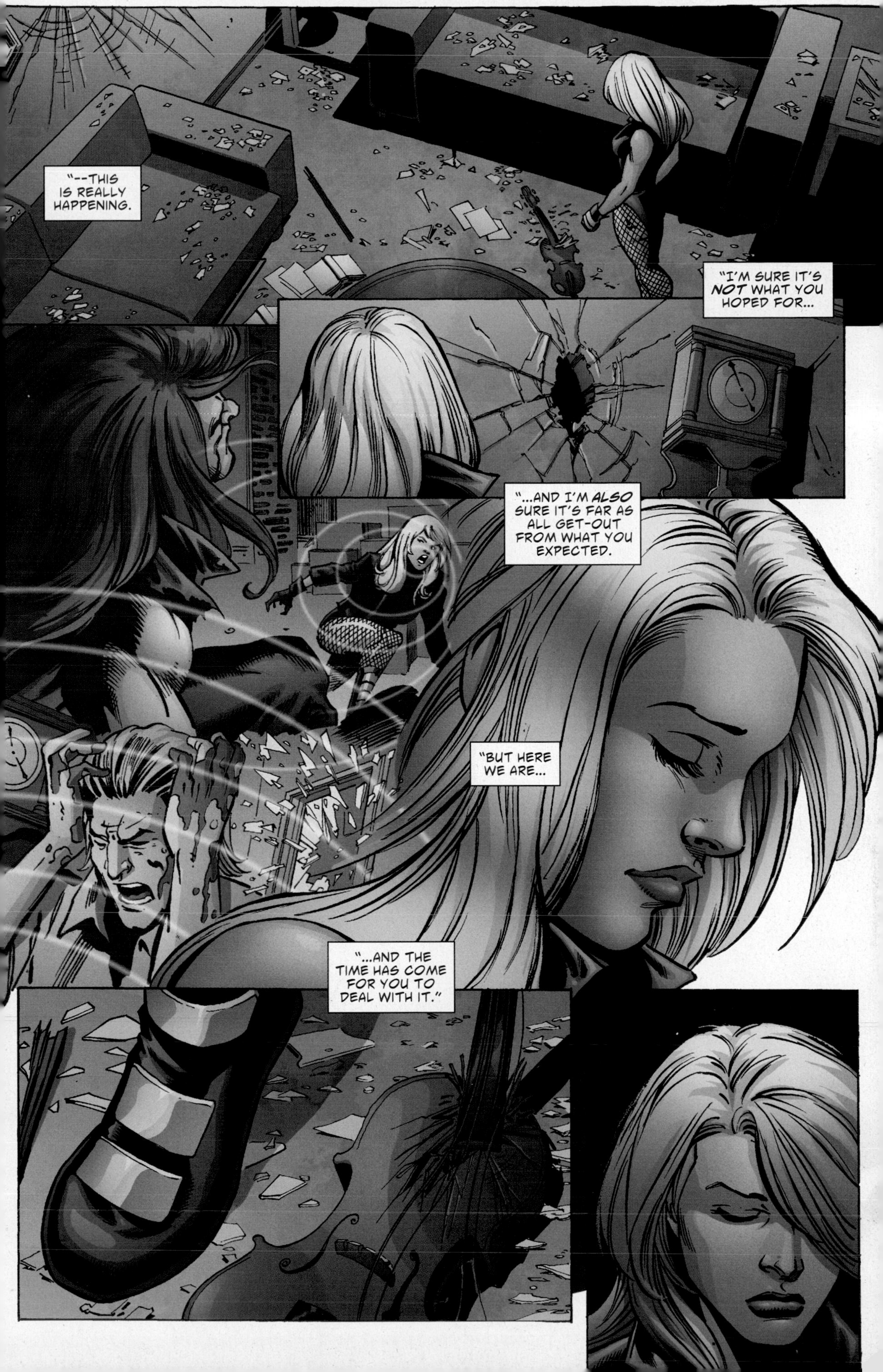
"--THIS IS REALLY HAPPENING.
"I'M SURE IT'S NOT WHAT YOU HOPED FOR...
"...AND I'M ALSO SURE IT'S FAR AS ALL GET-OUT FROM WHAT YOU EXPECTED.
"BUT HERE WE ARE...
"...AND THE TIME HAS COME FOR YOU TO DEAL WITH IT."

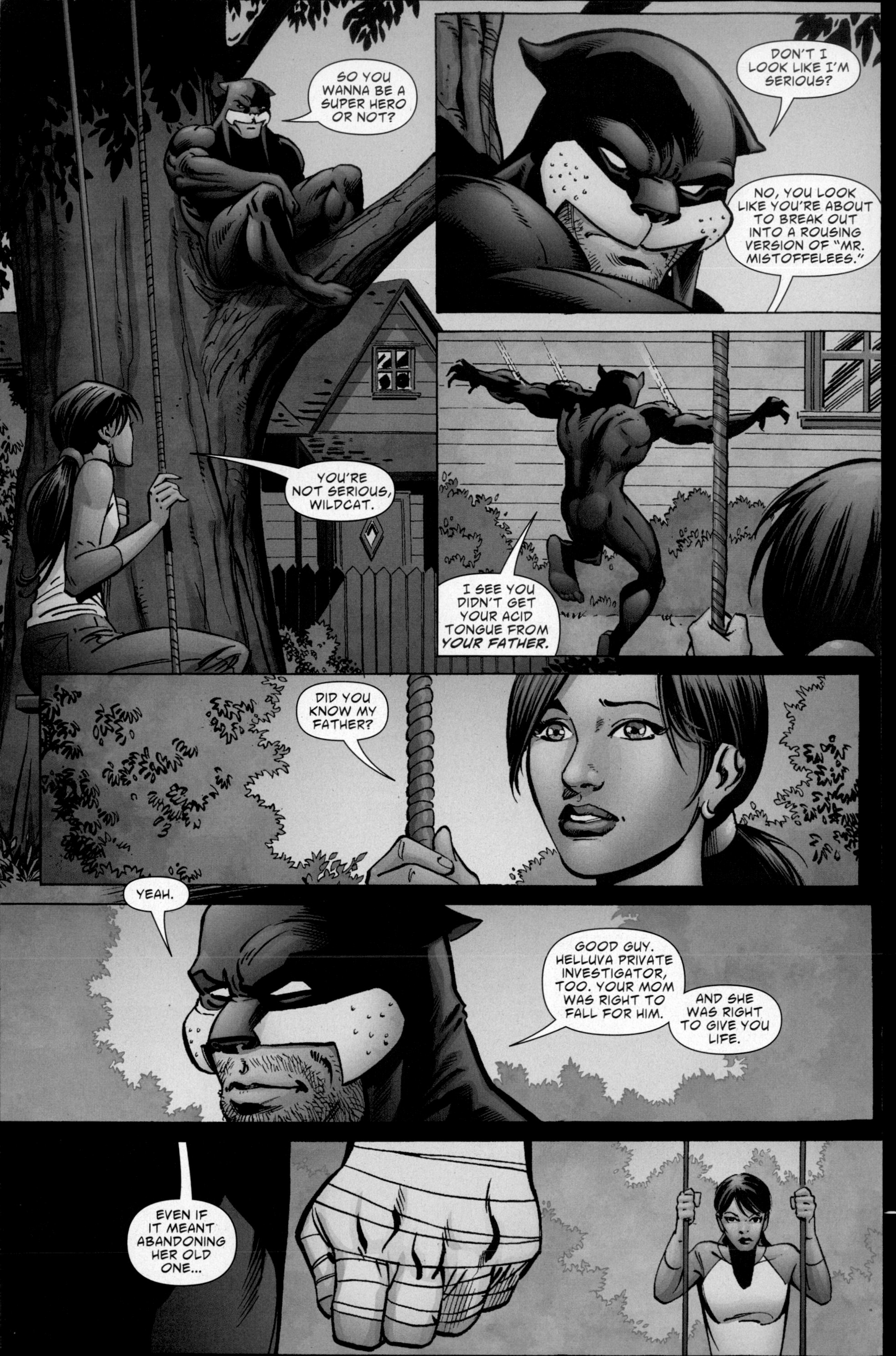

SO YOU WANNA BE A SUPER HERO OR NOT?
DON'T I LOOK LIKE I'M SERIOUS?
NO, YOU LOOK LIKE YOU'RE ABOUT TO BREAK OUT INTO A ROUSING VERSION OF "MR. MISTOFFELEES."
YOU'RE NOT SERIOUS, WILDCAT.
I SEE YOU DIDN'T GET YOUR ACID TONGUE FROM *YOUR FATHER.*
DID YOU KNOW MY FATHER?
YEAH.
GOOD GUY. HELLUVA PRIVATE INVESTIGATOR, TOO. YOUR MOM WAS RIGHT TO FALL FOR HIM.
AND SHE WAS RIGHT TO GIVE YOU LIFE.
EVEN IF IT MEANT ABANDONING HER OLD ONE...

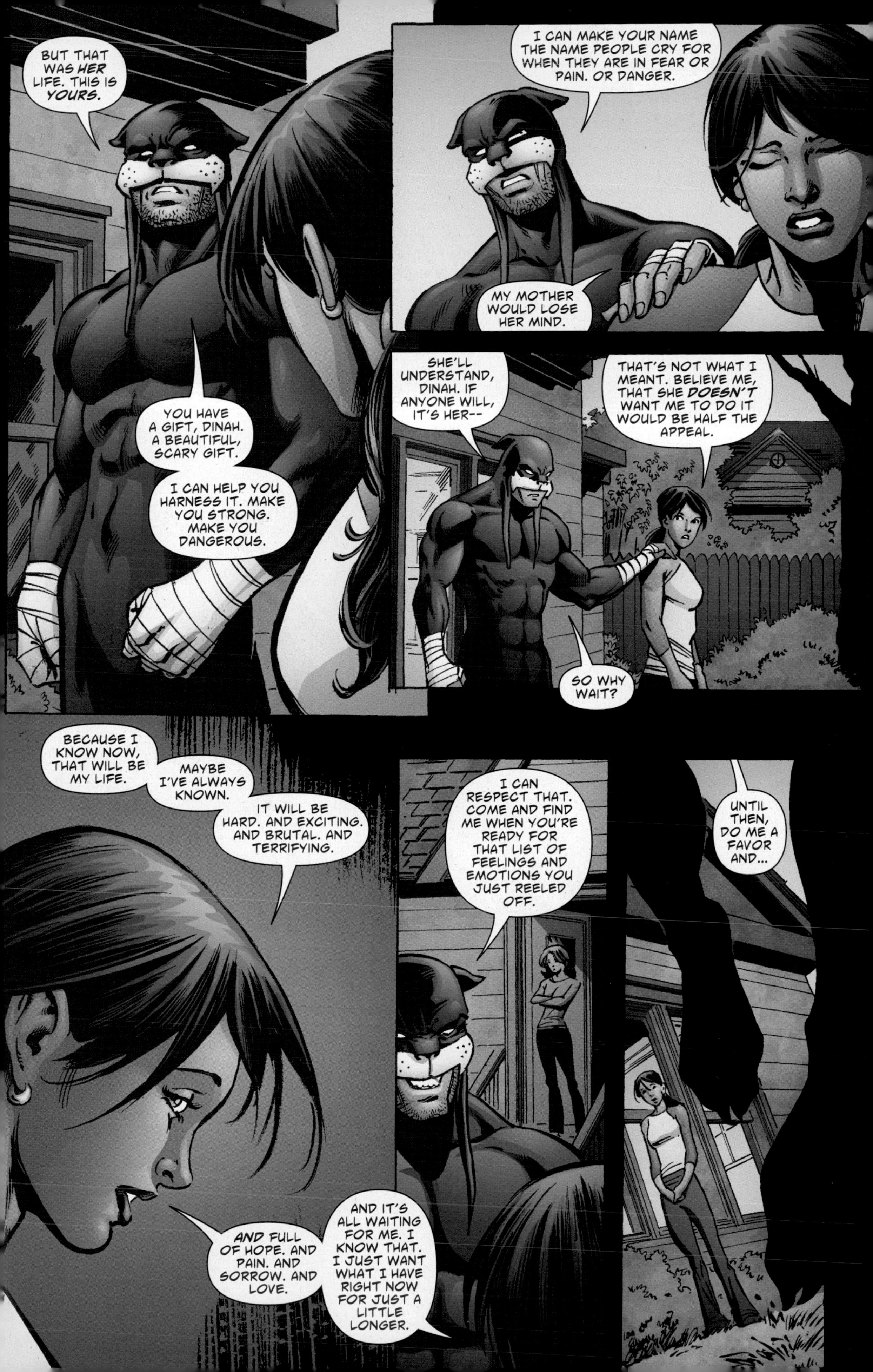
BUT THAT WAS HER LIFE. THIS IS YOURS.
YOU HAVE A GIFT, DINAH. A BEAUTIFUL, SCARY GIFT.
I CAN HELP YOU HARNESS IT. MAKE YOU STRONG. MAKE YOU DANGEROUS.
I CAN MAKE YOUR NAME THE NAME PEOPLE CRY FOR WHEN THEY ARE IN FEAR OR PAIN. OR DANGER.
MY MOTHER WOULD LOSE HER MIND.
SHE'LL UNDERSTAND, DINAH. IF ANYONE WILL, IT'S HER--
THAT'S NOT WHAT I MEANT. BELIEVE ME, THAT SHE DOESN'T WANT ME TO DO IT WOULD BE HALF THE APPEAL.
SO WHY WAIT?
BECAUSE I KNOW NOW, THAT WILL BE MY LIFE.
MAYBE I'VE ALWAYS KNOWN.
IT WILL BE HARD. AND EXCITING. AND BRUTAL. AND TERRIFYING.
AND FULL OF HOPE. AND PAIN. AND SORROW. AND LOVE.
AND IT'S ALL WAITING FOR ME. I KNOW THAT. I JUST WANT WHAT I HAVE RIGHT NOW FOR JUST A LITTLE LONGER.
I CAN RESPECT THAT. COME AND FIND ME WHEN YOU'RE READY FOR THAT LIST OF FEELINGS AND EMOTIONS YOU JUST REELED OFF.
UNTIL THEN, DO ME A FAVOR AND...

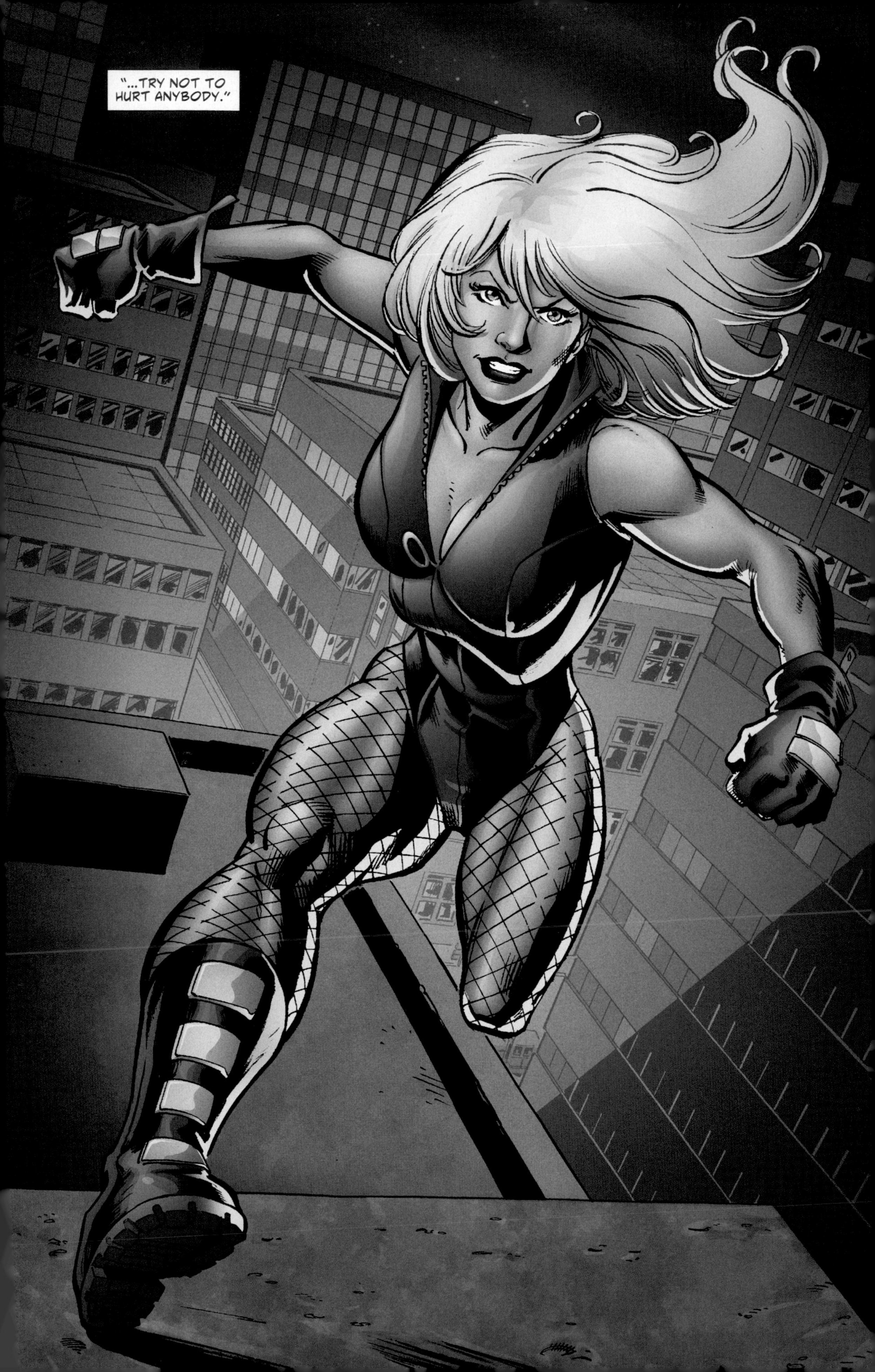
"...TRY NOT TO HURT ANYBODY."

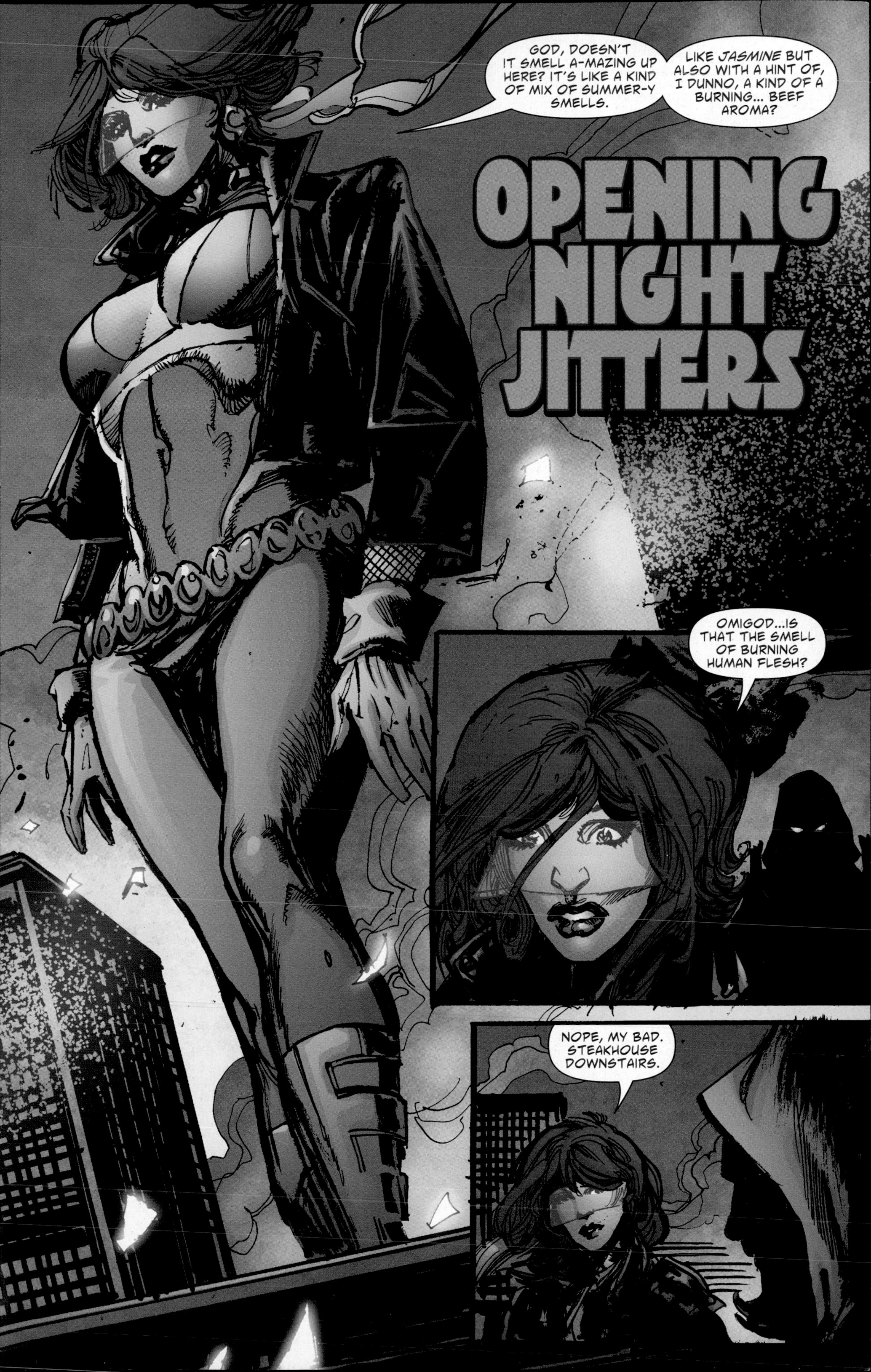
GOD, DOESN'T IT SMELL A-MAZING UP HERE? IT'S LIKE A KIND OF MIX OF SUMMER-Y SMELLS.
LIKE *JASMINE* BUT ALSO WITH A HINT OF, I DUNNO, A KIND OF A BURNING... BEEF AROMA?
OPENING NIGHT JITTERS
OMIGOD...IS THAT THE SMELL OF BURNING HUMAN FLESH?
NOPE, MY BAD. STEAKHOUSE DOWNSTAIRS.

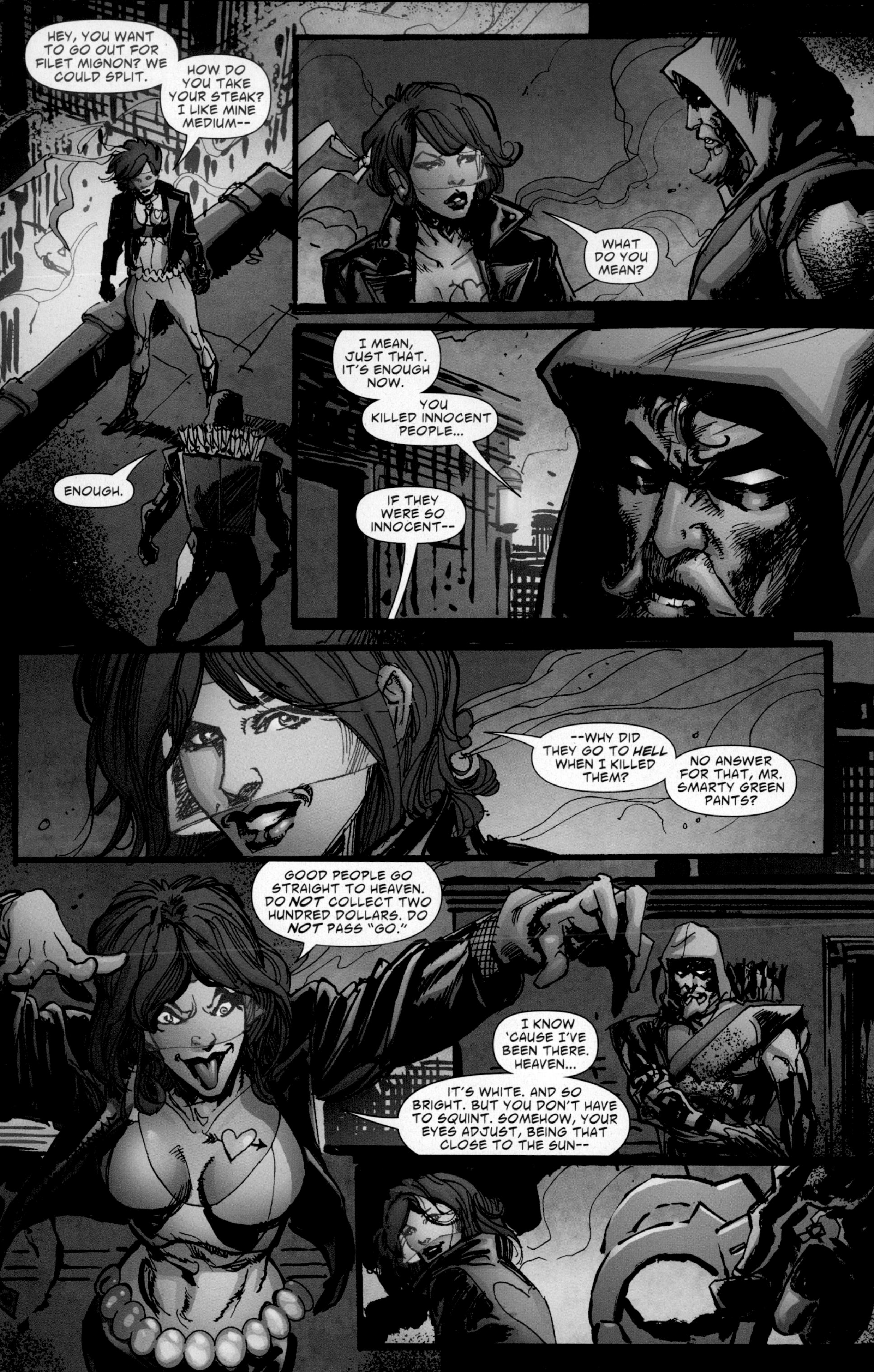
HEY, YOU WANT TO GO OUT FOR FILET MIGNON? WE COULD SPLIT.
HOW DO YOU TAKE YOUR STEAK? I LIKE MINE MEDIUM--
ENOUGH.
WHAT DO YOU MEAN?
I MEAN, JUST THAT. IT'S ENOUGH NOW.
YOU KILLED INNOCENT PEOPLE...
IF THEY WERE SO INNOCENT--
--WHY DID THEY GO TO HELL WHEN I KILLED THEM?
NO ANSWER FOR THAT, MR. SMARTY GREEN PANTS?
GOOD PEOPLE GO STRAIGHT TO HEAVEN. DO NOT COLLECT TWO HUNDRED DOLLARS. DO NOT PASS "GO."
I KNOW 'CAUSE I'VE BEEN THERE. HEAVEN...
IT'S WHITE. AND SO BRIGHT. BUT YOU DON'T HAVE TO SQUINT. SOMEHOW, YOUR EYES ADJUST, BEING THAT CLOSE TO THE SUN--

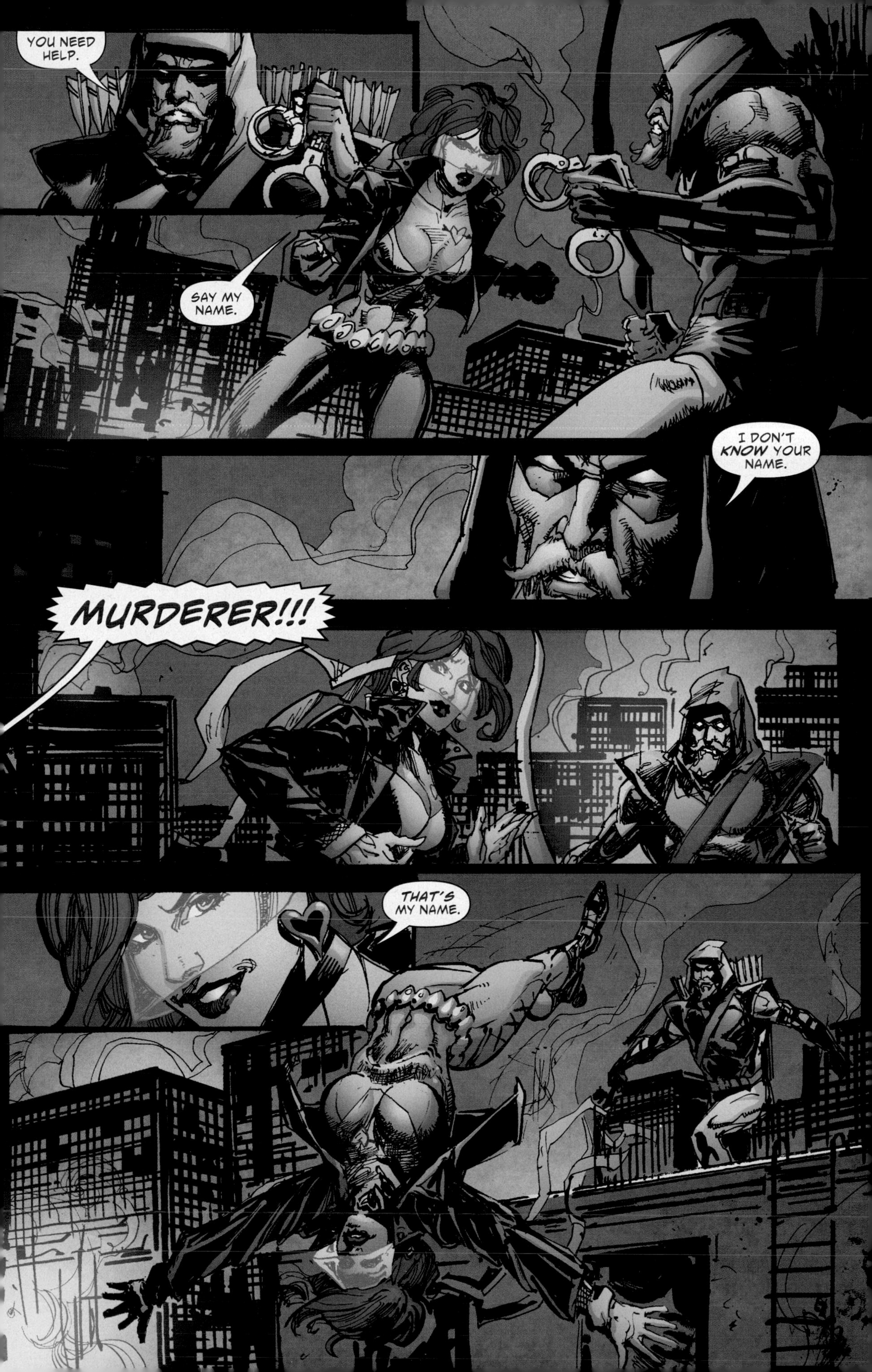
YOU NEED HELP.
SAY MY NAME.
I DON'T KNOW YOUR NAME.
MURDERER!!!
THAT'S MY NAME.

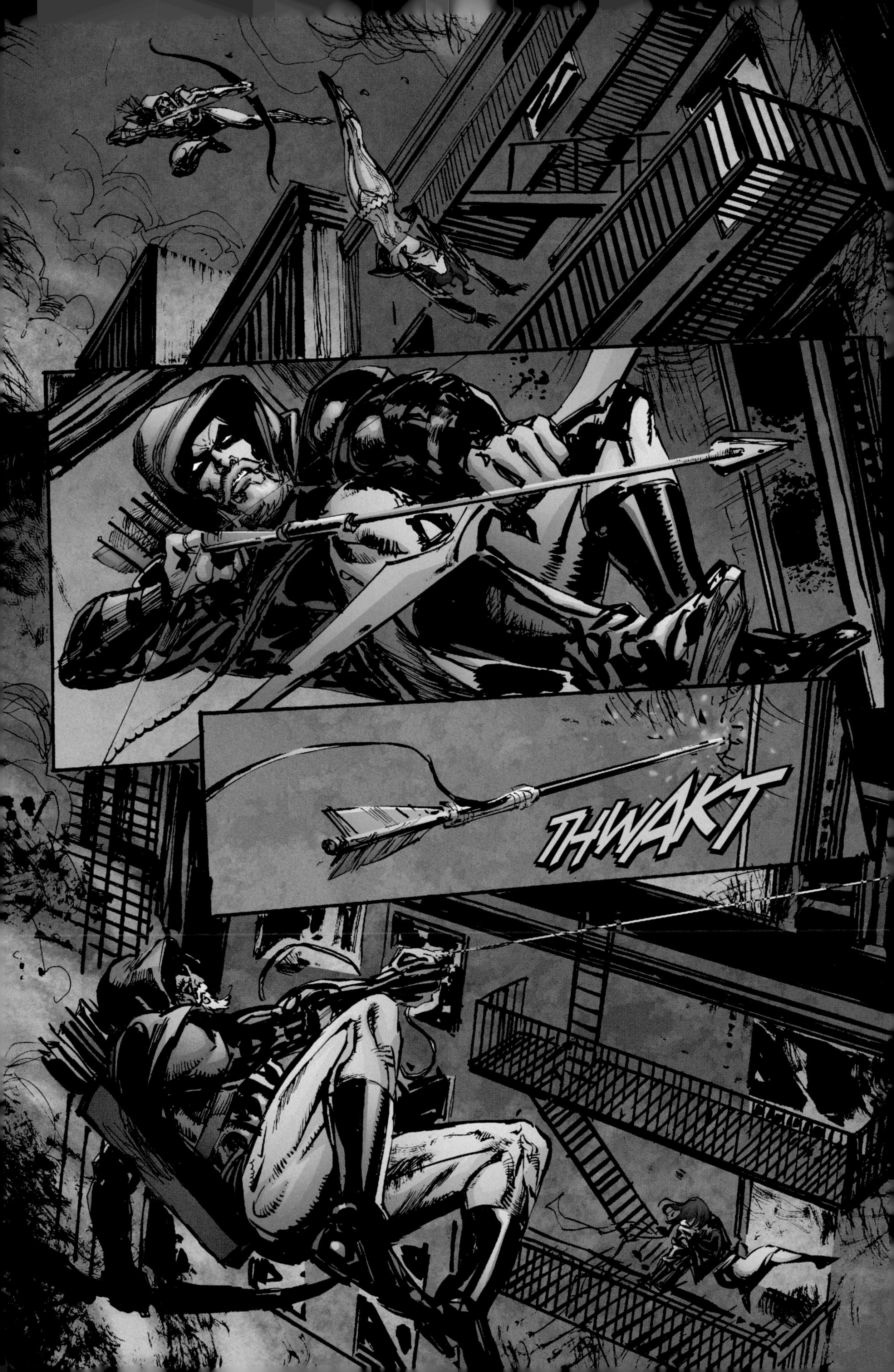
THWAKT

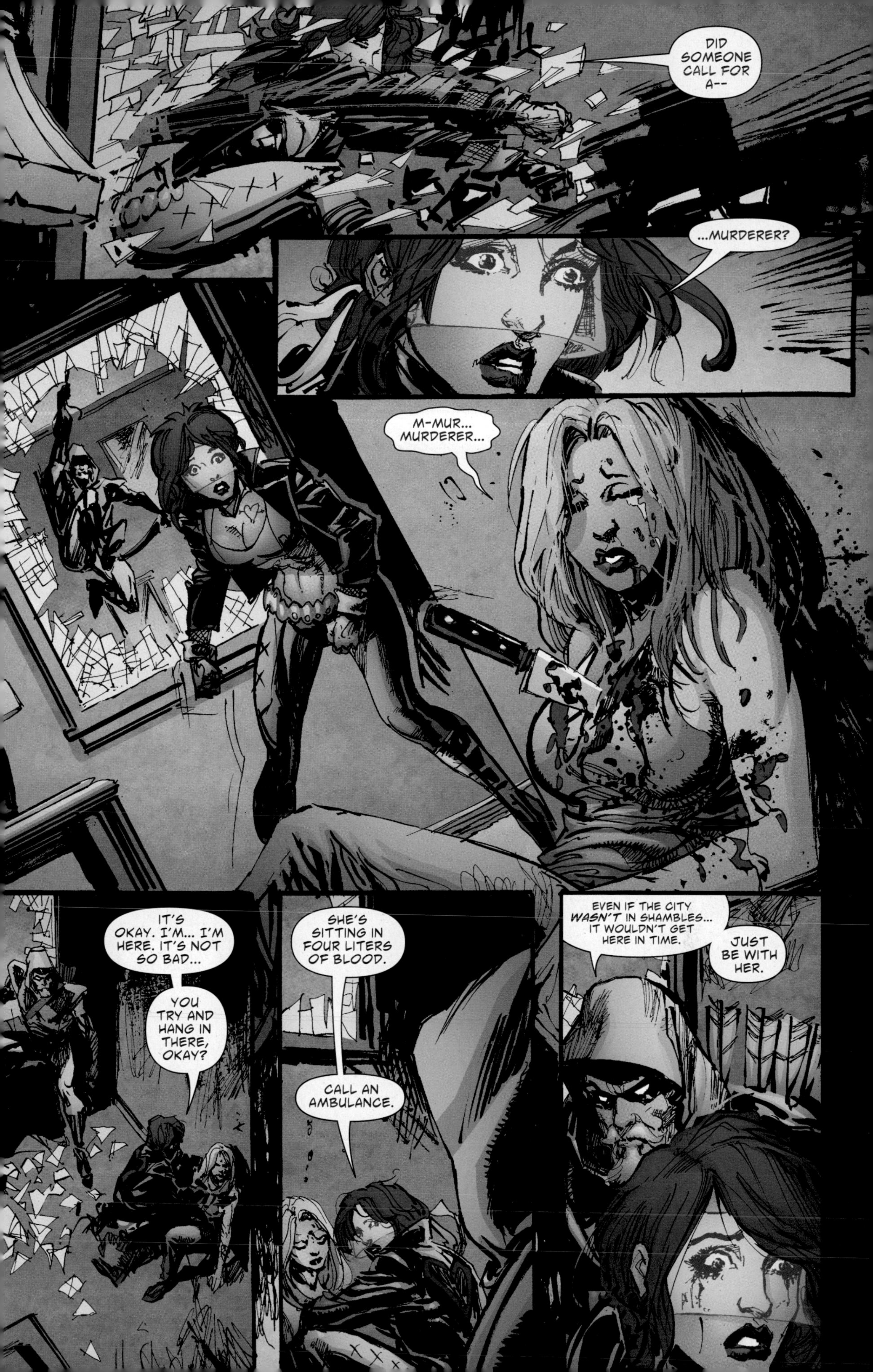
DID SOMEONE CALL FOR A--
...MURDERER?
M-MUR... MURDERER...
IT'S OKAY. I'M... I'M HERE. IT'S NOT SO BAD...
YOU TRY AND HANG IN THERE, OKAY?
SHE'S SITTING IN FOUR LITERS OF BLOOD.
CALL AN AMBULANCE.
EVEN IF THE CITY *WASN'T* IN SHAMBLES... IT WOULDN'T GET HERE IN TIME.
JUST BE WITH HER.

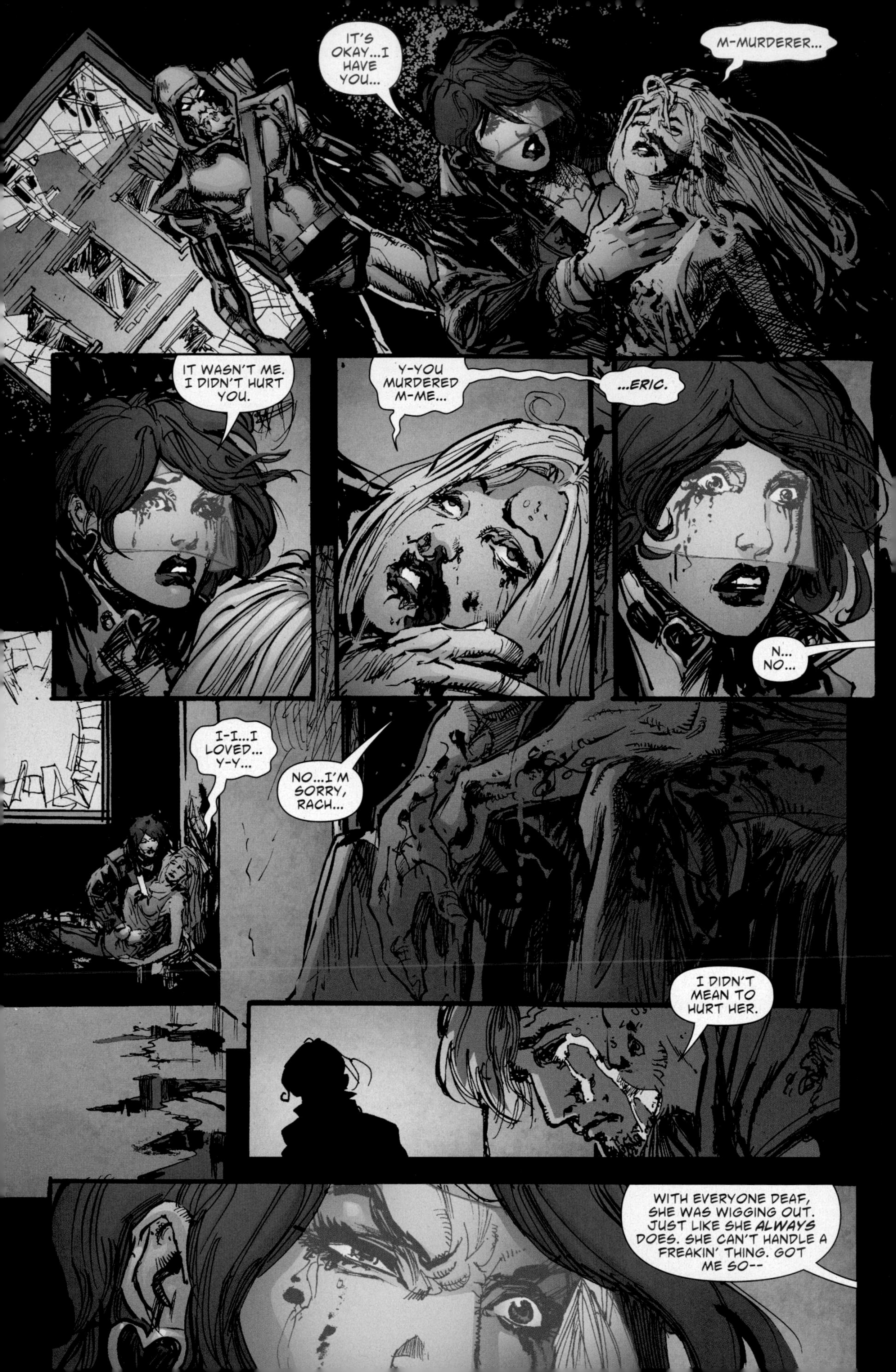
IT'S OKAY...I HAVE YOU...
M-MURDERER...
IT WASN'T ME. I DIDN'T HURT YOU.
Y-YOU MURDERED M-ME...
...ERIC.
N... NO...
I-I...I LOVED... Y-Y...
NO...I'M SORRY, RACH...
I DIDN'T MEAN TO HURT HER.
WITH EVERYONE DEAF, SHE WAS WIGGING OUT. JUST LIKE SHE ALWAYS DOES. SHE CAN'T HANDLE A FREAKIN' THING. GOT ME SO--

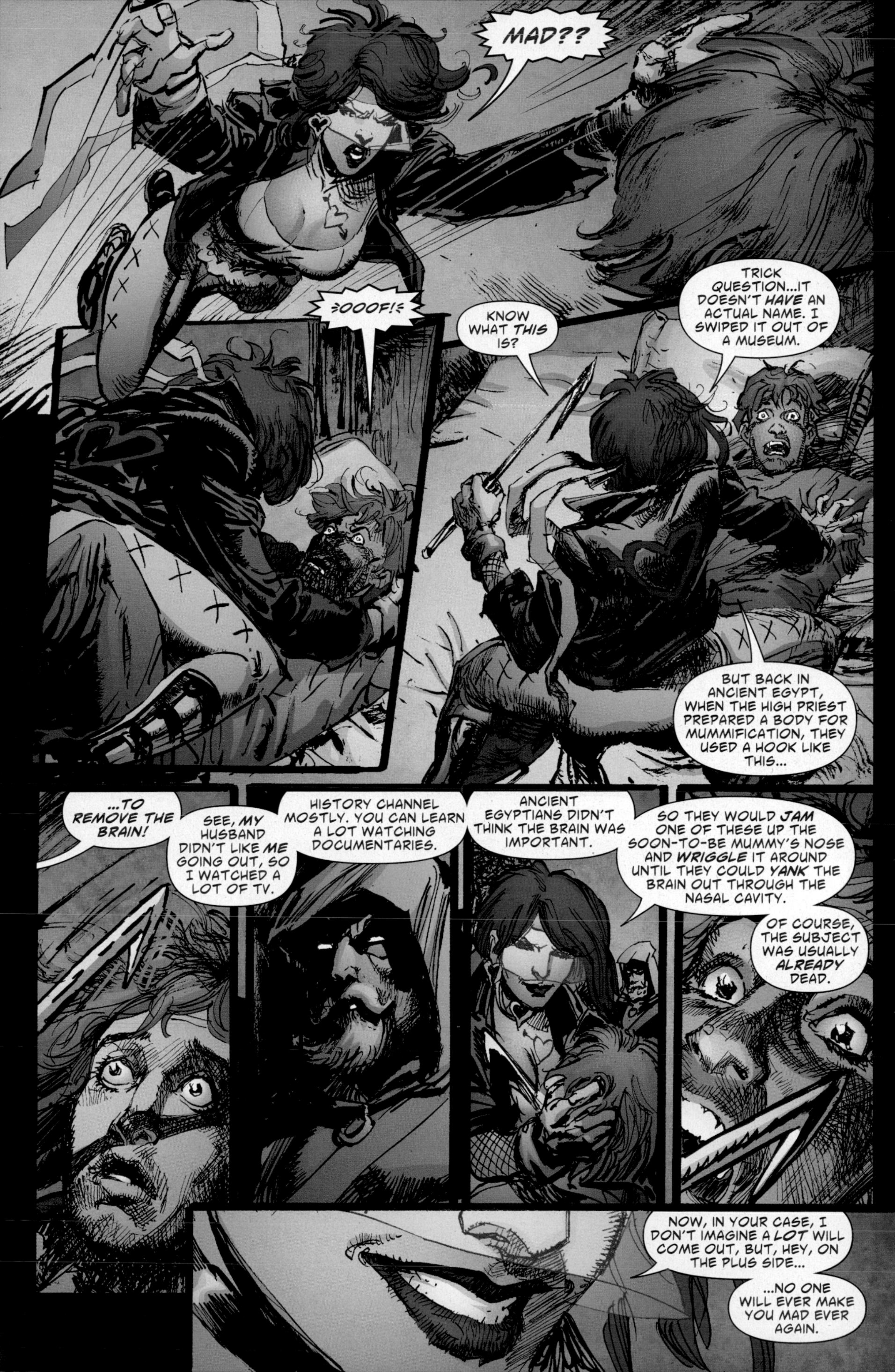
MAD??
OOOF!
KNOW WHAT THIS IS?
TRICK QUESTION...IT DOESN'T HAVE AN ACTUAL NAME. I SWIPED IT OUT OF A MUSEUM.
BUT BACK IN ANCIENT EGYPT, WHEN THE HIGH PRIEST PREPARED A BODY FOR MUMMIFICATION, THEY USED A HOOK LIKE THIS...
...TO REMOVE THE BRAIN!
SEE, MY HUSBAND DIDN'T LIKE ME GOING OUT, SO I WATCHED A LOT OF TV.
HISTORY CHANNEL MOSTLY. YOU CAN LEARN A LOT WATCHING DOCUMENTARIES.
ANCIENT EGYPTIANS DIDN'T THINK THE BRAIN WAS IMPORTANT.
SO THEY WOULD JAM ONE OF THESE UP THE SOON-TO-BE MUMMY'S NOSE AND WRIGGLE IT AROUND UNTIL THEY COULD YANK THE BRAIN OUT THROUGH THE NASAL CAVITY.
OF COURSE, THE SUBJECT WAS USUALLY ALREADY DEAD.
NOW, IN YOUR CASE, I DON'T IMAGINE A LOT WILL COME OUT, BUT, HEY, ON THE PLUS SIDE...
...NO ONE WILL EVER MAKE YOU MAD EVER AGAIN.

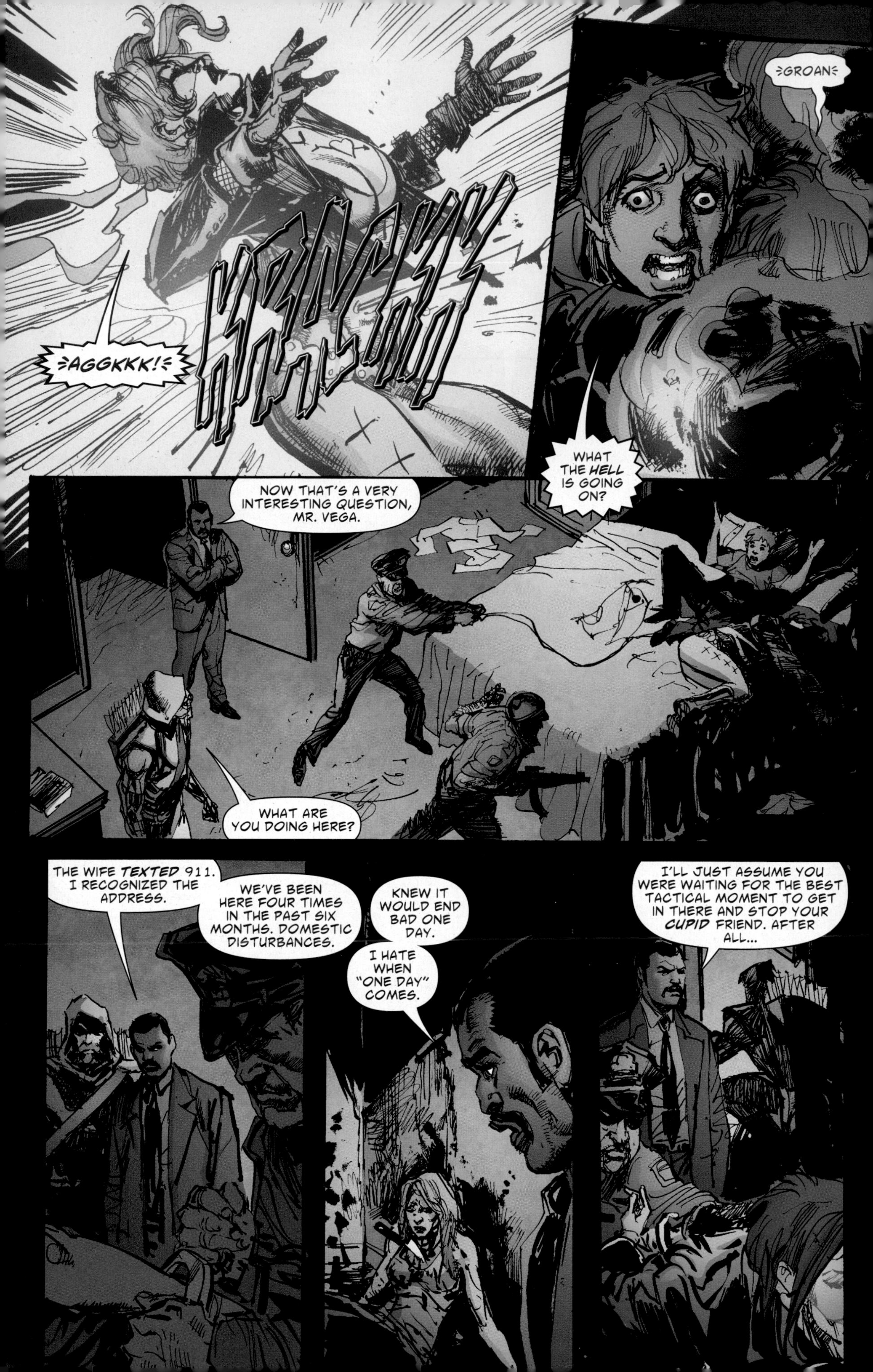
AGGKKK!
GROAN
WHAT THE HELL IS GOING ON?
NOW THAT'S A VERY INTERESTING QUESTION, MR. VEGA.
WHAT ARE YOU DOING HERE?
THE WIFE TEXTED 911. I RECOGNIZED THE ADDRESS.
WE'VE BEEN HERE FOUR TIMES IN THE PAST SIX MONTHS. DOMESTIC DISTURBANCES.
KNEW IT WOULD END BAD ONE DAY.
I HATE WHEN "ONE DAY" COMES.
I'LL JUST ASSUME YOU WERE WAITING FOR THE BEST TACTICAL MOMENT TO GET IN THERE AND STOP YOUR CUPID FRIEND. AFTER ALL...

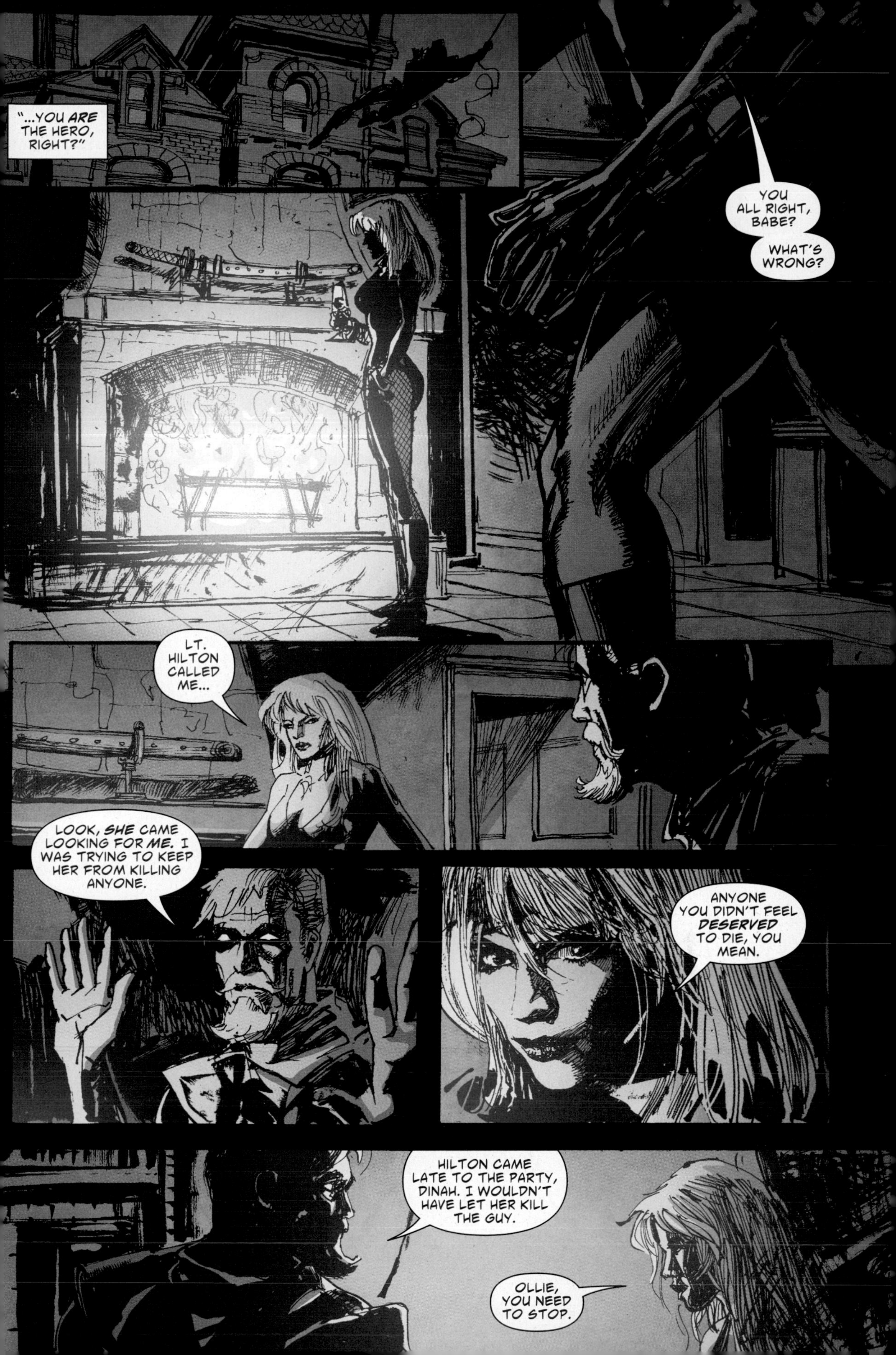
"...YOU ARE THE HERO, RIGHT?"
YOU ALL RIGHT, BABE?
WHAT'S WRONG?
LT. HILTON CALLED ME...
LOOK, SHE CAME LOOKING FOR ME. I WAS TRYING TO KEEP HER FROM KILLING ANYONE.
ANYONE YOU DIDN'T FEEL DESERVED TO DIE, YOU MEAN.
HILTON CAME LATE TO THE PARTY, DINAH. I WOULDN'T HAVE LET HER KILL THE GUY.
OLLIE, YOU NEED TO STOP.

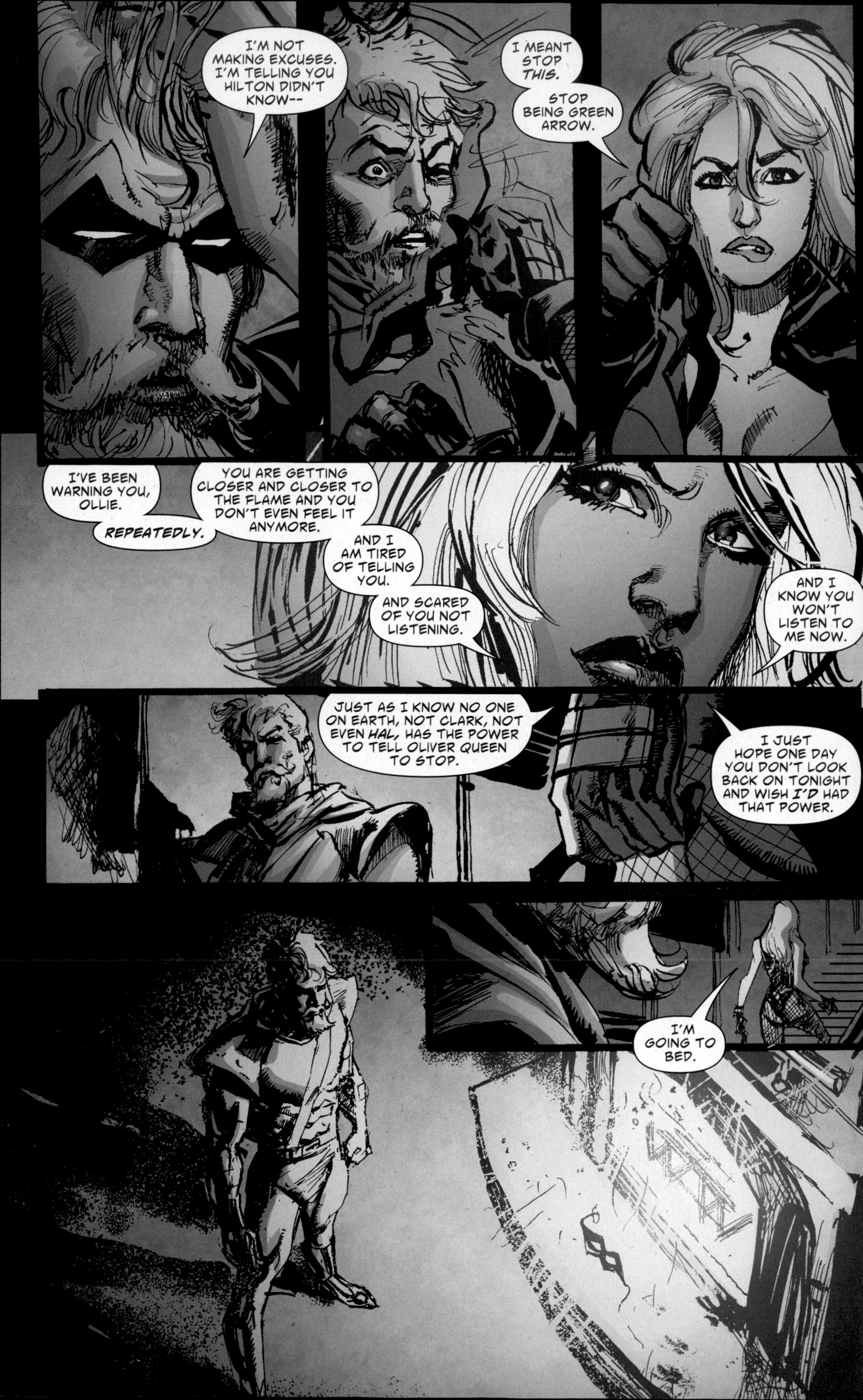

I'M NOT MAKING EXCUSES. I'M TELLING YOU HILTON DIDN'T KNOW--
I MEANT STOP *THIS.*
STOP BEING GREEN ARROW.
I'VE BEEN WARNING YOU, OLLIE.
REPEATEDLY.
YOU ARE GETTING CLOSER AND CLOSER TO THE FLAME AND YOU DON'T EVEN FEEL IT ANYMORE.
AND I AM TIRED OF TELLING YOU.
AND SCARED OF YOU NOT LISTENING.
AND I KNOW YOU WON'T LISTEN TO ME NOW.
JUST AS I KNOW NO ONE ON EARTH, NOT CLARK, NOT EVEN *HAL,* HAS THE POWER TO TELL OLIVER QUEEN TO STOP.
I JUST HOPE ONE DAY YOU DON'T LOOK BACK ON TONIGHT AND WISH *I'D* HAD THAT POWER.
I'M GOING TO BED.

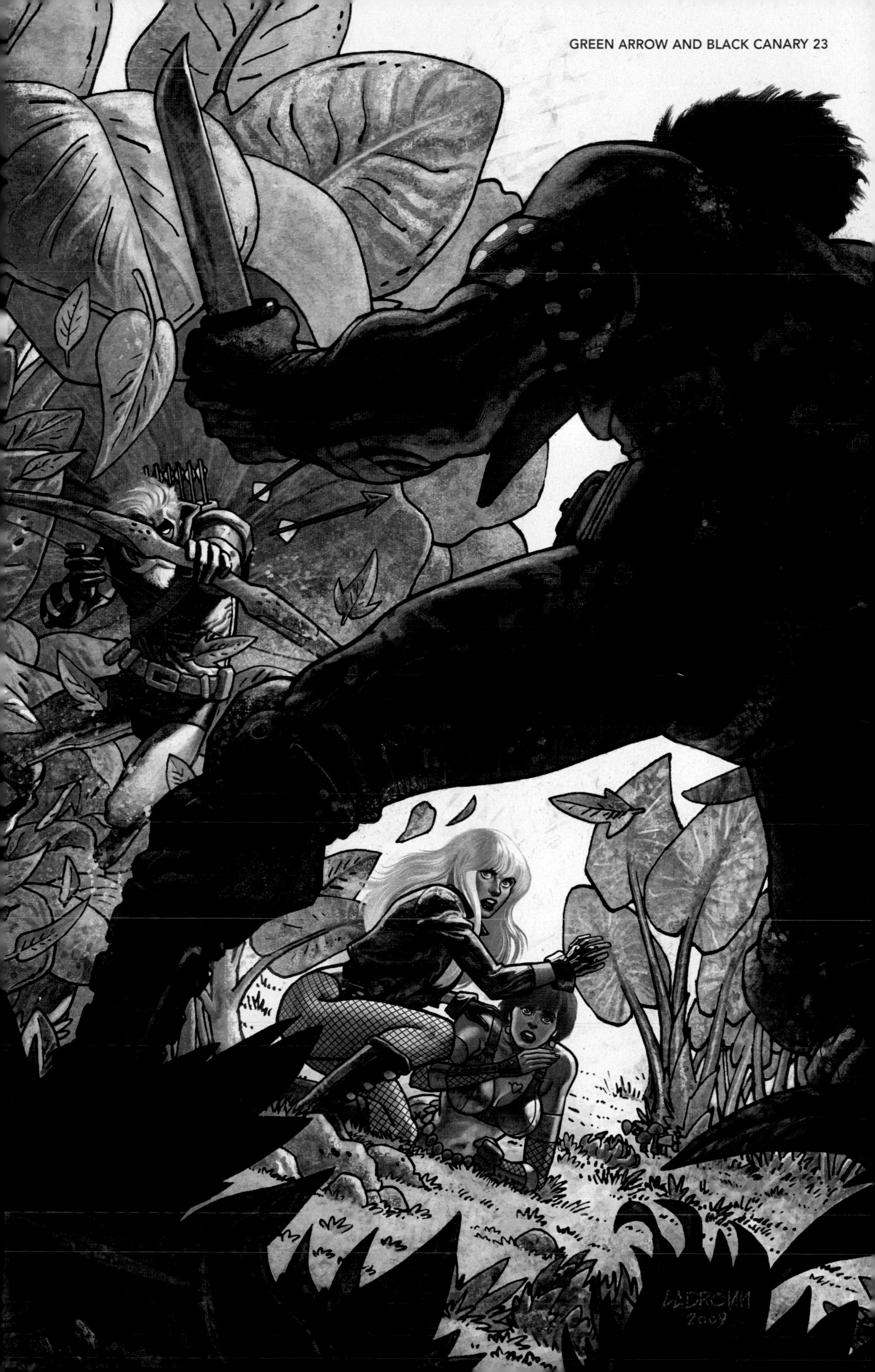
LADRONN
2009

THE GAME IS ON
Mike Norton Layouts
Bill Sienkiewicz Finishes

...IN A COAL MINE
Mike Norton Penciller
Joe Rubinstein Inker

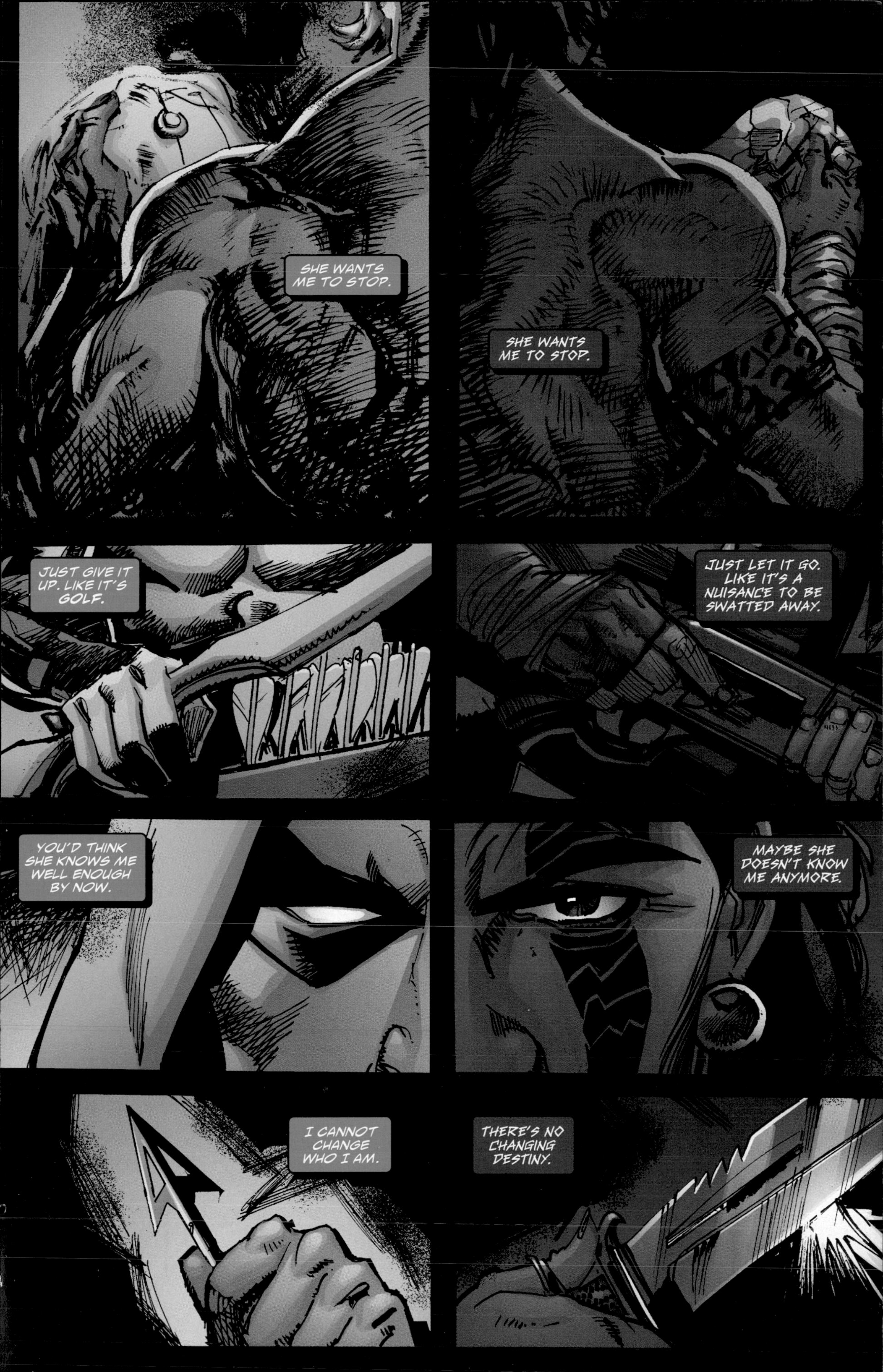
SHE WANTS ME TO STOP.
SHE WANTS ME TO STOP.
JUST GIVE IT UP. LIKE IT'S GOLF.
JUST LET IT GO. LIKE IT'S A NUISANCE TO BE SWATTED AWAY.
YOU'D THINK SHE KNOWS ME WELL ENOUGH BY NOW.
MAYBE SHE DOESN'T KNOW ME ANYMORE.
I CANNOT CHANGE WHO I AM.
THERE'S NO CHANGING DESTINY.

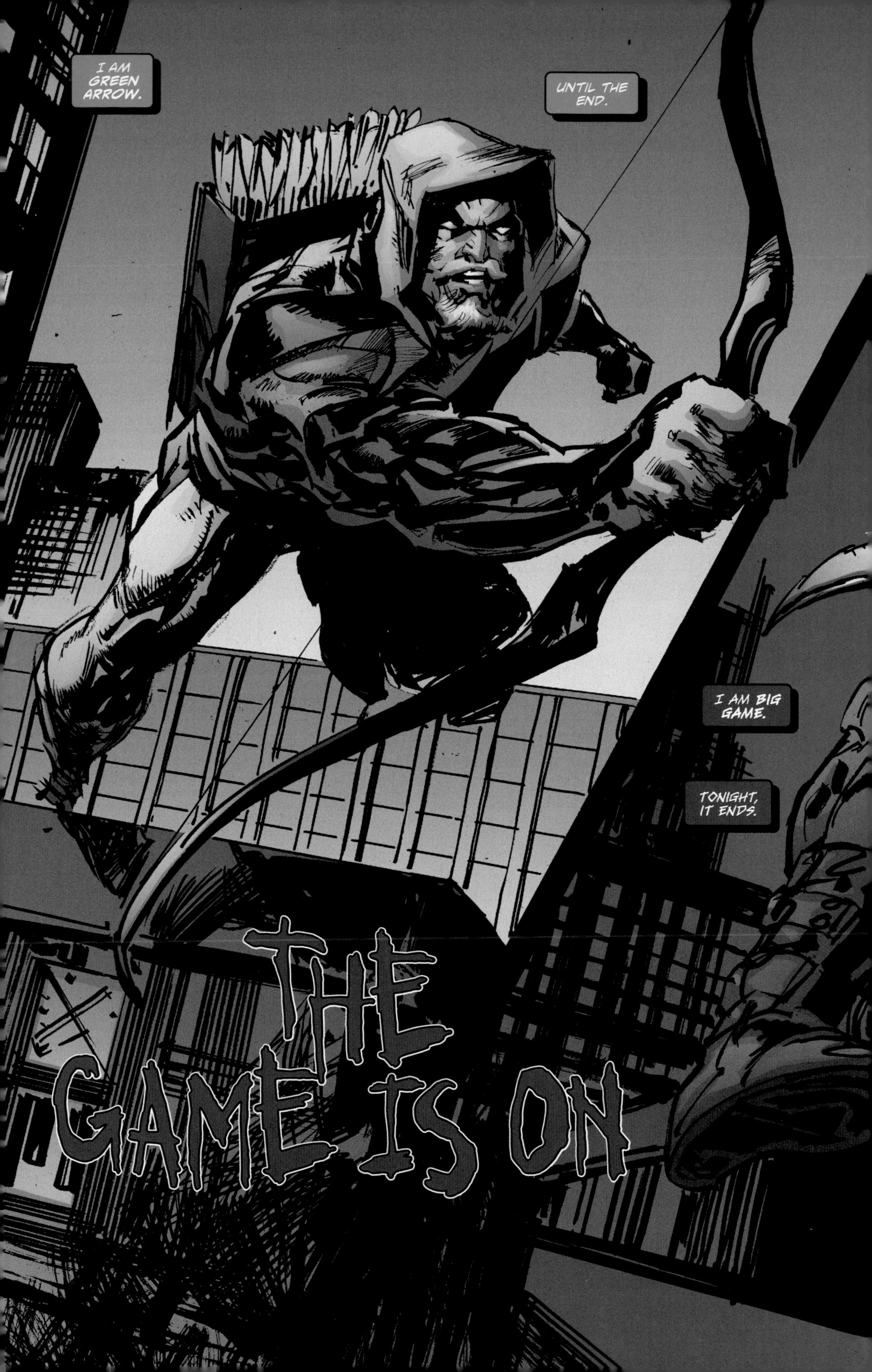
I AM GREEN ARROW.
UNTIL THE END.
I AM BIG GAME.
TONIGHT, IT ENDS.
THE GAME IS ON

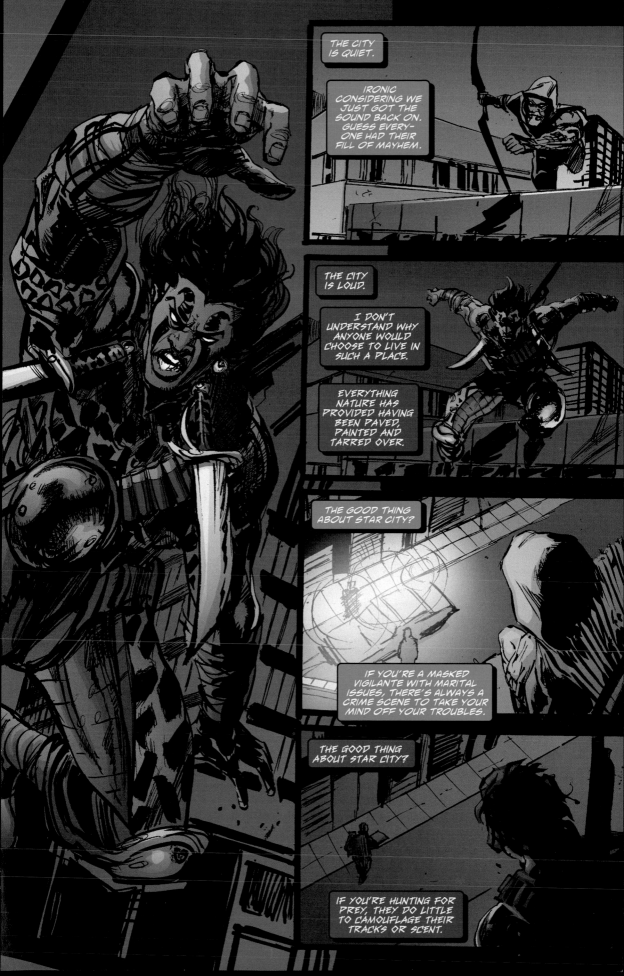

THE CITY IS QUIET.

IRONIC CONSIDERING WE JUST GOT THE SOUND BACK ON. GUESS EVERY-ONE HAD THEIR FILL OF MAYHEM.

THE CITY IS LOUD.

I DON'T UNDERSTAND WHY ANYONE WOULD CHOOSE TO LIVE IN SUCH A PLACE.

EVERYTHING NATURE HAS PROVIDED HAVING BEEN PAVED, PAINTED AND TARRED OVER.

THE GOOD THING ABOUT STAR CITY?

IF YOU'RE A MASKED VIGILANTE WITH MARITAL ISSUES, THERE'S ALWAYS A CRIME SCENE TO TAKE YOUR MIND OFF YOUR TROUBLES.

THE GOOD THING ABOUT STAR CITY?

IF YOU'RE HUNTING FOR PREY, THEY DO LITTLE TO CAMOUFLAGE THEIR TRACKS OR SCENT.

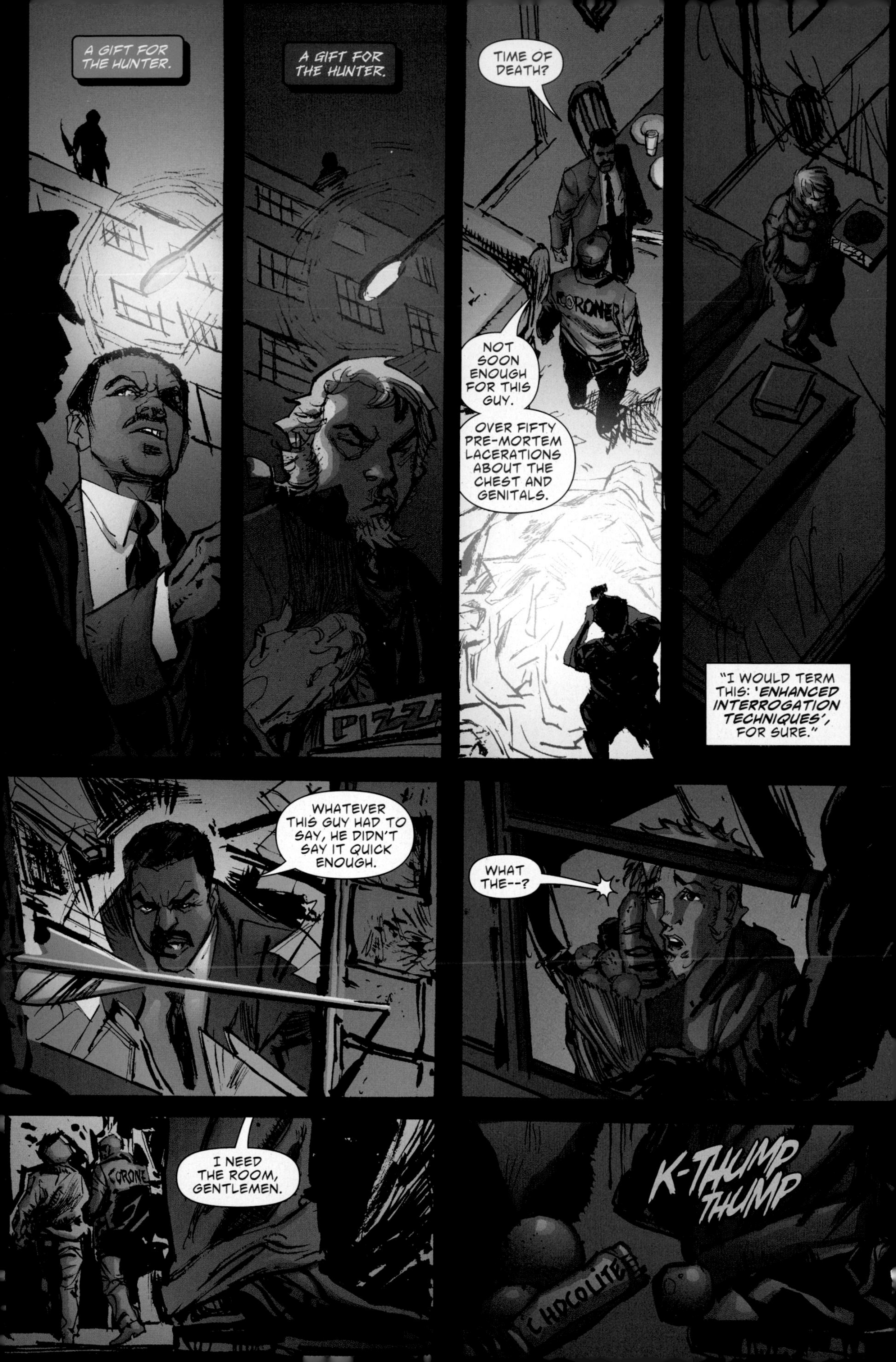
A GIFT FOR THE HUNTER.
A GIFT FOR THE HUNTER.
TIME OF DEATH?
NOT SOON ENOUGH FOR THIS GUY.
OVER FIFTY PRE-MORTEM LACERATIONS ABOUT THE CHEST AND GENITALS.
CORONER
PIZZA
"I WOULD TERM THIS: '*ENHANCED INTERROGATION TECHNIQUES*', FOR SURE."
WHATEVER THIS GUY HAD TO SAY, HE DIDN'T SAY IT QUICK ENOUGH.
WHAT THE--?
I NEED THE ROOM, GENTLEMEN.
K-THUMP THUMP
CHOCOLITE

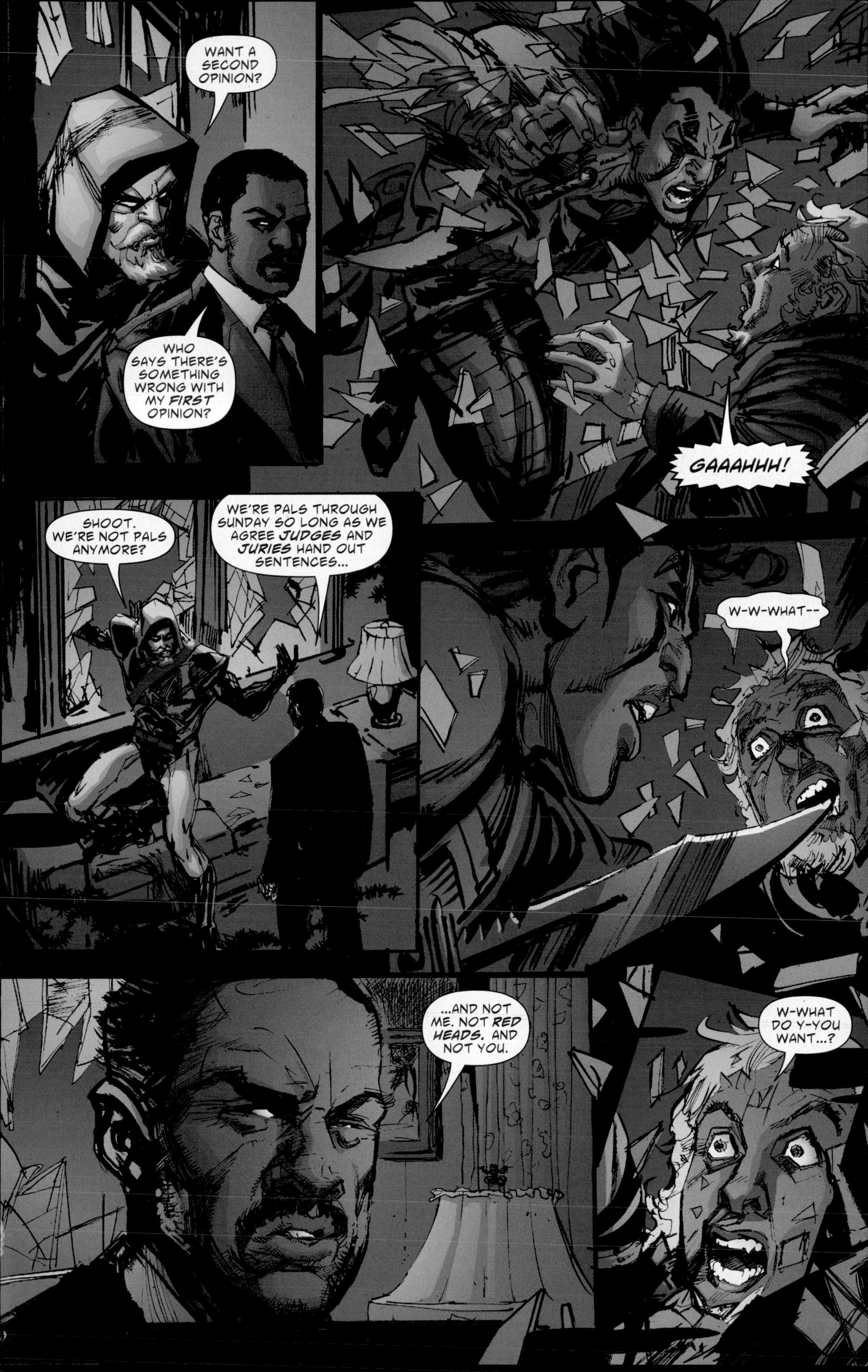
WANT A SECOND OPINION?
WHO SAYS THERE'S SOMETHING WRONG WITH MY *FIRST* OPINION?
GAAAHHH!
SHOOT. WE'RE NOT PALS ANYMORE?
WE'RE PALS THROUGH SUNDAY SO LONG AS WE AGREE **JUDGES** AND **JURIES** HAND OUT SENTENCES...
W-W-WHAT--
...AND NOT ME. NOT **RED HEADS.** AND NOT YOU.
W-WHAT DO Y-YOU WANT...?

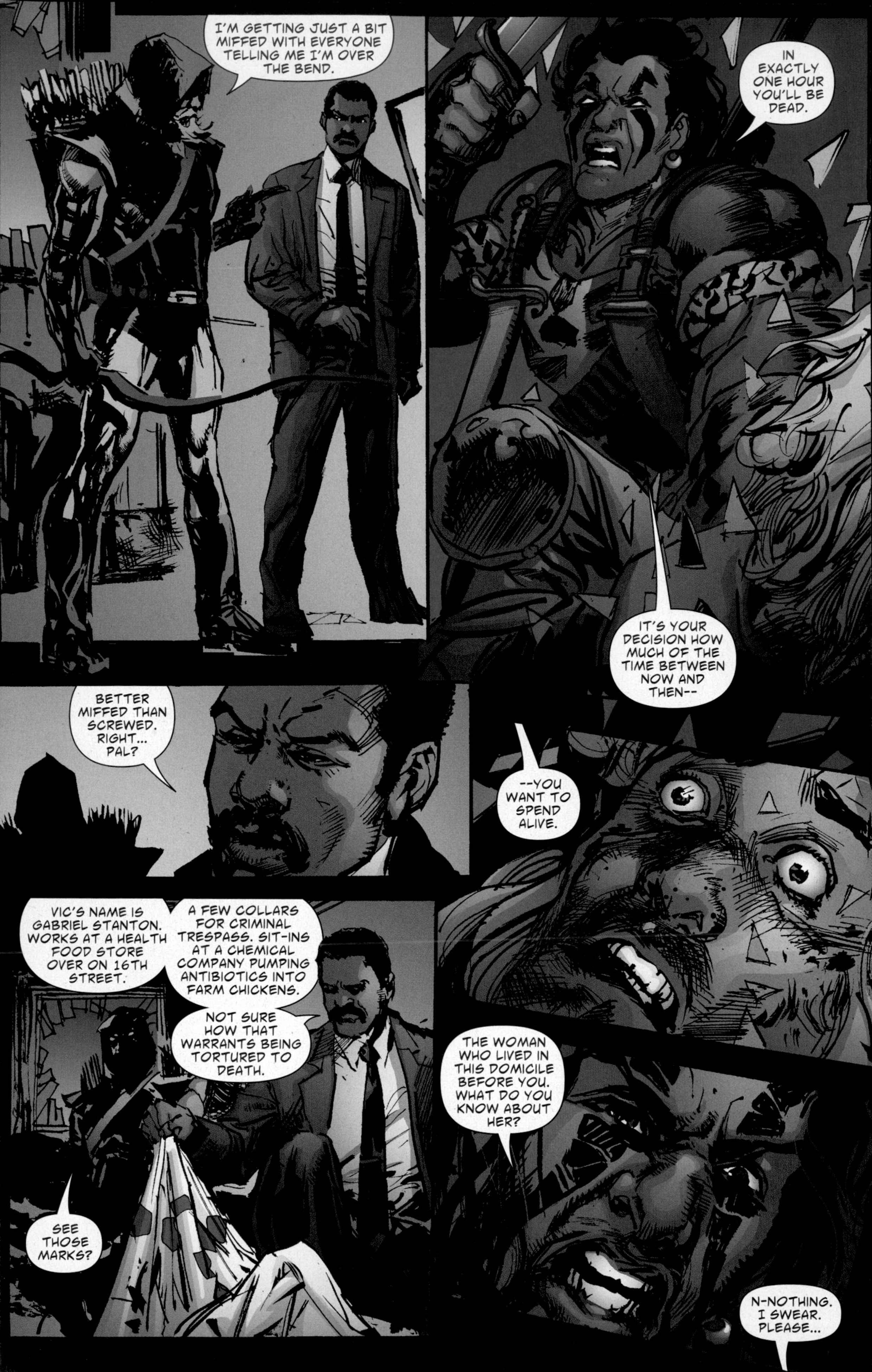
I'M GETTING JUST A BIT MIFFED WITH EVERYONE TELLING ME I'M OVER THE BEND.
IN EXACTLY ONE HOUR YOU'LL BE DEAD.
IT'S YOUR DECISION HOW MUCH OF THE TIME BETWEEN NOW AND THEN--
BETTER MIFFED THAN SCREWED. RIGHT... PAL?
--YOU WANT TO SPEND ALIVE.
VIC'S NAME IS GABRIEL STANTON. WORKS AT A HEALTH FOOD STORE OVER ON 16TH STREET.
A FEW COLLARS FOR CRIMINAL TRESPASS. SIT-INS AT A CHEMICAL COMPANY PUMPING ANTIBIOTICS INTO FARM CHICKENS.
NOT SURE HOW THAT WARRANTS BEING TORTURED TO DEATH.
SEE THOSE MARKS?
THE WOMAN WHO LIVED IN THIS DOMICILE BEFORE YOU. WHAT DO YOU KNOW ABOUT HER?
N-NOTHING. I SWEAR. PLEASE...

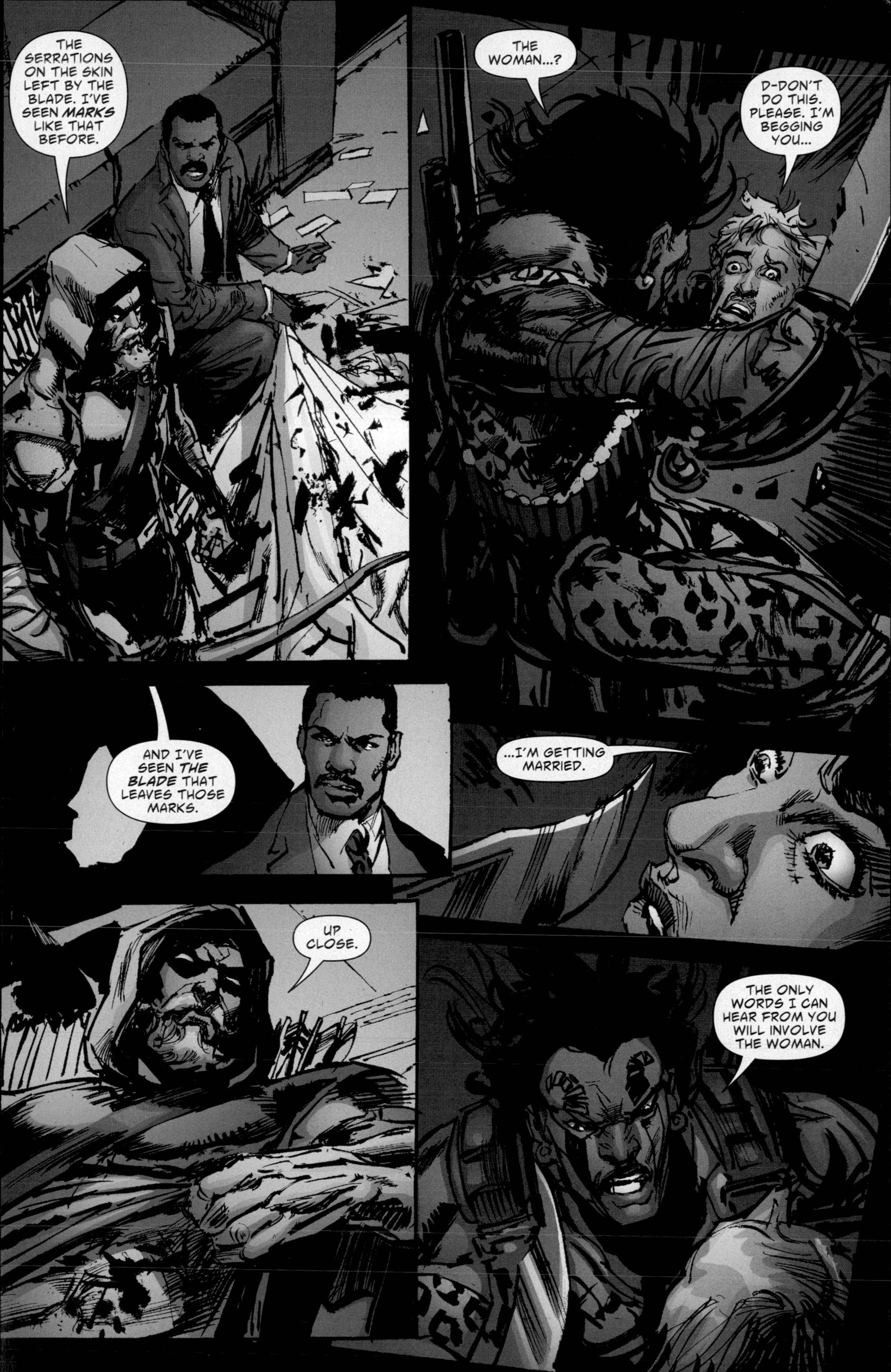
THE SERRATIONS ON THE SKIN LEFT BY THE BLADE. I'VE SEEN MARKS LIKE THAT BEFORE.
THE WOMAN...?
D-DON'T DO THIS. PLEASE. I'M BEGGING YOU...
AND I'VE SEEN THE BLADE THAT LEAVES THOSE MARKS.
UP CLOSE.
...I'M GETTING MARRIED.
THE ONLY WORDS I CAN HEAR FROM YOU WILL INVOLVE THE WOMAN.

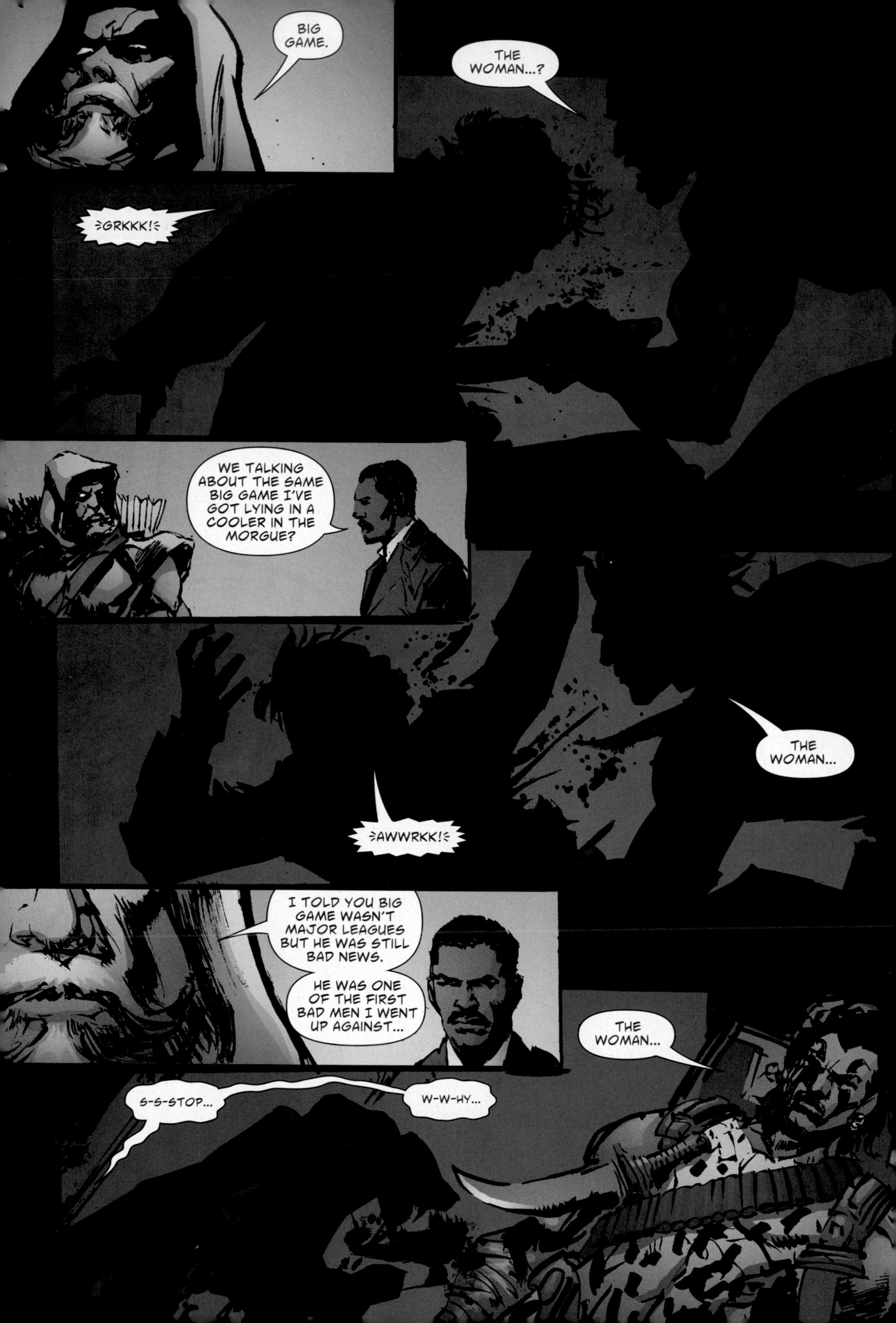
BIG GAME.
THE WOMAN...?
GRKKK!
WE TALKING ABOUT THE SAME BIG GAME I'VE GOT LYING IN A COOLER IN THE MORGUE?
THE WOMAN...
AWWRKK!
I TOLD YOU BIG GAME WASN'T MAJOR LEAGUES BUT HE WAS STILL BAD NEWS.
HE WAS ONE OF THE FIRST BAD MEN I WENT UP AGAINST...
THE WOMAN...
S-S-STOP...
W-W-HY...

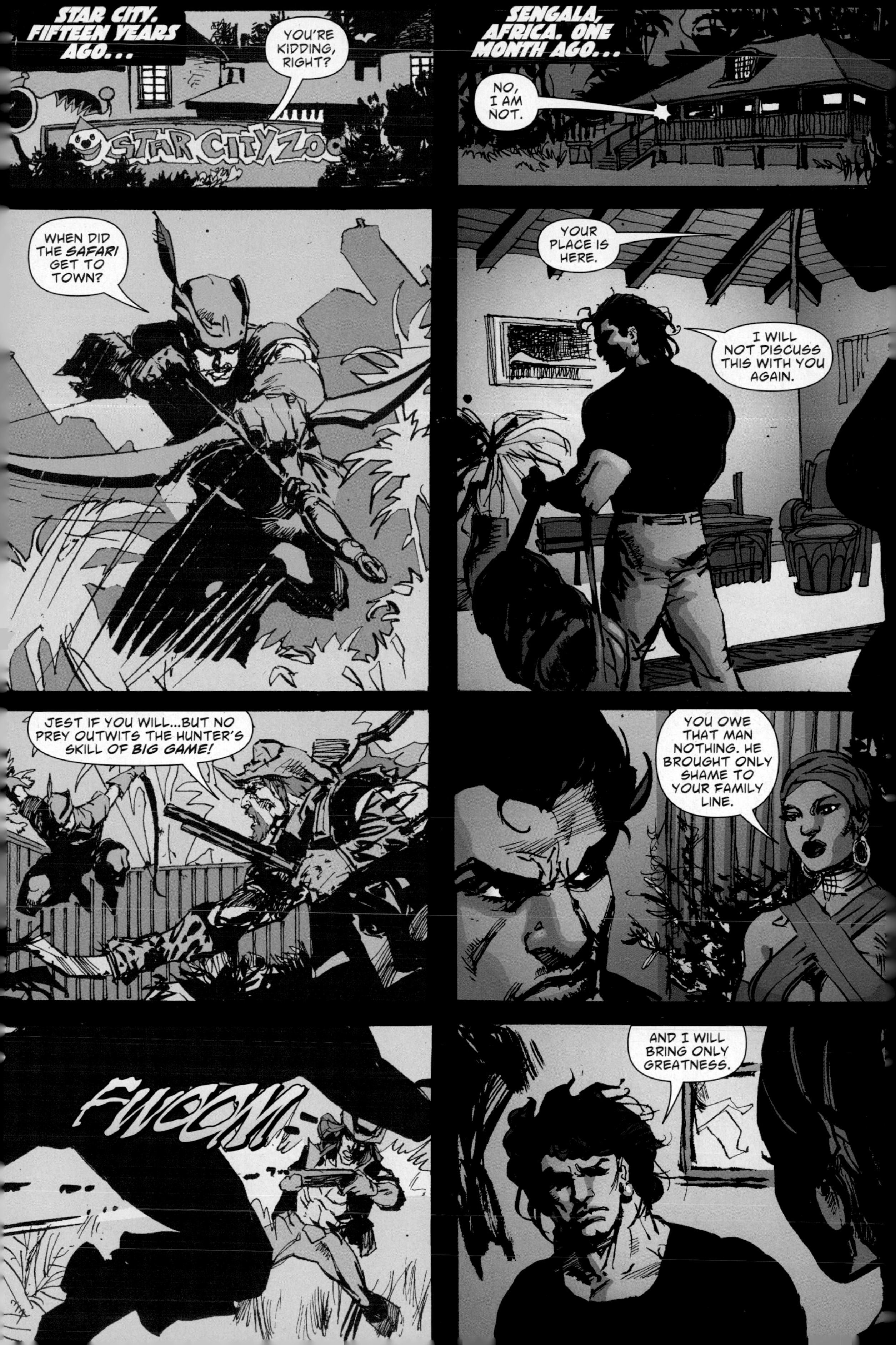
STAR CITY. FIFTEEN YEARS AGO...
YOU'RE KIDDING, RIGHT?
STAR CITY ZOO
SENGALA, AFRICA. ONE MONTH AGO...
NO, I AM NOT.
WHEN DID THE SAFARI GET TO TOWN?
YOUR PLACE IS HERE.
I WILL NOT DISCUSS THIS WITH YOU AGAIN.
JEST IF YOU WILL...BUT NO PREY OUTWITS THE HUNTER'S SKILL OF BIG GAME!
YOU OWE THAT MAN NOTHING. HE BROUGHT ONLY SHAME TO YOUR FAMILY LINE.
FWOOM-
AND I WILL BRING ONLY GREATNESS.

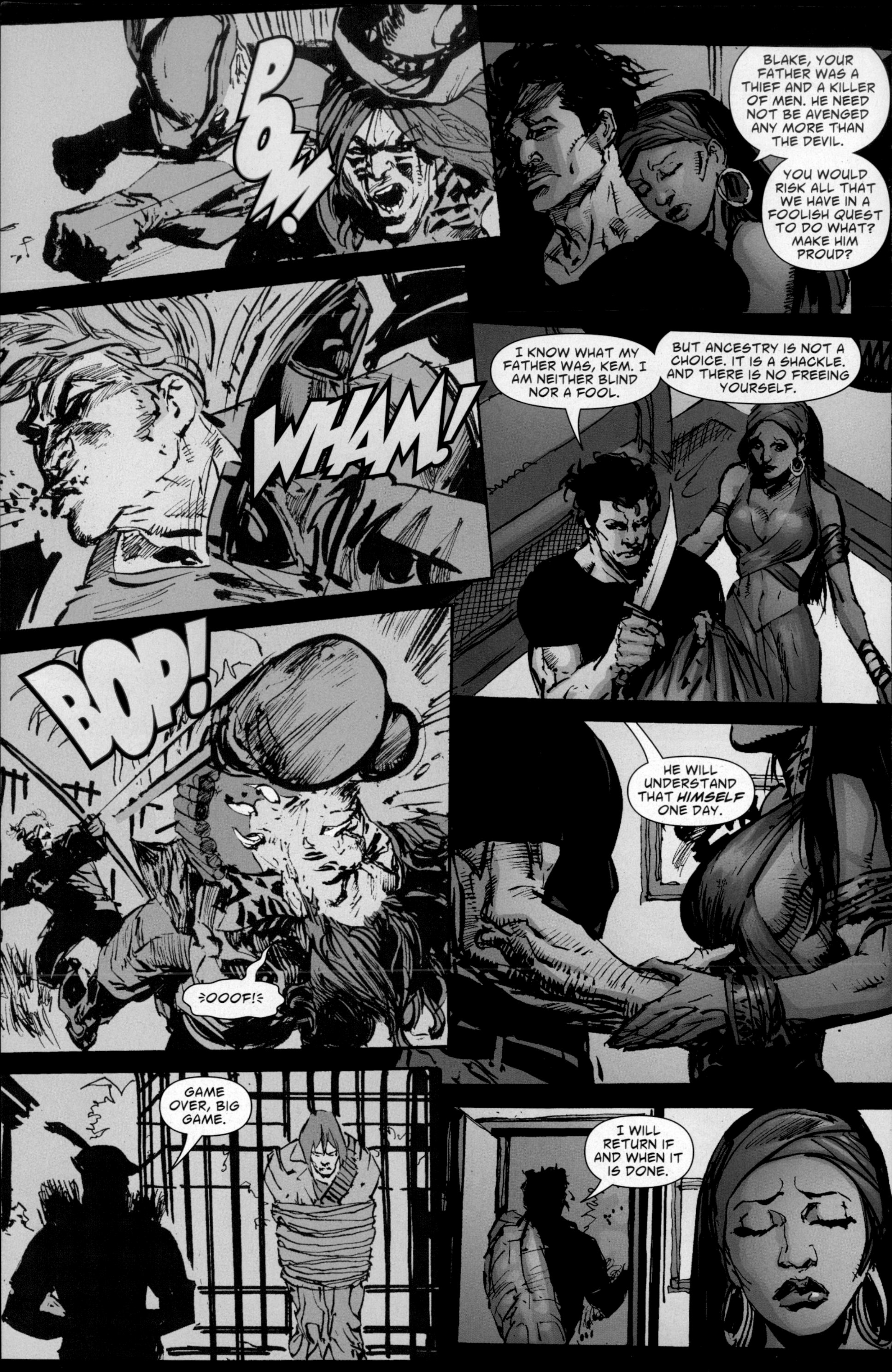
POW!
BLAKE, YOUR FATHER WAS A THIEF AND A KILLER OF MEN. HE NEED NOT BE AVENGED ANY MORE THAN THE DEVIL.
YOU WOULD RISK ALL THAT WE HAVE IN A FOOLISH QUEST TO DO WHAT? MAKE HIM PROUD?
WHAM!
I KNOW WHAT MY FATHER WAS, KEM. I AM NEITHER BLIND NOR A FOOL.
BUT ANCESTRY IS NOT A CHOICE. IT IS A SHACKLE. AND THERE IS NO FREEING YOURSELF.
BOP!
OOOF!
HE WILL UNDERSTAND THAT HIMSELF ONE DAY.
GAME OVER, BIG GAME.
I WILL RETURN IF AND WHEN IT IS DONE.

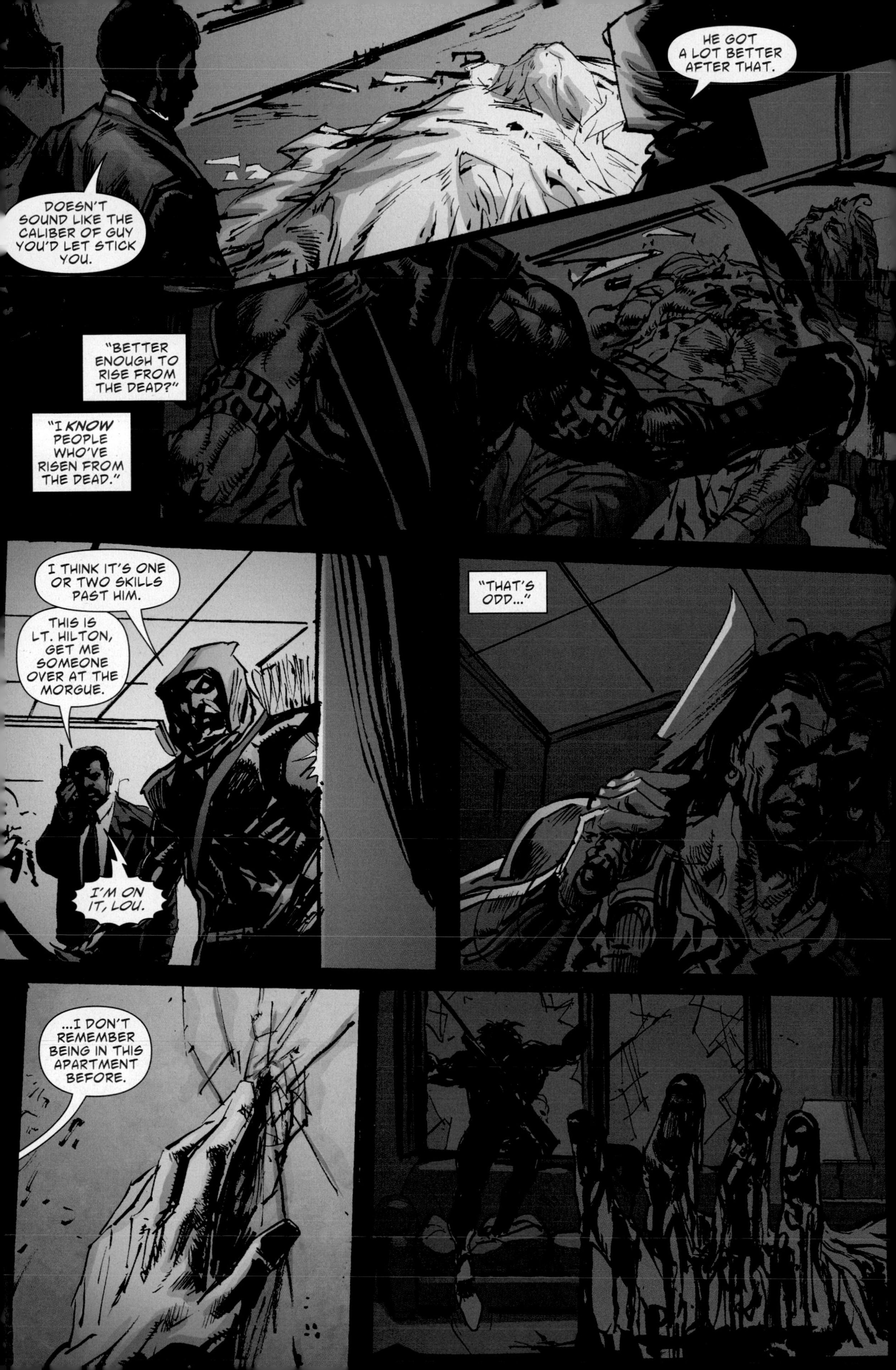
HE GOT A LOT BETTER AFTER THAT.
DOESN'T SOUND LIKE THE CALIBER OF GUY YOU'D LET STICK YOU.
"BETTER ENOUGH TO RISE FROM THE DEAD?"
"I KNOW PEOPLE WHO'VE RISEN FROM THE DEAD."
I THINK IT'S ONE OR TWO SKILLS PAST HIM.
THIS IS LT. HILTON, GET ME SOMEONE OVER AT THE MORGUE.
I'M ON IT, LOU.
"THAT'S ODD..."
...I DON'T REMEMBER BEING IN THIS APARTMENT BEFORE.

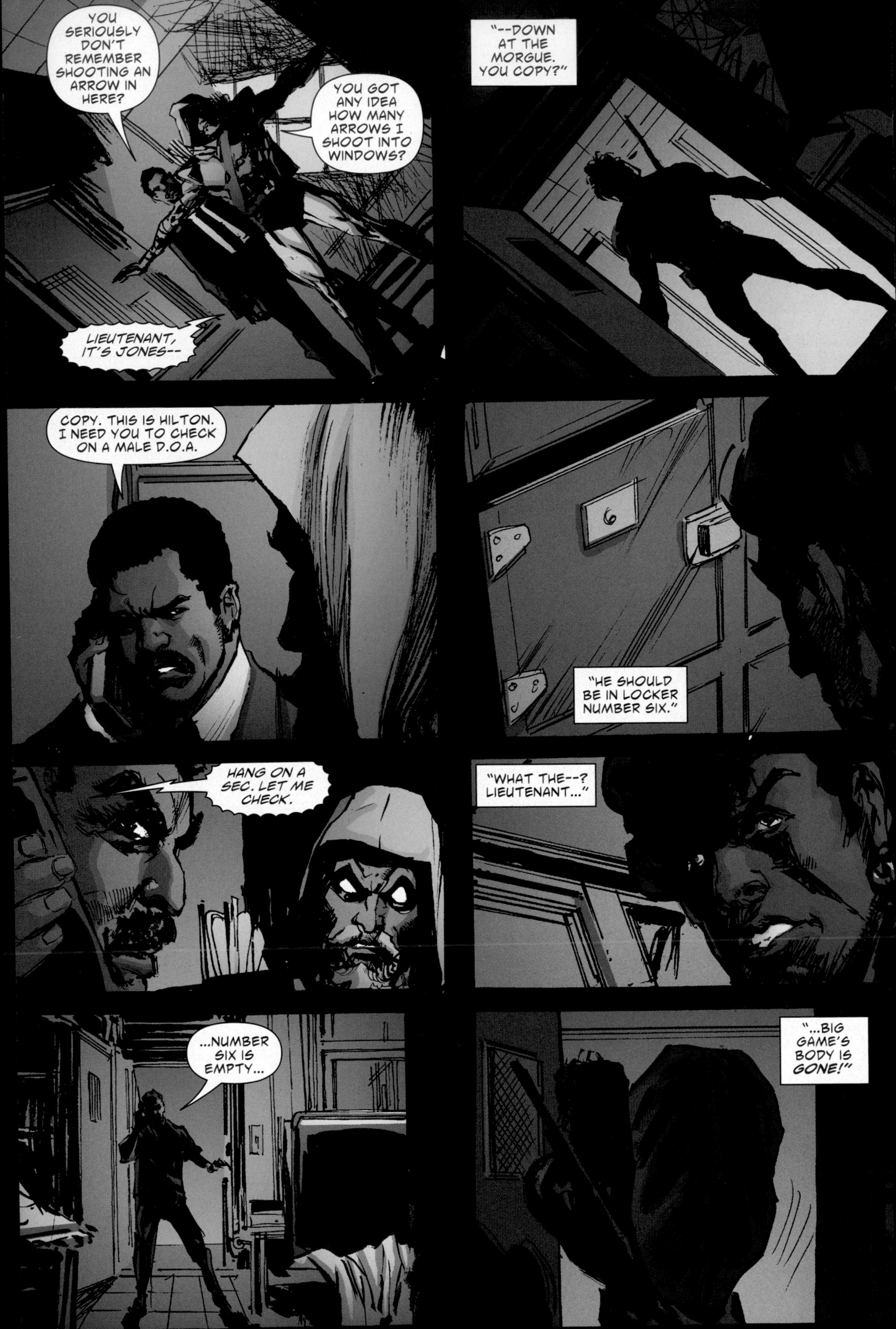

YOU SERIOUSLY DON'T REMEMBER SHOOTING AN ARROW IN HERE?
YOU GOT ANY IDEA HOW MANY ARROWS I SHOOT INTO WINDOWS?
LIEUTENANT, IT'S JONES--
"--DOWN AT THE MORGUE. YOU COPY?"
COPY. THIS IS HILTON. I NEED YOU TO CHECK ON A MALE D.O.A.
"HE SHOULD BE IN LOCKER NUMBER SIX."
HANG ON A SEC. LET ME CHECK.
"WHAT THE--? LIEUTENANT..."
...NUMBER SIX IS EMPTY...
"...BIG GAME'S BODY IS GONE!"

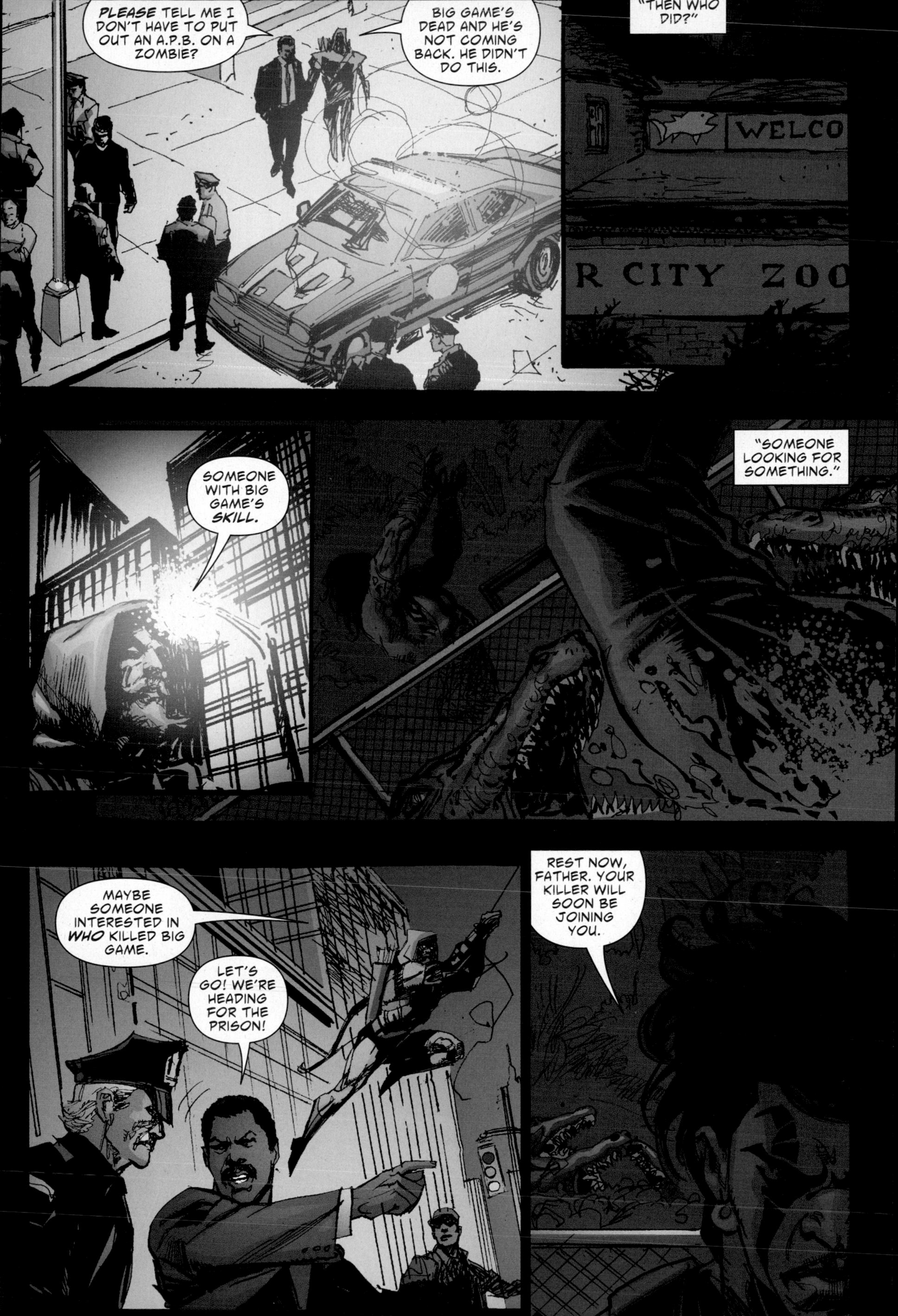
PLEASE TELL ME I DON'T HAVE TO PUT OUT AN A.P.B. ON A ZOMBIE?
BIG GAME'S DEAD AND HE'S NOT COMING BACK. HE DIDN'T DO THIS.
"THEN WHO DID?"
WELCO
R CITY ZOO
SOMEONE WITH BIG GAME'S SKILL.
"SOMEONE LOOKING FOR SOMETHING."
MAYBE SOMEONE INTERESTED IN WHO KILLED BIG GAME.
LET'S GO! WE'RE HEADING FOR THE PRISON!
REST NOW, FATHER. YOUR KILLER WILL SOON BE JOINING YOU.

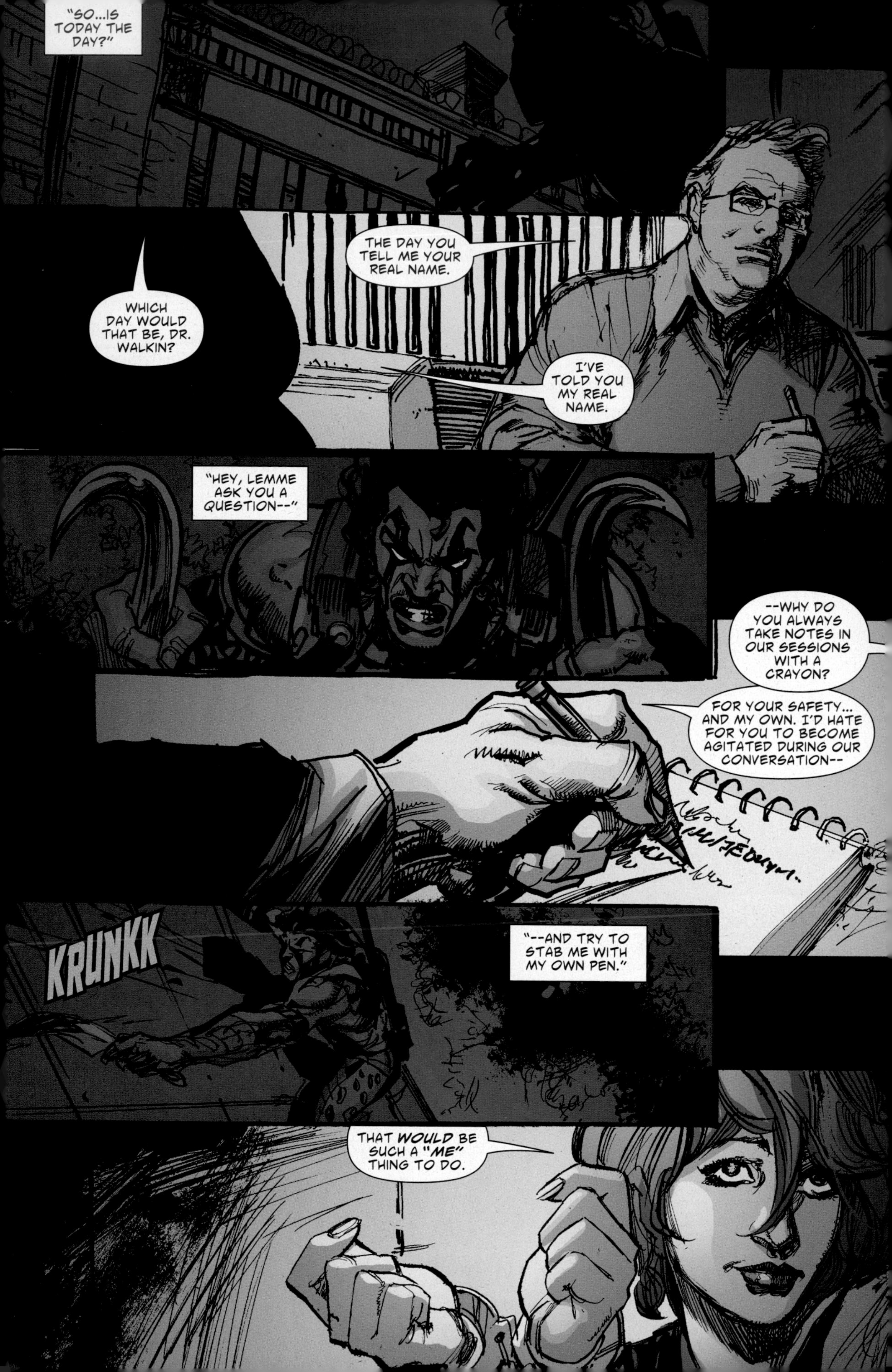
"SO...IS TODAY THE DAY?"
THE DAY YOU TELL ME YOUR REAL NAME.
WHICH DAY WOULD THAT BE, DR. WALKIN?
I'VE TOLD YOU MY REAL NAME.
"HEY, LEMME ASK YOU A QUESTION--"
--WHY DO YOU ALWAYS TAKE NOTES IN OUR SESSIONS WITH A CRAYON?
FOR YOUR SAFETY... AND MY OWN. I'D HATE FOR YOU TO BECOME AGITATED DURING OUR CONVERSATION--
KRUNKK
"--AND TRY TO STAB ME WITH MY OWN PEN."
THAT *WOULD* BE SUCH A *"ME"* THING TO DO.

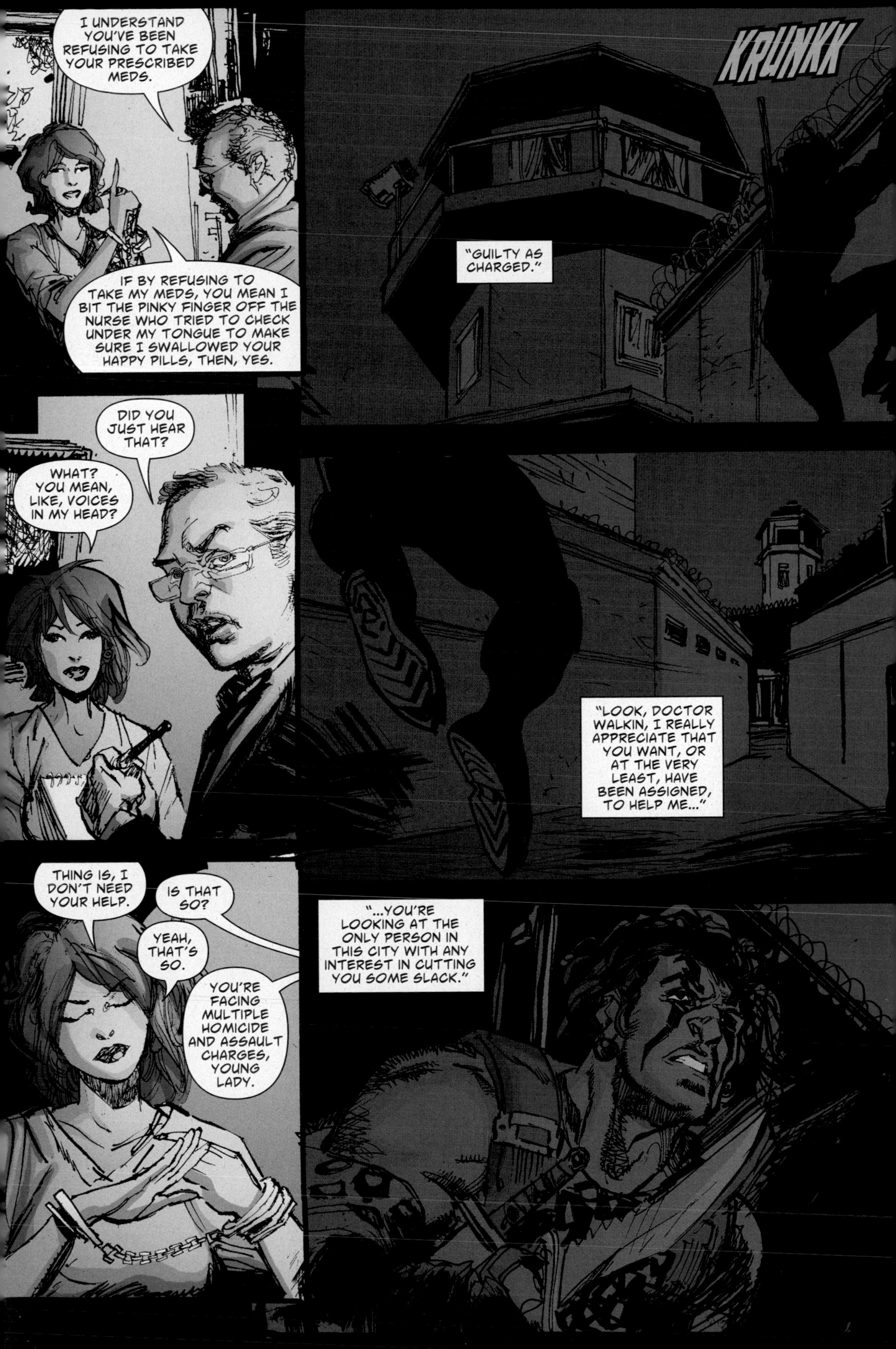
I UNDERSTAND YOU'VE BEEN REFUSING TO TAKE YOUR PRESCRIBED MEDS.
IF BY REFUSING TO TAKE MY MEDS, YOU MEAN I BIT THE PINKY FINGER OFF THE NURSE WHO TRIED TO CHECK UNDER MY TONGUE TO MAKE SURE I SWALLOWED YOUR HAPPY PILLS, THEN, YES.
KRUNKK
"GUILTY AS CHARGED."
DID YOU JUST HEAR THAT?
WHAT? YOU MEAN, LIKE, VOICES IN MY HEAD?
"LOOK, DOCTOR WALKIN, I REALLY APPRECIATE THAT YOU WANT, OR AT THE VERY LEAST, HAVE BEEN ASSIGNED, TO HELP ME..."
THING IS, I DON'T NEED YOUR HELP.
IS THAT SO?
YEAH, THAT'S SO.
YOU'RE FACING MULTIPLE HOMICIDE AND ASSAULT CHARGES, YOUNG LADY.
"...YOU'RE LOOKING AT THE ONLY PERSON IN THIS CITY WITH ANY INTEREST IN CUTTING YOU SOME SLACK."

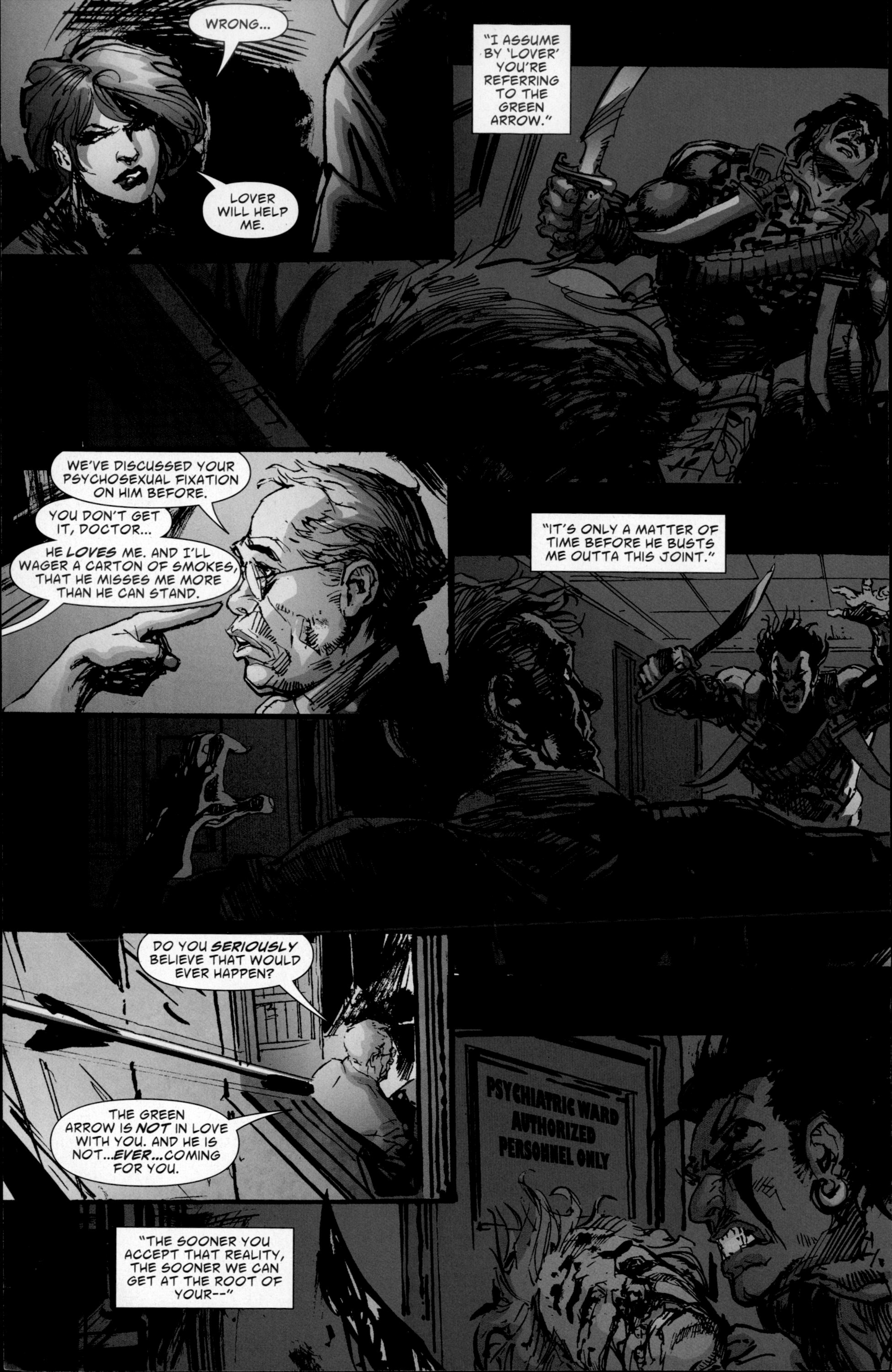
WRONG...
"I ASSUME BY 'LOVER' YOU'RE REFERRING TO THE GREEN ARROW."
LOVER WILL HELP ME.
WE'VE DISCUSSED YOUR PSYCHOSEXUAL FIXATION ON HIM BEFORE.
YOU DON'T GET IT, DOCTOR...
HE *LOVES* ME. AND I'LL WAGER A CARTON OF SMOKES, THAT HE MISSES ME MORE THAN HE CAN STAND.
"IT'S ONLY A MATTER OF TIME BEFORE HE BUSTS ME OUTTA THIS JOINT."
DO YOU *SERIOUSLY* BELIEVE THAT WOULD EVER HAPPEN?
THE GREEN ARROW IS *NOT* IN LOVE WITH YOU. AND HE IS NOT...*EVER*...COMING FOR YOU.
PSYCHIATRIC WARD AUTHORIZED PERSONNEL ONLY
"THE SOONER YOU ACCEPT THAT REALITY, THE SOONER WE CAN GET AT THE ROOT OF YOUR--"

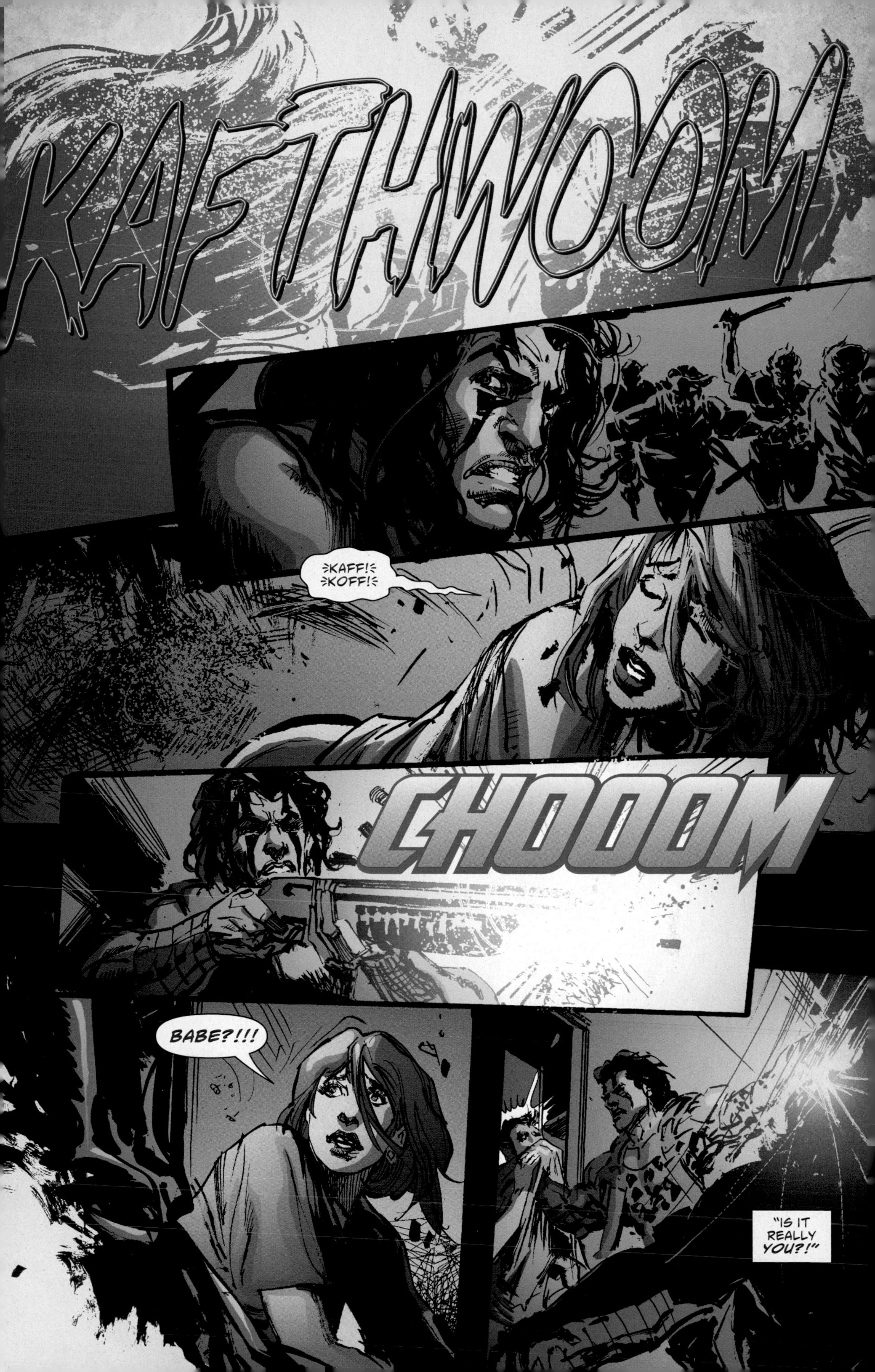
KAFTHWOOOM
KAFF! KOFF!
CHOOOM
BABE?!!!
"IS IT REALLY YOU?!"

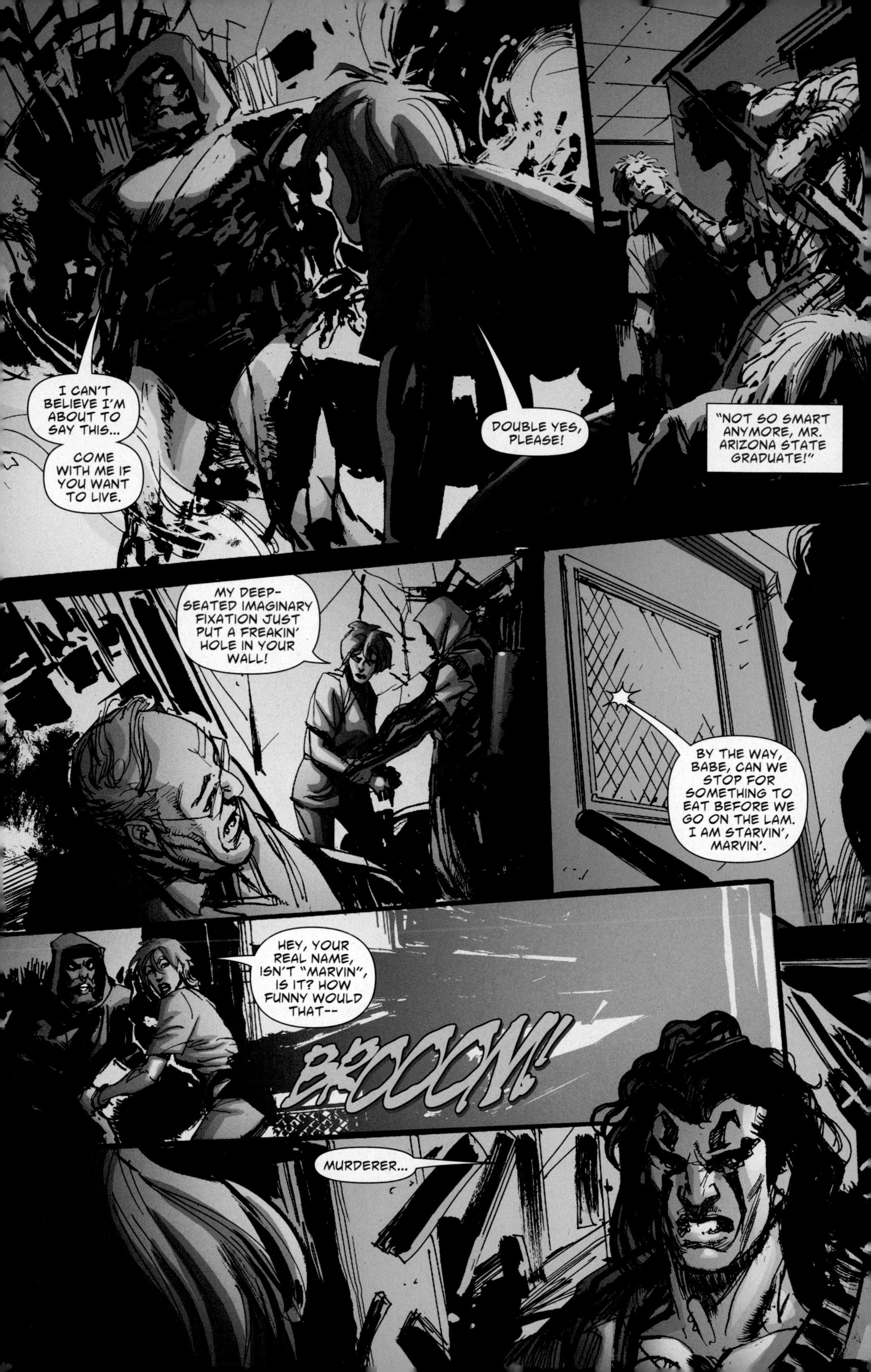
I CAN'T BELIEVE I'M ABOUT TO SAY THIS...
COME WITH ME IF YOU WANT TO LIVE.
DOUBLE YES, PLEASE!
"NOT SO SMART ANYMORE, MR. ARIZONA STATE GRADUATE!"
MY DEEP-SEATED IMAGINARY FIXATION JUST PUT A FREAKIN' HOLE IN YOUR WALL!
BY THE WAY, BABE, CAN WE STOP FOR SOMETHING TO EAT BEFORE WE GO ON THE LAM. I AM STARVIN', MARVIN'.
HEY, YOUR REAL NAME, ISN'T "MARVIN", IS IT? HOW FUNNY WOULD THAT--
BROOOM!
MURDERER...

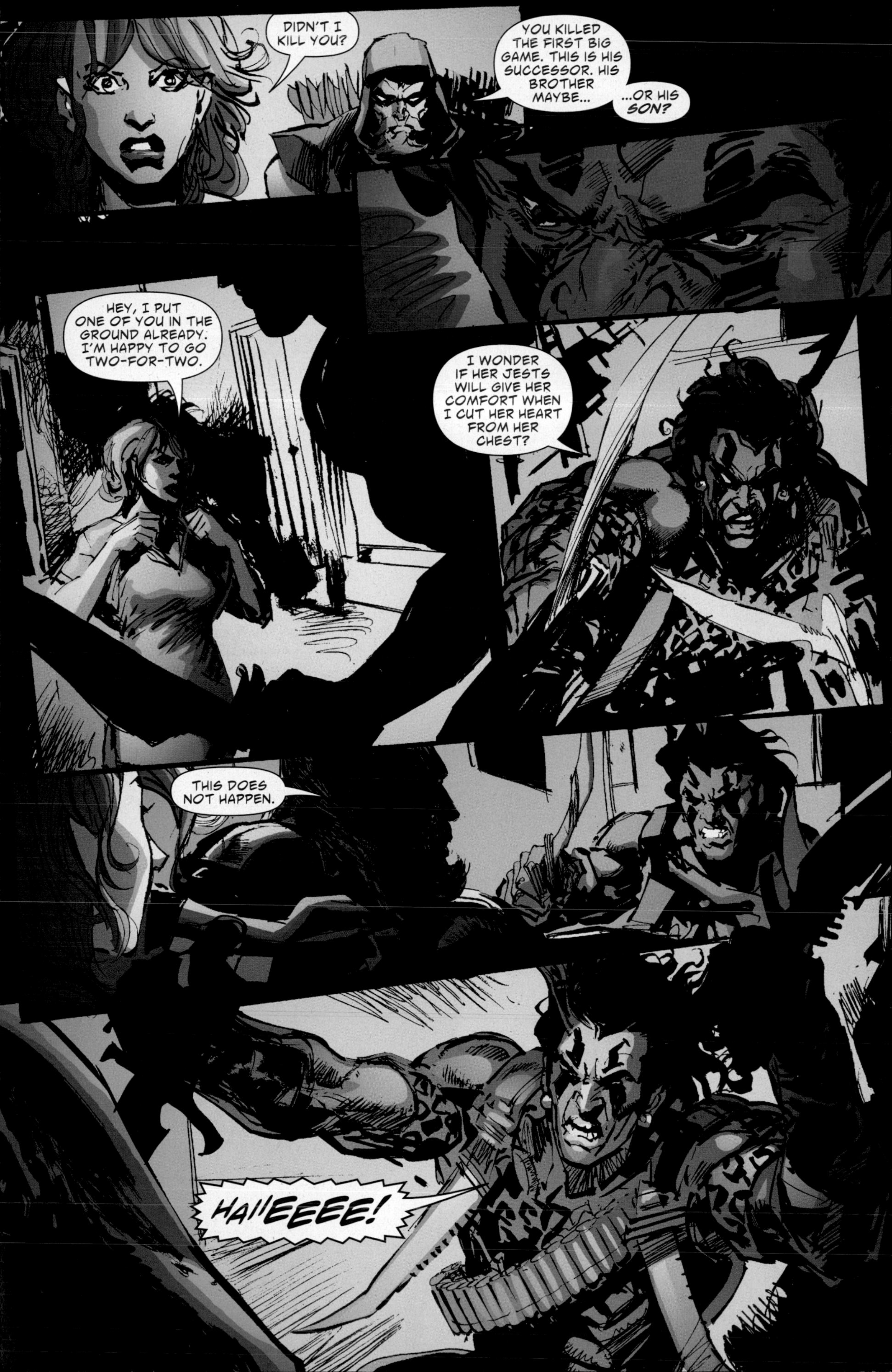
DIDN'T I KILL YOU?
YOU KILLED THE FIRST BIG GAME. THIS IS HIS SUCCESSOR. HIS BROTHER MAYBE...
...OR HIS SON?
HEY, I PUT ONE OF YOU IN THE GROUND ALREADY. I'M HAPPY TO GO TWO-FOR-TWO.
I WONDER IF HER JESTS WILL GIVE HER COMFORT WHEN I CUT HER HEART FROM HER CHEST?
THIS DOES NOT HAPPEN.
HAIIEEEE!

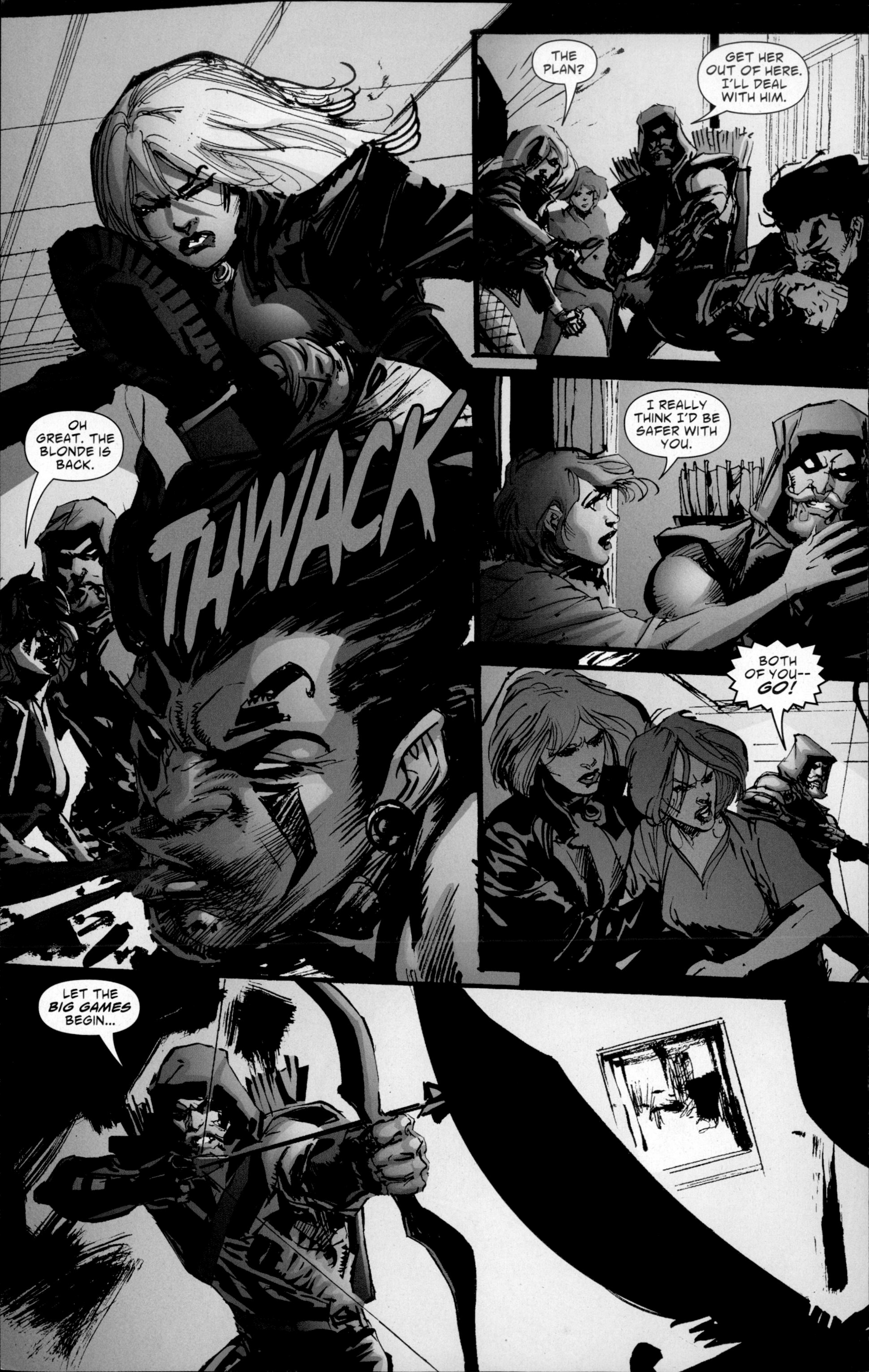
THE PLAN?
GET HER OUT OF HERE. I'LL DEAL WITH HIM.
OH GREAT. THE BLONDE IS BACK.
THWACK
I REALLY THINK I'D BE SAFER WITH YOU.
BOTH OF YOU-- GO!
LET THE BIG GAMES BEGIN...

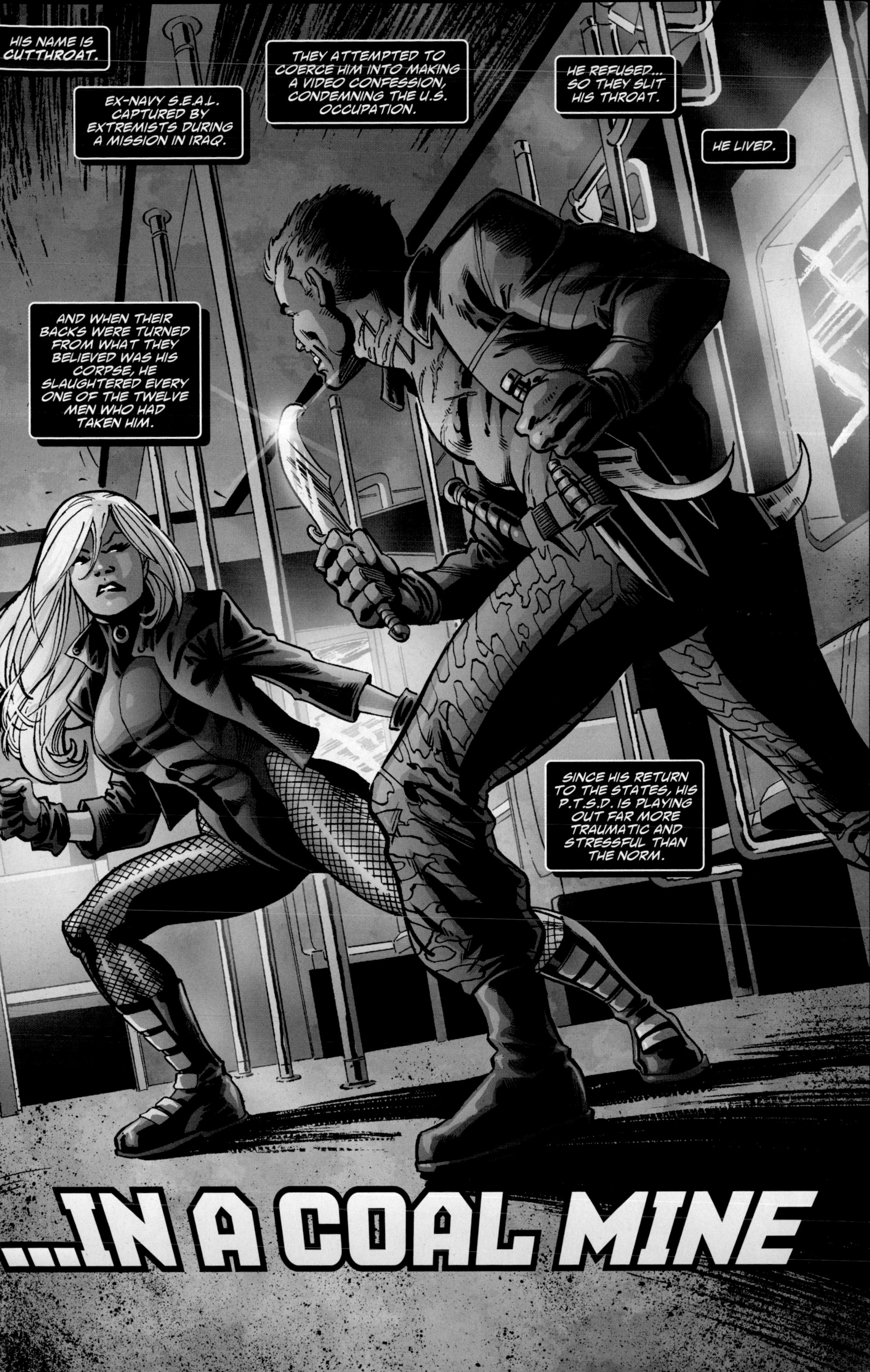

HIS NAME IS CUTTHROAT.
EX-NAVY S.E.A.L. CAPTURED BY EXTREMISTS DURING A MISSION IN IRAQ.
THEY ATTEMPTED TO COERCE HIM INTO MAKING A VIDEO CONFESSION, CONDEMNING THE U.S. OCCUPATION.
HE REFUSED... SO THEY SLIT HIS THROAT.
HE LIVED.
AND WHEN THEIR BACKS WERE TURNED FROM WHAT THEY BELIEVED WAS HIS CORPSE, HE SLAUGHTERED EVERY ONE OF THE TWELVE MEN WHO HAD TAKEN HIM.
SINCE HIS RETURN TO THE STATES, HIS P.T.S.D. IS PLAYING OUT FAR MORE TRAUMATIC AND STRESSFUL THAN THE NORM.
...IN A COAL MINE

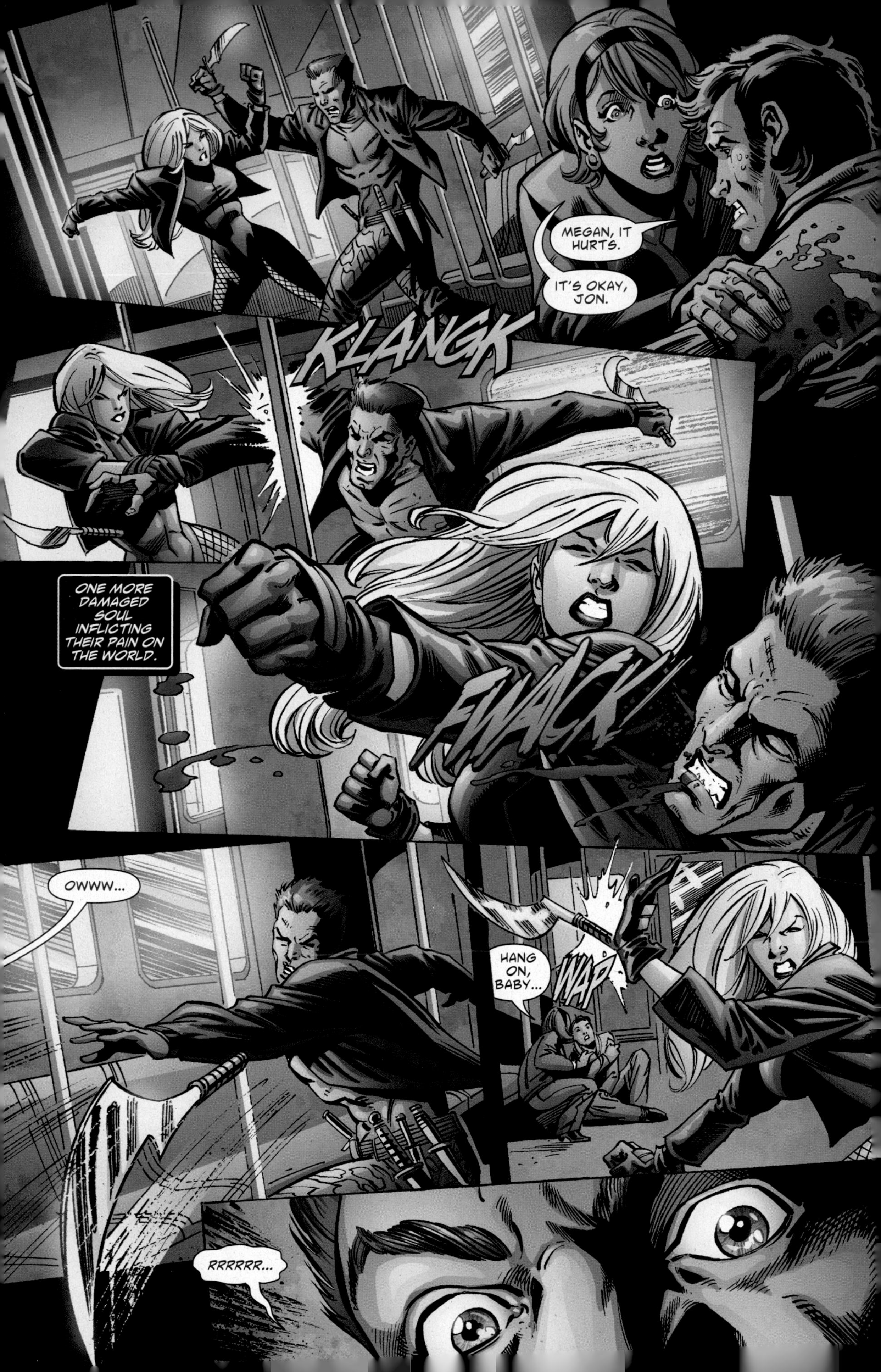

MEGAN, IT HURTS.
IT'S OKAY, JON.
KLANGK
ONE MORE DAMAGED SOUL INFLICTING THEIR PAIN ON THE WORLD.
FWACK
OWWW...
HANG ON, BABY...
WAP
RRRRRR...

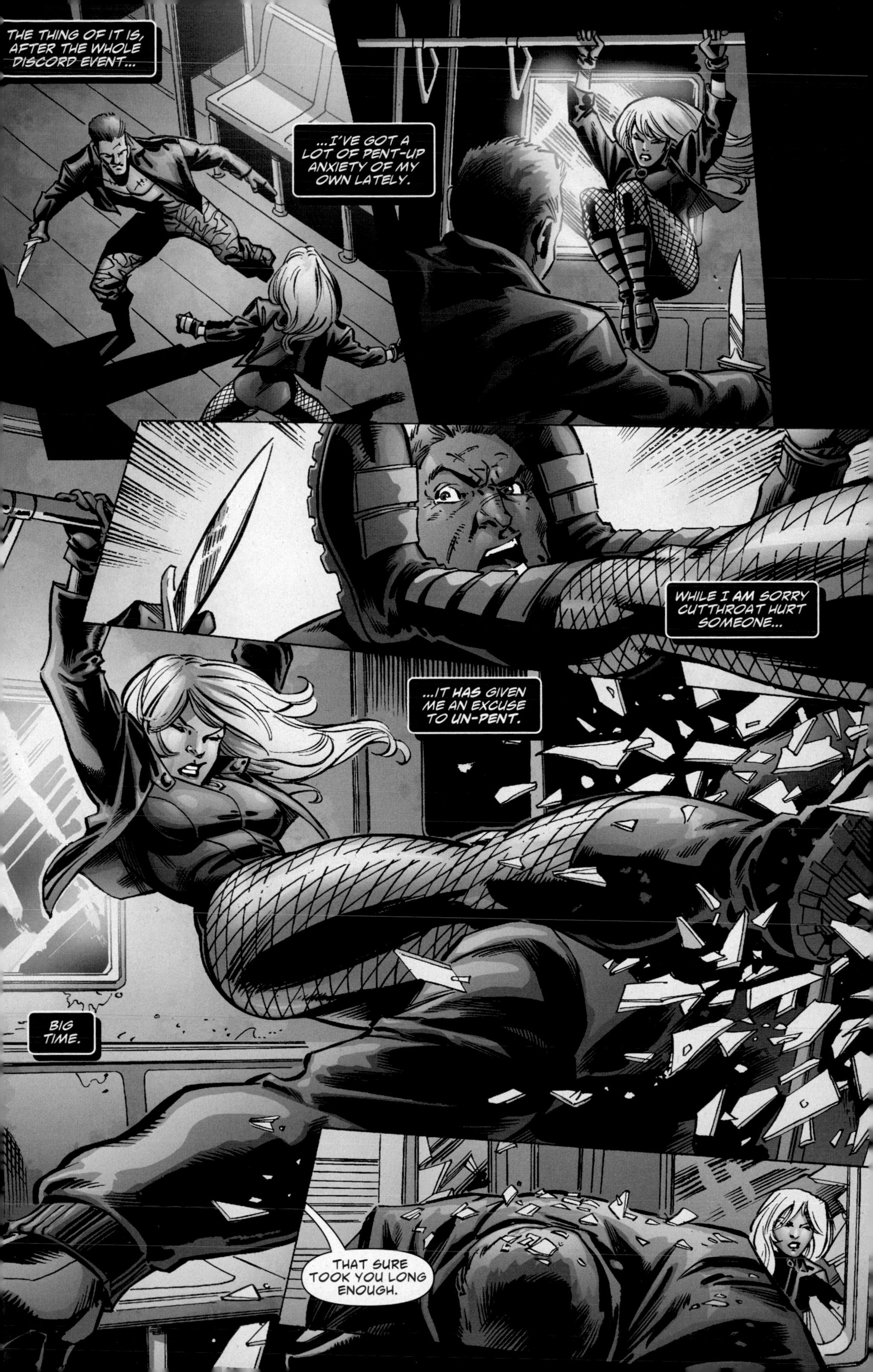
THE THING OF IT IS, AFTER THE WHOLE DISCORD EVENT...
...I'VE GOT A LOT OF PENT-UP ANXIETY OF MY OWN LATELY.
WHILE I AM SORRY CUTTHROAT HURT SOMEONE...
...IT HAS GIVEN ME AN EXCUSE TO UN-PENT.
BIG TIME.
THAT SURE TOOK YOU LONG ENOUGH.

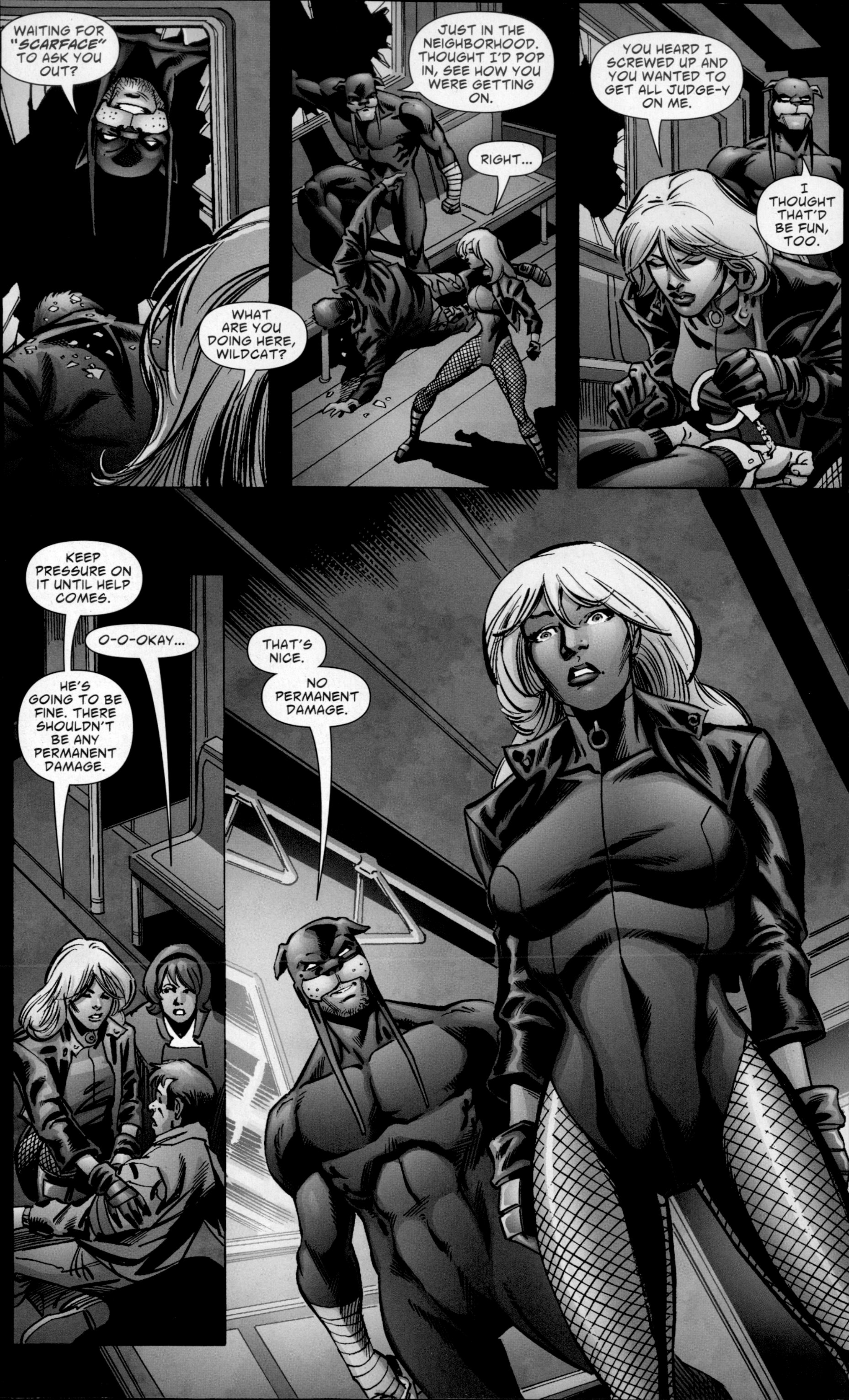
WAITING FOR "SCARFACE" TO ASK YOU OUT?
WHAT ARE YOU DOING HERE, WILDCAT?
JUST IN THE NEIGHBORHOOD. THOUGHT I'D POP IN, SEE HOW YOU WERE GETTING ON.
RIGHT...
YOU HEARD I SCREWED UP AND YOU WANTED TO GET ALL JUDGE-Y ON ME.
I THOUGHT THAT'D BE FUN, TOO.
KEEP PRESSURE ON IT UNTIL HELP COMES.
O-O-OKAY...
HE'S GOING TO BE FINE. THERE SHOULDN'T BE ANY PERMANENT DAMAGE.
THAT'S NICE.
NO PERMANENT DAMAGE.

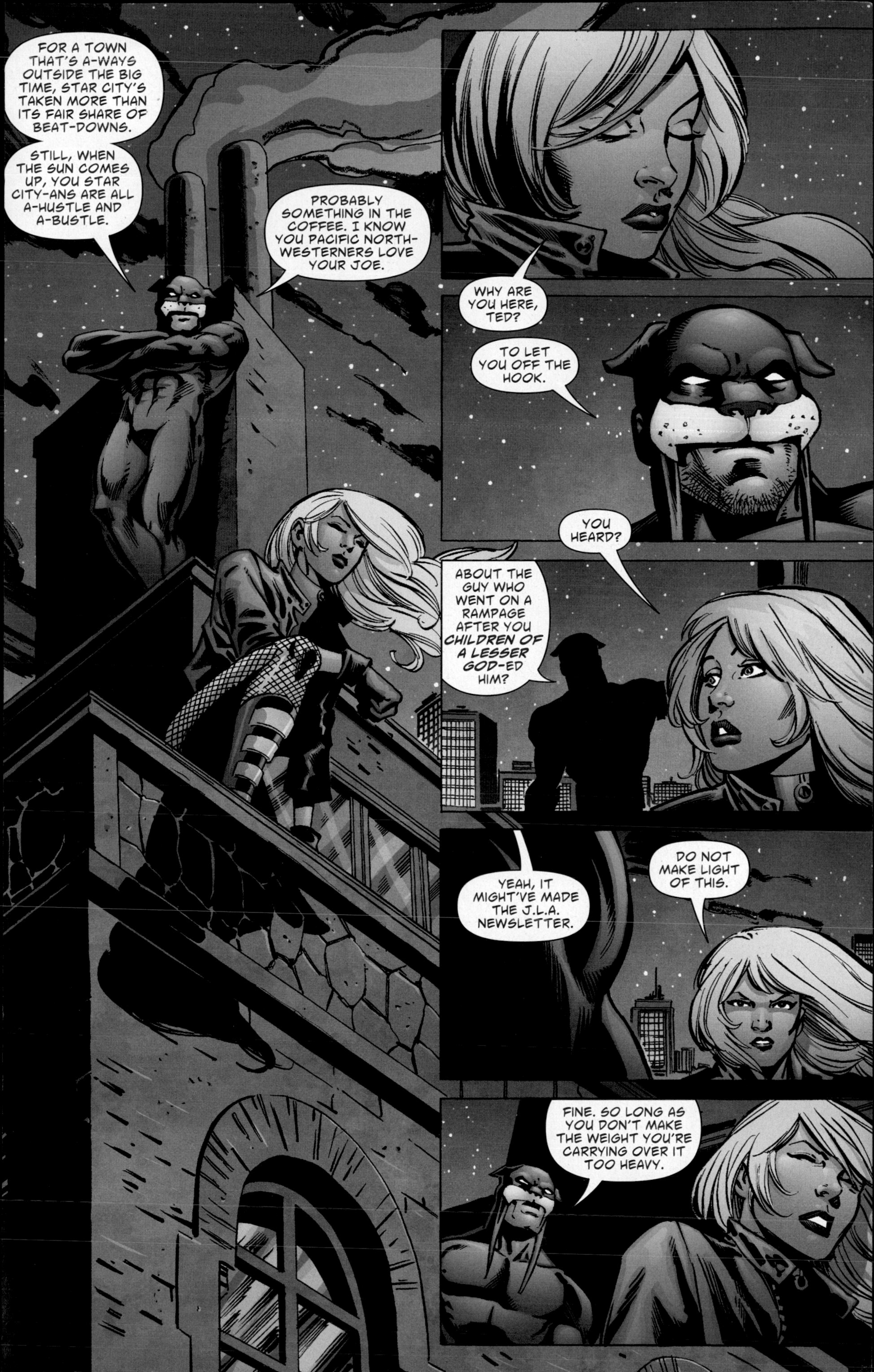
FOR A TOWN THAT'S A-WAYS OUTSIDE THE BIG TIME, STAR CITY'S TAKEN MORE THAN ITS FAIR SHARE OF BEAT-DOWNS.
STILL, WHEN THE SUN COMES UP, YOU STAR CITY-ANS ARE ALL A-HUSTLE AND A-BUSTLE.
PROBABLY SOMETHING IN THE COFFEE. I KNOW YOU PACIFIC NORTH-WESTERNERS LOVE YOUR JOE.
WHY ARE YOU HERE, TED?
TO LET YOU OFF THE HOOK.
YOU HEARD?
ABOUT THE GUY WHO WENT ON A RAMPAGE AFTER YOU CHILDREN OF A LESSER GOD-ED HIM?
YEAH, IT MIGHT'VE MADE THE J.L.A. NEWSLETTER.
DO NOT MAKE LIGHT OF THIS.
FINE. SO LONG AS YOU DON'T MAKE THE WEIGHT YOU'RE CARRYING OVER IT TOO HEAVY.

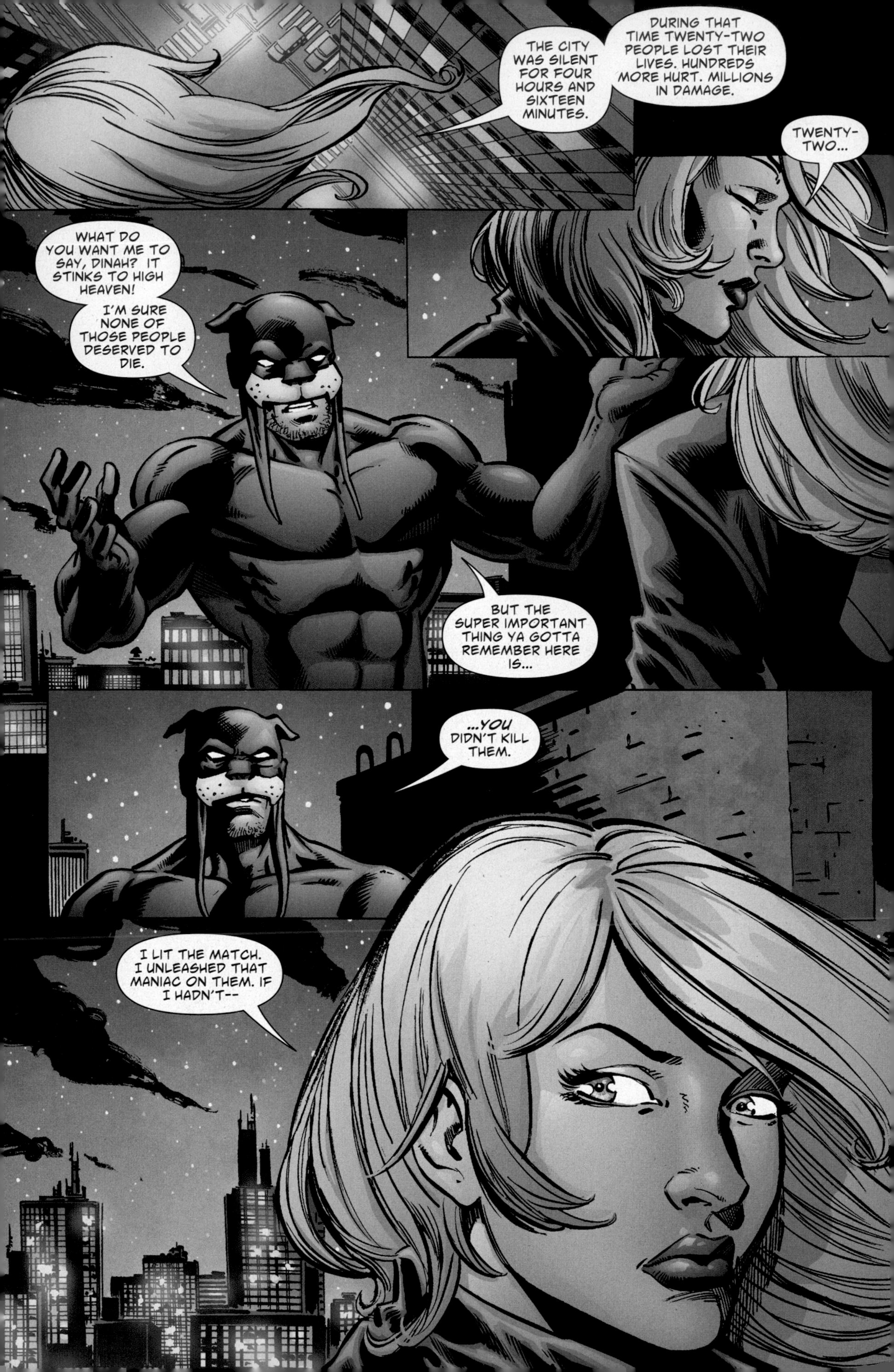
THE CITY WAS SILENT FOR FOUR HOURS AND SIXTEEN MINUTES.
DURING THAT TIME TWENTY-TWO PEOPLE LOST THEIR LIVES. HUNDREDS MORE HURT. MILLIONS IN DAMAGE.
TWENTY-TWO...
WHAT DO YOU WANT ME TO SAY, DINAH? IT STINKS TO HIGH HEAVEN!
I'M SURE NONE OF THOSE PEOPLE DESERVED TO DIE.
BUT THE SUPER IMPORTANT THING YA GOTTA REMEMBER HERE IS...
...YOU DIDN'T KILL THEM.
I LIT THE MATCH. I UNLEASHED THAT MANIAC ON THEM. IF I HADN'T--

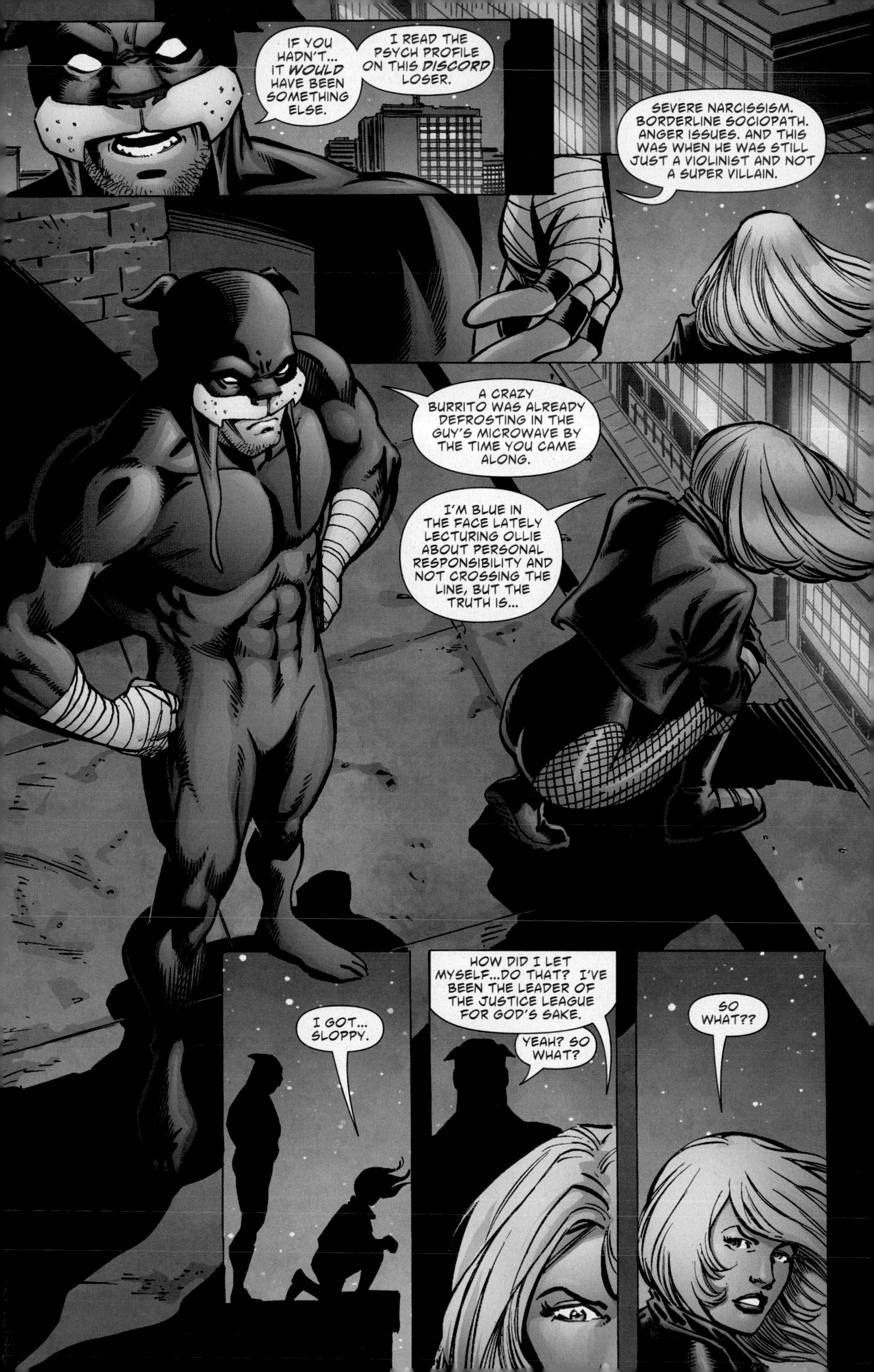
IF YOU HADN'T... IT WOULD HAVE BEEN SOMETHING ELSE.
I READ THE PSYCH PROFILE ON THIS DISCORD LOSER.
SEVERE NARCISSISM. BORDERLINE SOCIOPATH. ANGER ISSUES. AND THIS WAS WHEN HE WAS STILL JUST A VIOLINIST AND NOT A SUPER VILLAIN.
A CRAZY BURRITO WAS ALREADY DEFROSTING IN THE GUY'S MICROWAVE BY THE TIME YOU CAME ALONG.
I'M BLUE IN THE FACE LATELY LECTURING OLLIE ABOUT PERSONAL RESPONSIBILITY AND NOT CROSSING THE LINE, BUT THE TRUTH IS...
I GOT... SLOPPY.
HOW DID I LET MYSELF...DO THAT? I'VE BEEN THE LEADER OF THE JUSTICE LEAGUE FOR GOD'S SAKE.
YEAH? SO WHAT?
SO WHAT??

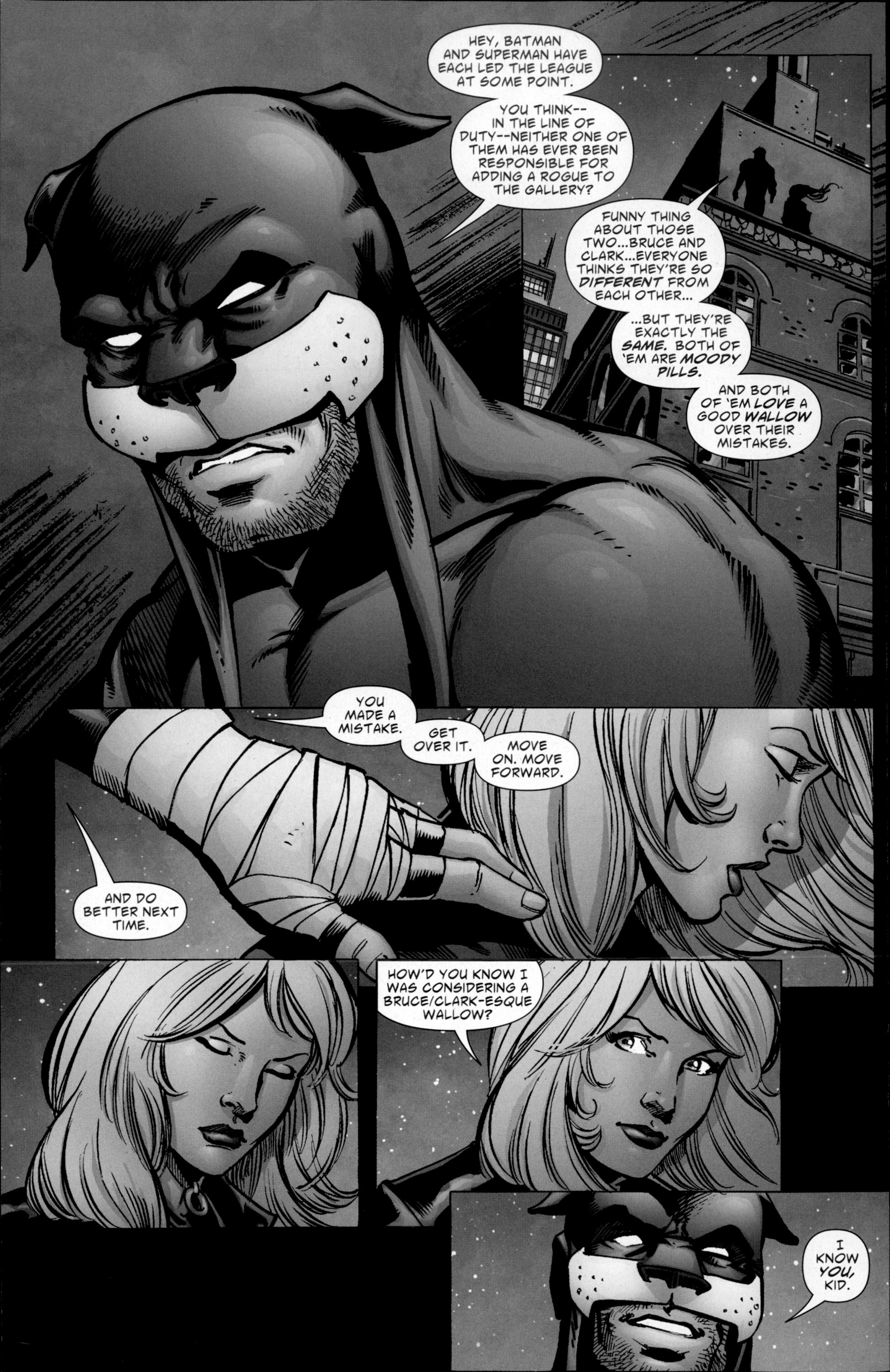
HEY, BATMAN AND SUPERMAN HAVE EACH LED THE LEAGUE AT SOME POINT.
YOU THINK-- IN THE LINE OF DUTY--NEITHER ONE OF THEM HAS EVER BEEN RESPONSIBLE FOR ADDING A ROGUE TO THE GALLERY?
FUNNY THING ABOUT THOSE TWO...BRUCE AND CLARK...EVERYONE THINKS THEY'RE SO DIFFERENT FROM EACH OTHER...
...BUT THEY'RE EXACTLY THE SAME. BOTH OF 'EM ARE MOODY PILLS.
AND BOTH OF 'EM LOVE A GOOD WALLOW OVER THEIR MISTAKES.
YOU MADE A MISTAKE.
GET OVER IT.
MOVE ON. MOVE FORWARD.
AND DO BETTER NEXT TIME.
HOW'D YOU KNOW I WAS CONSIDERING A BRUCE/CLARK-ESQUE WALLOW?
I KNOW YOU, KID.

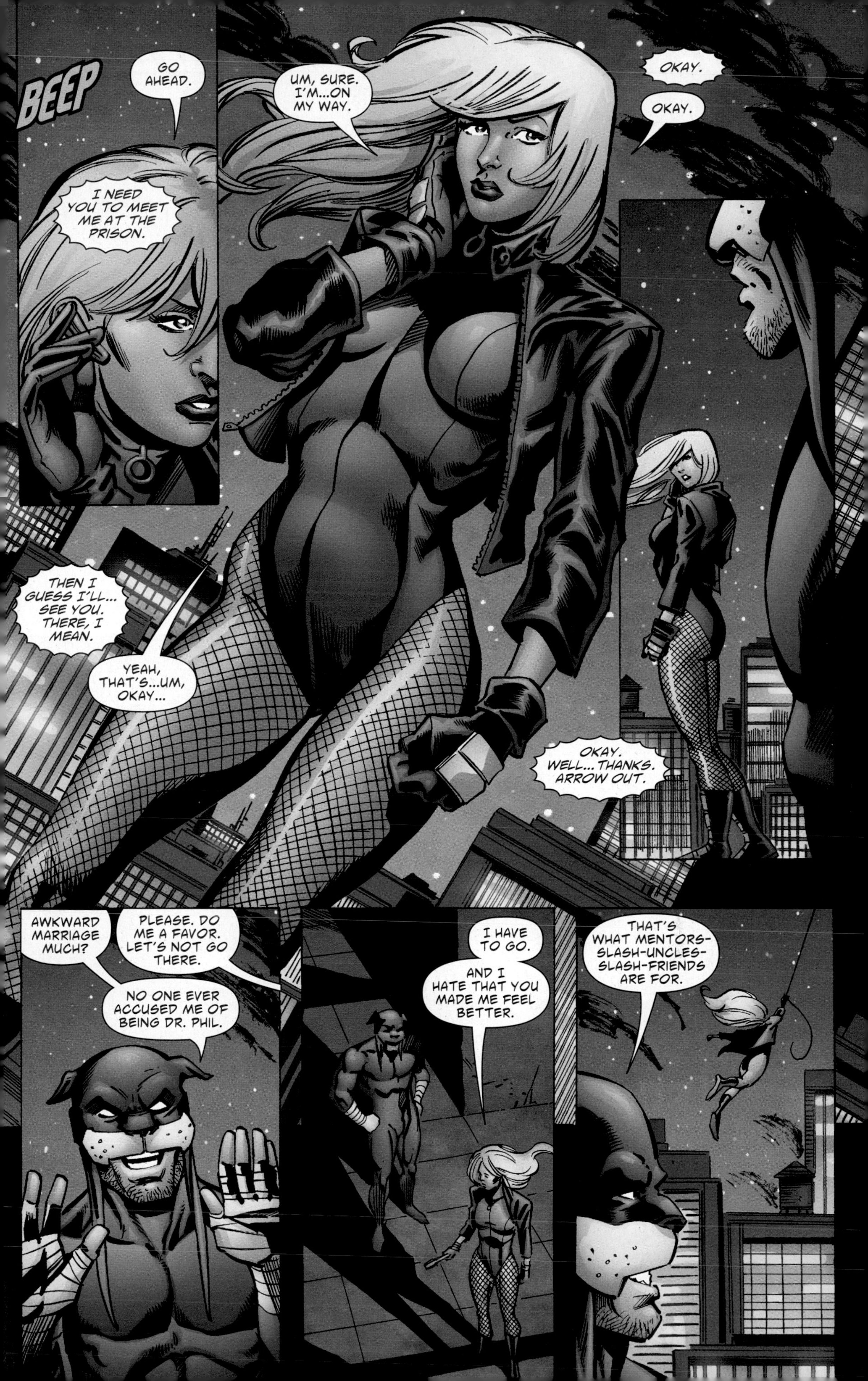
BEEP
GO AHEAD.
I NEED YOU TO MEET ME AT THE PRISON.
UM, SURE. I'M...ON MY WAY.
OKAY.
OKAY.
THEN I GUESS I'LL... SEE YOU. THERE, I MEAN.
YEAH, THAT'S...UM, OKAY...
OKAY. WELL... THANKS. ARROW OUT.
AWKWARD MARRIAGE MUCH?
PLEASE. DO ME A FAVOR. LET'S NOT GO THERE.
NO ONE EVER ACCUSED ME OF BEING DR. PHIL.
I HAVE TO GO.
AND I HATE THAT YOU MADE ME FEEL BETTER.
THAT'S WHAT MENTORS-SLASH-UNCLES-SLASH-FRIENDS ARE FOR.

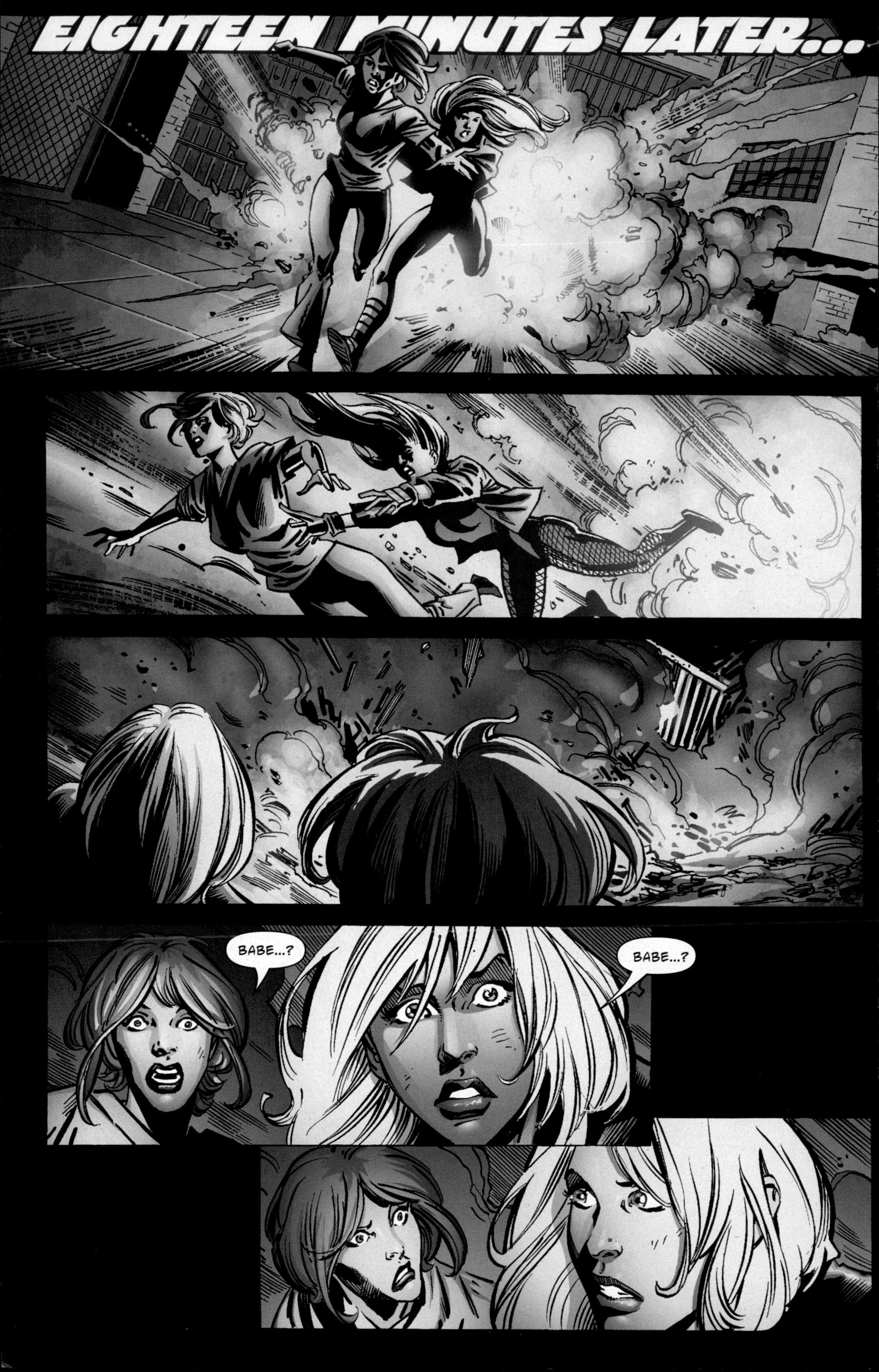
EIGHTEEN MINUTES LATER...
BABE...?
BABE...?

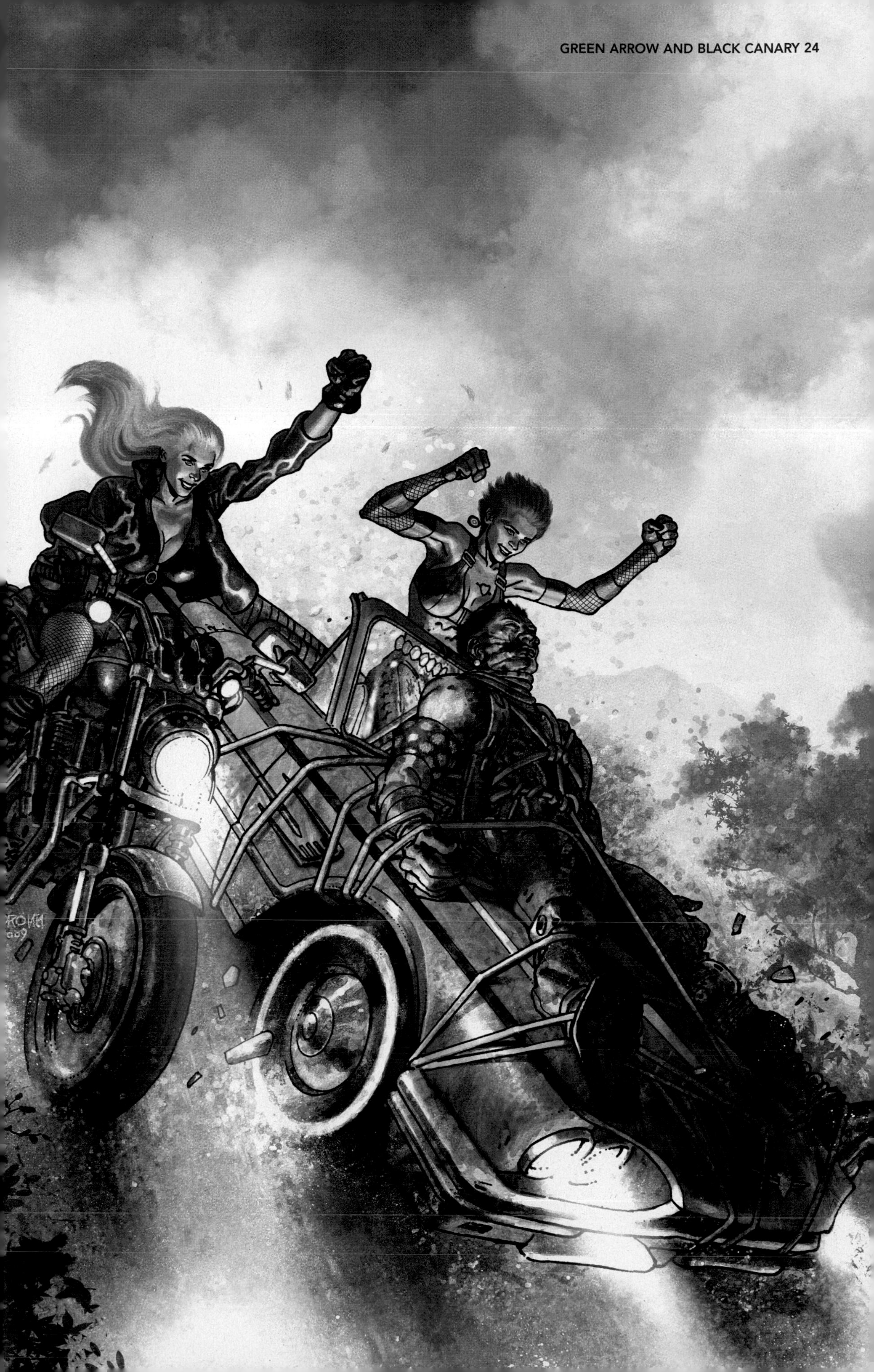

WE, PREY
Mike Norton Penciller
Joe Rubinstein Inker

HOMETOWN GIRL MAKES GOOD
Mike Norton Layouts
Bill Sienkiewicz Finishes

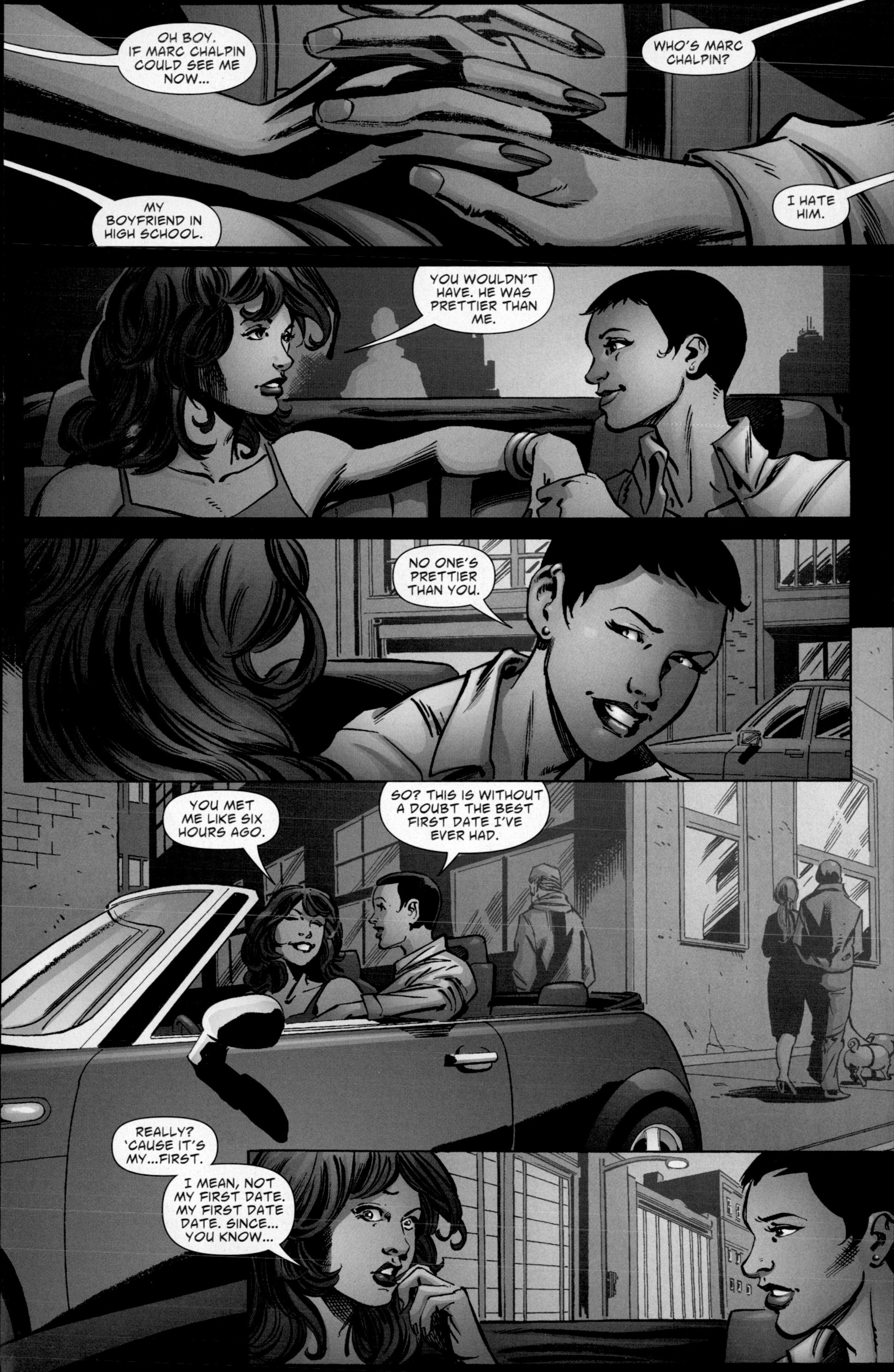
OH BOY. IF MARC CHALPIN COULD SEE ME NOW...
WHO'S MARC CHALPIN?
MY BOYFRIEND IN HIGH SCHOOL.
I HATE HIM.
YOU WOULDN'T HAVE. HE WAS PRETTIER THAN ME.
NO ONE'S PRETTIER THAN YOU.
YOU MET ME LIKE SIX HOURS AGO.
SO? THIS IS WITHOUT A DOUBT THE BEST FIRST DATE I'VE EVER HAD.
REALLY? 'CAUSE IT'S MY...FIRST.
I MEAN, NOT MY FIRST DATE. MY FIRST DATE DATE. SINCE... YOU KNOW...

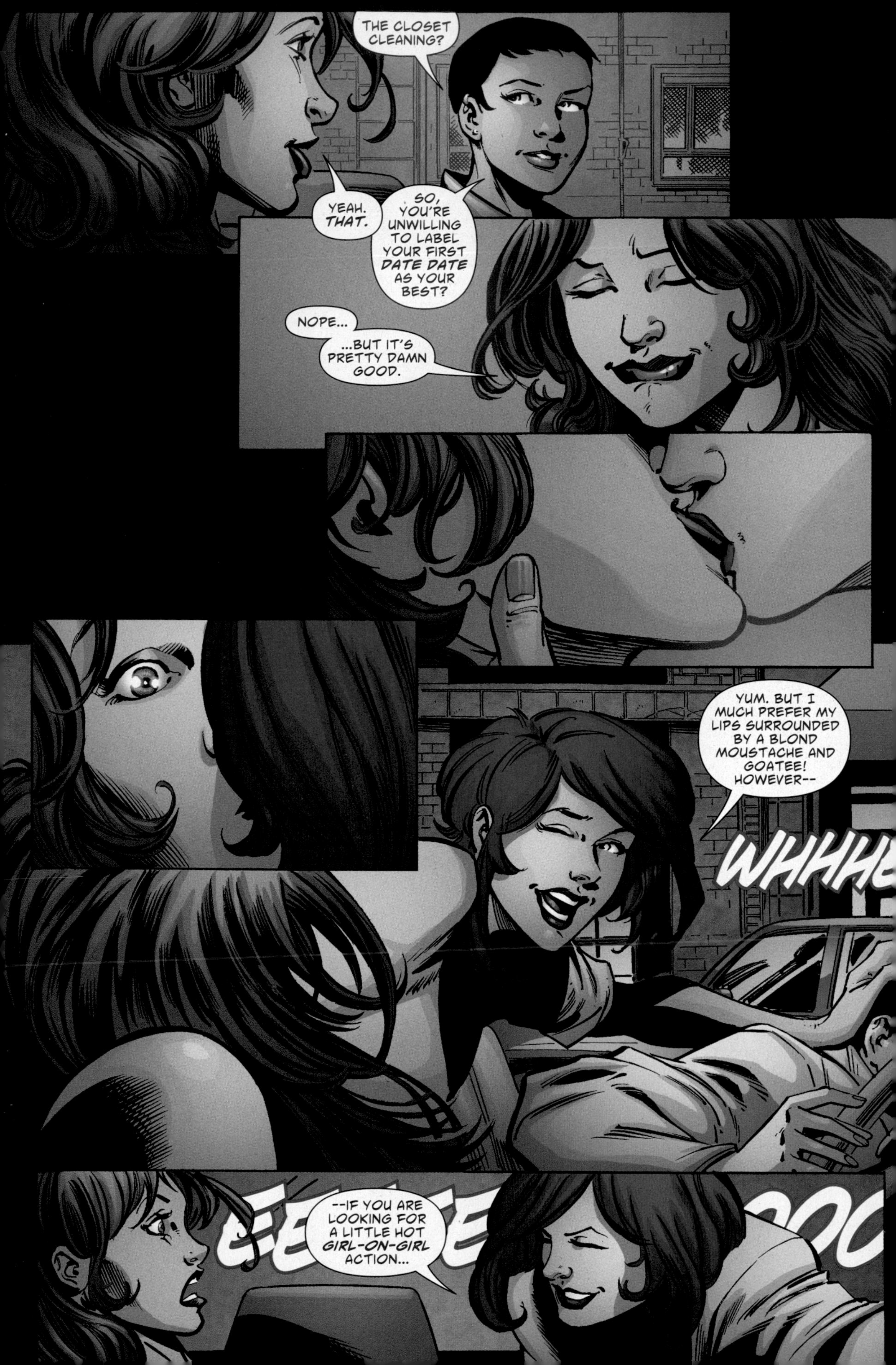
THE CLOSET CLEANING?
YEAH. THAT.
SO, YOU'RE UNWILLING TO LABEL YOUR FIRST DATE DATE AS YOUR BEST?
NOPE...
...BUT IT'S PRETTY DAMN GOOD.
YUM. BUT I MUCH PREFER MY LIPS SURROUNDED BY A BLOND MOUSTACHE AND GOATEE! HOWEVER--
WHHHE
--IF YOU ARE LOOKING FOR A LITTLE HOT GIRL-ON-GIRL ACTION...

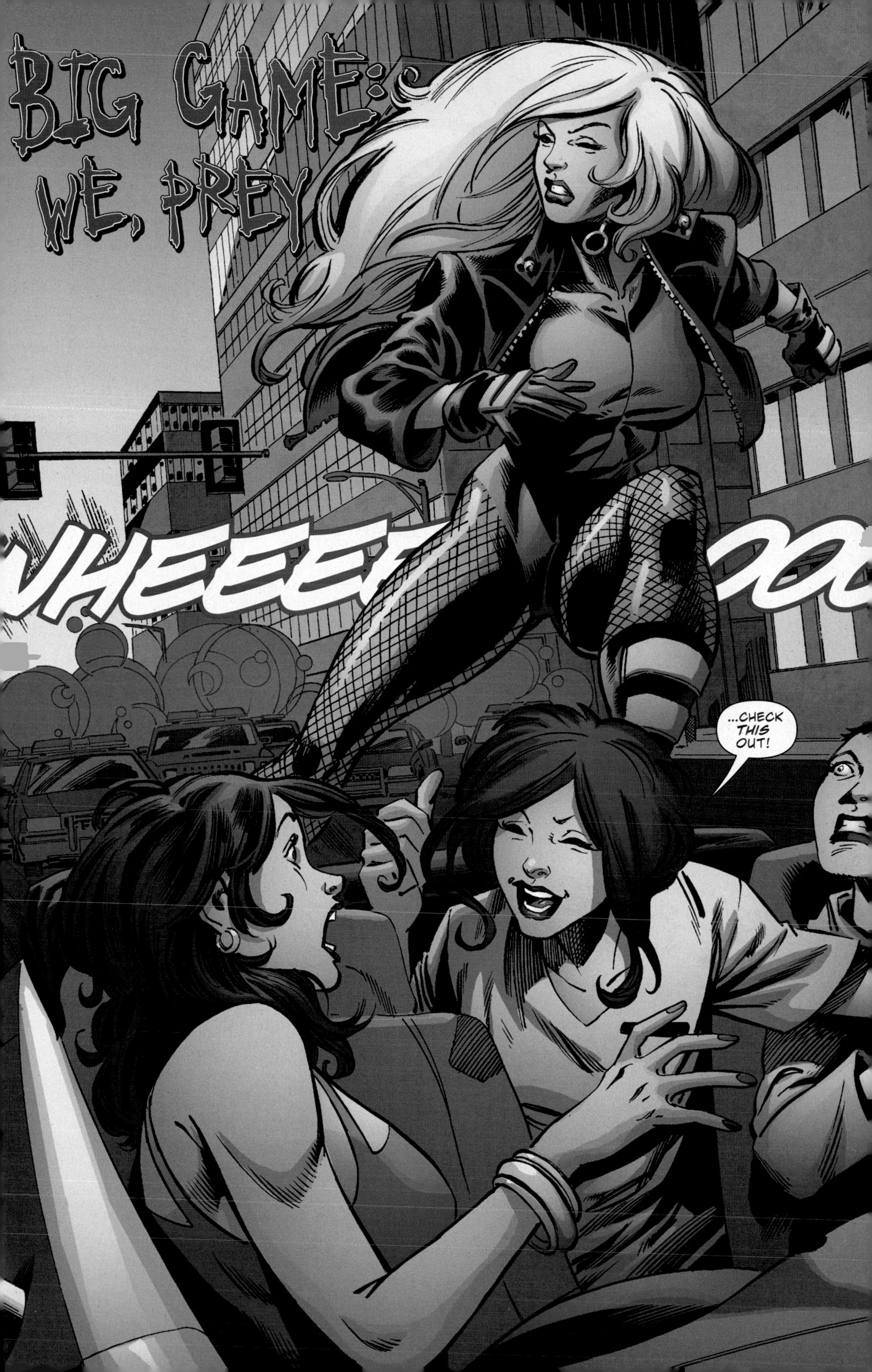
BIG GAME:
WE, PREY
...CHECK THIS OUT!

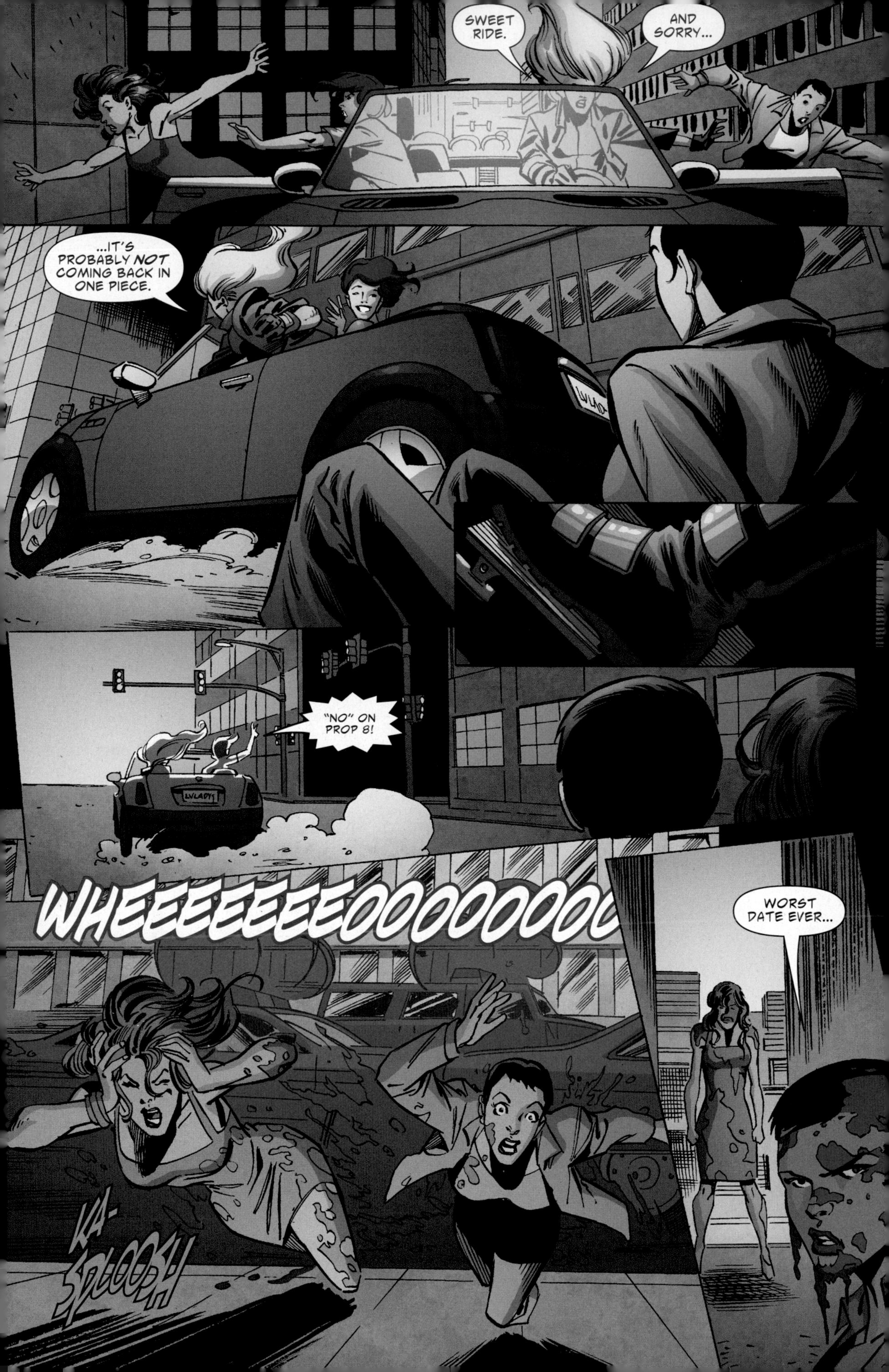
SWEET RIDE.
AND SORRY...
...IT'S PROBABLY NOT COMING BACK IN ONE PIECE.
"NO" ON PROP 8!
WHEEEEEEEEOOOOOOOO
KA-SPLOOSH
WORST DATE EVER...

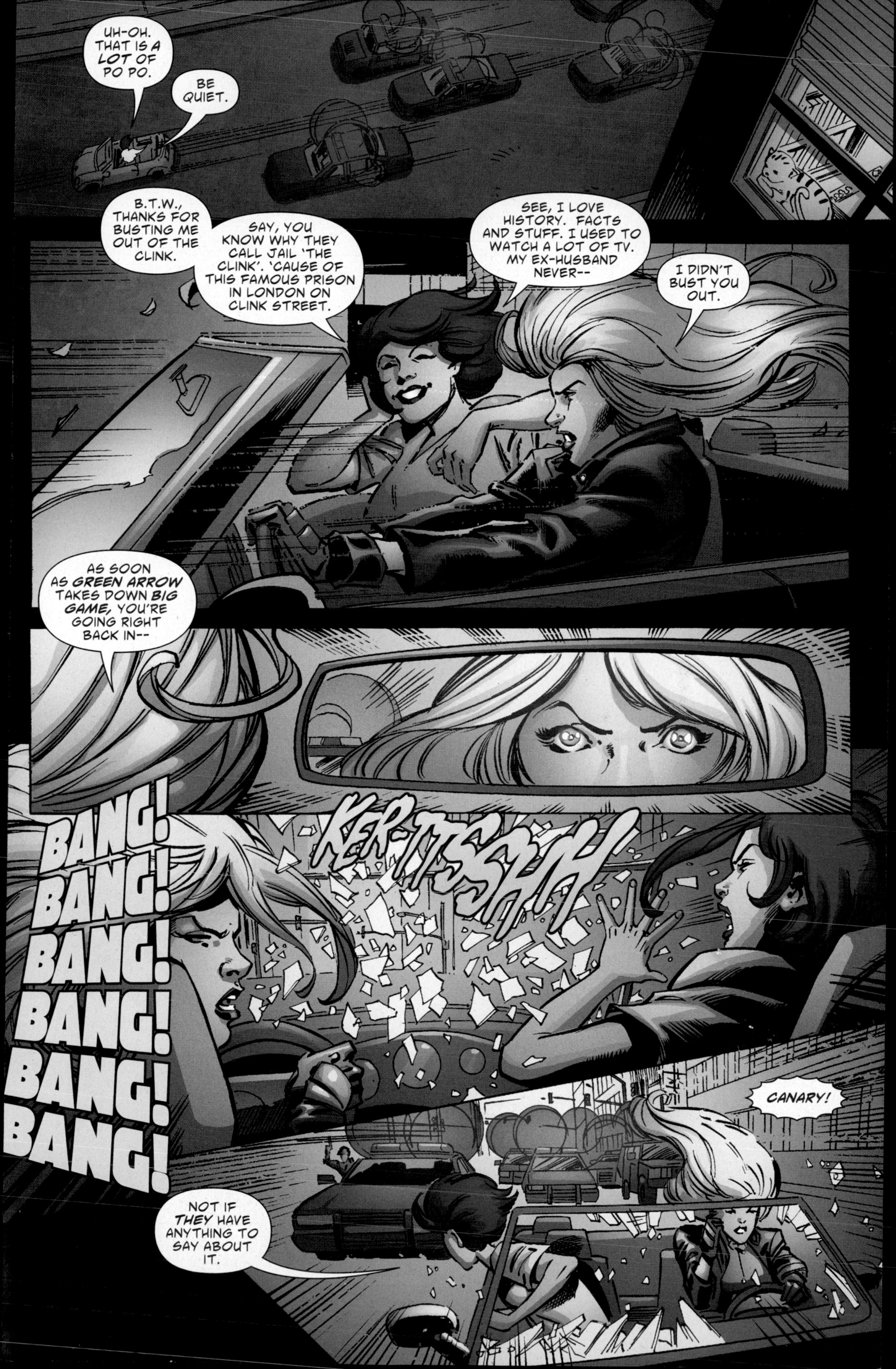
UH-OH. THAT IS A LOT OF PO PO.
BE QUIET.
B.T.W., THANKS FOR BUSTING ME OUT OF THE CLINK.
SAY, YOU KNOW WHY THEY CALL JAIL 'THE CLINK'. 'CAUSE OF THIS FAMOUS PRISON IN LONDON ON CLINK STREET.
SEE, I LOVE HISTORY. FACTS AND STUFF. I USED TO WATCH A LOT OF TV. MY EX-HUSBAND NEVER--
I DIDN'T BUST YOU OUT.
AS SOON AS GREEN ARROW TAKES DOWN BIG GAME, YOU'RE GOING RIGHT BACK IN--
BANG! BANG! BANG! BANG! BANG! BANG!
KER-TTSSHH
CANARY!
NOT IF THEY HAVE ANYTHING TO SAY ABOUT IT.

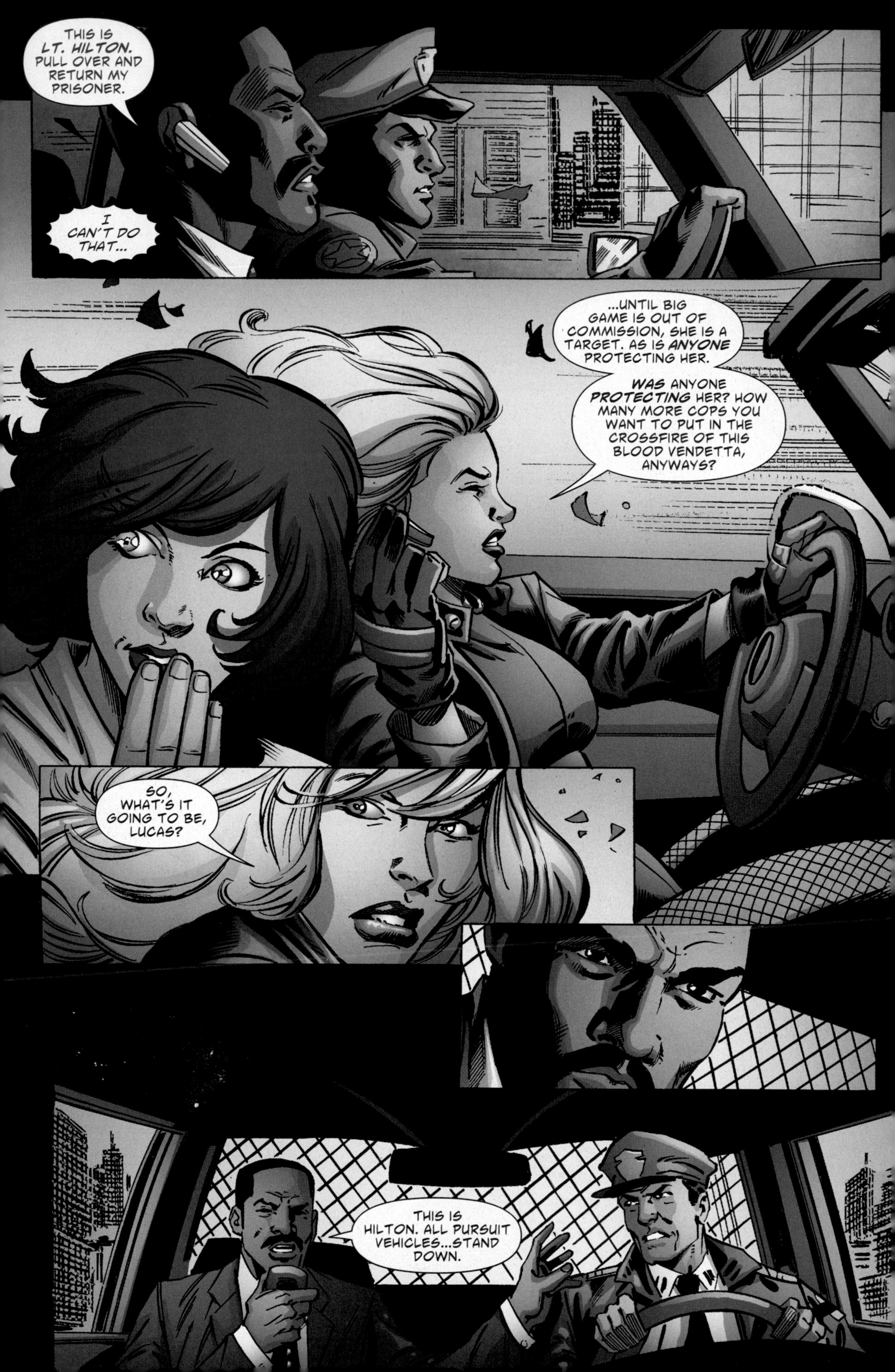
THIS IS LT. HILTON. PULL OVER AND RETURN MY PRISONER.
I CAN'T DO THAT...
...UNTIL BIG GAME IS OUT OF COMMISSION, SHE IS A TARGET. AS IS ANYONE PROTECTING HER.
WAS ANYONE PROTECTING HER? HOW MANY MORE COPS YOU WANT TO PUT IN THE CROSSFIRE OF THIS BLOOD VENDETTA, ANYWAYS?
SO, WHAT'S IT GOING TO BE, LUCAS?
THIS IS HILTON. ALL PURSUIT VEHICLES...STAND DOWN.

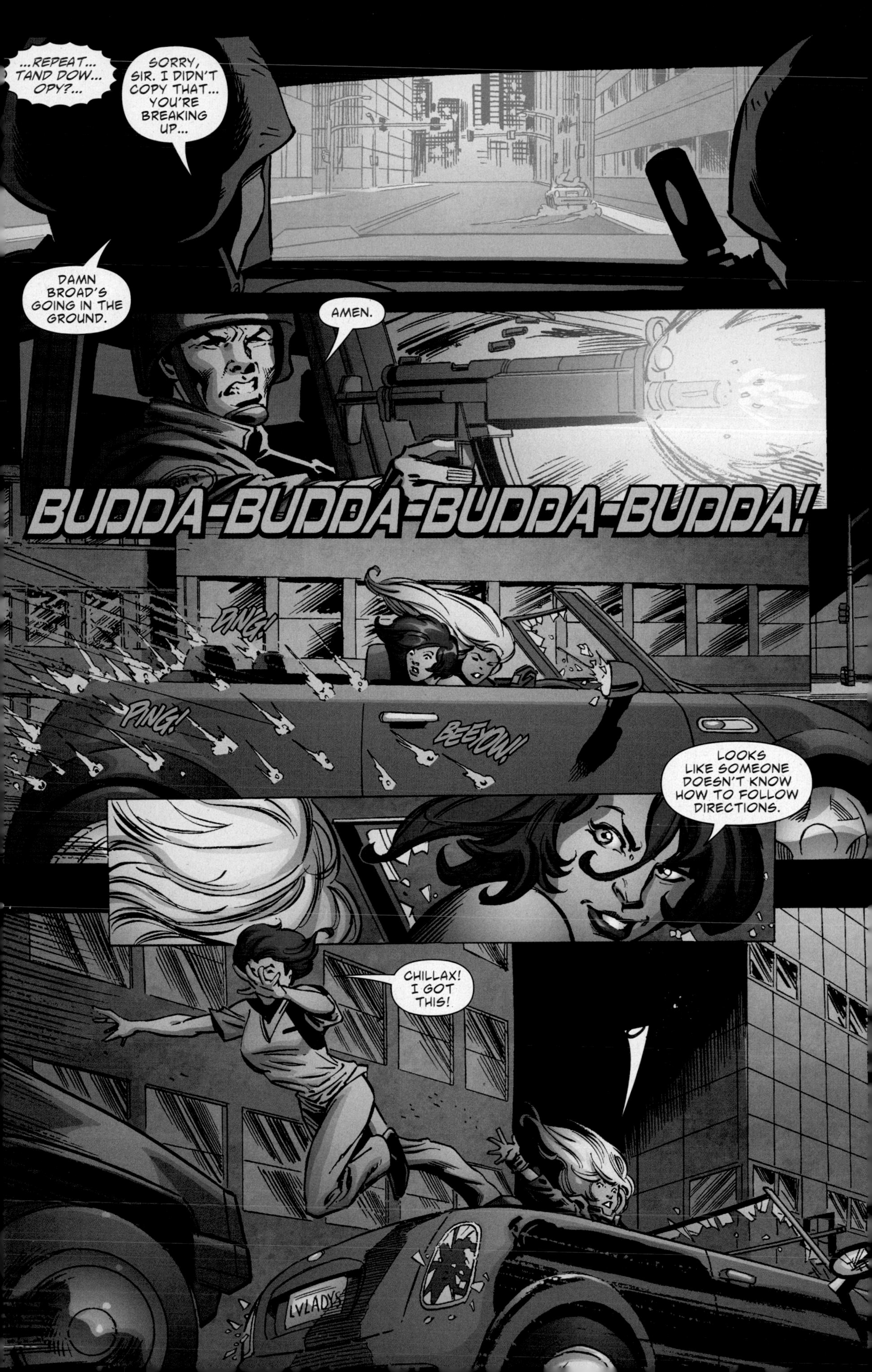
...REPEAT... TAND DOW... OPY?...
SORRY, SIR. I DIDN'T COPY THAT... YOU'RE BREAKING UP...
DAMN BROAD'S GOING IN THE GROUND.
AMEN.
BUDDA-BUDDA-BUDDA-BUDDA!
DING!
PING!
BEEYOW!
LOOKS LIKE SOMEONE DOESN'T KNOW HOW TO FOLLOW DIRECTIONS.
CHILLAX! I GOT THIS!
LVLADYS

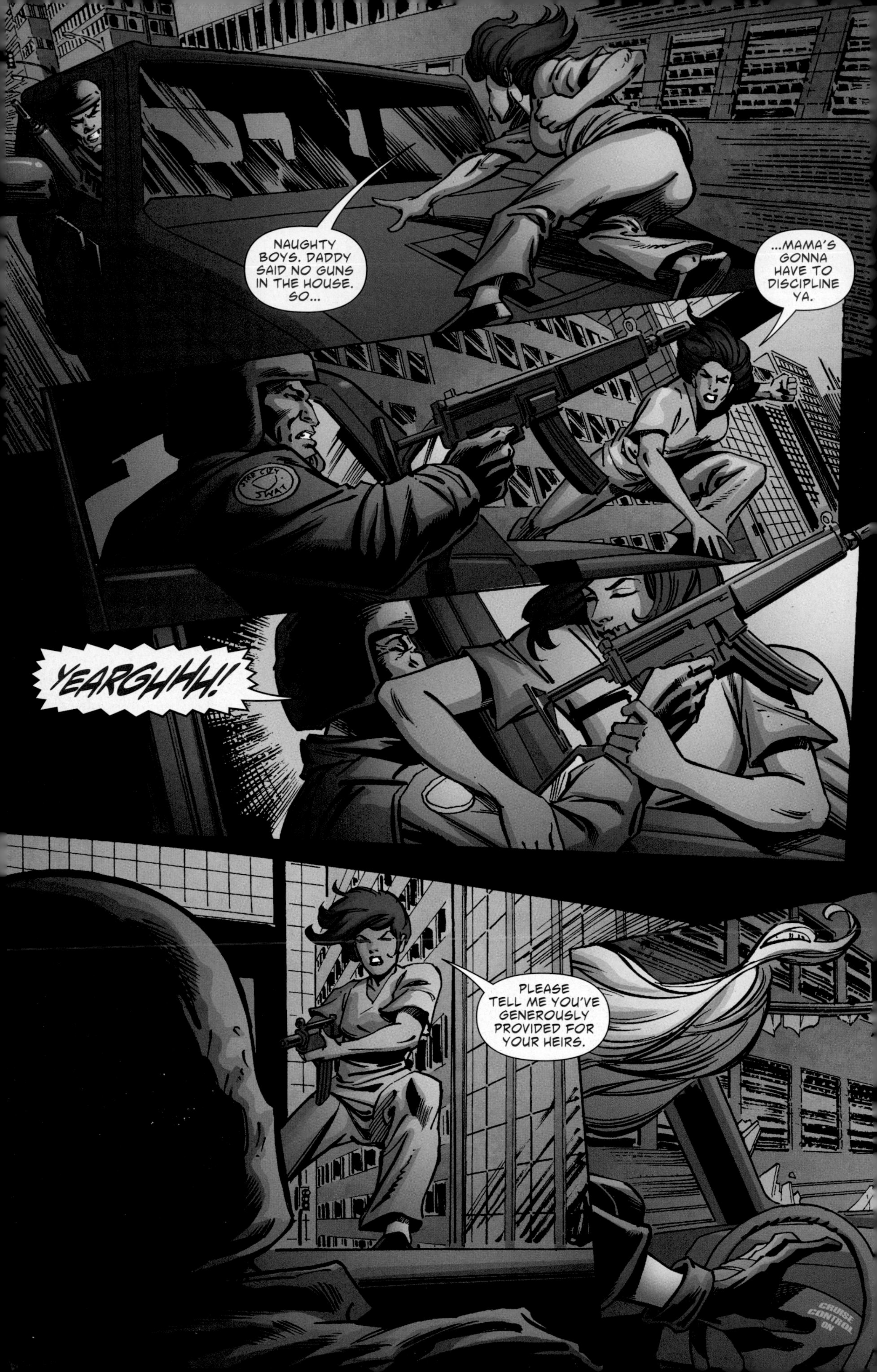
NAUGHTY BOYS. DADDY SAID NO GUNS IN THE HOUSE. SO...
...MAMA'S GONNA HAVE TO DISCIPLINE YA.
STAR CITY SWAT
YEARGHHH!
PLEASE TELL ME YOU'VE GENEROUSLY PROVIDED FOR YOUR HEIRS.
CRUISE CONTROL ON

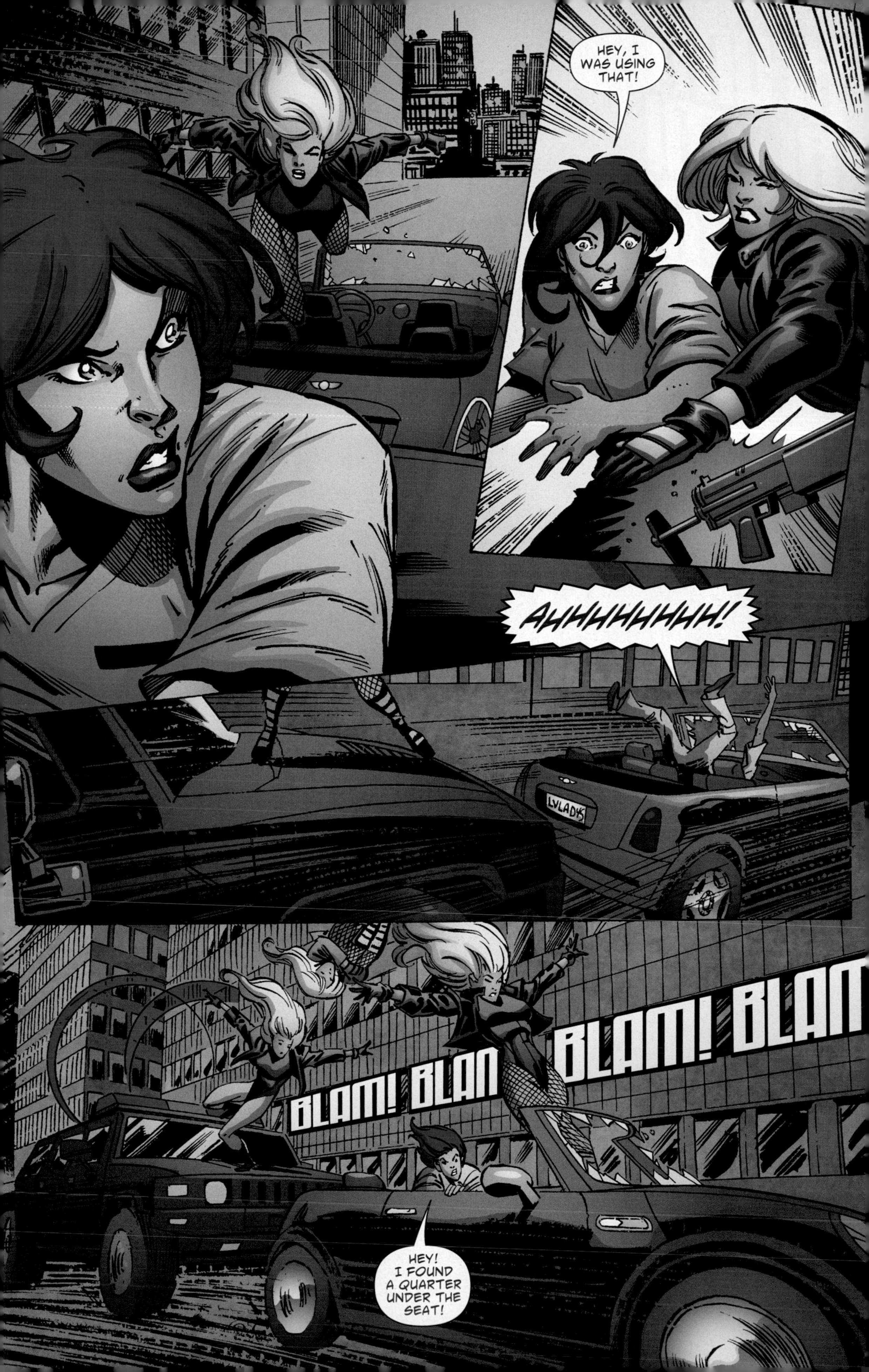

HEY, I WAS USING THAT!
AHHHHHHHH!
LVLADYS
BLAM! BLAM
BLAM! BLAM
HEY! I FOUND A QUARTER UNDER THE SEAT!

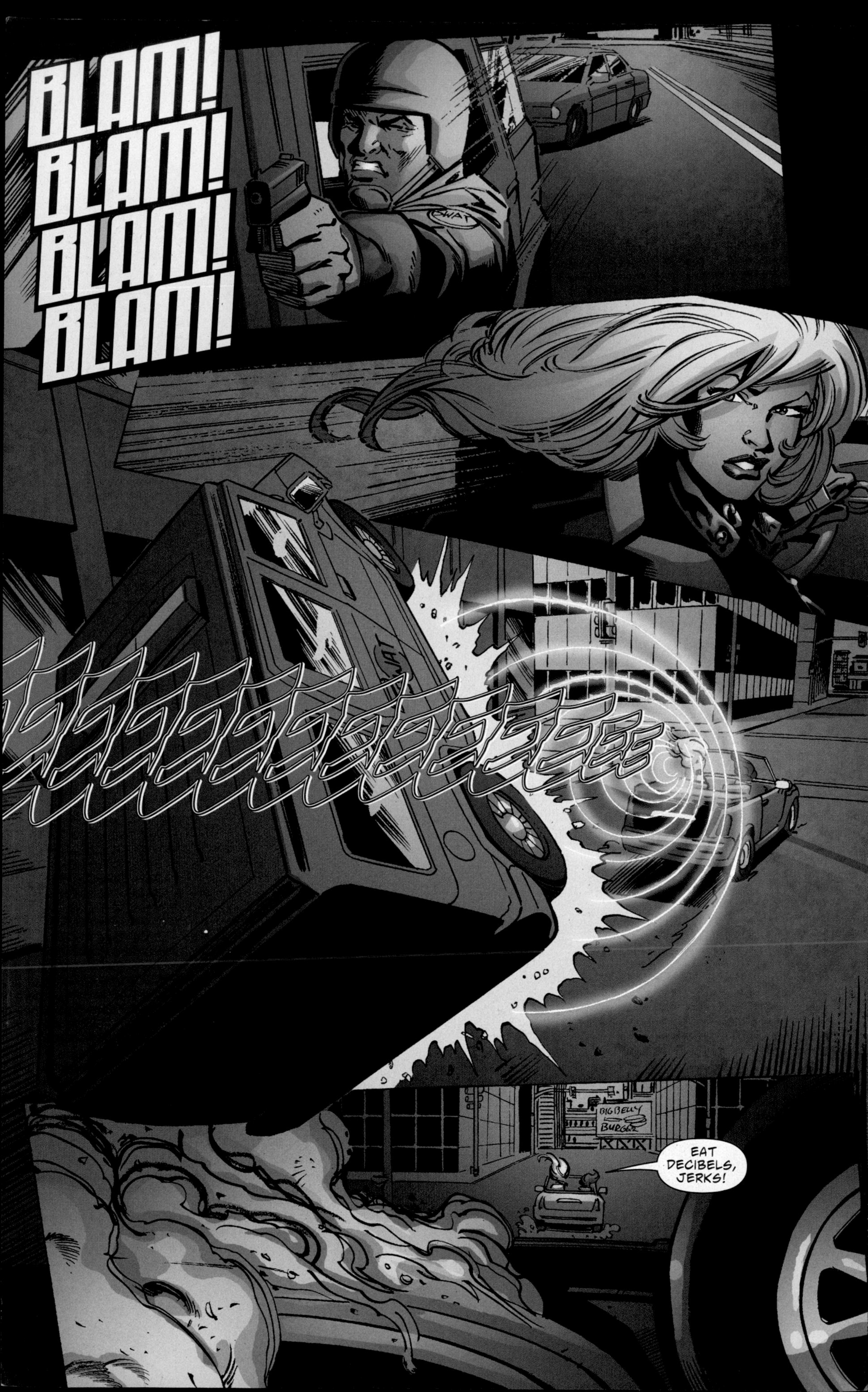
BLAM! BLAM! BLAM! BLAM!
SWAT
BIG BELLY BURGER
EAT DECIBELS, JERKS!

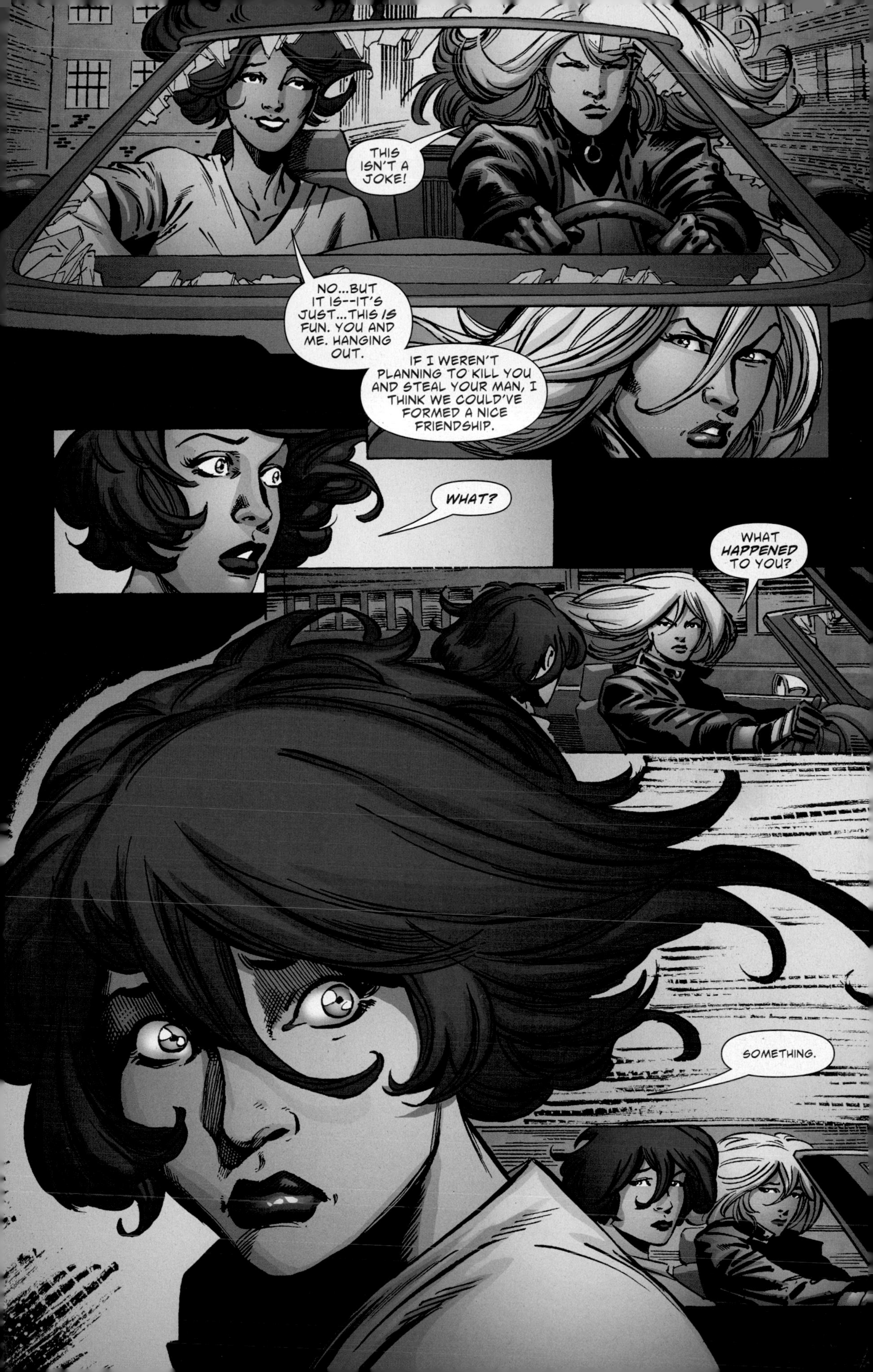
THIS ISN'T A JOKE!
NO...BUT IT IS--IT'S JUST...THIS *IS* FUN. YOU AND ME. HANGING OUT.
IF I WEREN'T PLANNING TO KILL YOU AND STEAL YOUR MAN, I THINK WE COULD'VE FORMED A NICE FRIENDSHIP.
WHAT?
WHAT *HAPPENED* TO YOU?
SOMETHING.

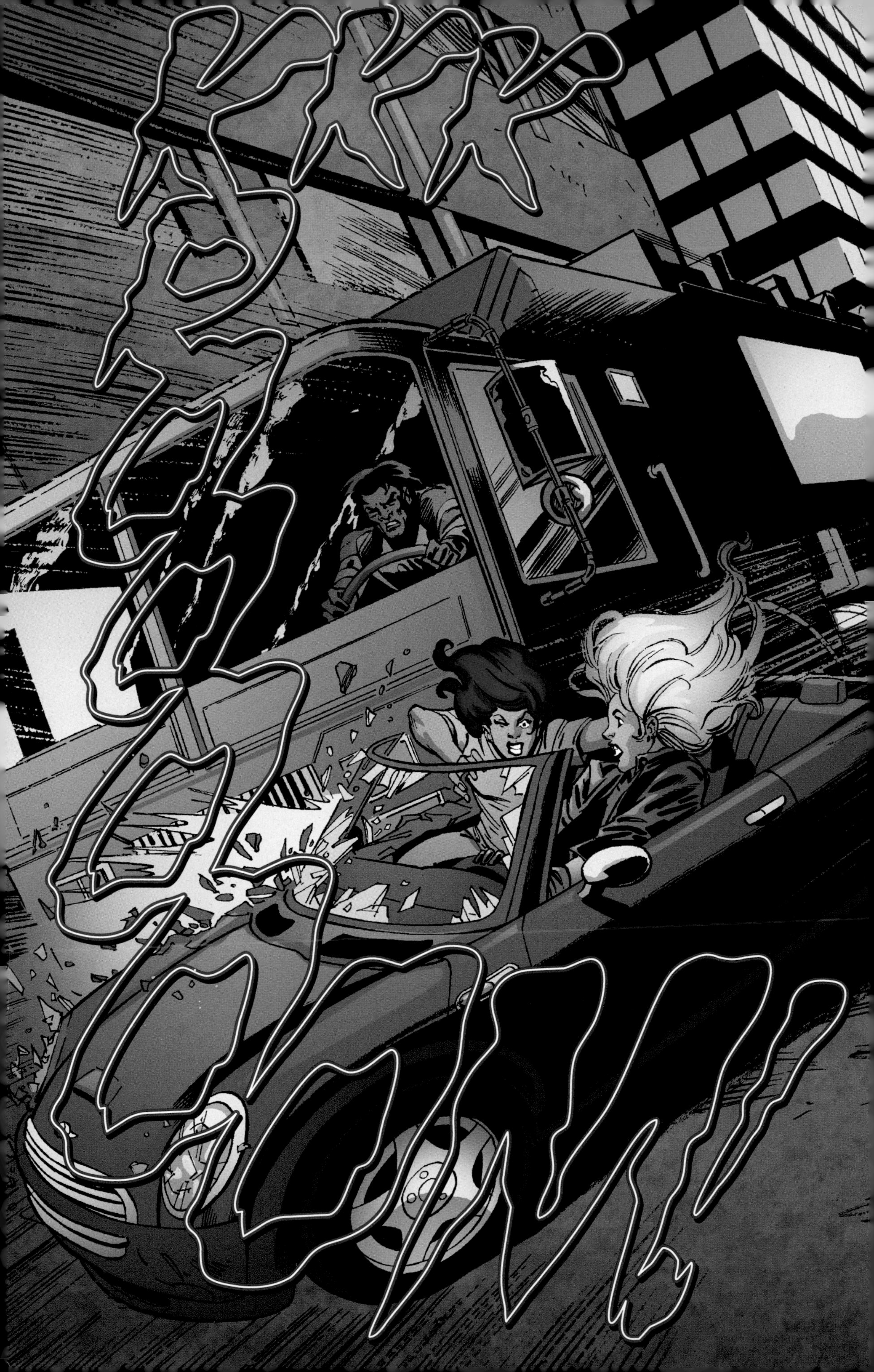

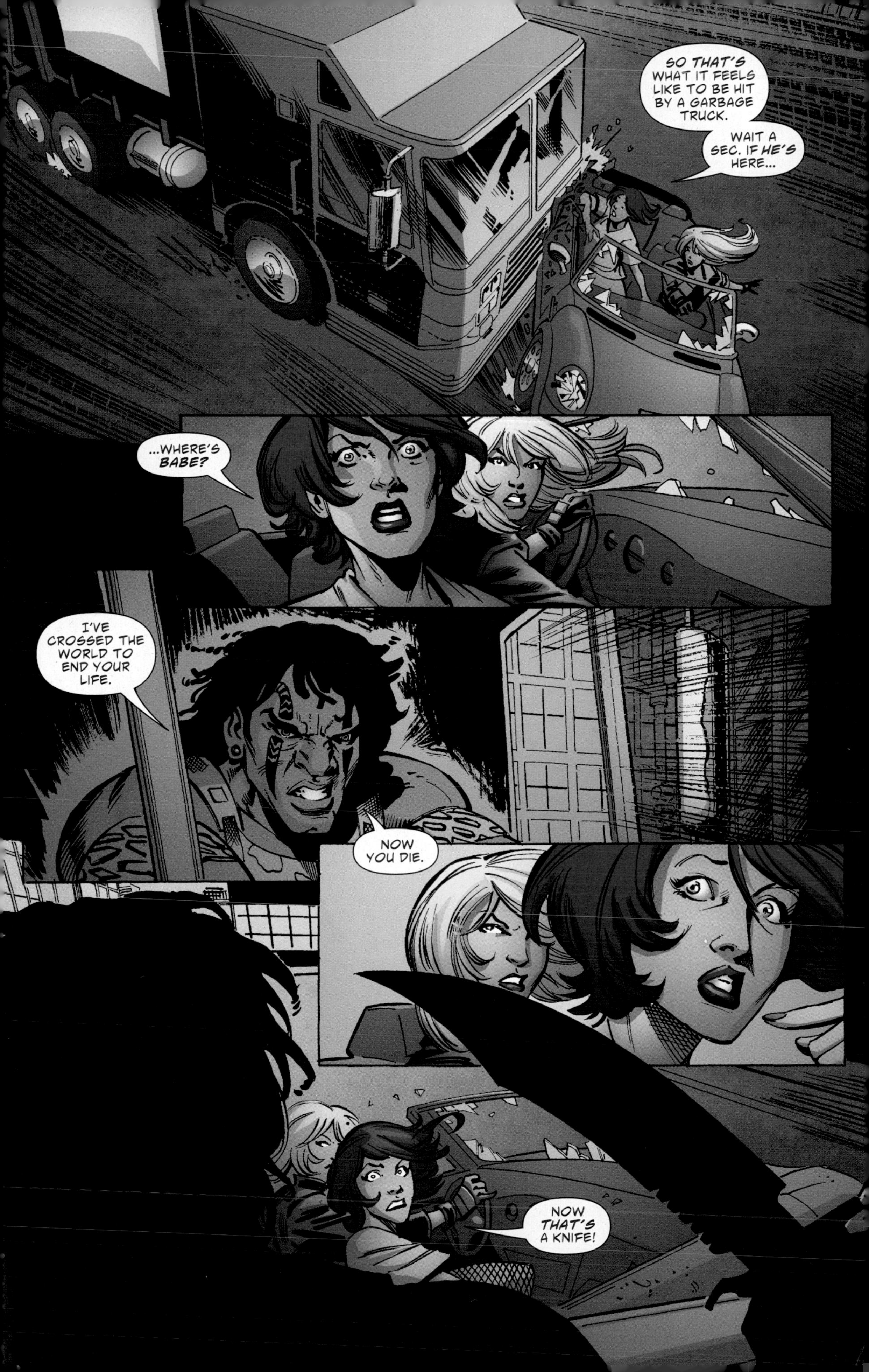
SO THAT'S WHAT IT FEELS LIKE TO BE HIT BY A GARBAGE TRUCK.
WAIT A SEC. IF HE'S HERE...
...WHERE'S BABE?
I'VE CROSSED THE WORLD TO END YOUR LIFE.
NOW YOU DIE.
NOW THAT'S A KNIFE!

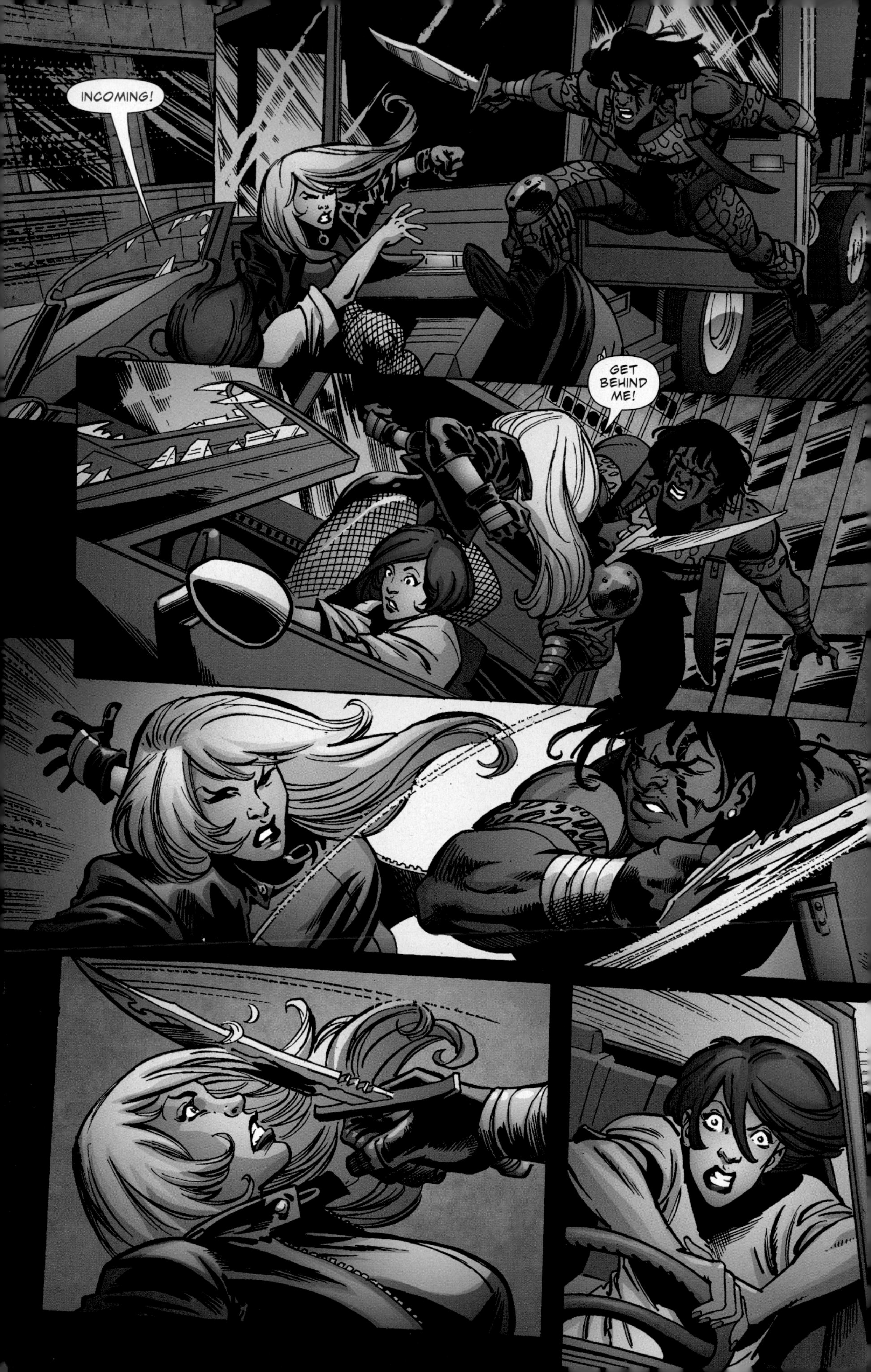
INCOMING!
GET BEHIND ME!

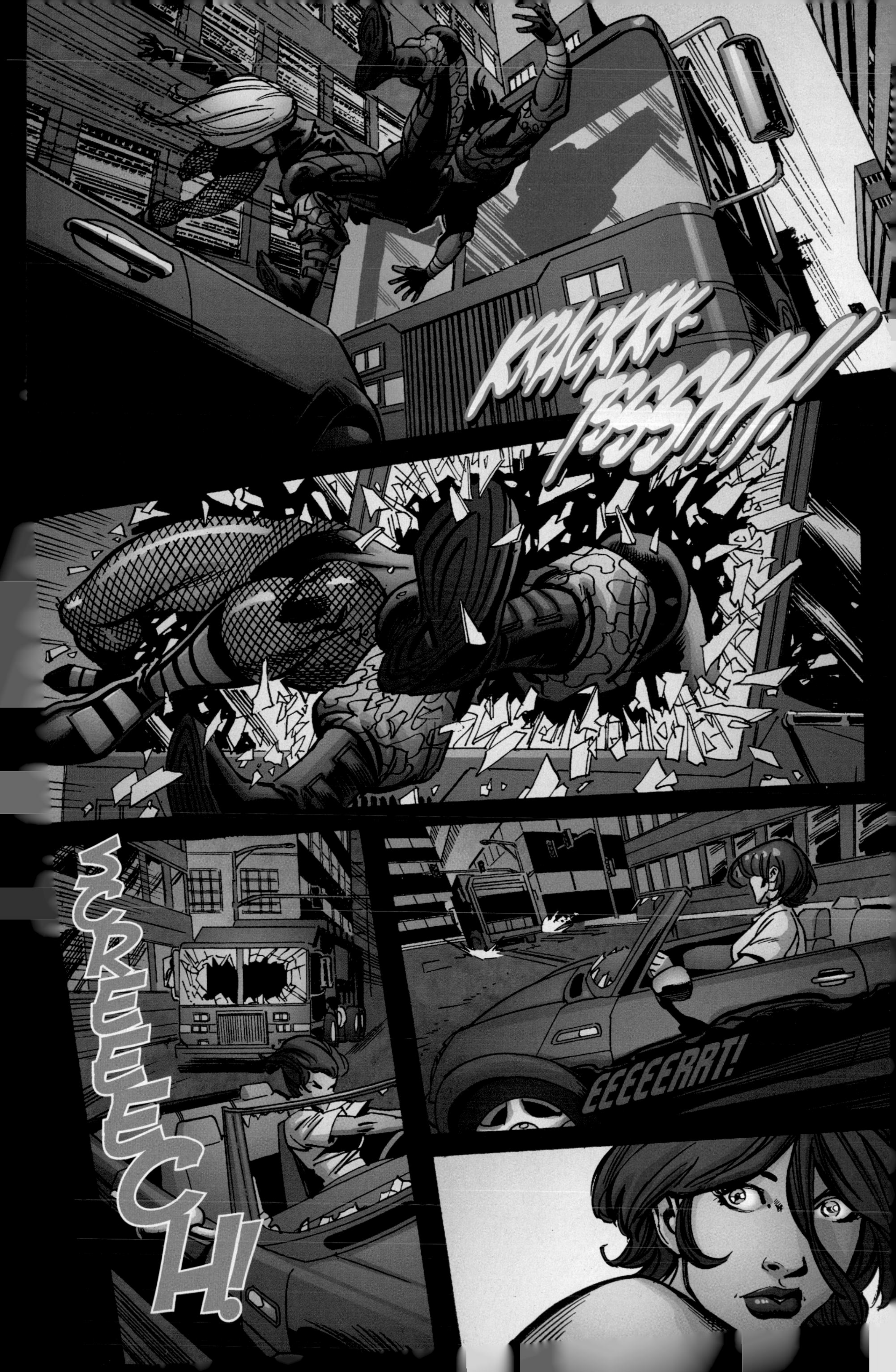
KRACKKK-TSSSHH!!
SCREEEEECH!
EEEEERRT!

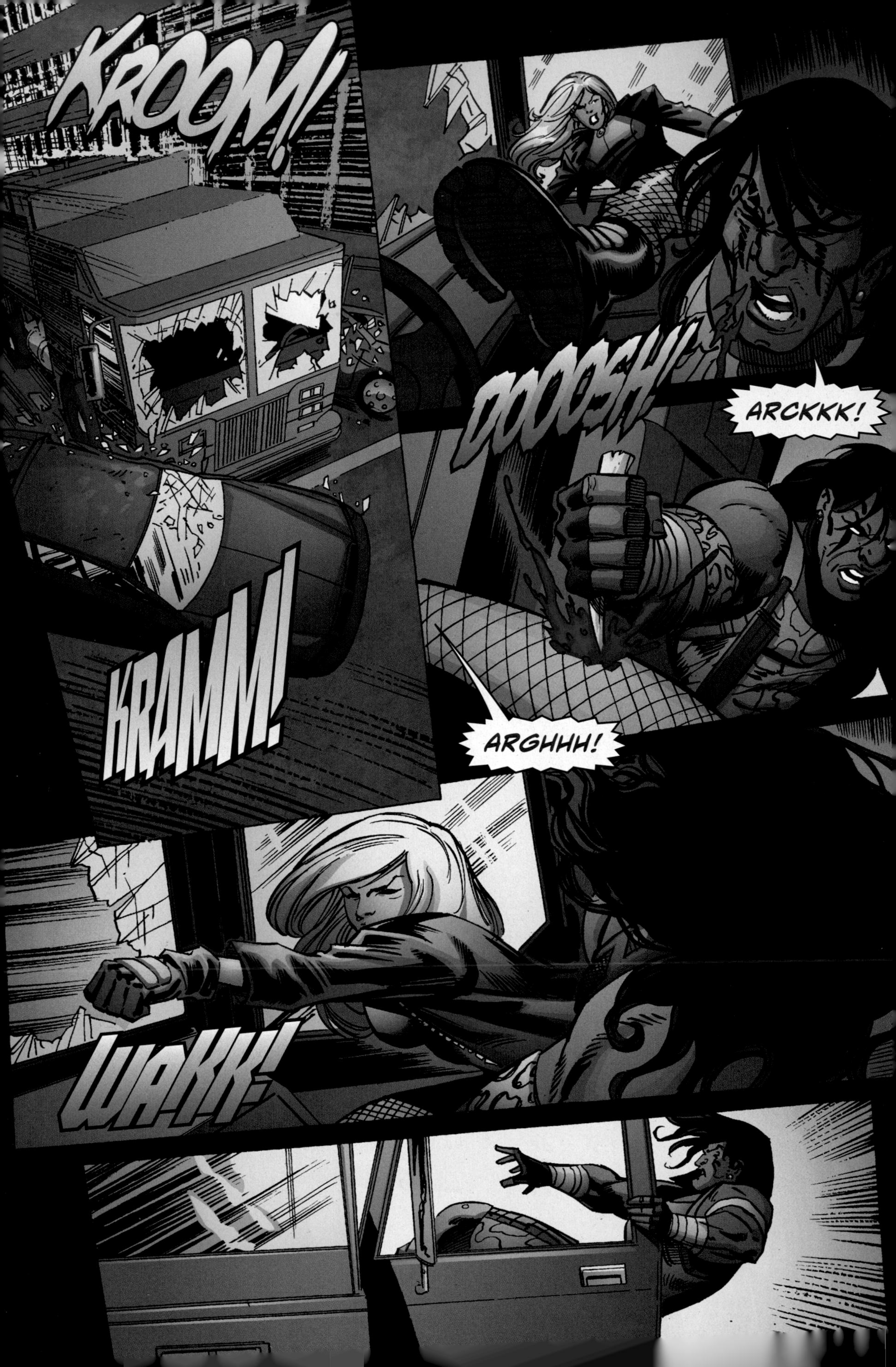
KROOM!!
DOOOSH!
ARCKKK!
KRAMM!
ARGHHH!
WAKK!

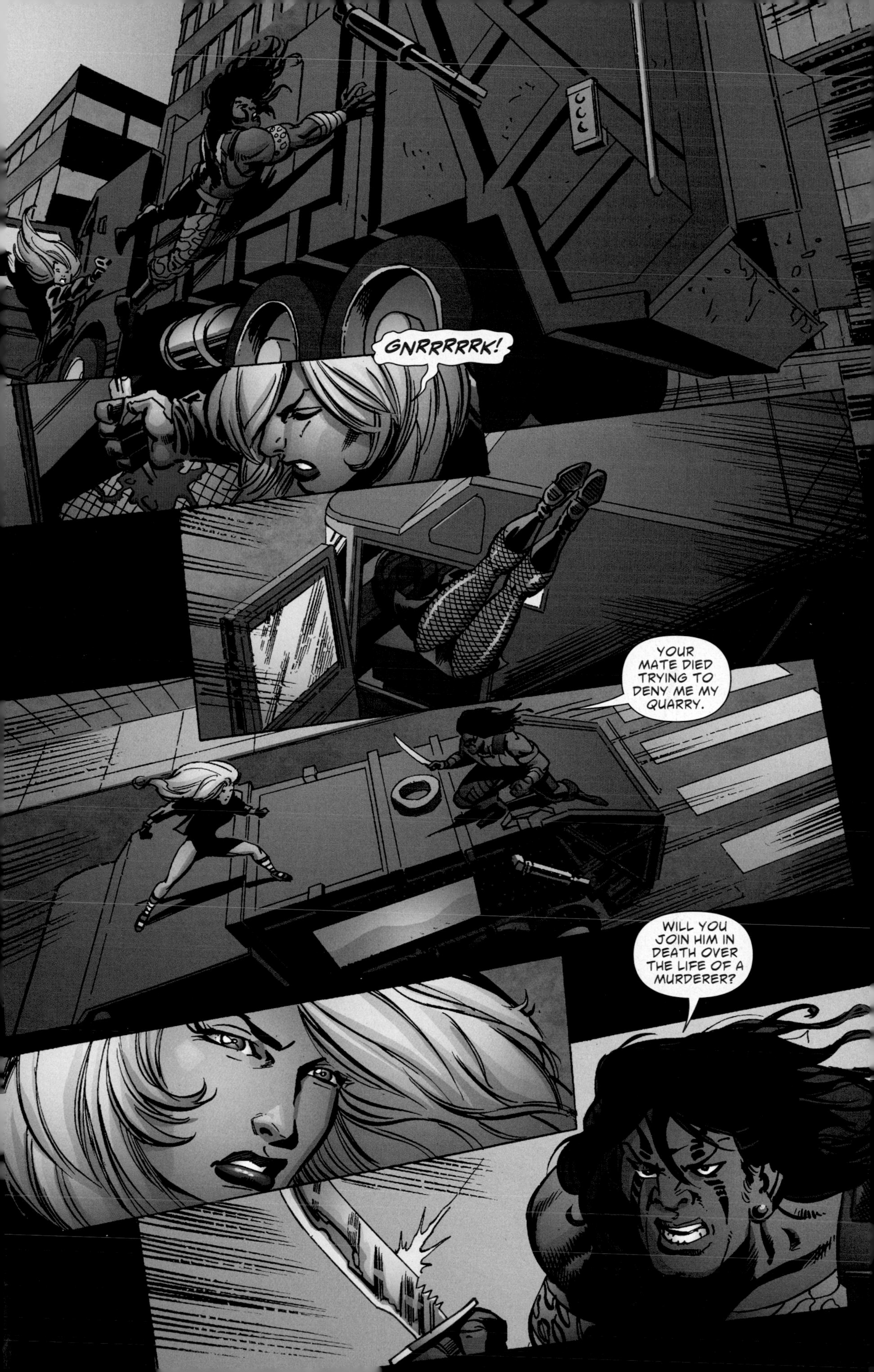
GNRRRRRK!
YOUR MATE DIED TRYING TO DENY ME MY QUARRY.
WILL YOU JOIN HIM IN DEATH OVER THE LIFE OF A MURDERER?

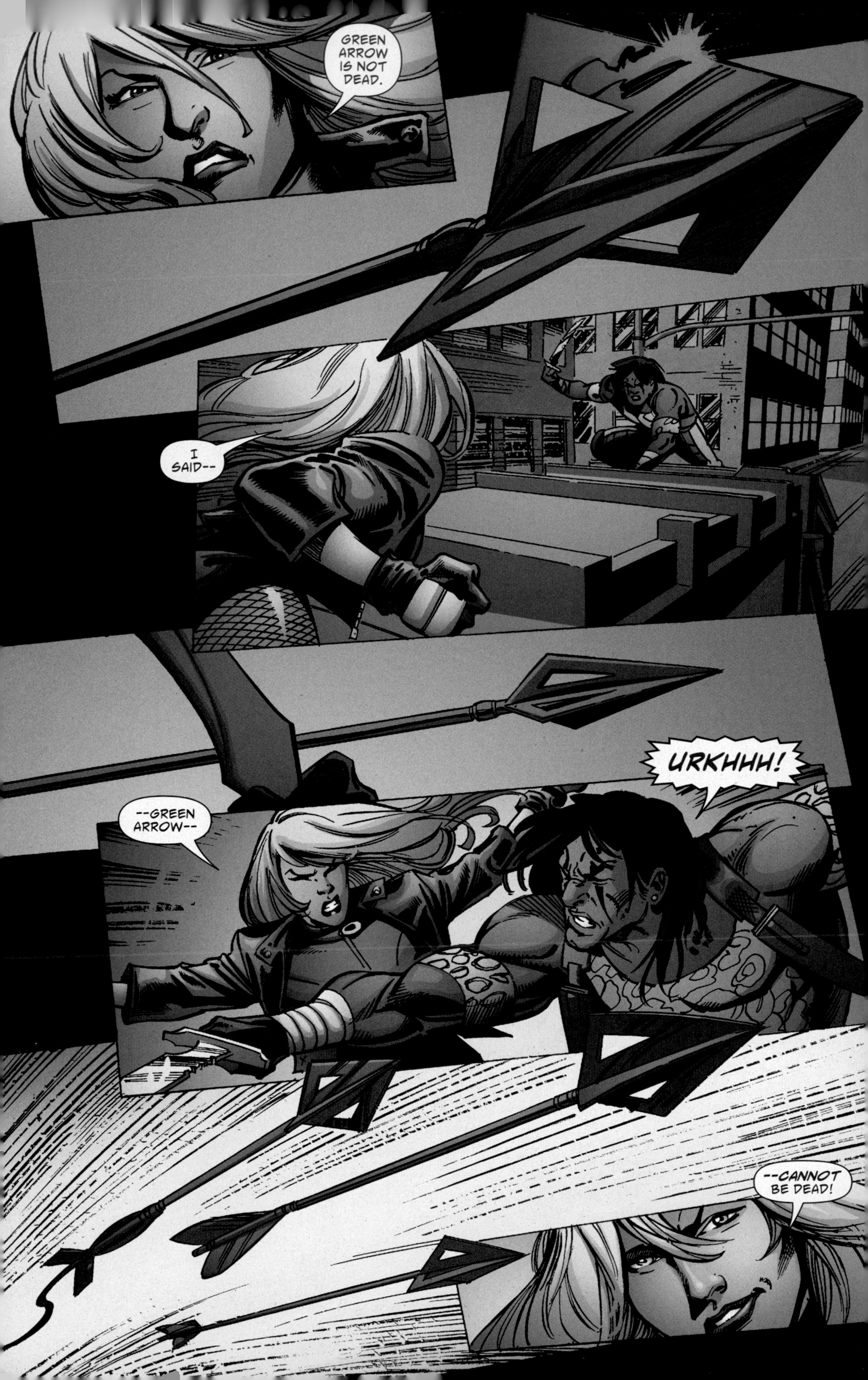
GREEN ARROW IS NOT DEAD.
I SAID--
URKHHH!
--GREEN ARROW--
--CANNOT BE DEAD!

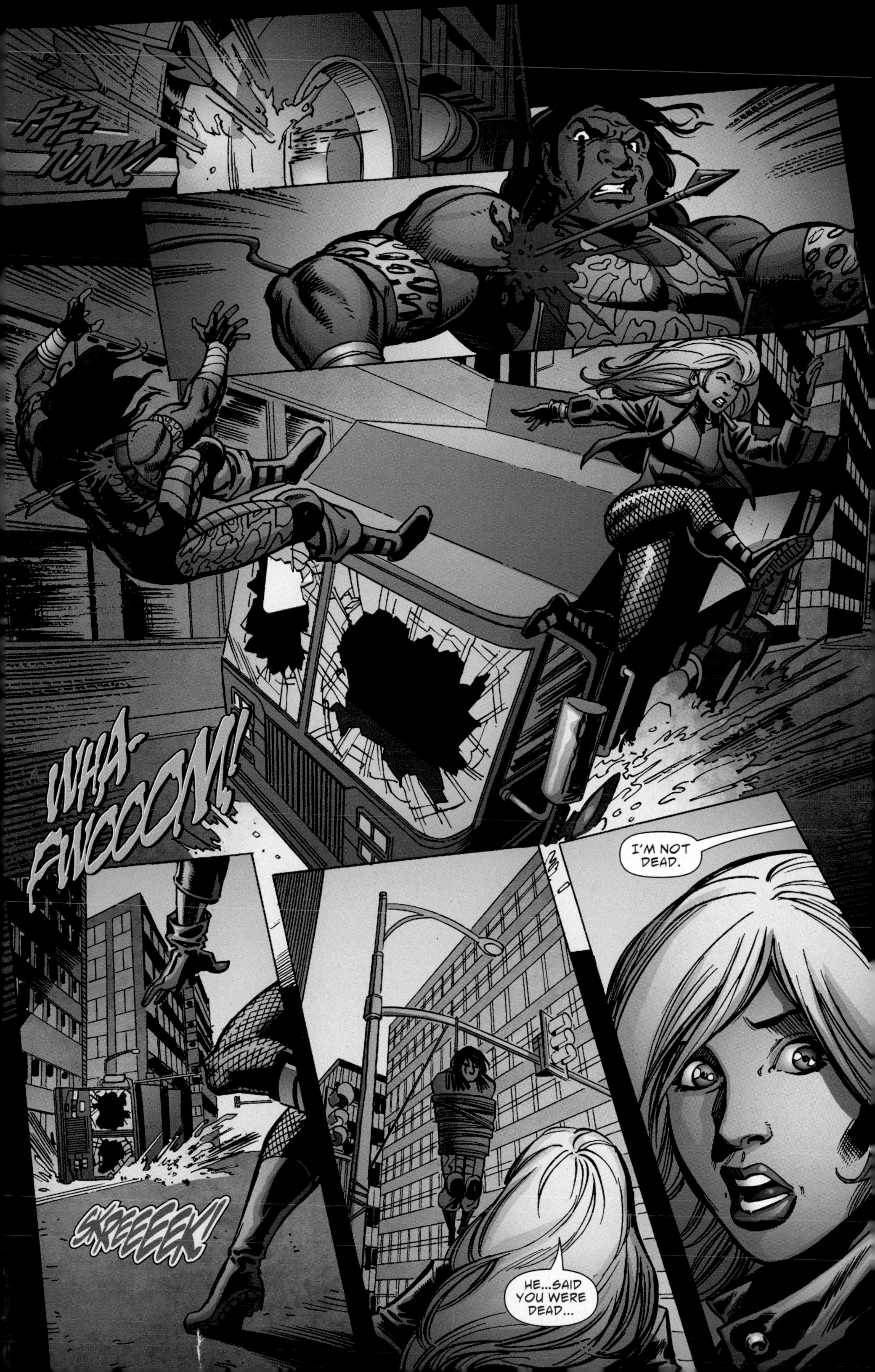
FFF-TUNK!
WHA-FWOOOM!
SKREEEEK!
I'M NOT DEAD.
HE...SAID YOU WERE DEAD...

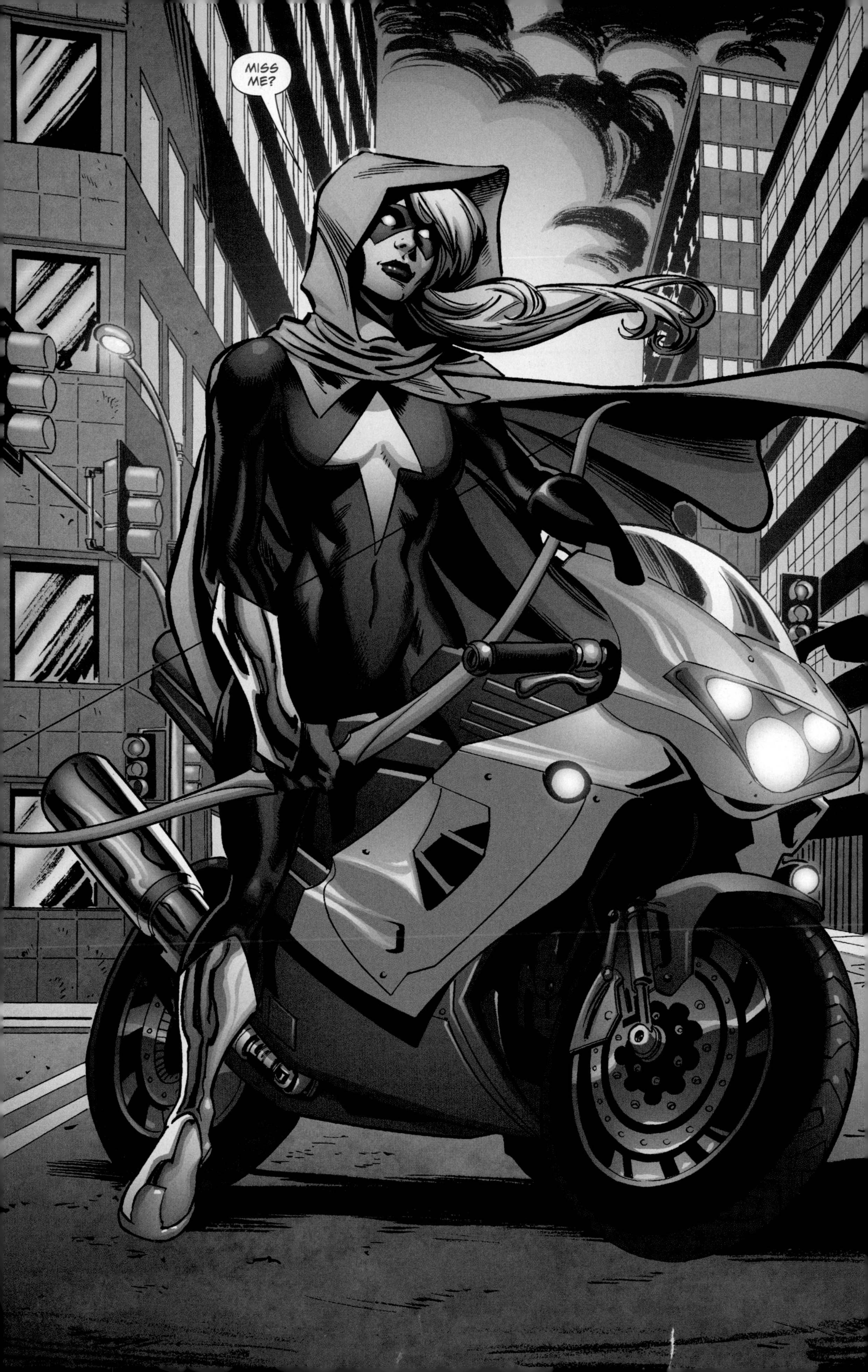
MISS ME?

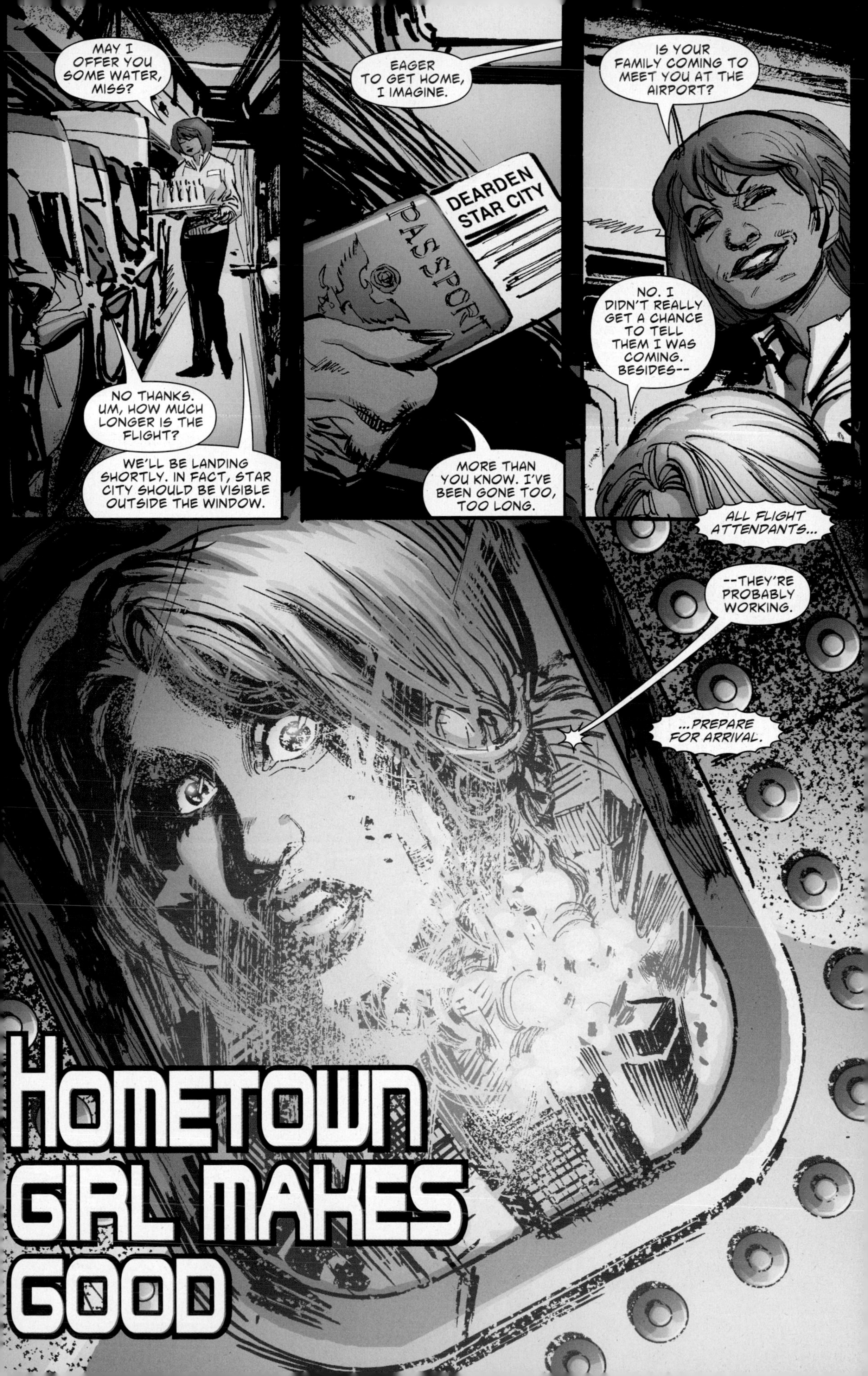
MAY I OFFER YOU SOME WATER, MISS?
NO THANKS. UM, HOW MUCH LONGER IS THE FLIGHT?
WE'LL BE LANDING SHORTLY. IN FACT, STAR CITY SHOULD BE VISIBLE OUTSIDE THE WINDOW.
EAGER TO GET HOME, I IMAGINE.
DEARDEN STAR CITY
PASSPORT
MORE THAN YOU KNOW. I'VE BEEN GONE TOO, TOO LONG.
IS YOUR FAMILY COMING TO MEET YOU AT THE AIRPORT?
NO. I DIDN'T REALLY GET A CHANCE TO TELL THEM I WAS COMING. BESIDES--
ALL FLIGHT ATTENDANTS...
--THEY'RE PROBABLY WORKING.
...PREPARE FOR ARRIVAL.
HOMETOWN GIRL MAKES GOOD

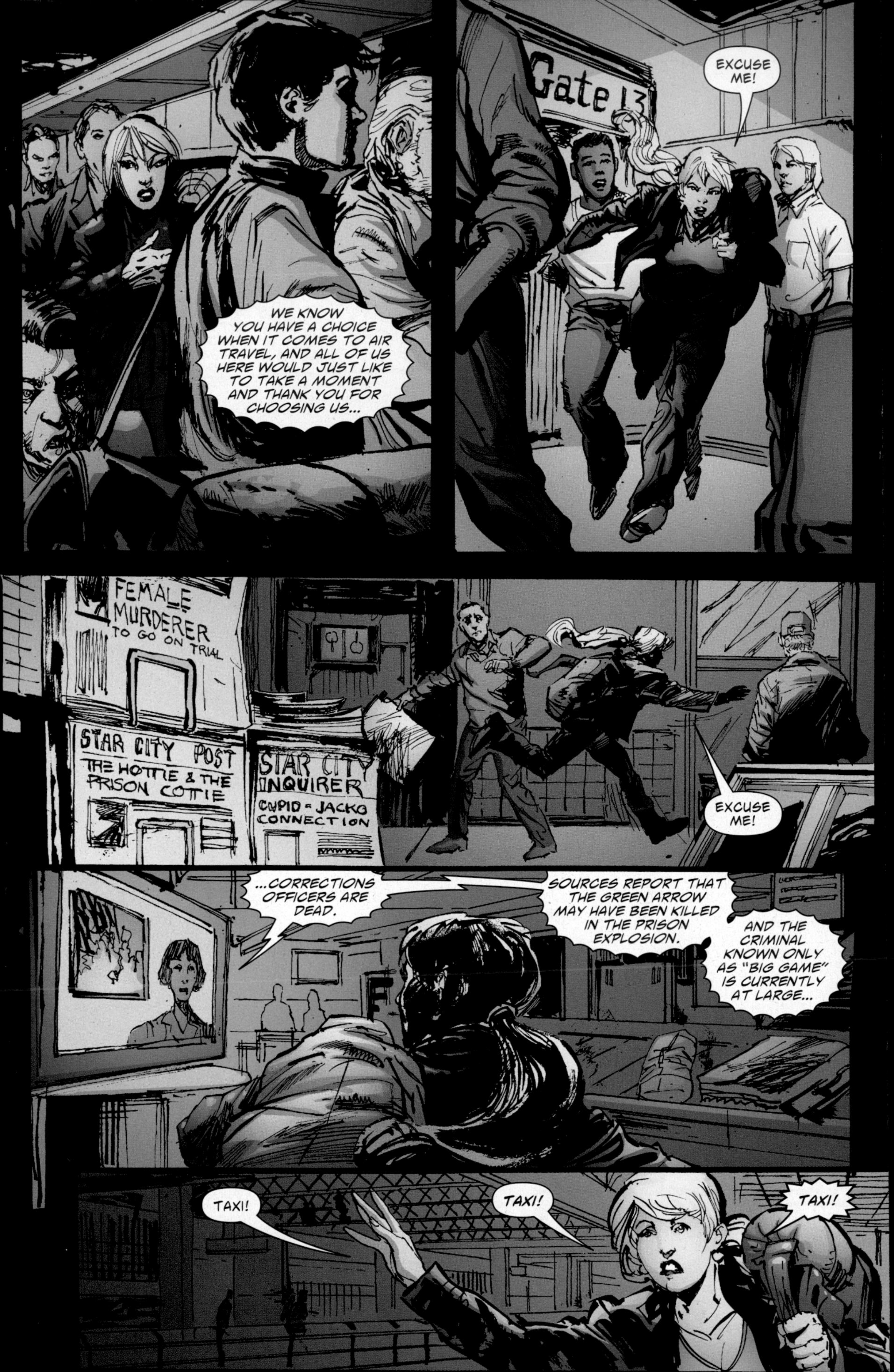
WE KNOW YOU HAVE A CHOICE WHEN IT COMES TO AIR TRAVEL, AND ALL OF US HERE WOULD JUST LIKE TO TAKE A MOMENT AND THANK YOU FOR CHOOSING US...
Gate 13
EXCUSE ME!
FEMALE MURDERER TO GO ON TRIAL
STAR CITY POST
THE HOTTIE & THE PRISON COTTIE
STAR CITY INQUIRER
CUPID = JACKO CONNECTION
EXCUSE ME!
...CORRECTIONS OFFICERS ARE DEAD.
SOURCES REPORT THAT THE GREEN ARROW MAY HAVE BEEN KILLED IN THE PRISON EXPLOSION.
AND THE CRIMINAL KNOWN ONLY AS "BIG GAME" IS CURRENTLY AT LARGE...
TAXI!
TAXI!
TAXI!

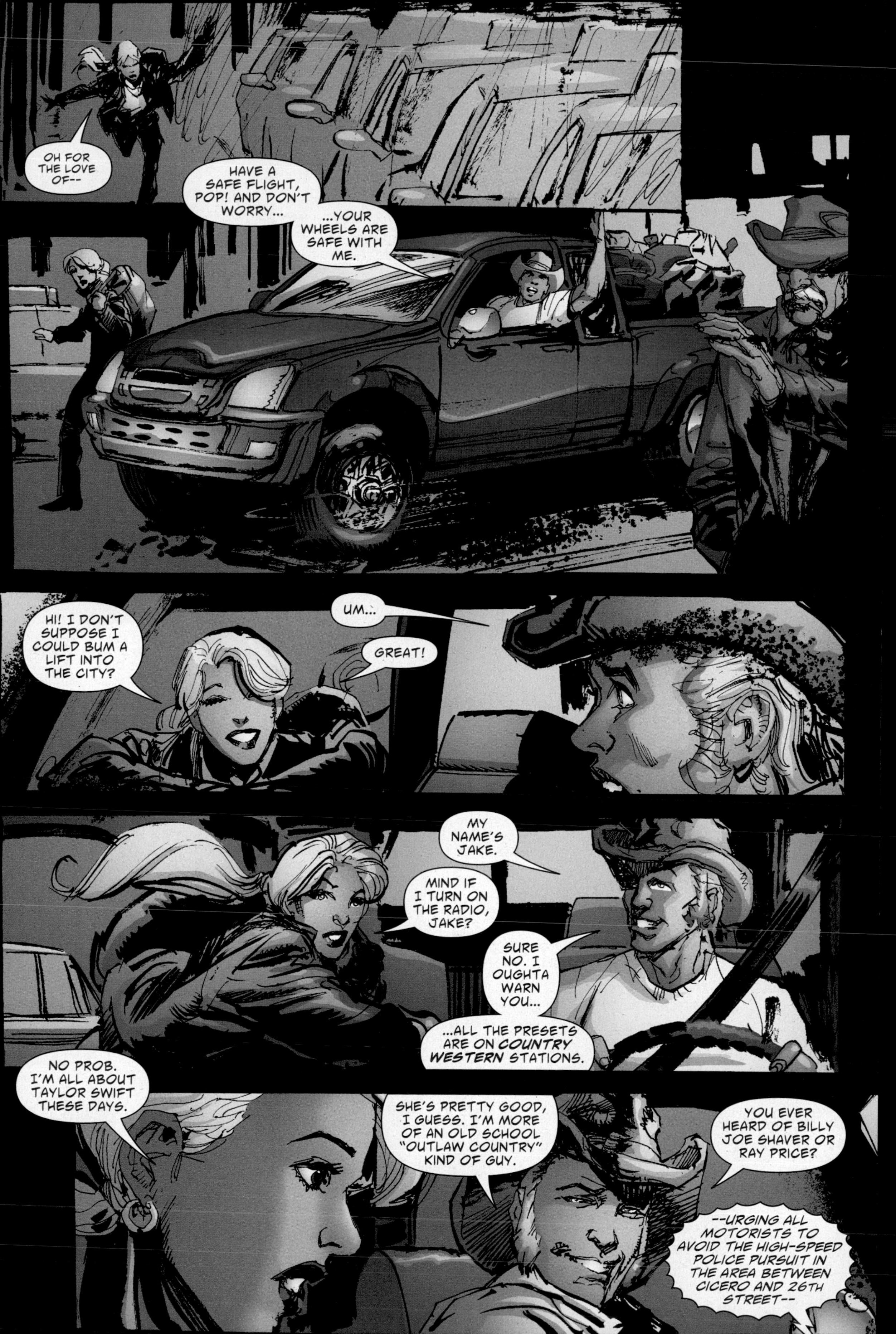
OH FOR THE LOVE OF--
HAVE A SAFE FLIGHT, POP! AND DON'T WORRY...
...YOUR WHEELS ARE SAFE WITH ME.
HI! I DON'T SUPPOSE I COULD BUM A LIFT INTO THE CITY?
UM...
GREAT!
MY NAME'S JAKE.
MIND IF I TURN ON THE RADIO, JAKE?
SURE NO. I OUGHTA WARN YOU...
...ALL THE PRESETS ARE ON COUNTRY WESTERN STATIONS.
NO PROB. I'M ALL ABOUT TAYLOR SWIFT THESE DAYS.
SHE'S PRETTY GOOD, I GUESS. I'M MORE OF AN OLD SCHOOL "OUTLAW COUNTRY" KIND OF GUY.
YOU EVER HEARD OF BILLY JOE SHAVER OR RAY PRICE?
--URGING ALL MOTORISTS TO AVOID THE HIGH-SPEED POLICE PURSUIT IN THE AREA BETWEEN CICERO AND 26TH STREET--

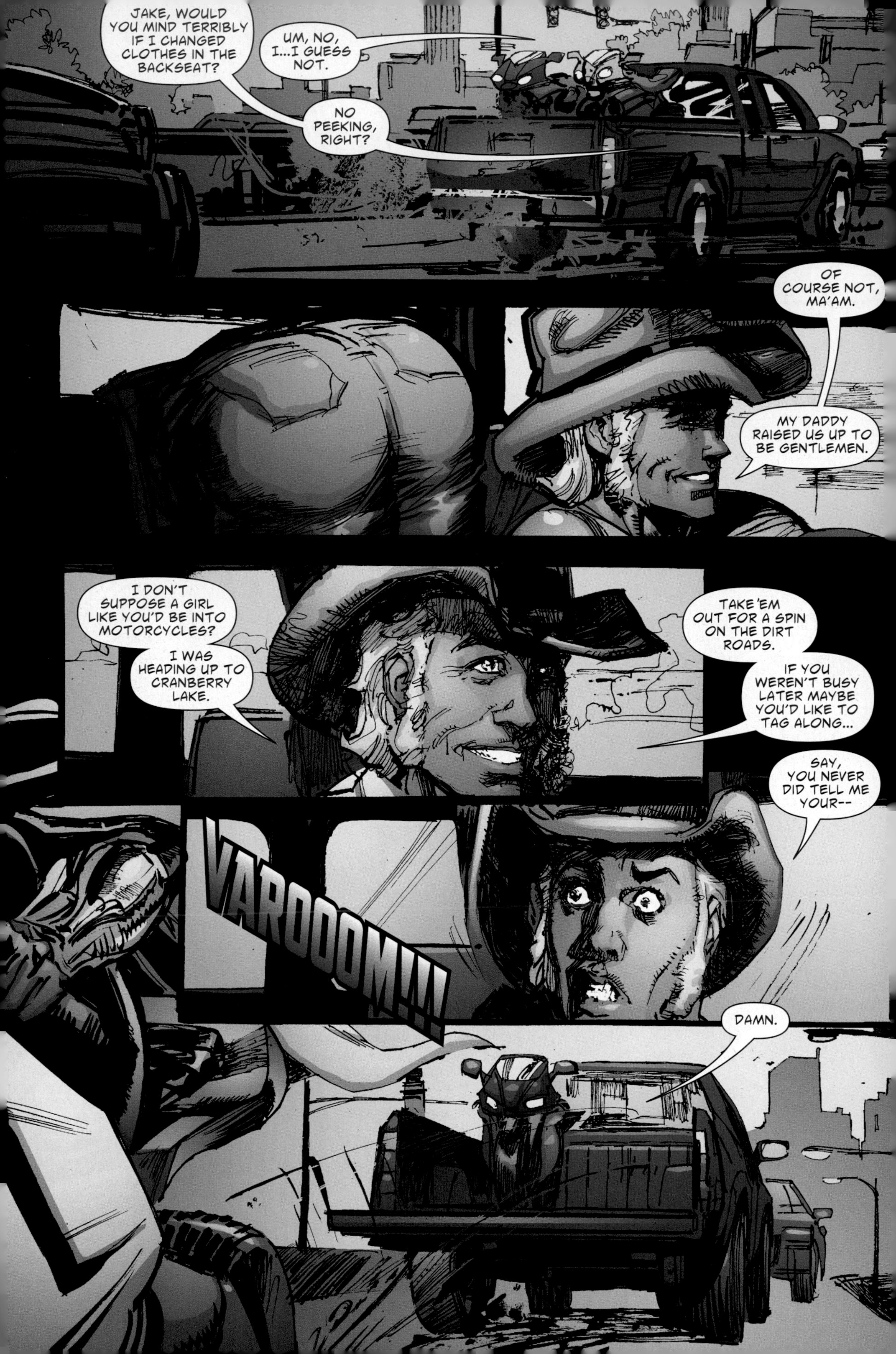
JAKE, WOULD YOU MIND TERRIBLY IF I CHANGED CLOTHES IN THE BACKSEAT?
UM, NO, I...I GUESS NOT.
NO PEEKING, RIGHT?
OF COURSE NOT, MA'AM.
MY DADDY RAISED US UP TO BE GENTLEMEN.
I DON'T SUPPOSE A GIRL LIKE YOU'D BE INTO MOTORCYCLES?
I WAS HEADING UP TO CRANBERRY LAKE.
TAKE 'EM OUT FOR A SPIN ON THE DIRT ROADS.
IF YOU WEREN'T BUSY LATER MAYBE YOU'D LIKE TO TAG ALONG...
SAY, YOU NEVER DID TELL ME YOUR--
VAROOOM!!!
DAMN.

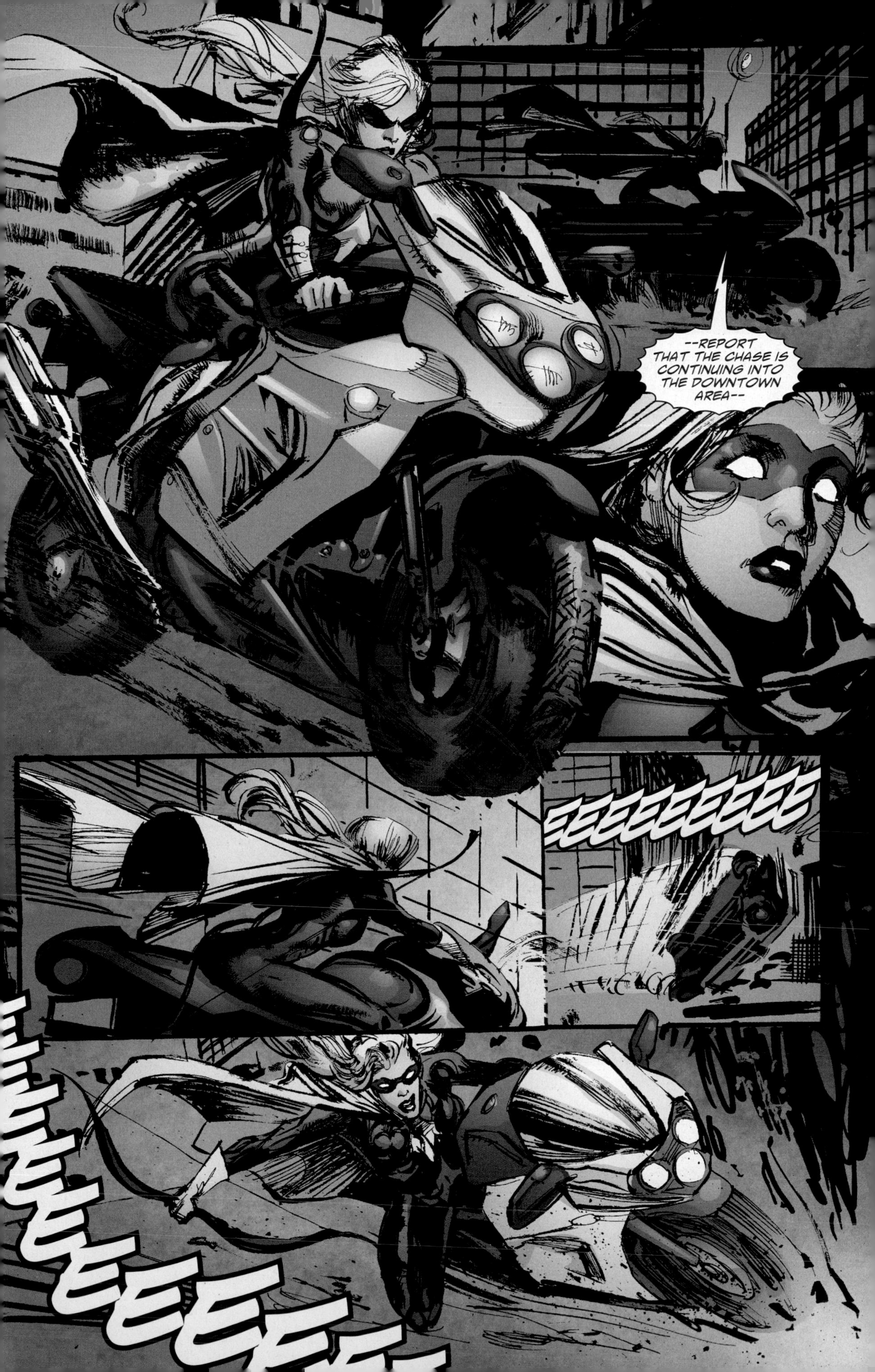
--REPORT THAT THE CHASE IS CONTINUING INTO THE DOWNTOWN AREA--
EEEEEEEEE
WHHHEEEEEEE

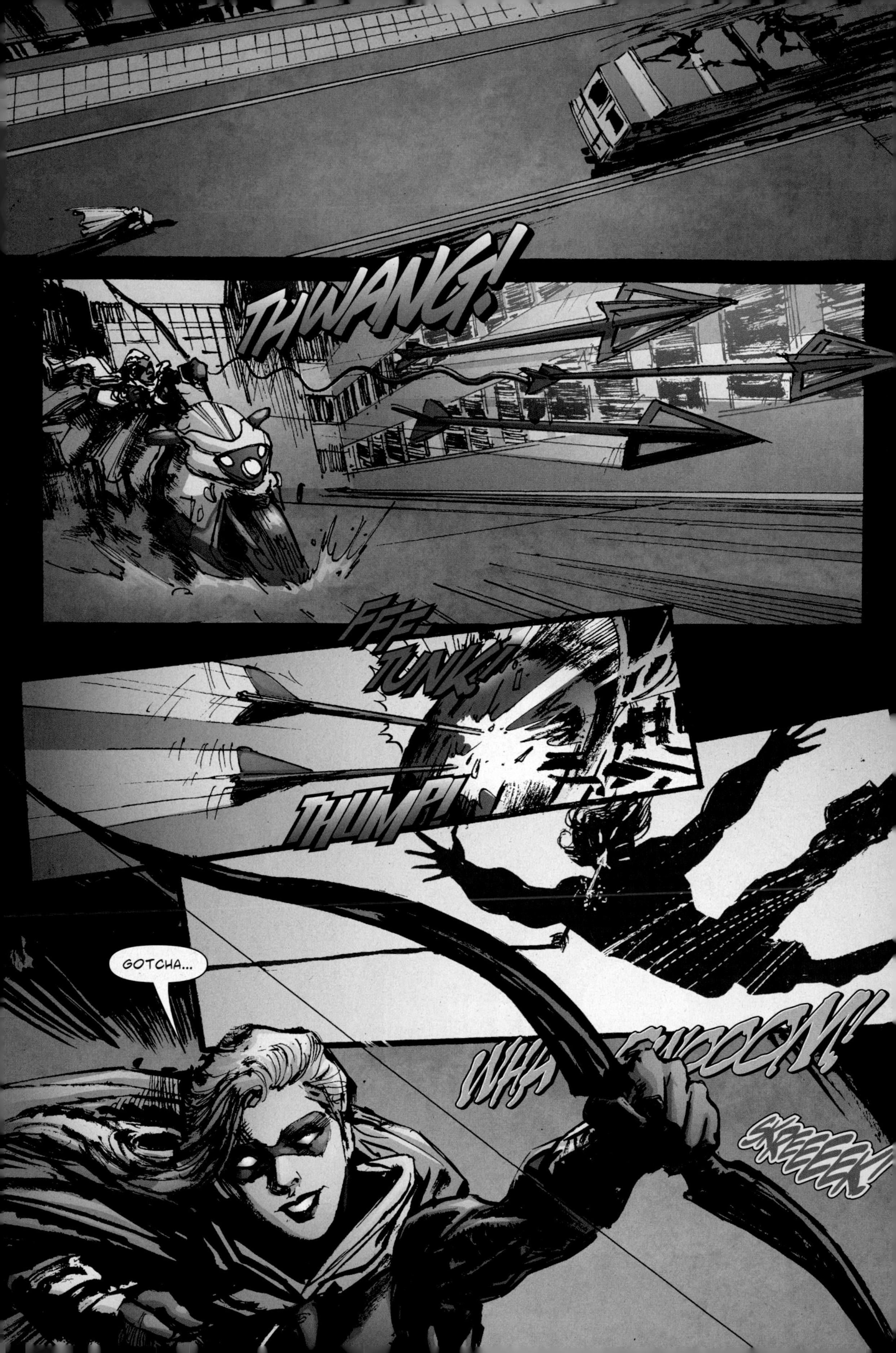
THWANG!
FFF-
TUNK!
THUMP!
GOTCHA...
WHA
OOOM!
SKREEEEK!

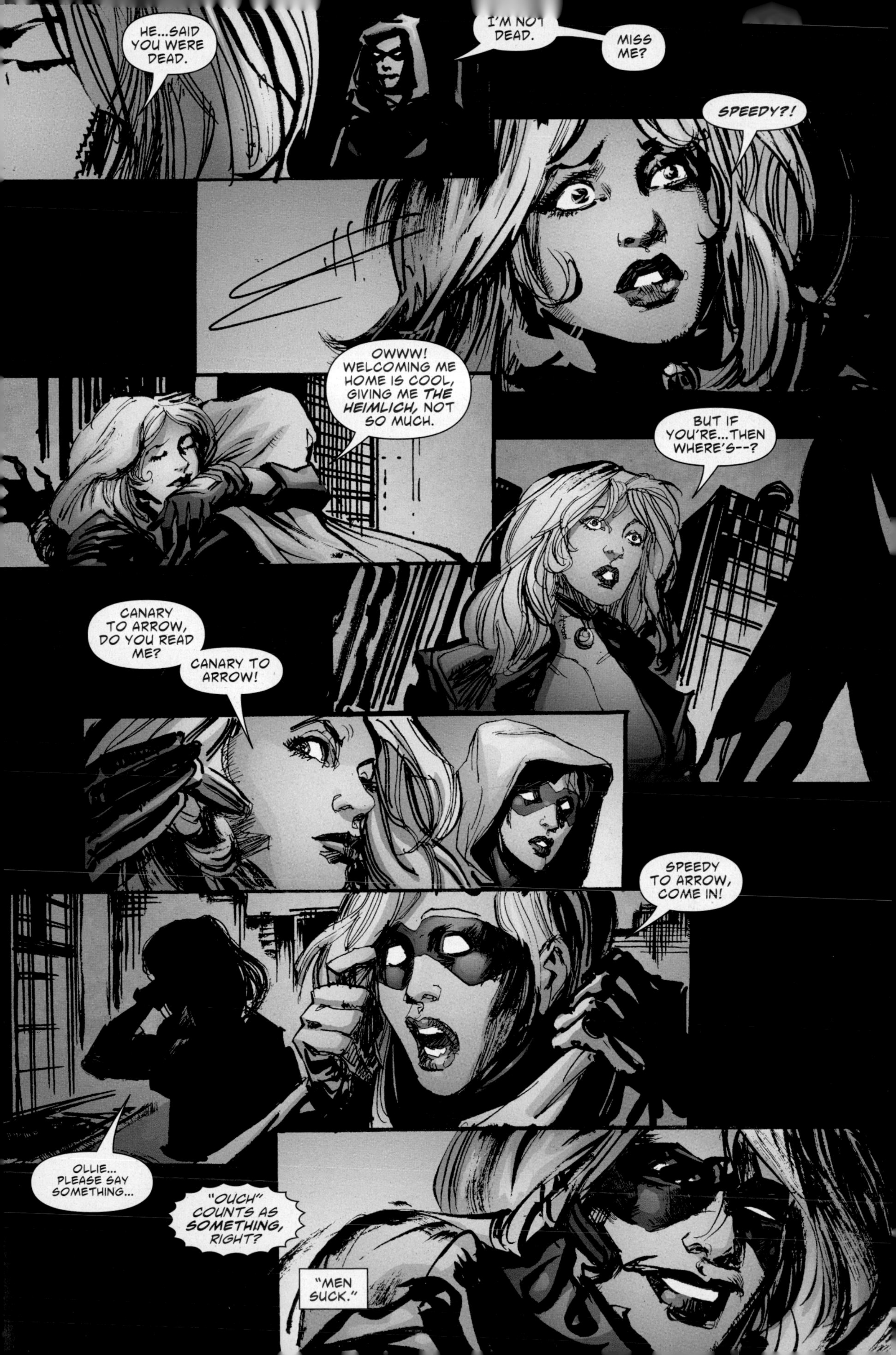

HE...SAID YOU WERE DEAD.
I'M NOT DEAD.
MISS ME?
SPEEDY?!
OWWW! WELCOMING ME HOME IS COOL, GIVING ME THE HEIMLICH, NOT SO MUCH.
BUT IF YOU'RE...THEN WHERE'S--?
CANARY TO ARROW, DO YOU READ ME?
CANARY TO ARROW!
SPEEDY TO ARROW, COME IN!
OLLIE... PLEASE SAY SOMETHING...
"OUCH" COUNTS AS SOMETHING, RIGHT?
"MEN SUCK."

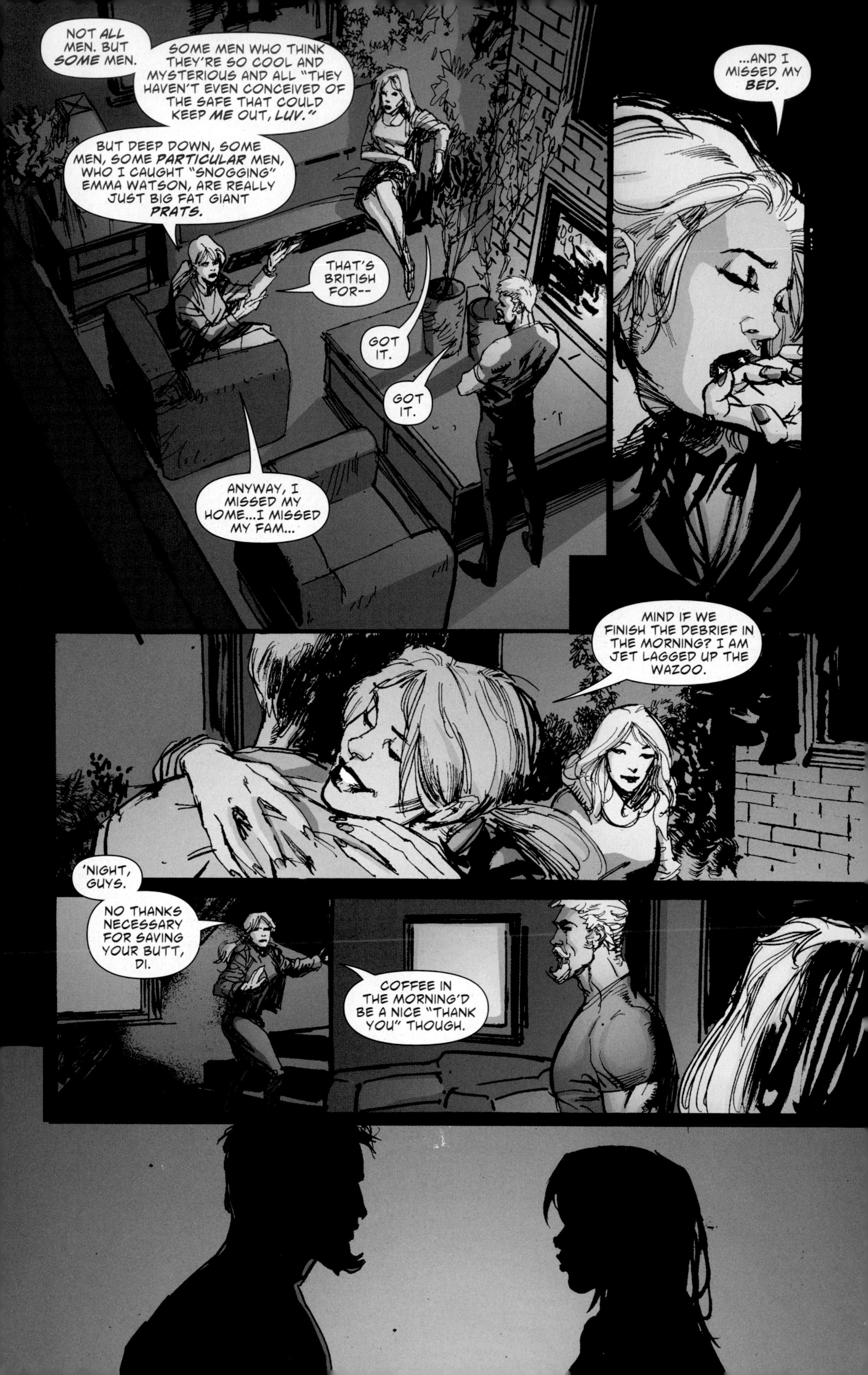
NOT *ALL* MEN. BUT *SOME* MEN.
SOME MEN WHO THINK THEY'RE SO COOL AND MYSTERIOUS AND ALL "THEY HAVEN'T EVEN CONCEIVED OF THE SAFE THAT COULD KEEP *ME* OUT, *LUV*."
BUT DEEP DOWN, SOME MEN, SOME *PARTICULAR* MEN, WHO I CAUGHT "SNOGGING" EMMA WATSON, ARE REALLY JUST BIG FAT GIANT *PRATS*.
THAT'S BRITISH FOR--
GOT IT.
GOT IT.
ANYWAY, I MISSED MY HOME...I MISSED MY FAM...
...AND I MISSED MY *BED*.
MIND IF WE FINISH THE DEBRIEF IN THE MORNING? I AM JET LAGGED UP THE WAZOO.
'NIGHT, GUYS.
NO THANKS NECESSARY FOR SAVING YOUR BUTT, DI.
COFFEE IN THE MORNING'D BE A NICE "THANK YOU" THOUGH.

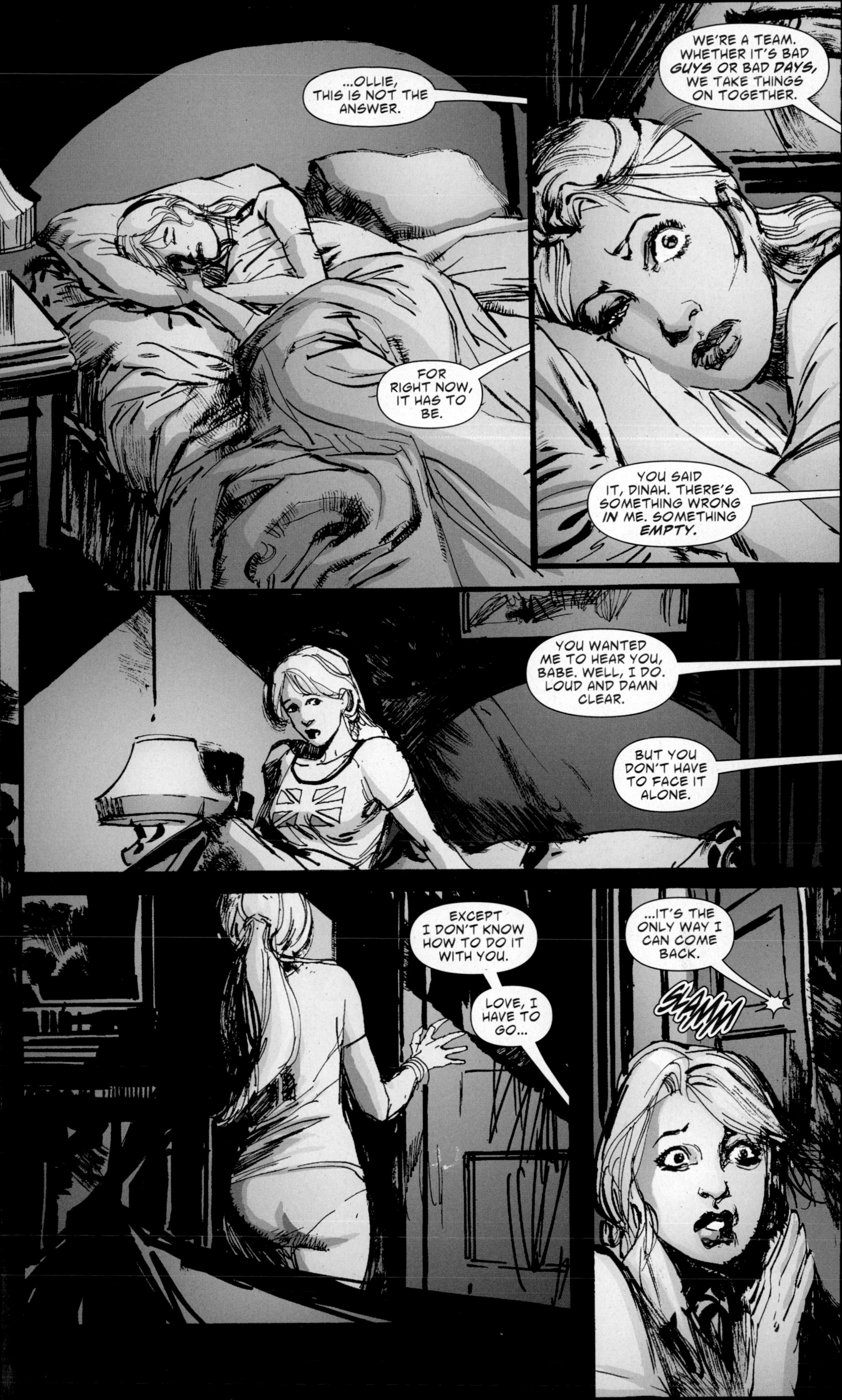
...OLLIE, THIS IS NOT THE ANSWER.
FOR RIGHT NOW, IT HAS TO BE.
WE'RE A TEAM. WHETHER IT'S BAD GUYS OR BAD DAYS, WE TAKE THINGS ON TOGETHER.
YOU SAID IT, DINAH. THERE'S SOMETHING WRONG IN ME. SOMETHING EMPTY.
YOU WANTED ME TO HEAR YOU, BABE. WELL, I DO. LOUD AND DAMN CLEAR.
BUT YOU DON'T HAVE TO FACE IT ALONE.
EXCEPT I DON'T KNOW HOW TO DO IT WITH YOU.
LOVE, I HAVE TO GO...
...IT'S THE ONLY WAY I CAN COME BACK.
SLAMM

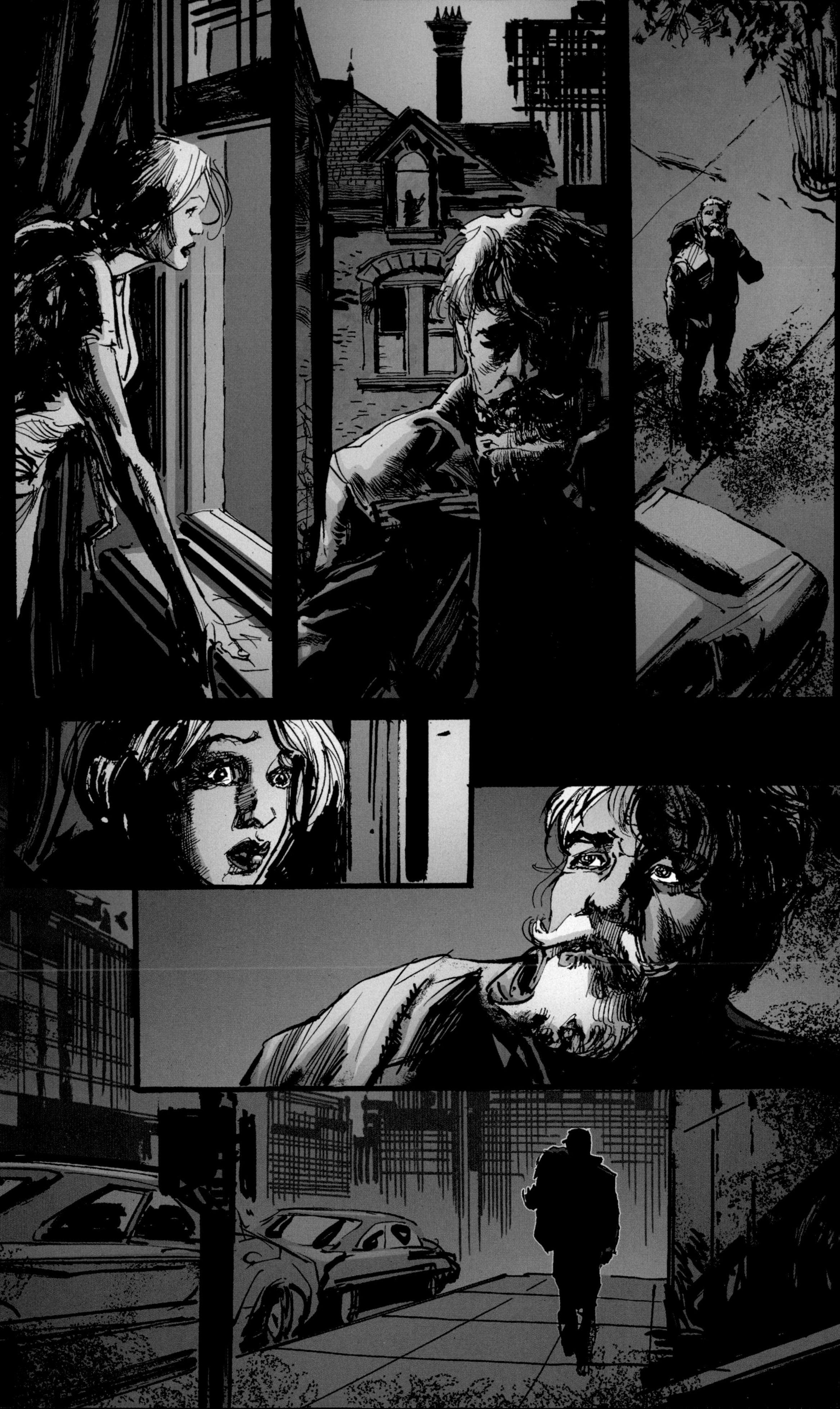

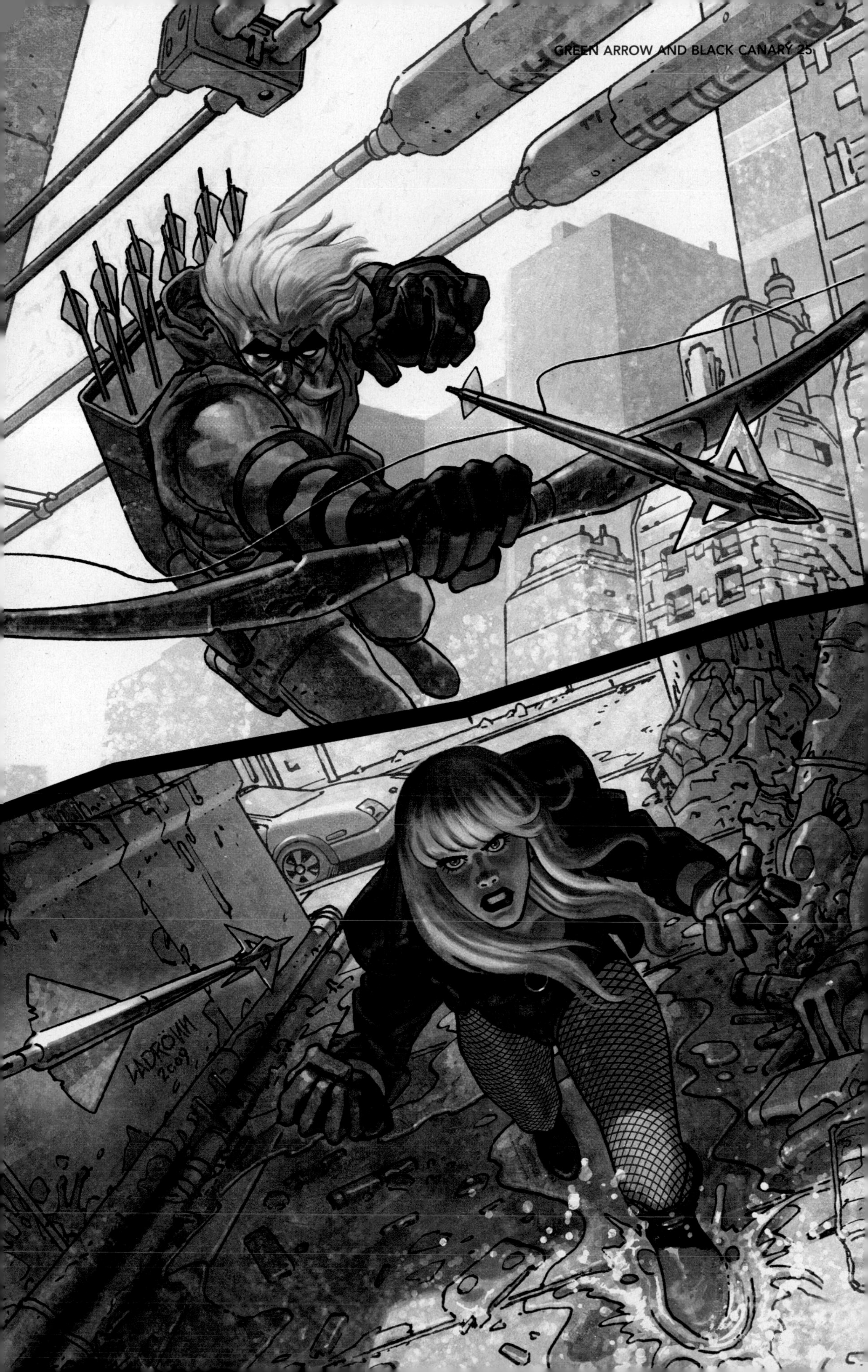
LADRÖNN
2009

DENIAL

Mike Norton Layouts

Bill Sienkiewicz Finishes

BEDTIME STORIES

Renato Guedes Penciller

José Wilson Magalhaes Inker

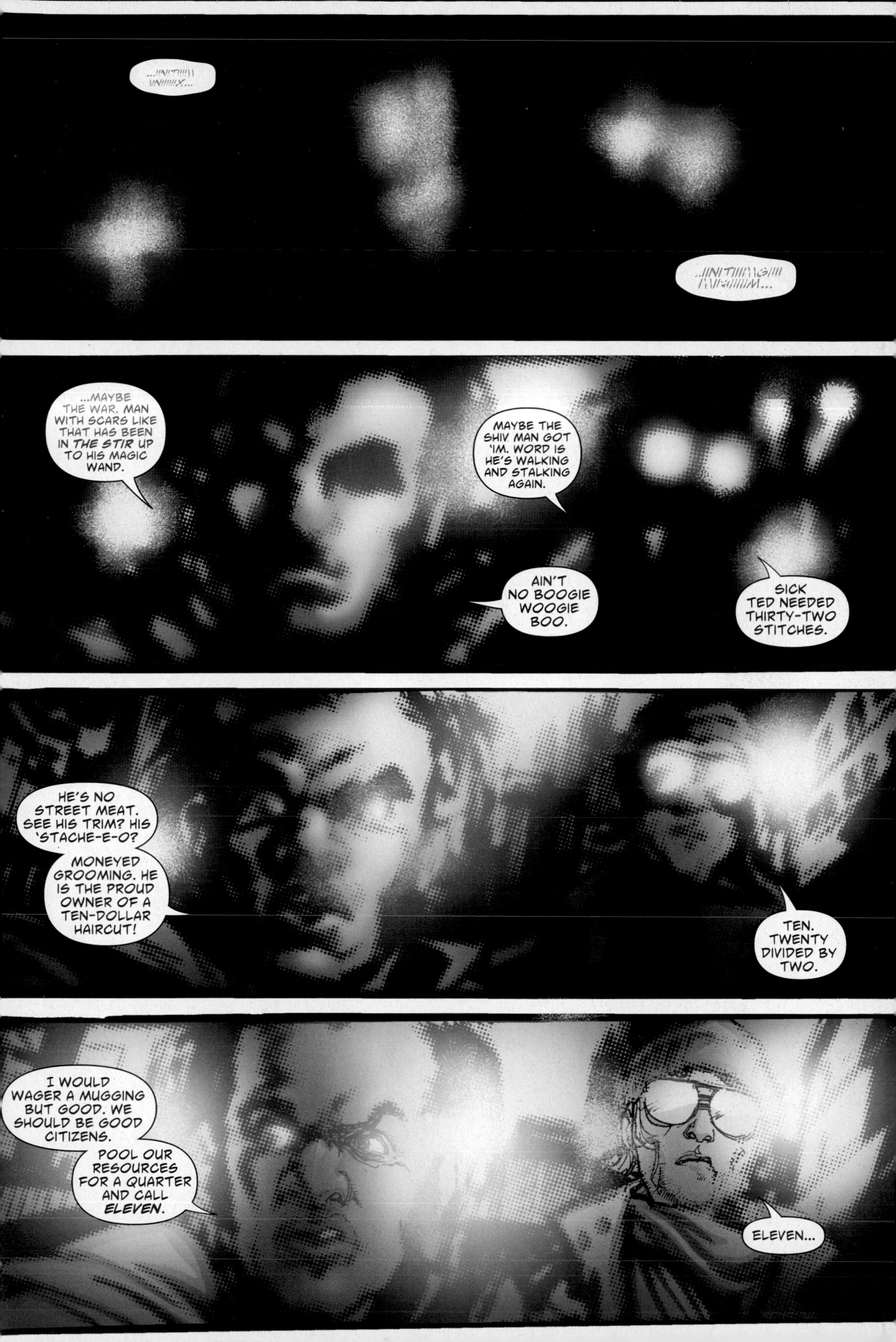
...MAYBE THE WAR. MAN WITH SCARS LIKE THAT HAS BEEN IN *THE STIR* UP TO HIS MAGIC WAND.
MAYBE THE SHIV MAN GOT 'IM. WORD IS HE'S WALKING AND STALKING AGAIN.
AIN'T NO BOOGIE WOOGIE BOO.
SICK TED NEEDED THIRTY-TWO STITCHES.
HE'S NO STREET MEAT. SEE HIS TRIM? HIS 'STACHE-E-O?
MONEYED GROOMING. HE IS THE PROUD OWNER OF A TEN-DOLLAR HAIRCUT!
TEN. TWENTY DIVIDED BY TWO.
I WOULD WAGER A MUGGING BUT GOOD. WE SHOULD BE GOOD CITIZENS.
POOL OUR RESOURCES FOR A QUARTER AND CALL *ELEVEN*.
ELEVEN...

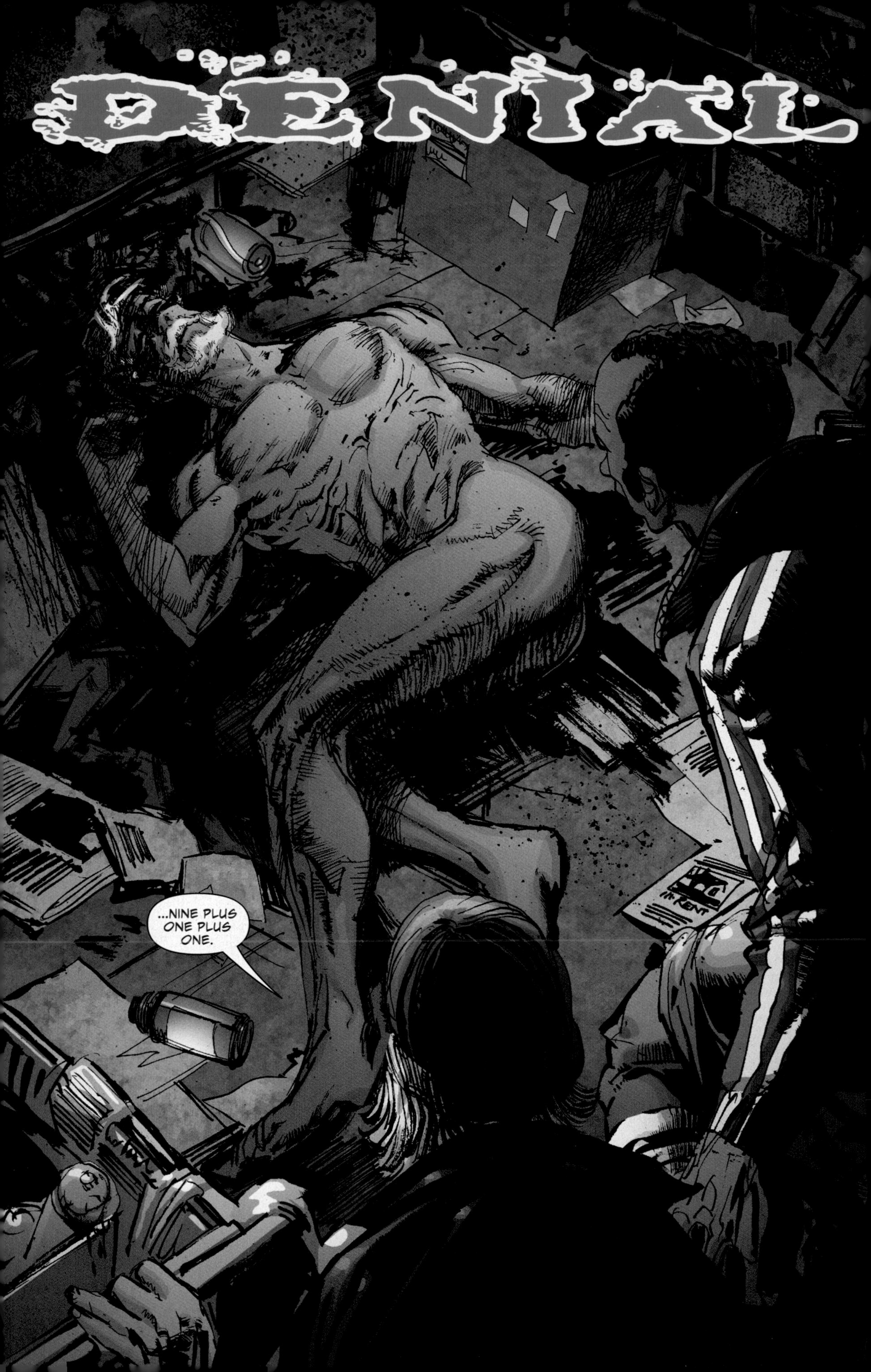
DENIAL
...NINE PLUS ONE PLUS ONE.
FOR RENT

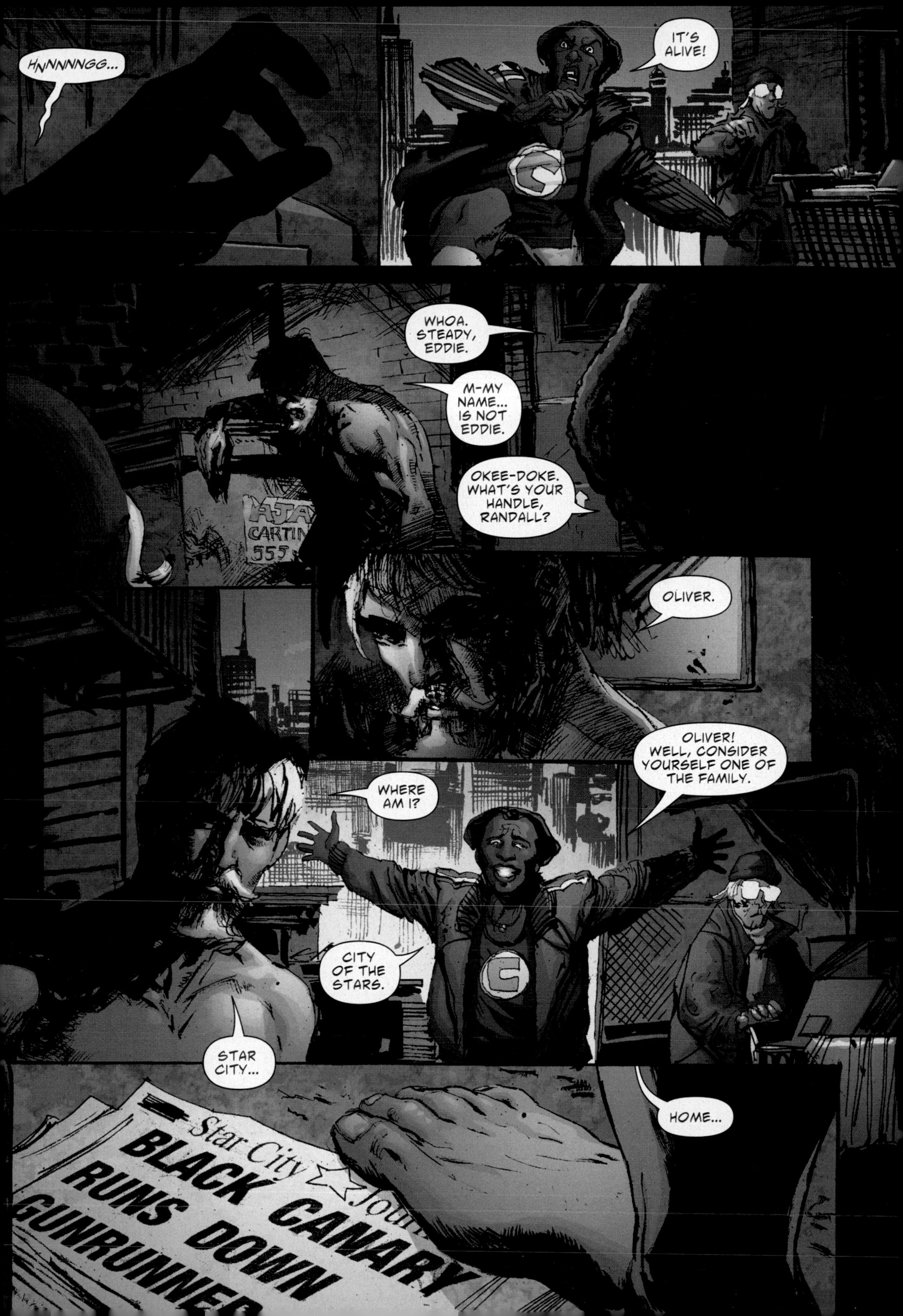
HNNNNNGG...
IT'S ALIVE!
WHOA. STEADY, EDDIE.
M-MY NAME... IS NOT EDDIE.
OKEE-DOKE. WHAT'S YOUR HANDLE, RANDALL?
OLIVER.
OLIVER! WELL, CONSIDER YOURSELF ONE OF THE FAMILY.
WHERE AM I?
CITY OF THE STARS.
STAR CITY...
HOME...
Star City Journal
BLACK CANARY RUNS DOWN GUNRUNNER

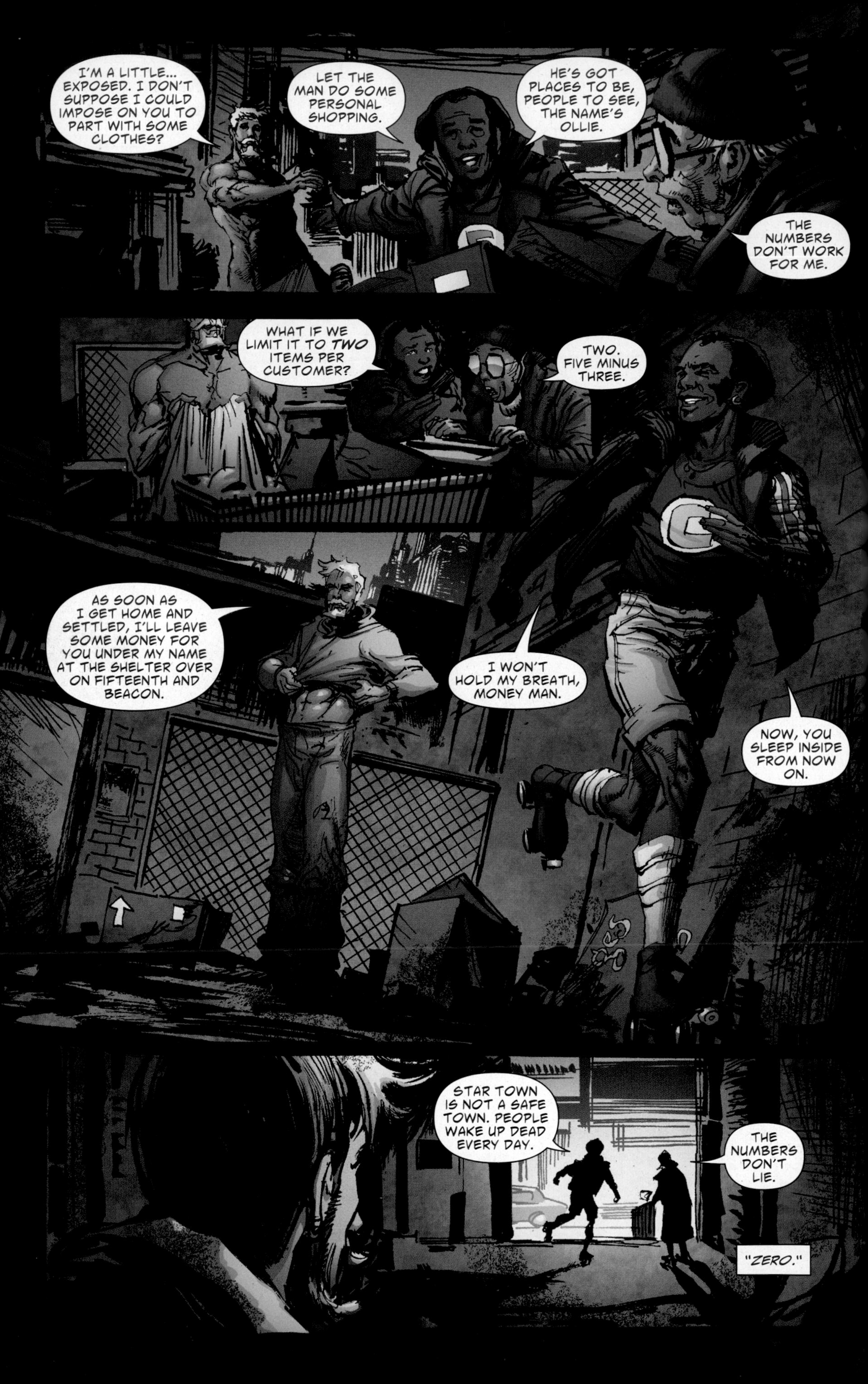
I'M A LITTLE... EXPOSED. I DON'T SUPPOSE I COULD IMPOSE ON YOU TO PART WITH SOME CLOTHES?
LET THE MAN DO SOME PERSONAL SHOPPING.
HE'S GOT PLACES TO BE, PEOPLE TO SEE, THE NAME'S OLLIE.
THE NUMBERS DON'T WORK FOR ME.
WHAT IF WE LIMIT IT TO *TWO* ITEMS PER CUSTOMER?
TWO. FIVE MINUS THREE.
AS SOON AS I GET HOME AND SETTLED, I'LL LEAVE SOME MONEY FOR YOU UNDER MY NAME AT THE SHELTER OVER ON FIFTEENTH AND BEACON.
I WON'T HOLD MY BREATH, MONEY MAN.
NOW, YOU SLEEP INSIDE FROM NOW ON.
STAR TOWN IS NOT A SAFE TOWN. PEOPLE WAKE UP DEAD EVERY DAY.
THE NUMBERS DON'T LIE.
"ZERO."

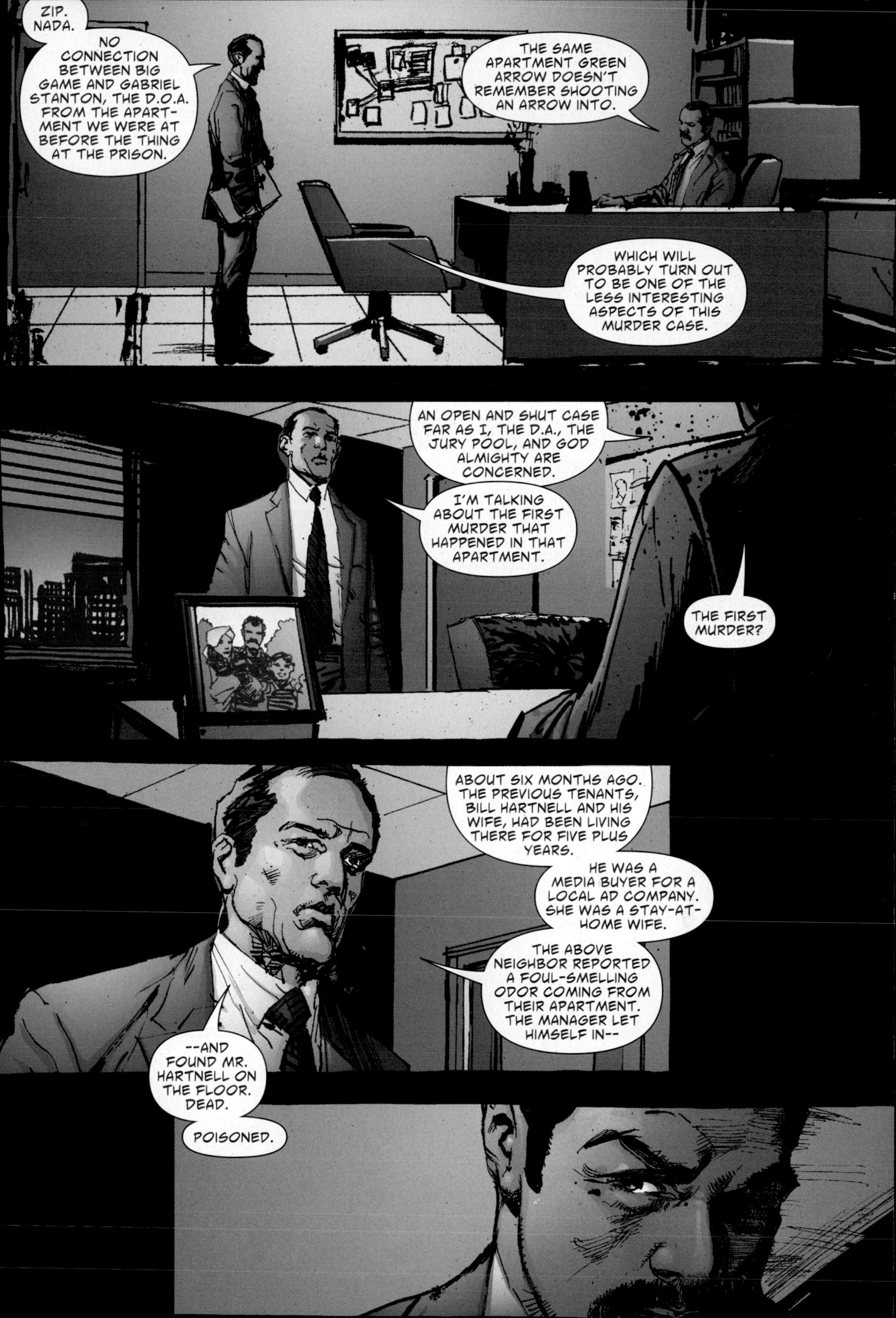
ZIP. NADA.
NO CONNECTION BETWEEN BIG GAME AND GABRIEL STANTON, THE D.O.A. FROM THE APARTMENT WE WERE AT BEFORE THE THING AT THE PRISON.
THE SAME APARTMENT GREEN ARROW DOESN'T REMEMBER SHOOTING AN ARROW INTO.
WHICH WILL PROBABLY TURN OUT TO BE ONE OF THE LESS INTERESTING ASPECTS OF THIS MURDER CASE.
AN OPEN AND SHUT CASE FAR AS I, THE D.A., THE JURY POOL, AND GOD ALMIGHTY ARE CONCERNED.
I'M TALKING ABOUT THE FIRST MURDER THAT HAPPENED IN THAT APARTMENT.
THE FIRST MURDER?
ABOUT SIX MONTHS AGO. THE PREVIOUS TENANTS, BILL HARTNELL AND HIS WIFE, HAD BEEN LIVING THERE FOR FIVE PLUS YEARS.
HE WAS A MEDIA BUYER FOR A LOCAL AD COMPANY. SHE WAS A STAY-AT-HOME WIFE.
THE ABOVE NEIGHBOR REPORTED A FOUL-SMELLING ODOR COMING FROM THEIR APARTMENT. THE MANAGER LET HIMSELF IN--
--AND FOUND MR. HARTNELL ON THE FLOOR. DEAD.
POISONED.

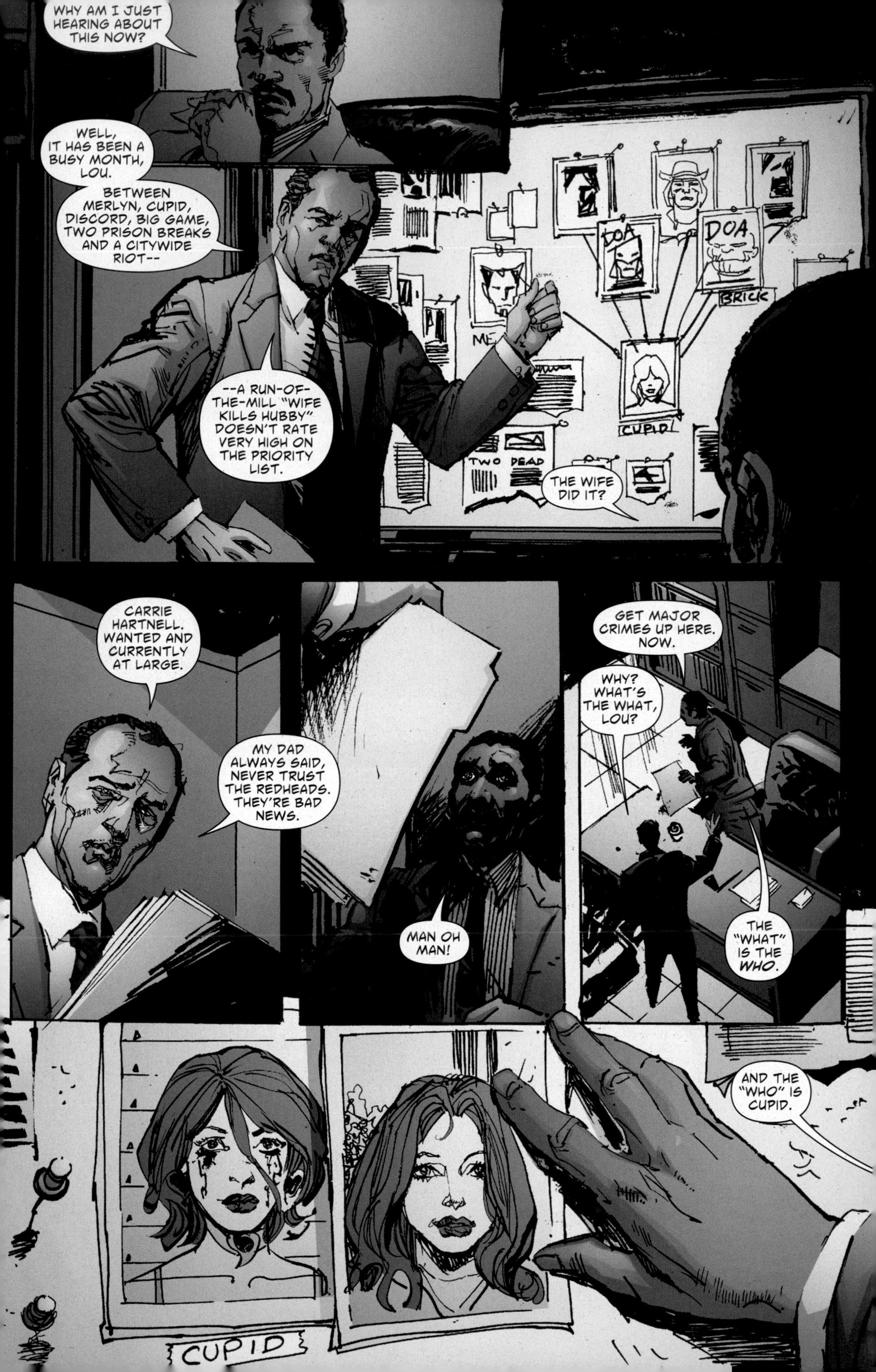
WHY AM I JUST HEARING ABOUT THIS NOW?
WELL, IT HAS BEEN A BUSY MONTH, LOU.
BETWEEN MERLYN, CUPID, DISCORD, BIG GAME, TWO PRISON BREAKS AND A CITYWIDE RIOT--
--A RUN-OF-THE-MILL "WIFE KILLS HUBBY" DOESN'T RATE VERY HIGH ON THE PRIORITY LIST.
THE WIFE DID IT?
DOA
DOA
BRICK
CUPID
TWO DEAD
CARRIE HARTNELL. WANTED AND CURRENTLY AT LARGE.
MY DAD ALWAYS SAID, NEVER TRUST THE REDHEADS. THEY'RE BAD NEWS.
MAN OH MAN!
GET MAJOR CRIMES UP HERE. NOW.
WHY? WHAT'S THE WHAT, LOU?
THE "WHAT" IS THE WHO.
AND THE "WHO" IS CUPID.
CUPID

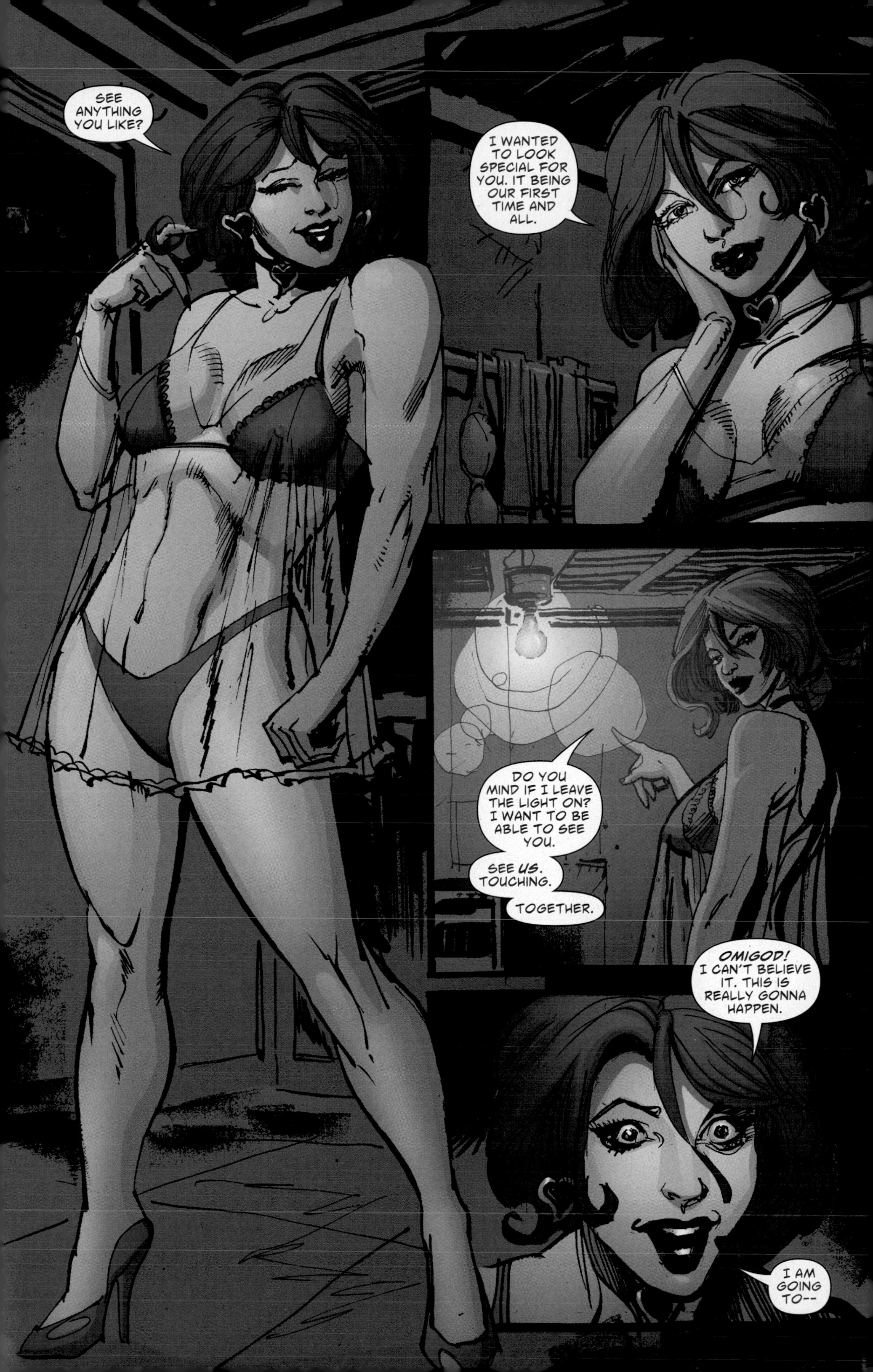
SEE ANYTHING YOU LIKE?
I WANTED TO LOOK SPECIAL FOR YOU. IT BEING OUR FIRST TIME AND ALL.
DO YOU MIND IF I LEAVE THE LIGHT ON? I WANT TO BE ABLE TO SEE YOU.
SEE *US*. TOUCHING.
TOGETHER.
OMIGOD! I CAN'T BELIEVE IT. THIS IS REALLY GONNA HAPPEN.
I AM GOING TO--

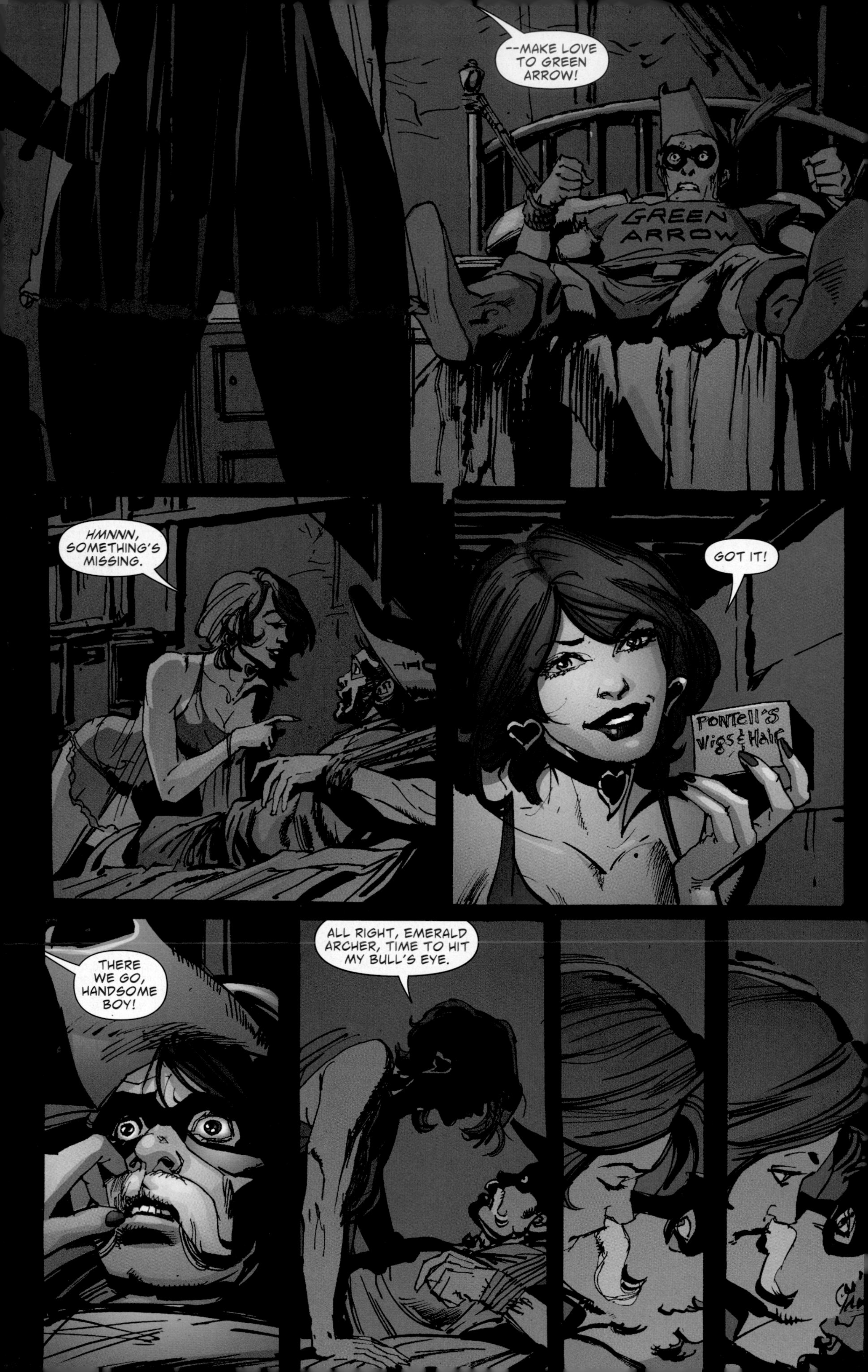
--MAKE LOVE TO GREEN ARROW!
GREEN ARROW
HMNNN, SOMETHING'S MISSING.
GOT IT!
PONTELL'S Wigs & Hair
THERE WE GO, HANDSOME BOY!
ALL RIGHT, EMERALD ARCHER, TIME TO HIT MY BULL'S EYE.

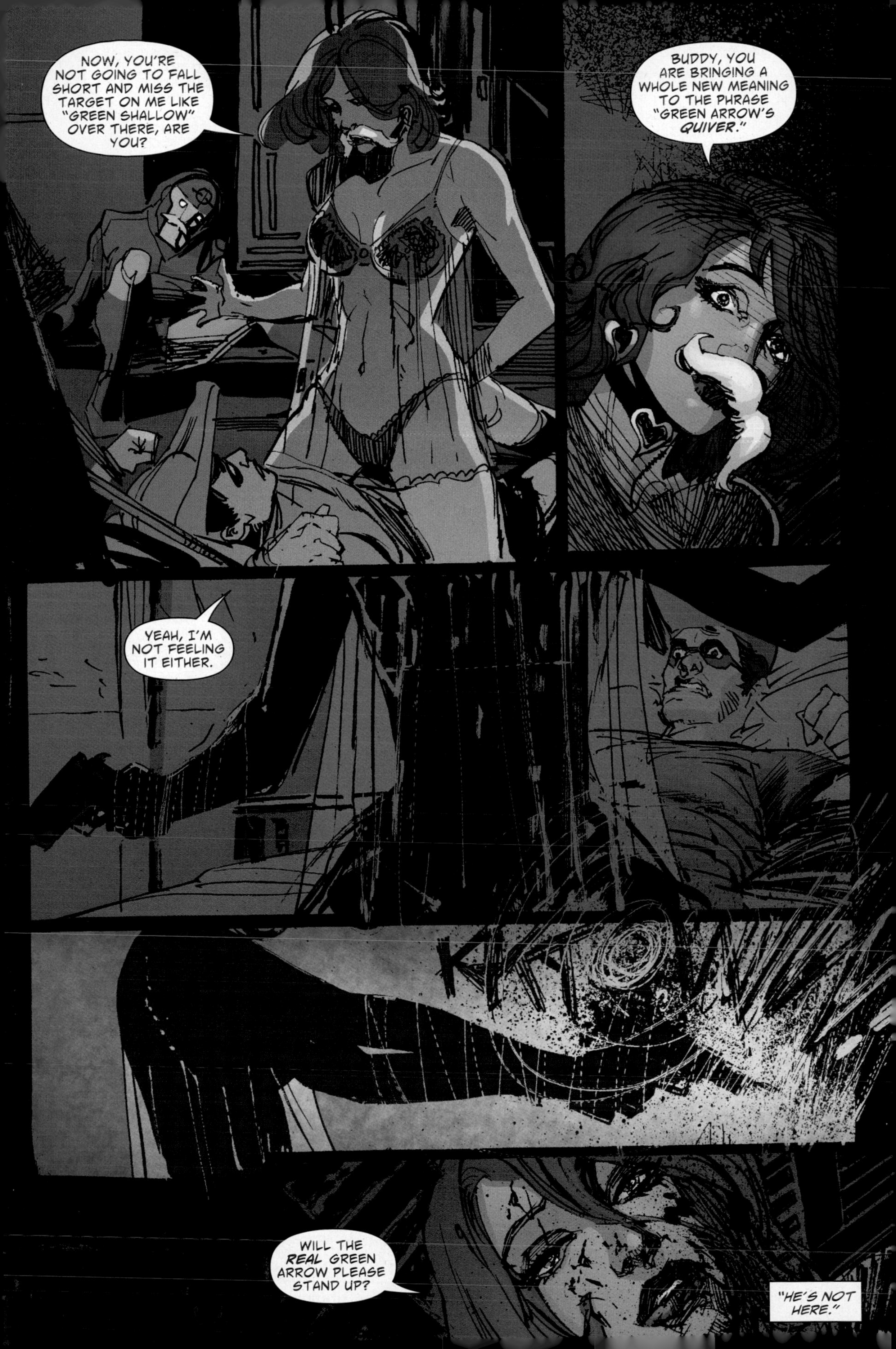
NOW, YOU'RE NOT GOING TO FALL SHORT AND MISS THE TARGET ON ME LIKE "GREEN SHALLOW" OVER THERE, ARE YOU?
BUDDY, YOU ARE BRINGING A WHOLE NEW MEANING TO THE PHRASE "GREEN ARROW'S QUIVER."
YEAH, I'M NOT FEELING IT EITHER.
WILL THE REAL GREEN ARROW PLEASE STAND UP?
"HE'S NOT HERE."

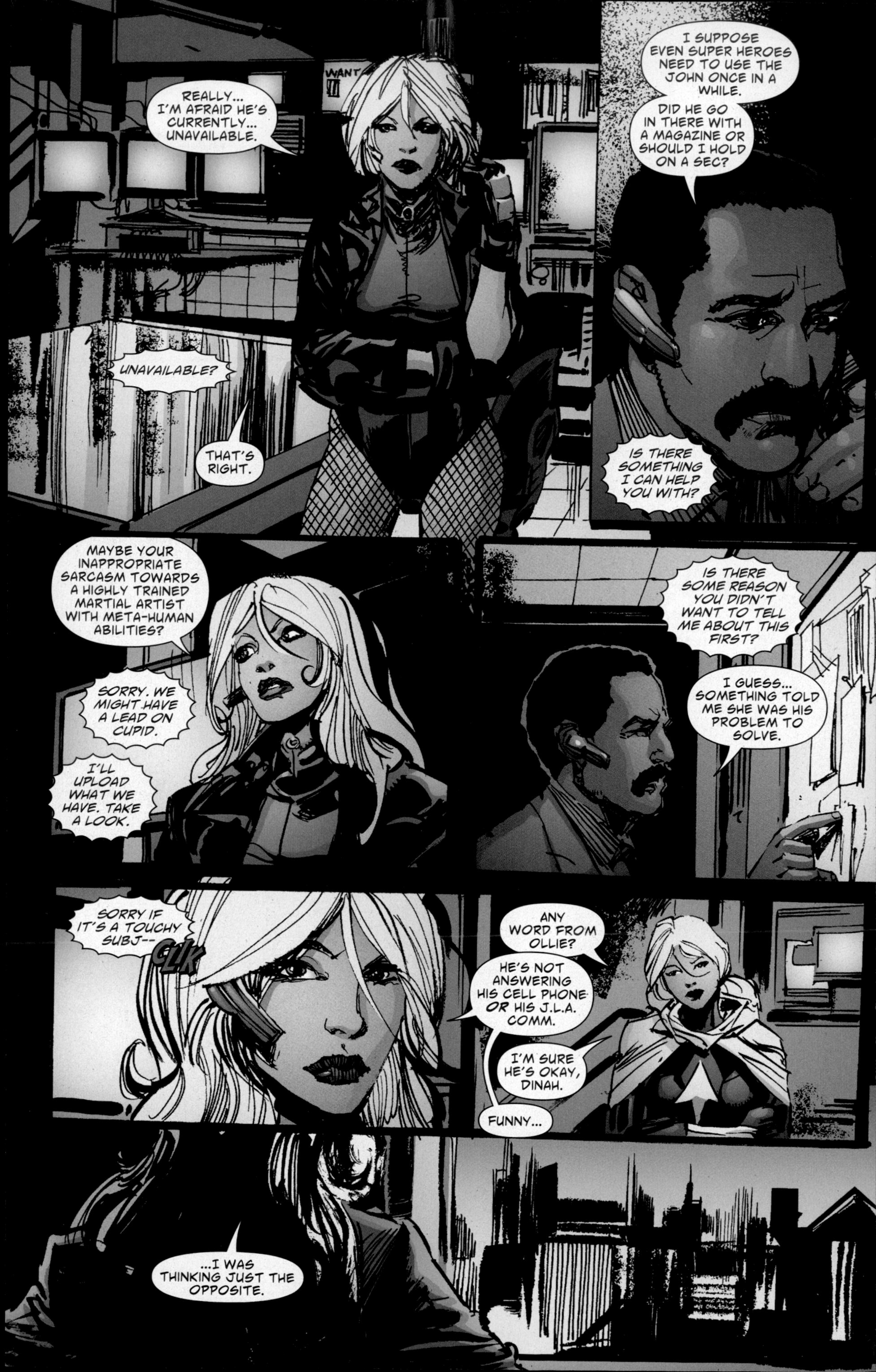

WANT
REALLY... I'M AFRAID HE'S CURRENTLY... UNAVAILABLE.
I SUPPOSE EVEN SUPER HEROES NEED TO USE THE JOHN ONCE IN A WHILE.
DID HE GO IN THERE WITH A MAGAZINE OR SHOULD I HOLD ON A SEC?
UNAVAILABLE?
THAT'S RIGHT.
IS THERE SOMETHING I CAN HELP YOU WITH?
MAYBE YOUR INAPPROPRIATE SARCASM TOWARDS A HIGHLY TRAINED MARTIAL ARTIST WITH META-HUMAN ABILITIES?
SORRY. WE MIGHT HAVE A LEAD ON CUPID.
I'LL UPLOAD WHAT WE HAVE. TAKE A LOOK.
IS THERE SOME REASON YOU DIDN'T WANT TO TELL ME ABOUT THIS FIRST?
I GUESS... SOMETHING TOLD ME SHE WAS HIS PROBLEM TO SOLVE.
SORRY IF IT'S A TOUCHY SUBJ--
CLIK
ANY WORD FROM OLLIE?
HE'S NOT ANSWERING HIS CELL PHONE OR HIS J.L.A. COMM.
I'M SURE HE'S OKAY, DINAH.
FUNNY...
...I WAS THINKING JUST THE OPPOSITE.

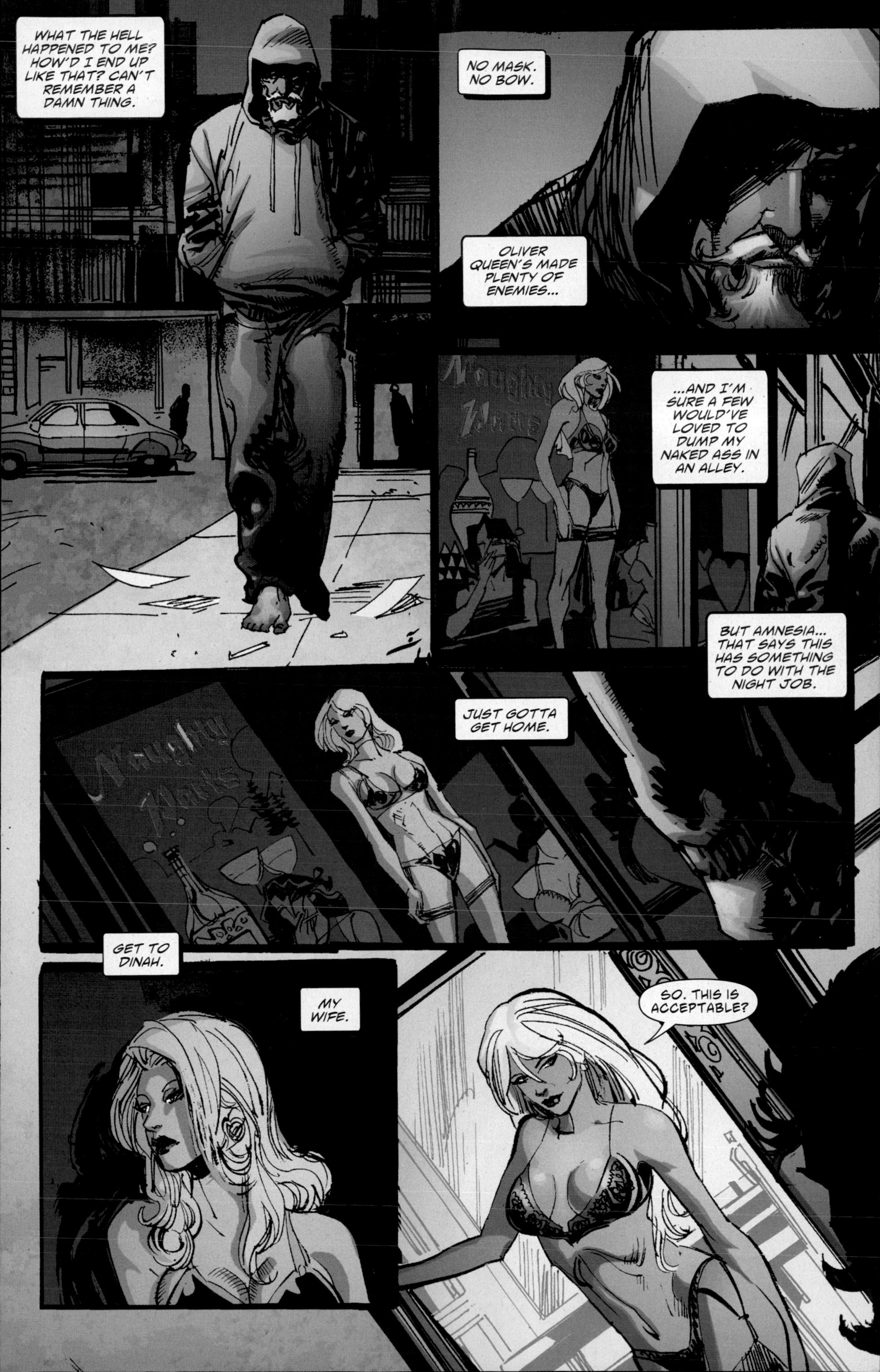
WHAT THE HELL HAPPENED TO ME? HOW'D I END UP LIKE THAT? CAN'T REMEMBER A DAMN THING.
NO MASK. NO BOW.
OLIVER QUEEN'S MADE PLENTY OF ENEMIES...
...AND I'M SURE A FEW WOULD'VE LOVED TO DUMP MY NAKED ASS IN AN ALLEY.
BUT AMNESIA... THAT SAYS THIS HAS SOMETHING TO DO WITH THE NIGHT JOB.
JUST GOTTA GET HOME.
GET TO DINAH.
MY WIFE.
SO. THIS IS ACCEPTABLE?

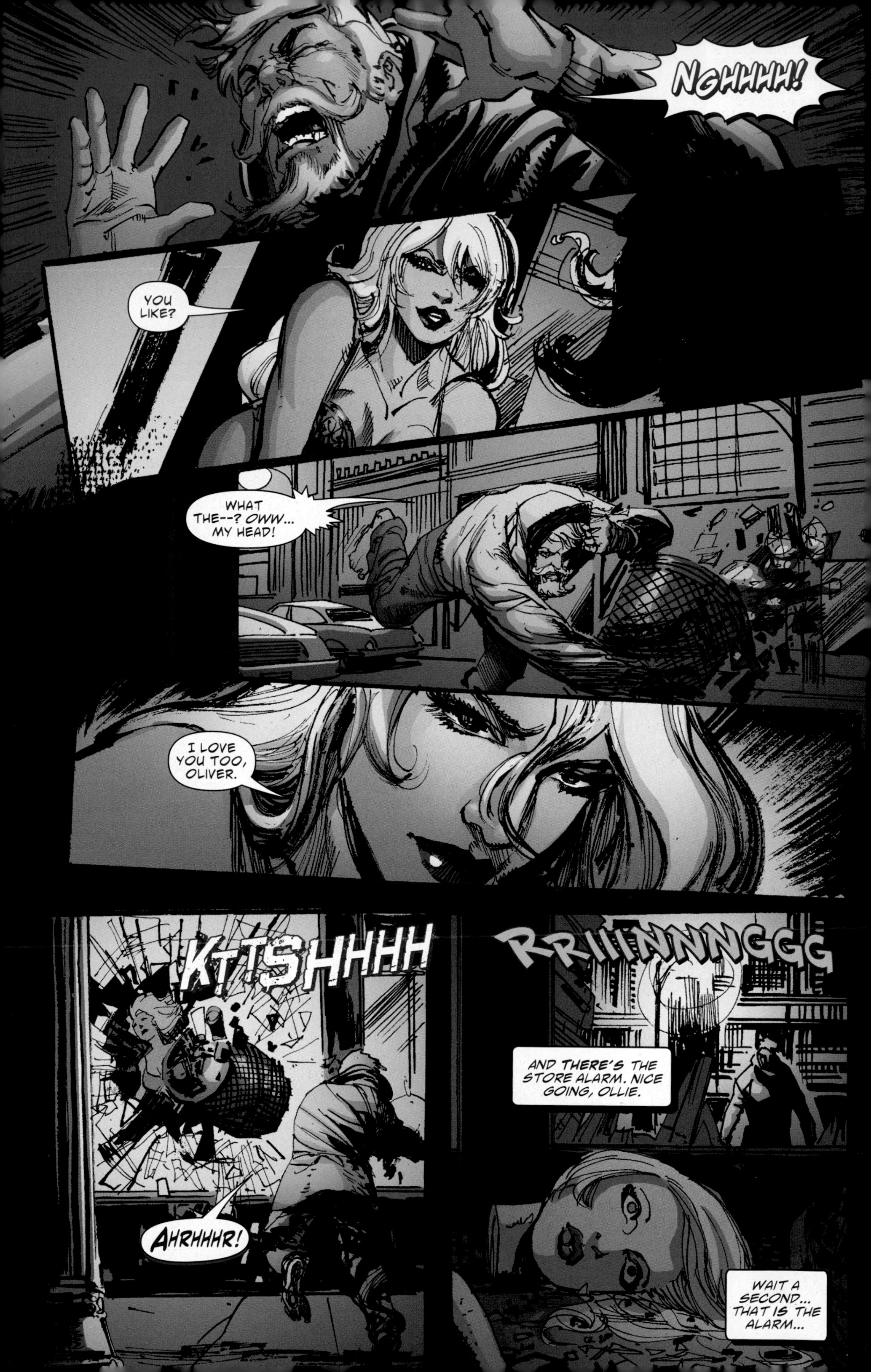

NGHHHH!
YOU LIKE?
WHAT THE--? OWW... MY HEAD!
I LOVE YOU TOO, OLIVER.
KTTSHHHH
AHRHHHR!
RRIIINNNGGG
AND THERE'S THE STORE ALARM. NICE GOING, OLLIE.
WAIT A SECOND... THAT IS THE ALARM...

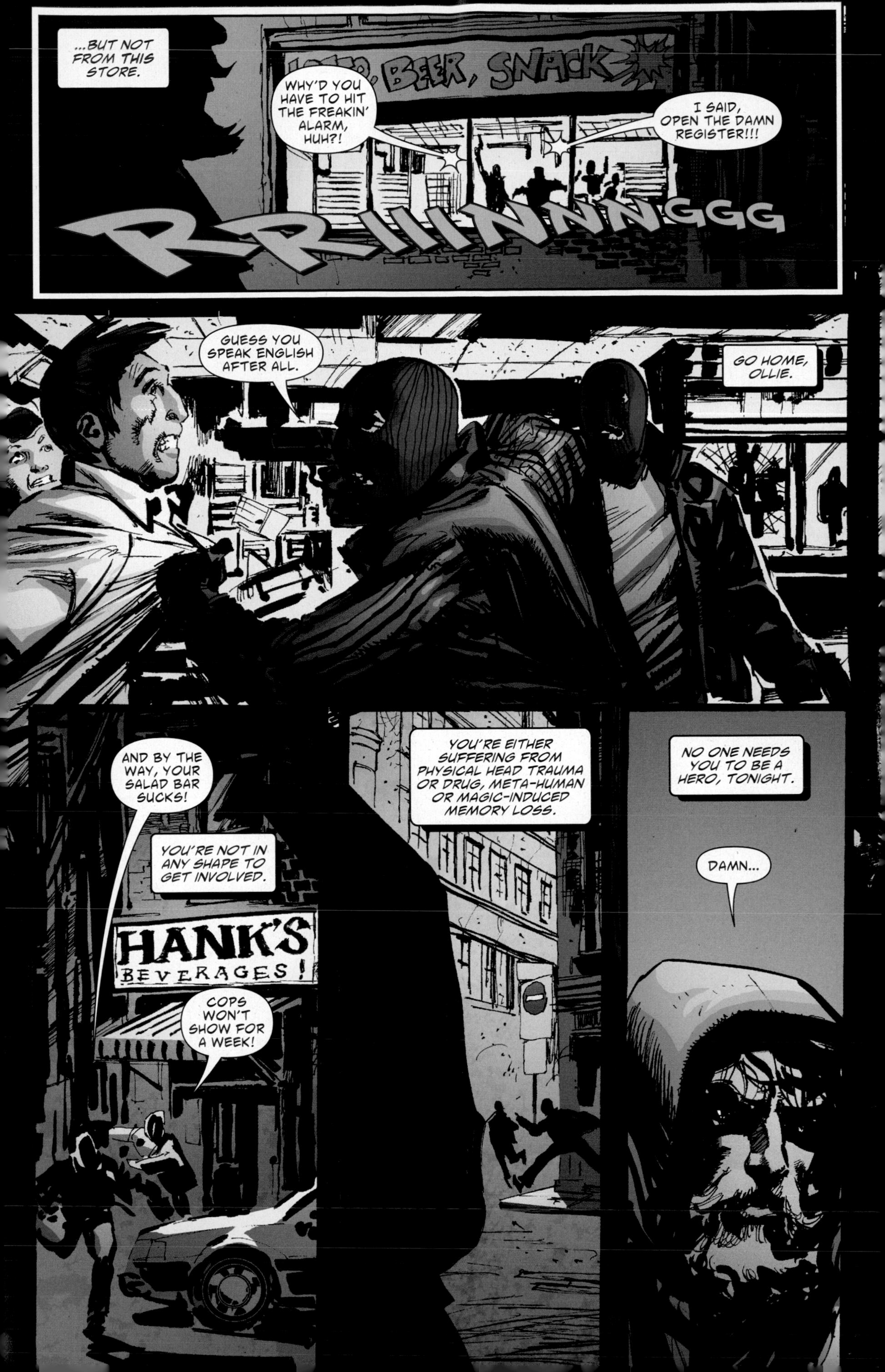
...BUT NOT FROM THIS STORE.
BEER, SNACK
WHY'D YOU HAVE TO HIT THE FREAKIN' ALARM, HUH?!
I SAID, OPEN THE DAMN REGISTER!!!
RRIIINNNGGG
GUESS YOU SPEAK ENGLISH AFTER ALL.
GO HOME, OLLIE.
AND BY THE WAY, YOUR SALAD BAR SUCKS!
YOU'RE NOT IN ANY SHAPE TO GET INVOLVED.
HANK'S BEVERAGES!
COPS WON'T SHOW FOR A WEEK!
YOU'RE EITHER SUFFERING FROM PHYSICAL HEAD TRAUMA OR DRUG, META-HUMAN OR MAGIC-INDUCED MEMORY LOSS.
NO ONE NEEDS YOU TO BE A HERO, TONIGHT.
DAMN...

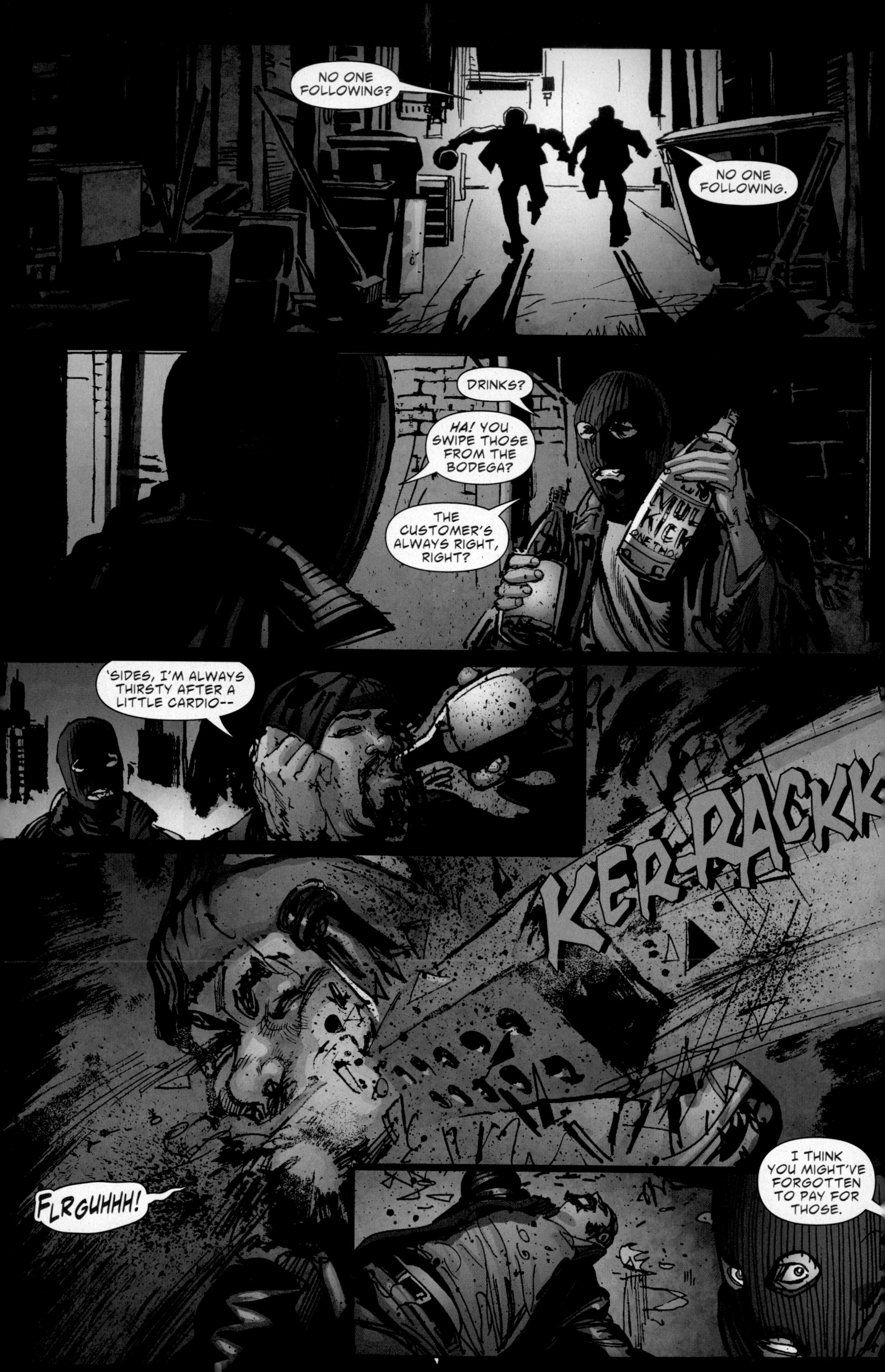

NO ONE FOLLOWING?
NO ONE FOLLOWING.
DRINKS?
HA! YOU SWIPE THOSE FROM THE BODEGA?
THE CUSTOMER'S ALWAYS RIGHT, RIGHT?
'SIDES, I'M ALWAYS THIRSTY AFTER A LITTLE CARDIO--
KER-RACKK
FLRGUHHH!
I THINK YOU MIGHT'VE FORGOTTEN TO PAY FOR THOSE.

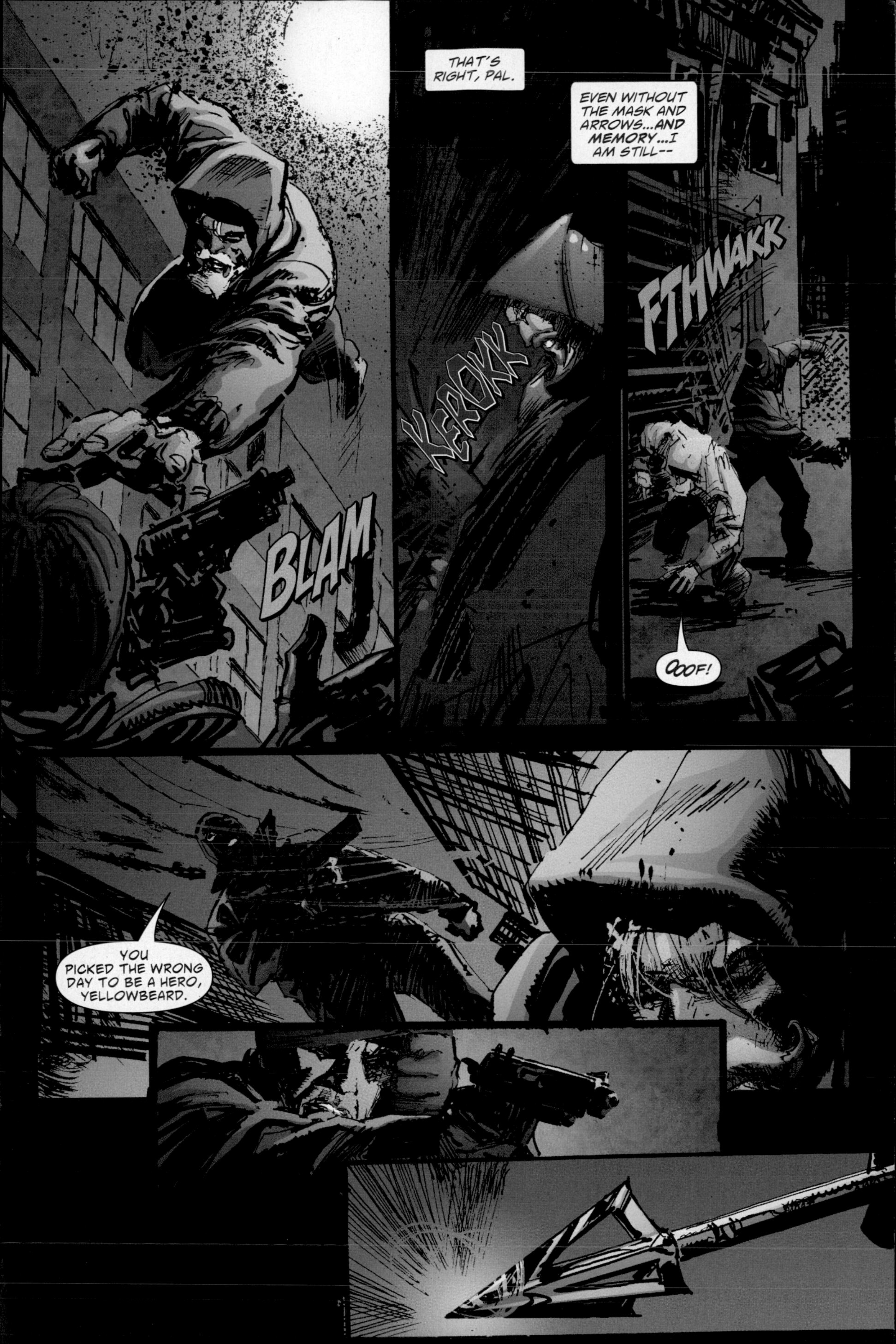
BLAM
THAT'S RIGHT, PAL.
EVEN WITHOUT THE MASK AND ARROWS...AND MEMORY...I AM STILL--
KEROKK
FTHWAKK
OOOF!
YOU PICKED THE WRONG DAY TO BE A HERO, YELLOWBEARD.

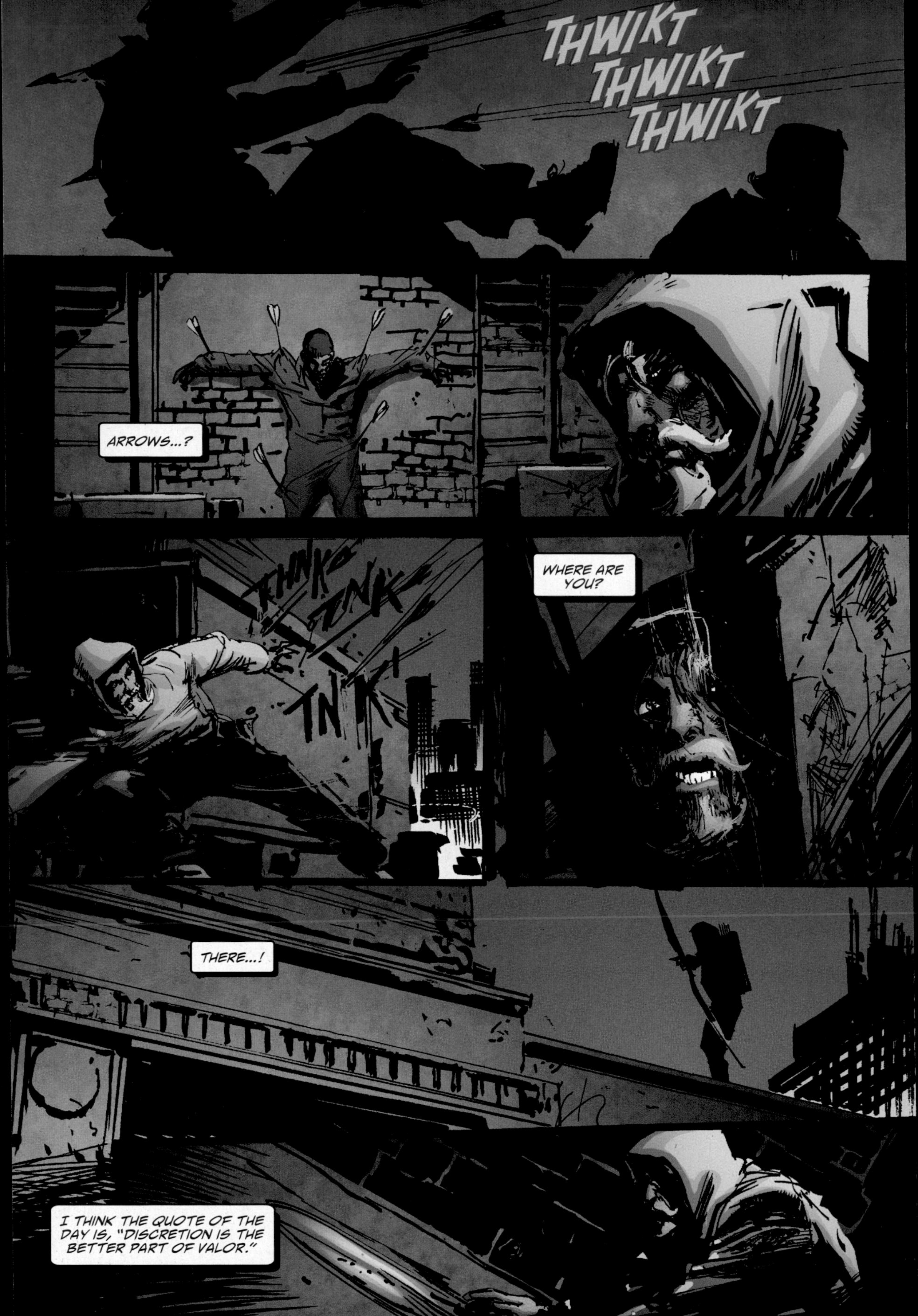
THWIKT
THWIKT
THWIKT
ARROWS...?
THNK
TZNK
TNK
WHERE ARE YOU?
THERE...!
I THINK THE QUOTE OF THE DAY IS, "DISCRETION IS THE BETTER PART OF VALOR."

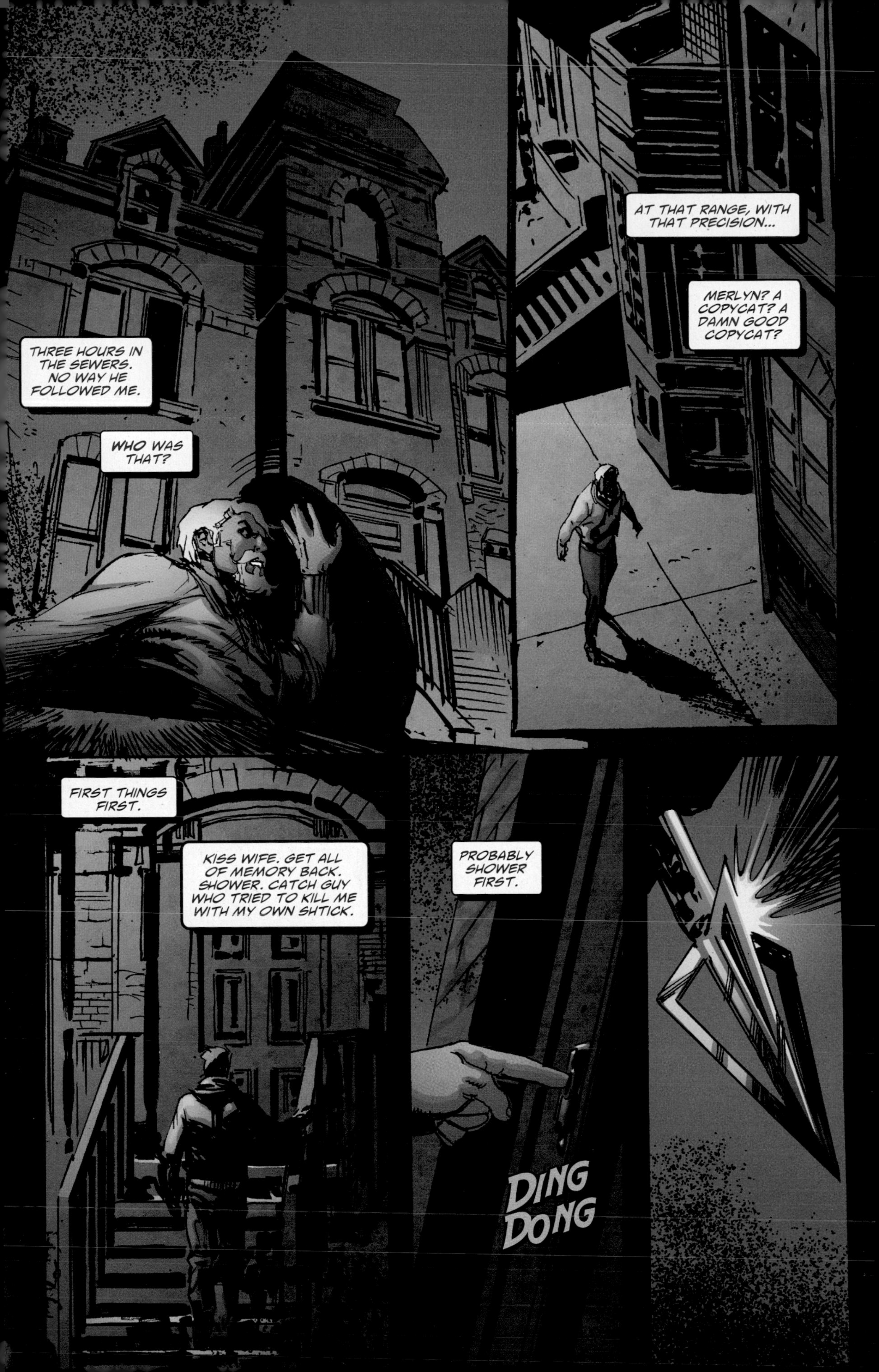
THREE HOURS IN THE SEWERS. NO WAY HE FOLLOWED ME.
WHO WAS THAT?
AT THAT RANGE, WITH THAT PRECISION...
MERLYN? A COPYCAT? A DAMN GOOD COPYCAT?
FIRST THINGS FIRST.
KISS WIFE. GET ALL OF MEMORY BACK. SHOWER. CATCH GUY WHO TRIED TO KILL ME WITH MY OWN SHTICK.
PROBABLY SHOWER FIRST.
DING DONG

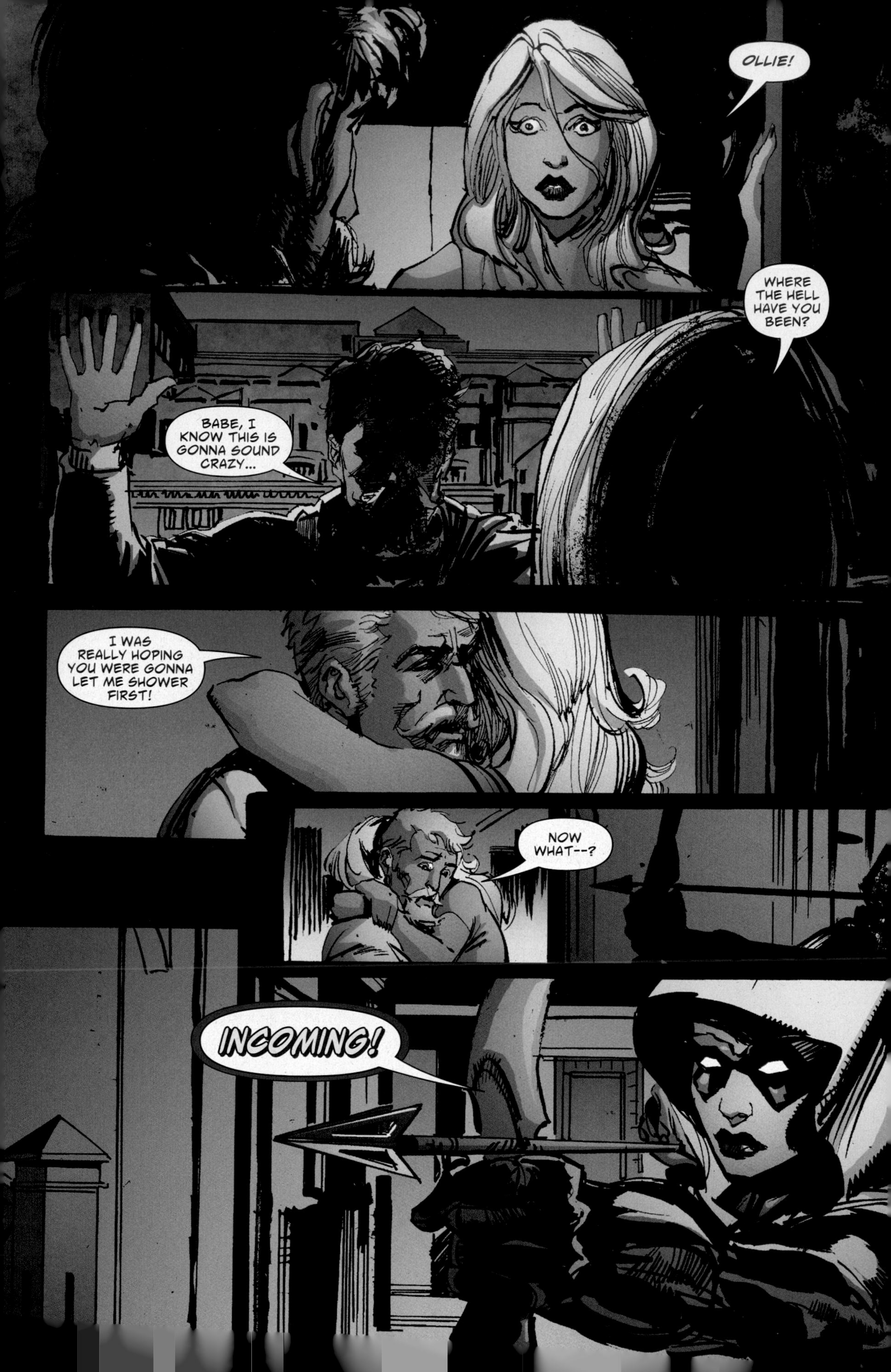
OLLIE!
WHERE THE HELL HAVE YOU BEEN?
BABE, I KNOW THIS IS GONNA SOUND CRAZY...
I WAS REALLY HOPING YOU WERE GONNA LET ME SHOWER FIRST!
NOW WHAT--?
INCOMING!

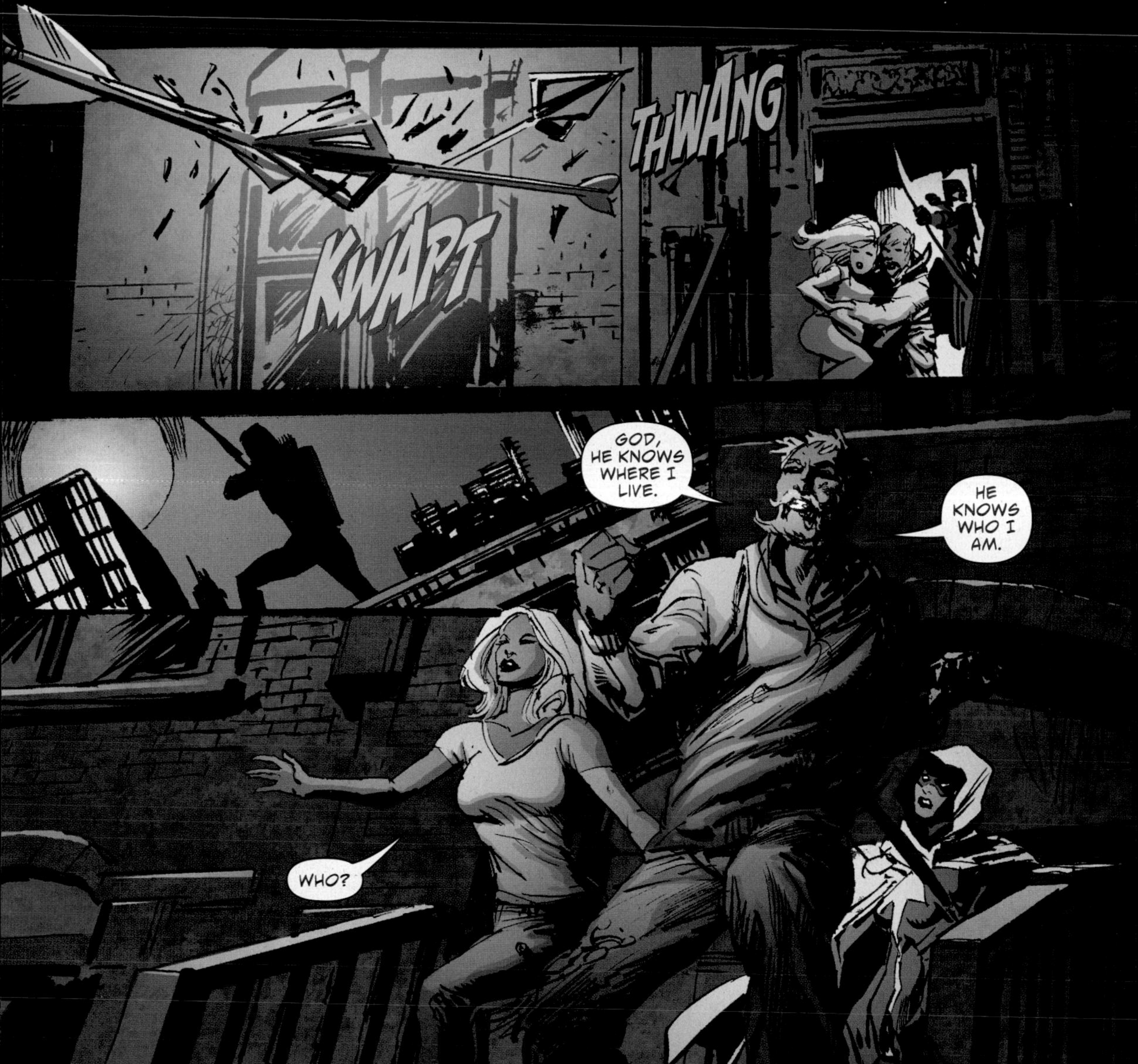
KWAPT
THWANG
GOD, HE KNOWS WHERE I LIVE.
HE KNOWS WHO I AM.
WHO?

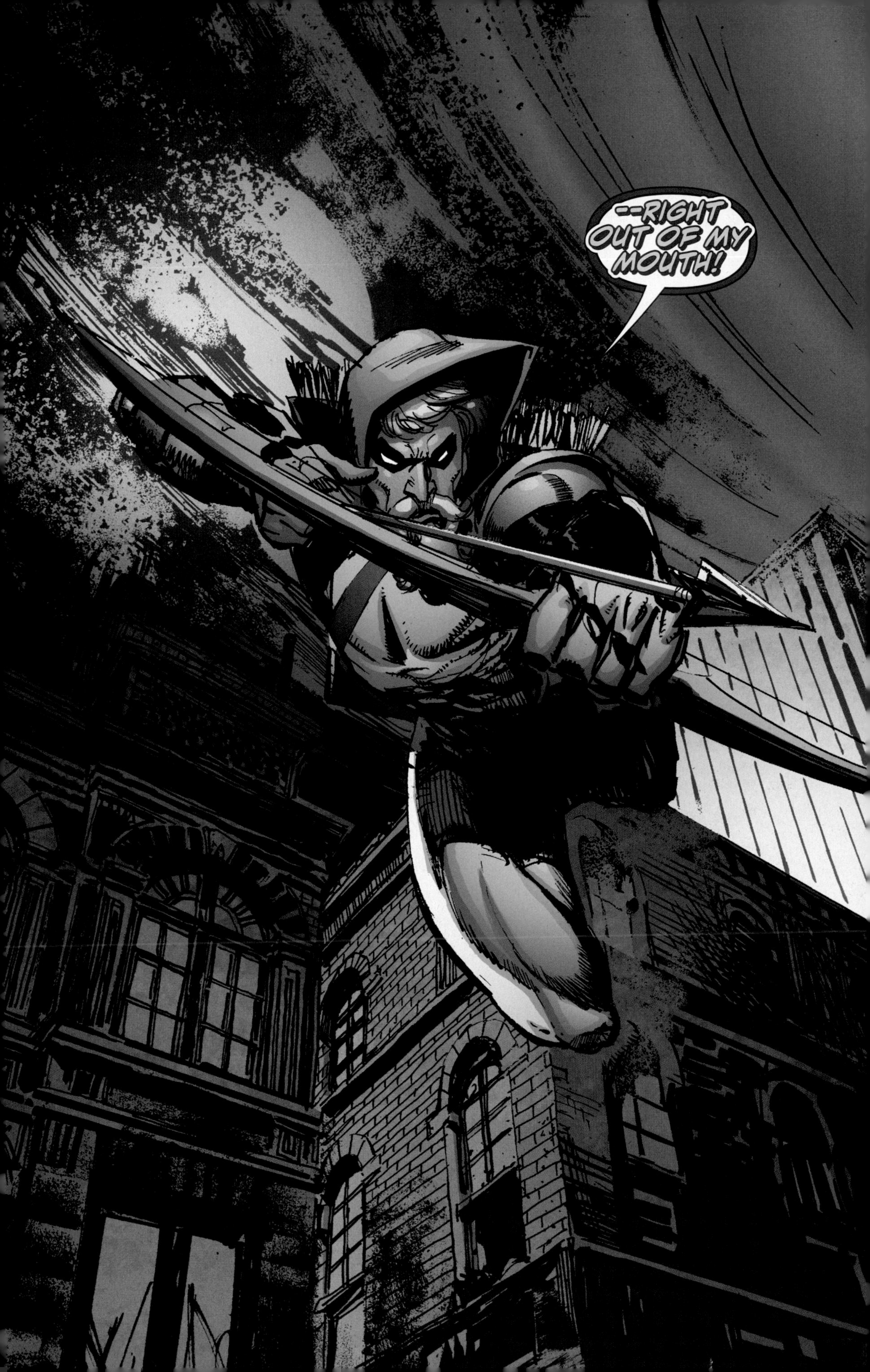
--RIGHT OUT OF MY MOUTH!

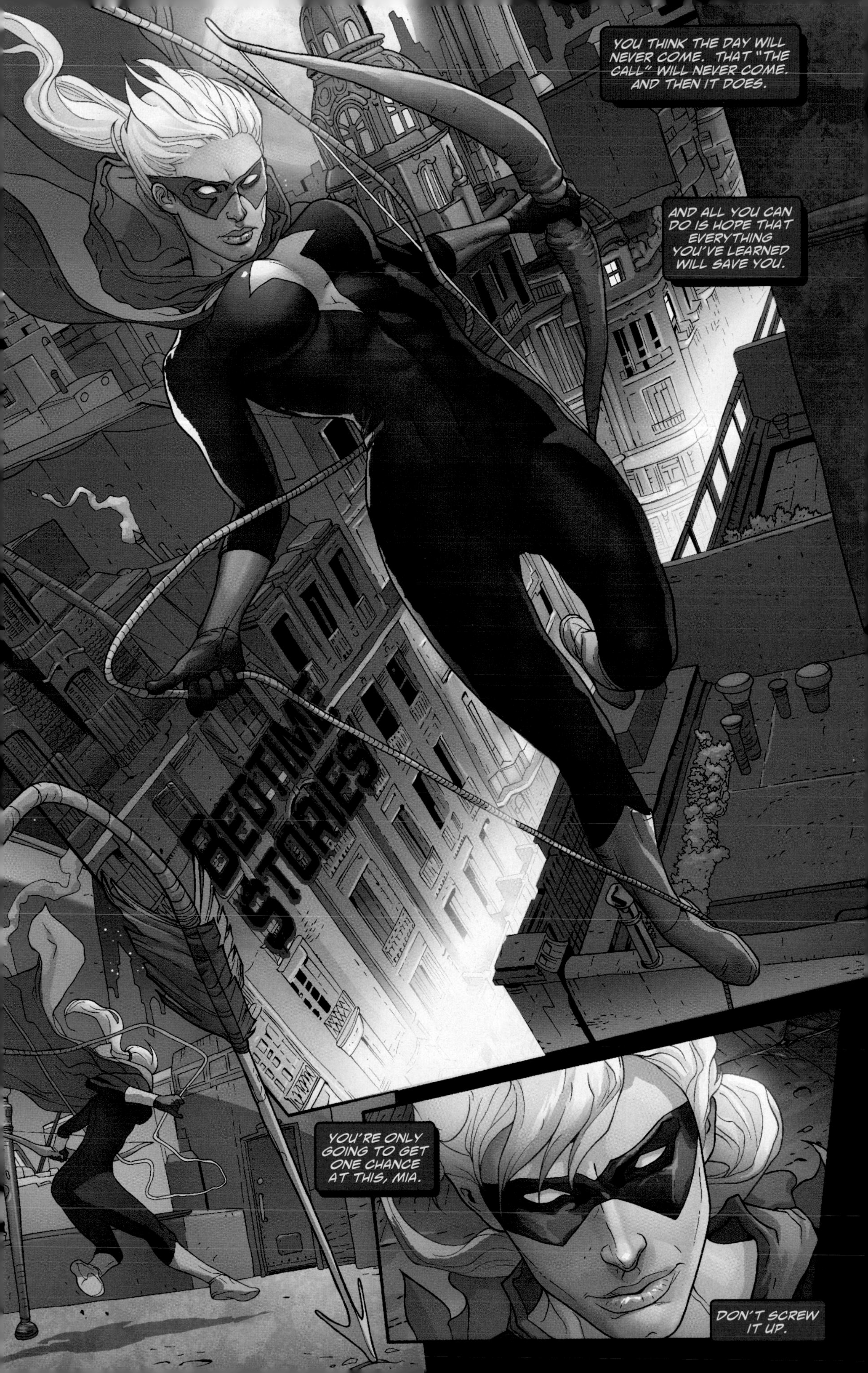
YOU THINK THE DAY WILL NEVER COME. THAT "THE CALL" WILL NEVER COME. AND THEN IT DOES.
AND ALL YOU CAN DO IS HOPE THAT EVERYTHING YOU'VE LEARNED WILL SAVE YOU.
BEDTIME STORIES
YOU'RE ONLY GOING TO GET ONE CHANCE AT THIS, MIA.
DON'T SCREW IT UP.

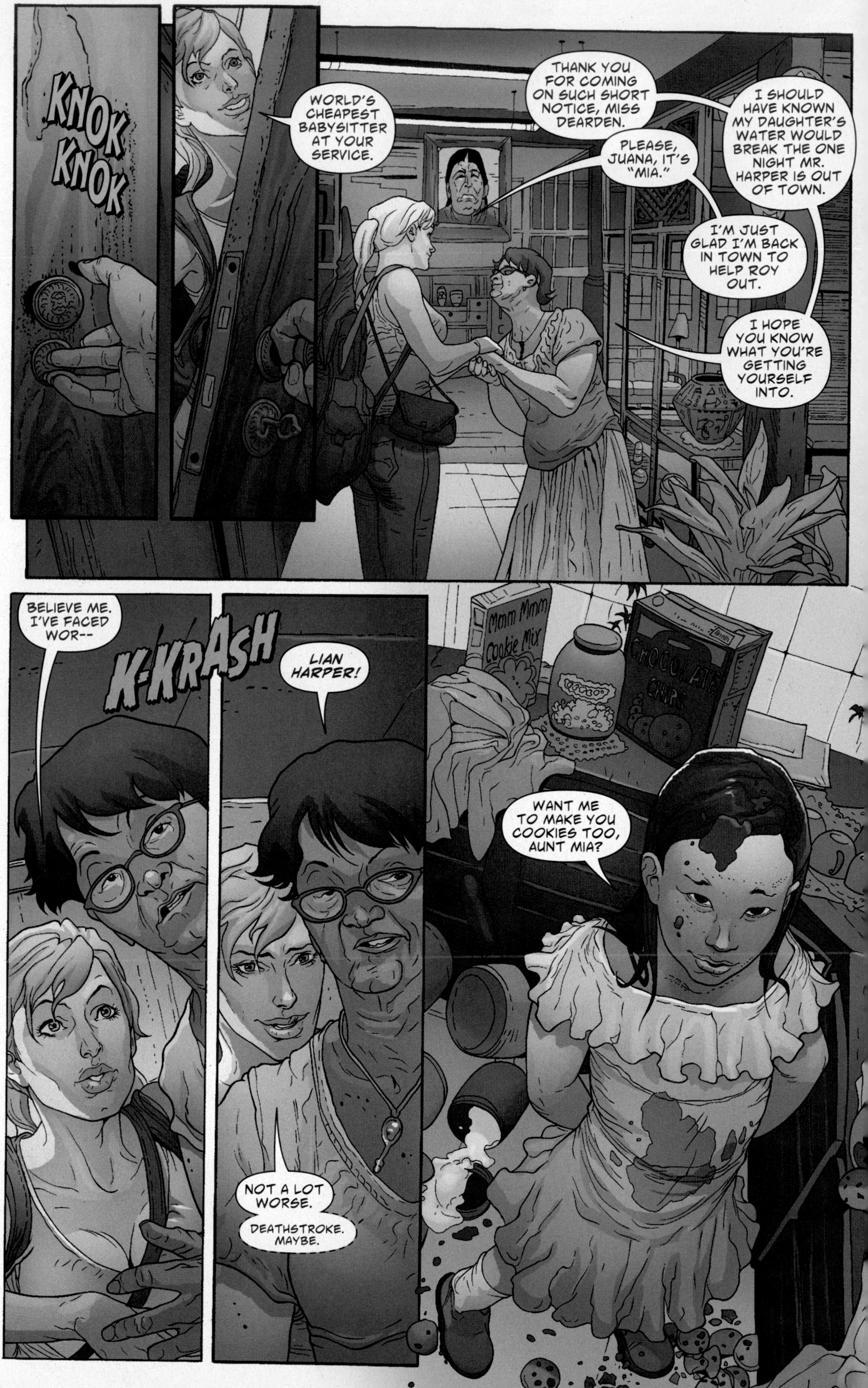

KNOK KNOK
WORLD'S CHEAPEST BABYSITTER AT YOUR SERVICE.
THANK YOU FOR COMING ON SUCH SHORT NOTICE, MISS DEARDEN.
PLEASE, JUANA, IT'S "MIA."
I SHOULD HAVE KNOWN MY DAUGHTER'S WATER WOULD BREAK THE ONE NIGHT MR. HARPER IS OUT OF TOWN.
I'M JUST GLAD I'M BACK IN TOWN TO HELP ROY OUT.
I HOPE YOU KNOW WHAT YOU'RE GETTING YOURSELF INTO.
BELIEVE ME. I'VE FACED WOR--
K-KRASH
LIAN HARPER!
NOT A LOT WORSE.
DEATHSTROKE. MAYBE.
Mmm Mmm Cookie Mix
CHOCOLATE CHIPS
WANT ME TO MAKE YOU COOKIES TOO, AUNT MIA?

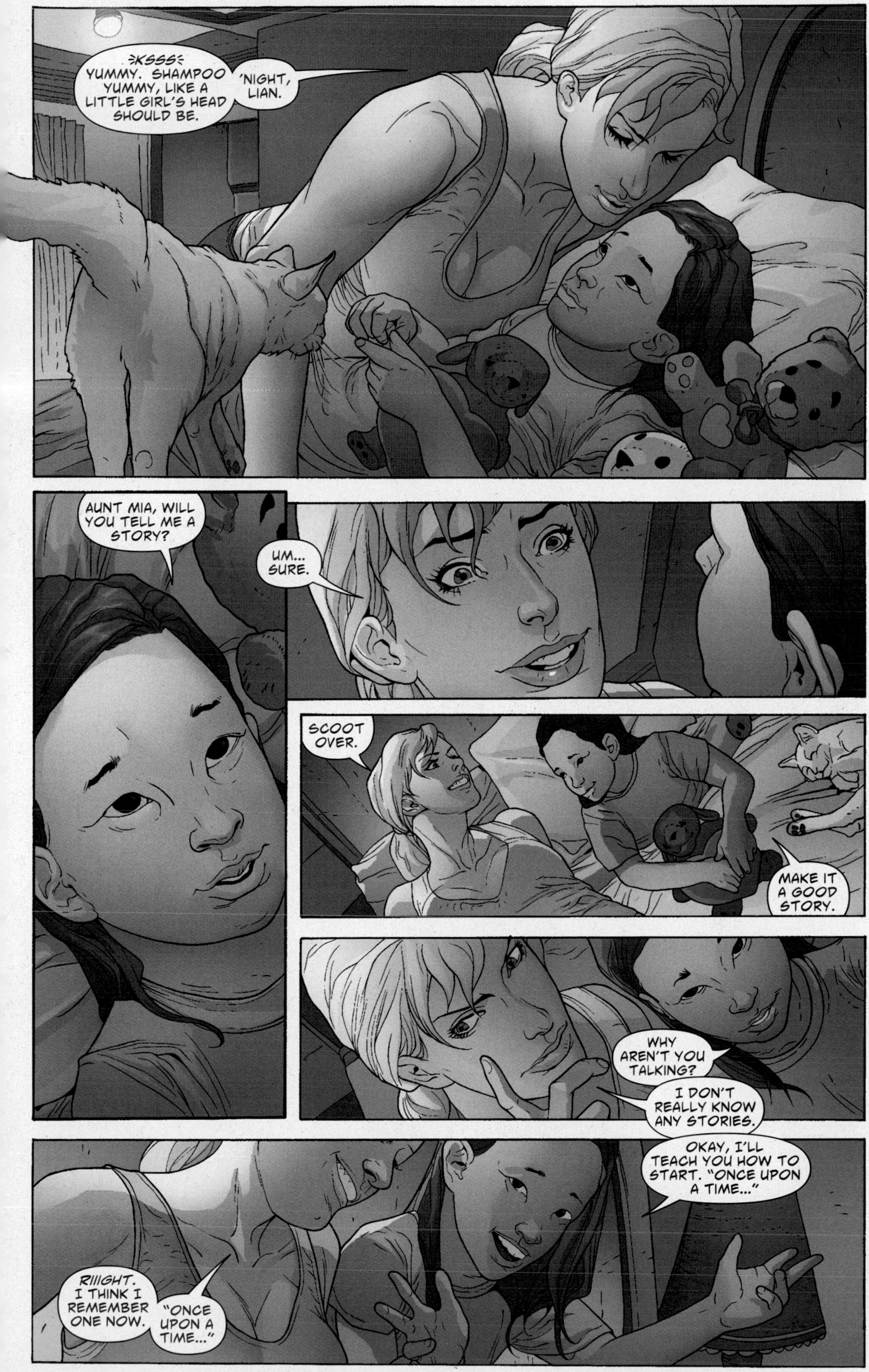

⩩KSSS⩩
YUMMY. SHAMPOO YUMMY, LIKE A LITTLE GIRL'S HEAD SHOULD BE.
'NIGHT, LIAN.
AUNT MIA, WILL YOU TELL ME A STORY?
UM... SURE.
SCOOT OVER.
MAKE IT A GOOD STORY.
WHY AREN'T YOU TALKING?
I DON'T REALLY KNOW ANY STORIES.
OKAY, I'LL TEACH YOU HOW TO START. "ONCE UPON A TIME..."
RIIIGHT. I THINK I REMEMBER ONE NOW.
"ONCE UPON A TIME..."

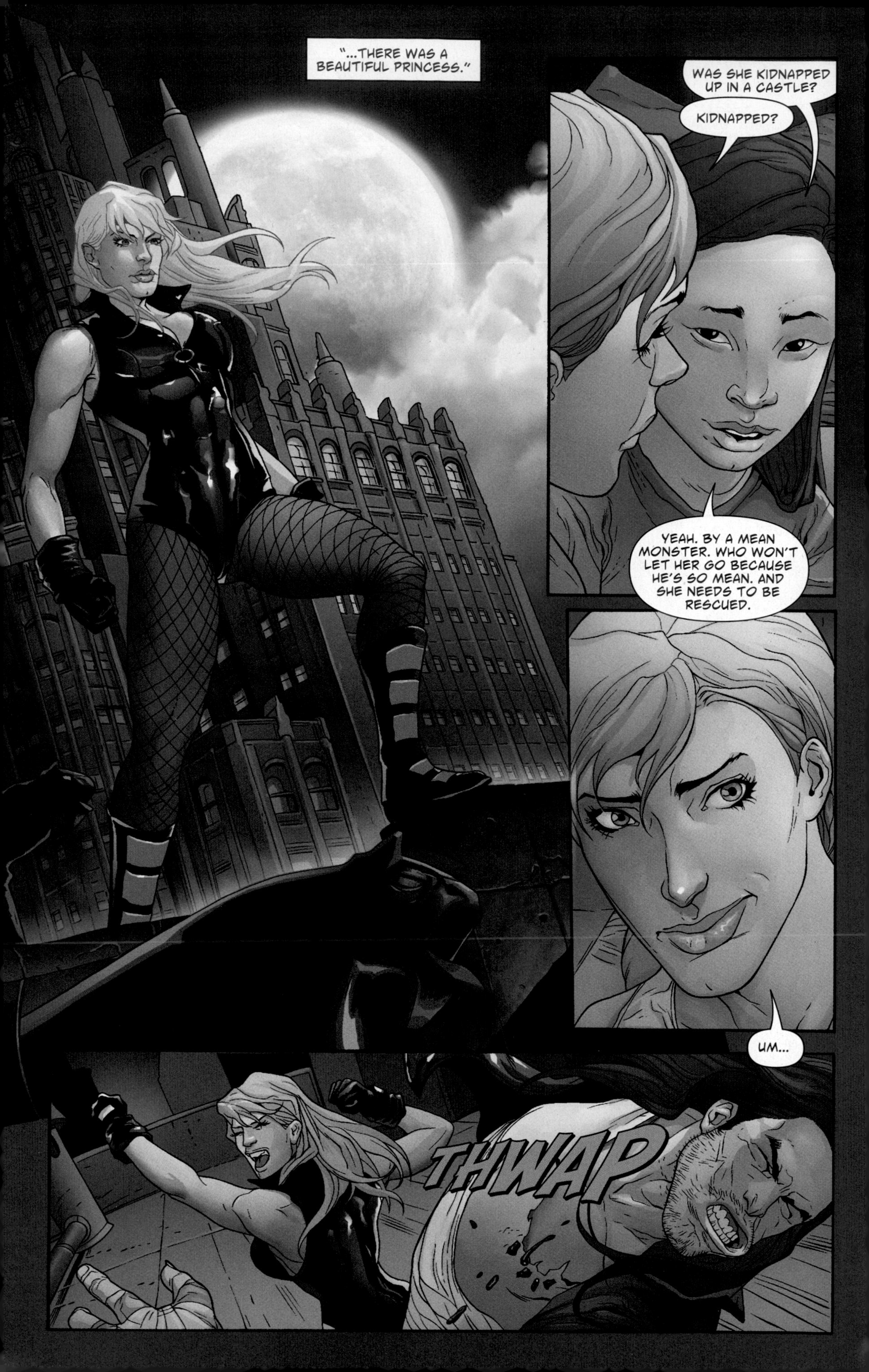
"...THERE WAS A BEAUTIFUL PRINCESS."
WAS SHE KIDNAPPED UP IN A CASTLE?
KIDNAPPED?
YEAH. BY A MEAN MONSTER. WHO WON'T LET HER GO BECAUSE HE'S SO MEAN. AND SHE NEEDS TO BE RESCUED.
UM...
THWAP

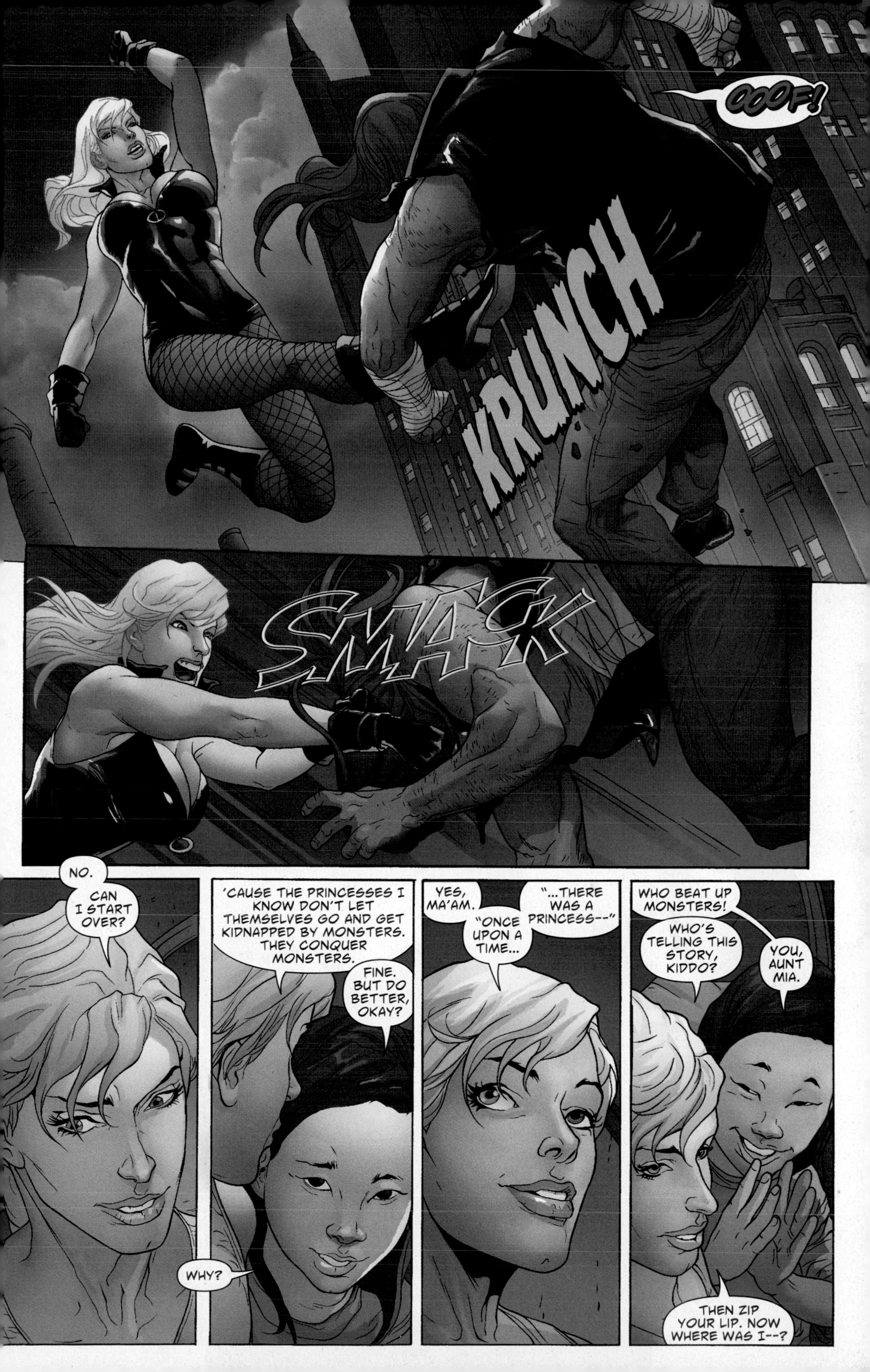
OOOF!
KRUNCH
SMACK
NO.
CAN I START OVER?
WHY?
'CAUSE THE PRINCESSES I KNOW DON'T LET THEMSELVES GO AND GET KIDNAPPED BY MONSTERS. THEY CONQUER MONSTERS.
FINE. BUT DO BETTER, OKAY?
YES, MA'AM.
"ONCE UPON A TIME...
"...THERE WAS A PRINCESS--"
WHO BEAT UP MONSTERS!
WHO'S TELLING THIS STORY, KIDDO?
YOU, AUNT MIA.
THEN ZIP YOUR LIP. NOW WHERE WAS I--?

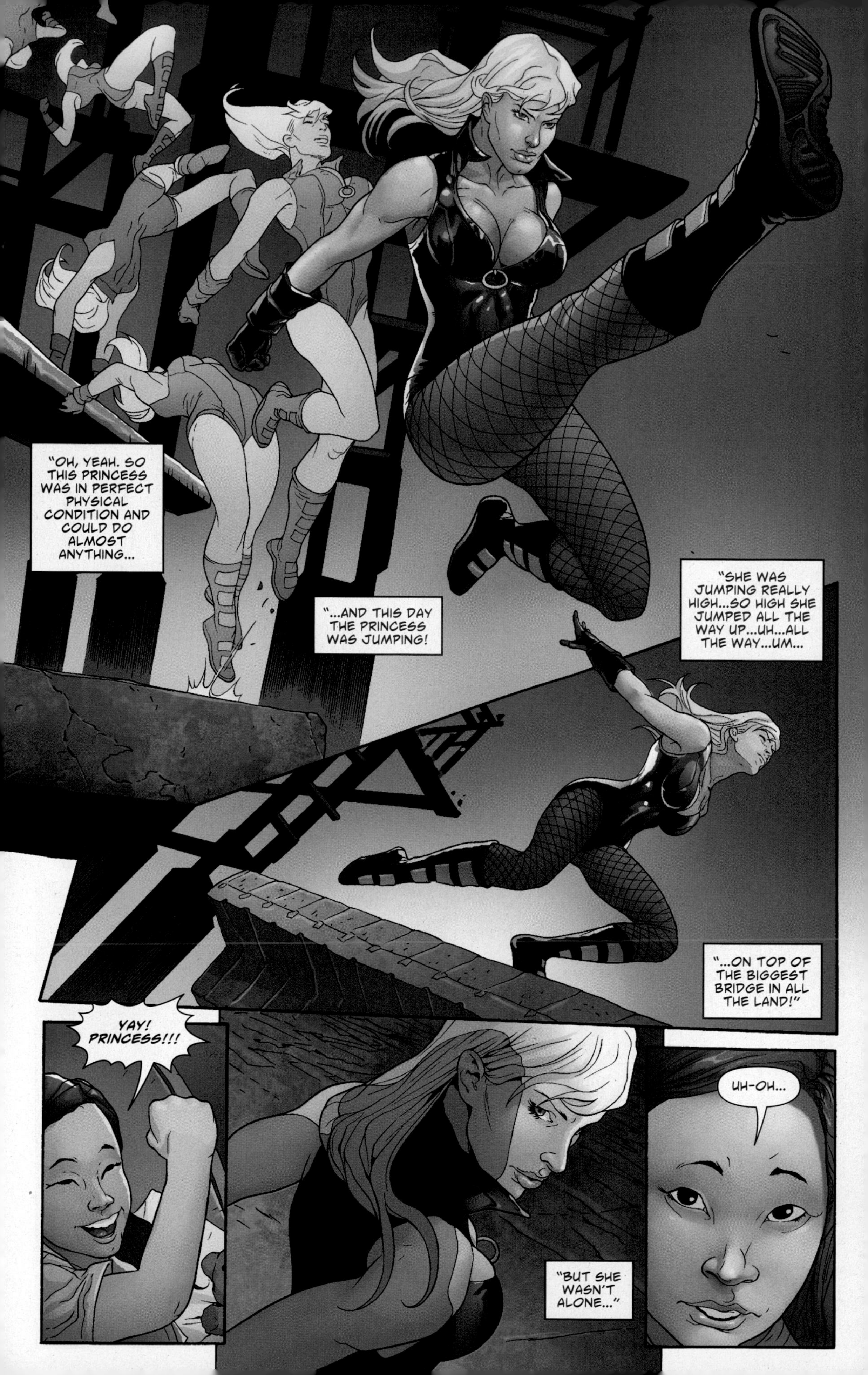

"OH, YEAH. SO THIS PRINCESS WAS IN PERFECT PHYSICAL CONDITION AND COULD DO ALMOST ANYTHING...
"...AND THIS DAY THE PRINCESS WAS JUMPING!
"SHE WAS JUMPING REALLY HIGH...SO HIGH SHE JUMPED ALL THE WAY UP...UH...ALL THE WAY...UM...
"...ON TOP OF THE BIGGEST BRIDGE IN ALL THE LAND!"
YAY! PRINCESS!!!
"BUT SHE WASN'T ALONE..."
UH-OH...

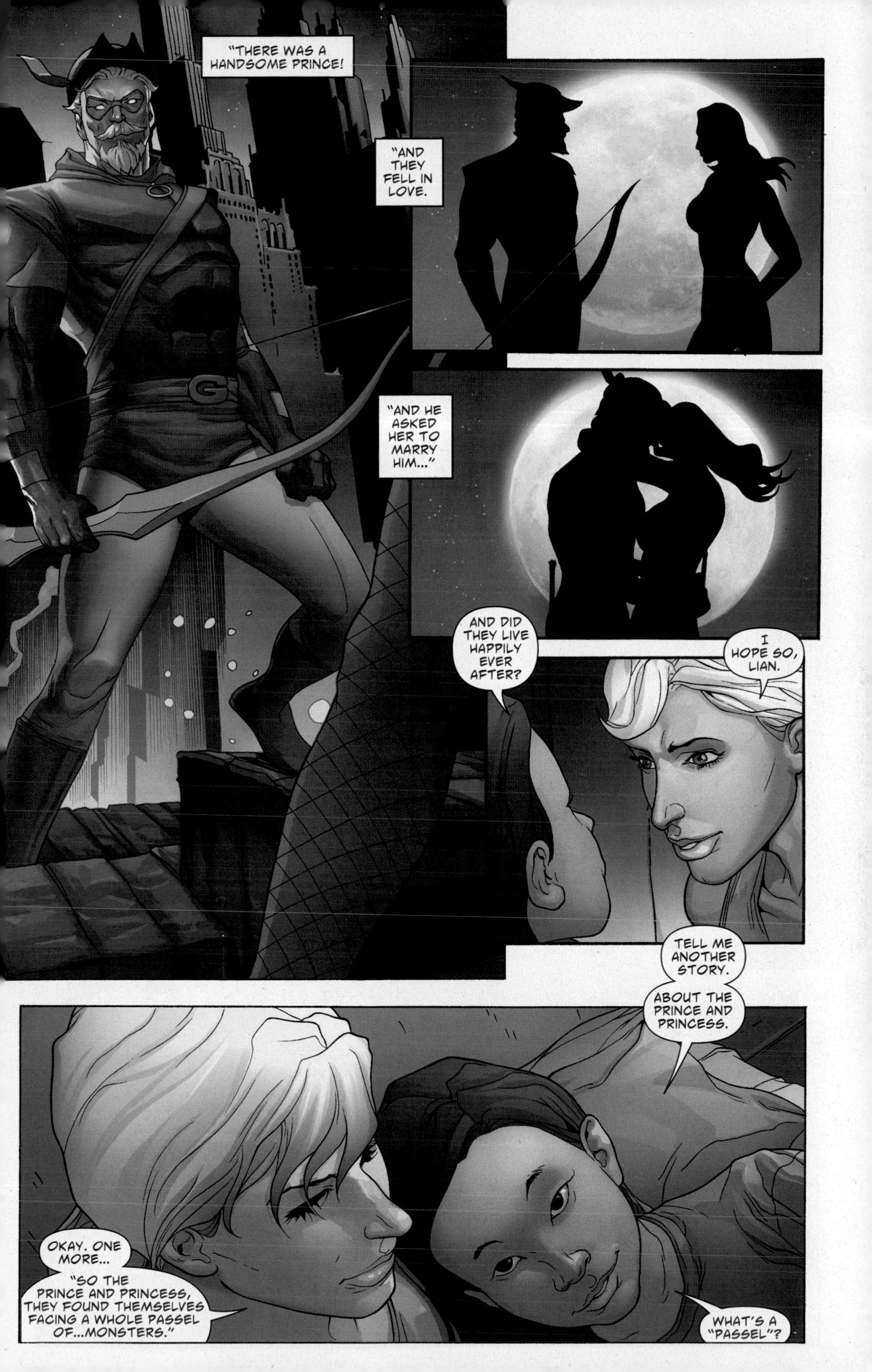
"THERE WAS A HANDSOME PRINCE!
"AND THEY FELL IN LOVE.
"AND HE ASKED HER TO MARRY HIM..."
AND DID THEY LIVE HAPPILY EVER AFTER?
I HOPE SO, LIAN.
TELL ME ANOTHER STORY.
ABOUT THE PRINCE AND PRINCESS.
OKAY. ONE MORE...
"SO THE PRINCE AND PRINCESS, THEY FOUND THEMSELVES FACING A WHOLE PASSEL OF...MONSTERS."
WHAT'S A "PASSEL"?

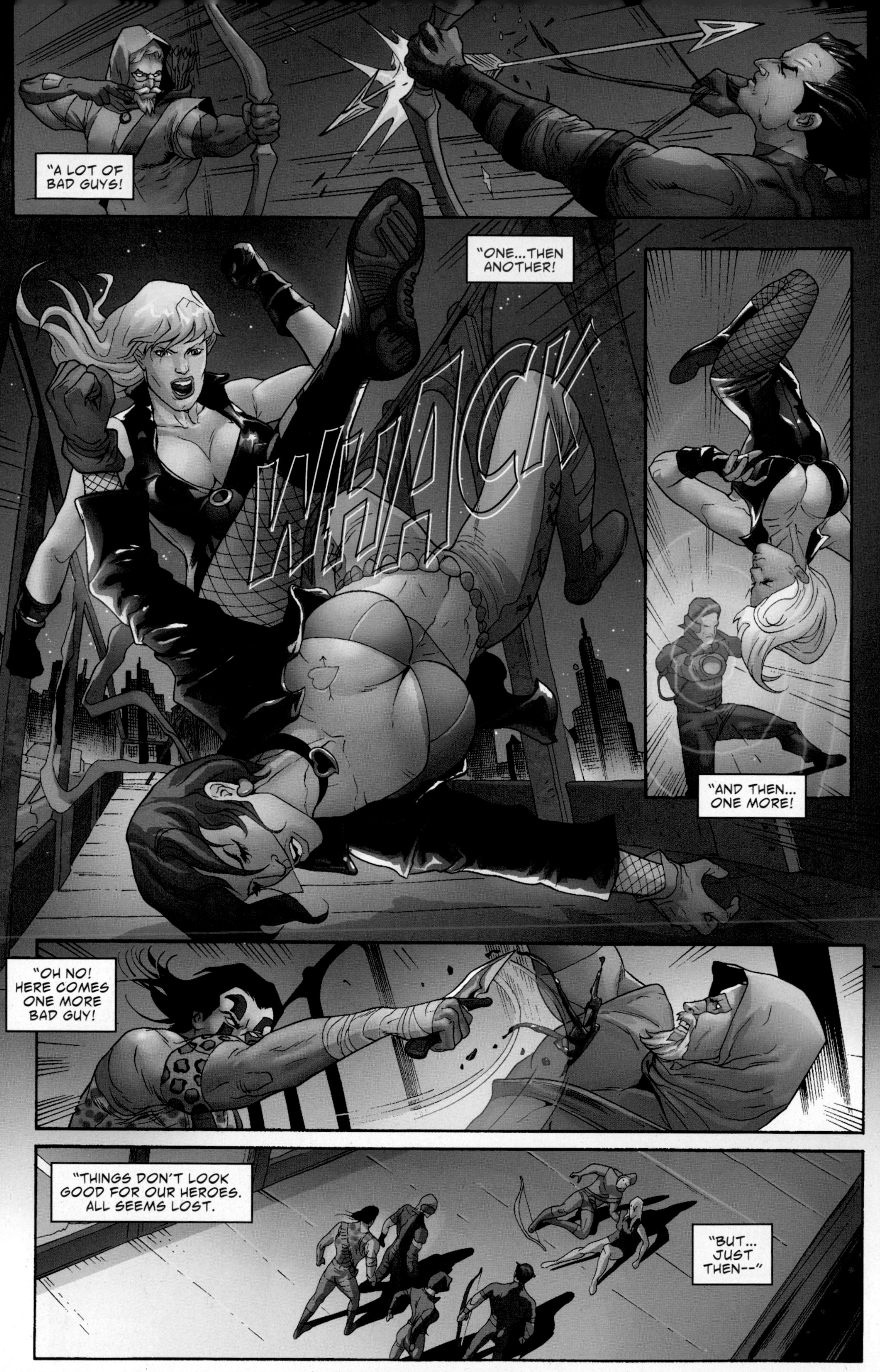
"A LOT OF
BAD GUYS!
"ONE...THEN
ANOTHER!
WHACK
"AND THEN...
ONE MORE!
"OH NO!
HERE COMES
ONE MORE
BAD GUY!
"THINGS DON'T LOOK
GOOD FOR OUR HEROES.
ALL SEEMS LOST.
"BUT...
JUST
THEN--"

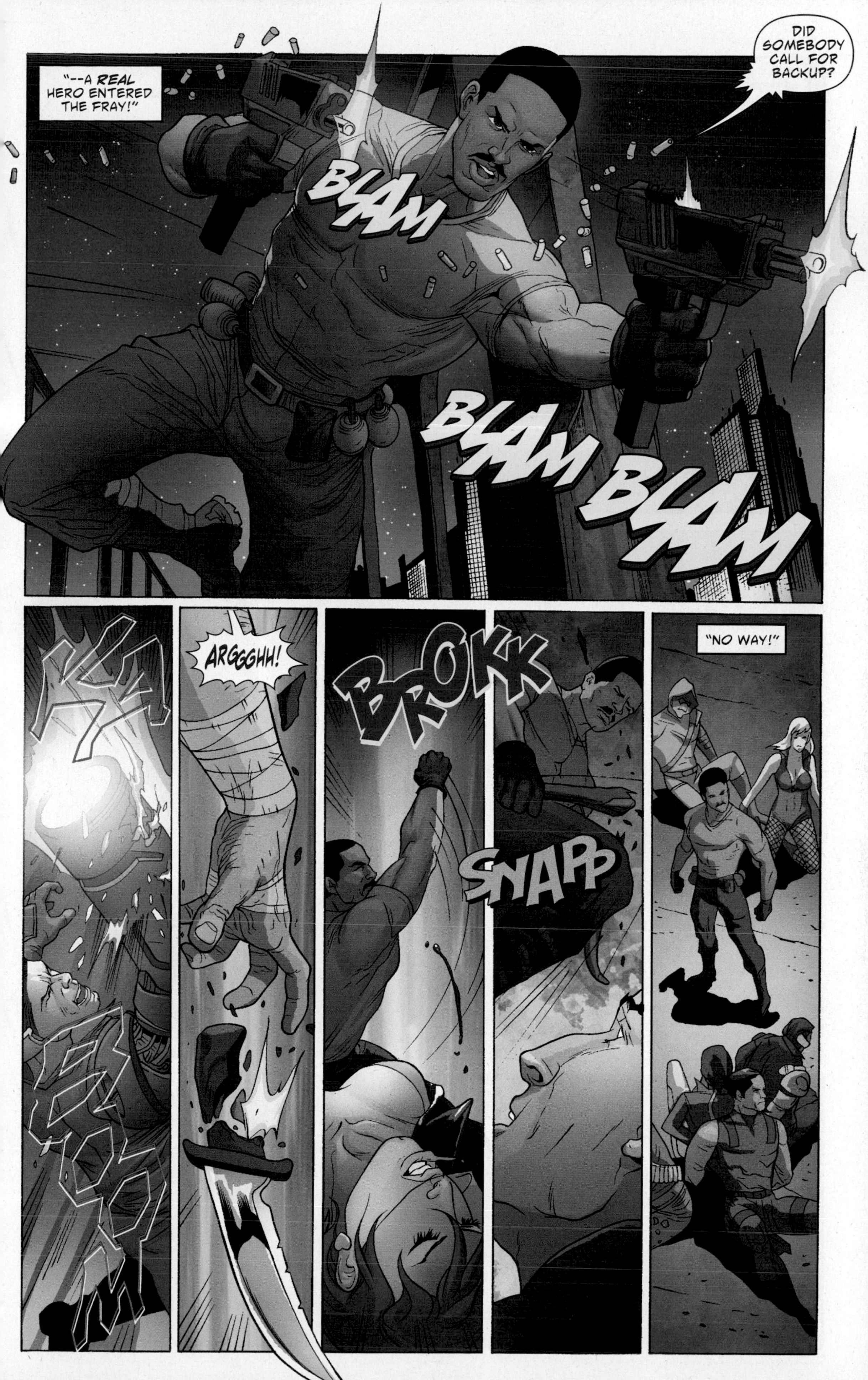
"--A *REAL* HERO ENTERED THE FRAY!"
DID SOMEBODY CALL FOR BACKUP?
BLAM
BLAM BLAM BLAM
ARGGGHH!
BROKK
SNAPP
"NO WAY!"

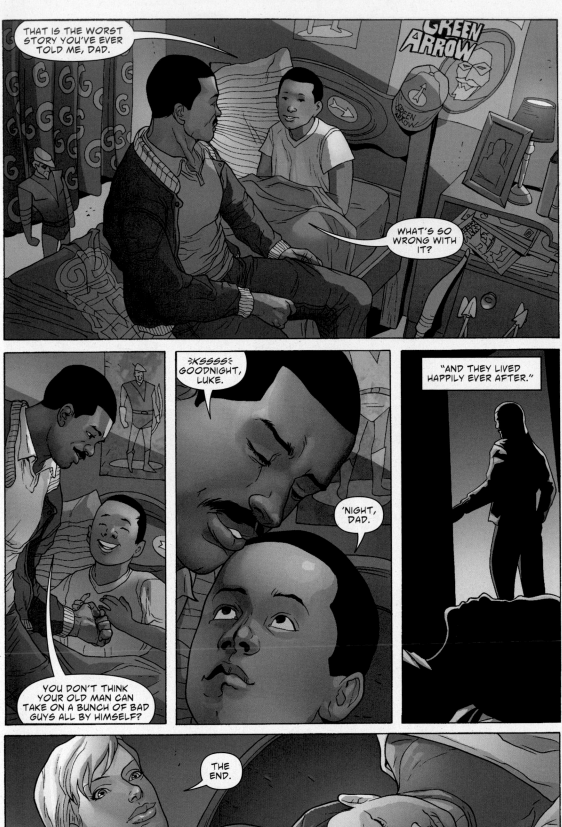

THAT IS THE WORST STORY YOU'VE EVER TOLD ME, DAD.

WHAT'S SO WRONG WITH IT?

≳KSSSS≲ GOODNIGHT, LUKE.

"AND THEY LIVED HAPPILY EVER AFTER."

'NIGHT, DAD.

YOU DON'T THINK YOUR OLD MAN CAN TAKE ON A BUNCH OF BAD GUYS ALL BY HIMSELF?

THE END.

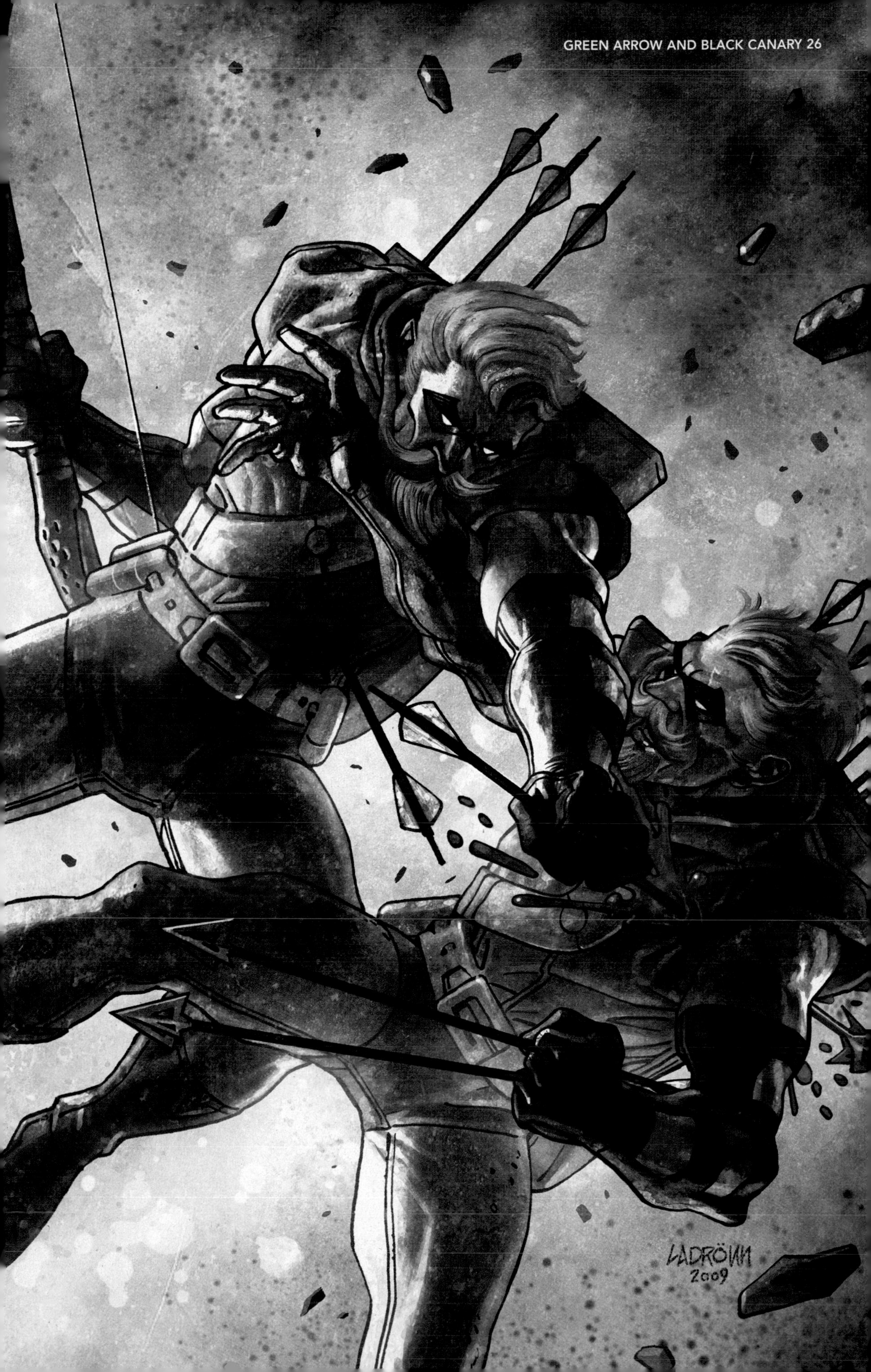
LADRÖNN
2009

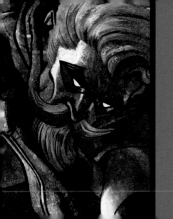

OLIVER SQUARED
Mike Norton Layouts
Bill Sienkiewicz Finishes

ANGER
Renato Guedes Penciller
José Wilson Magalhaes Inker

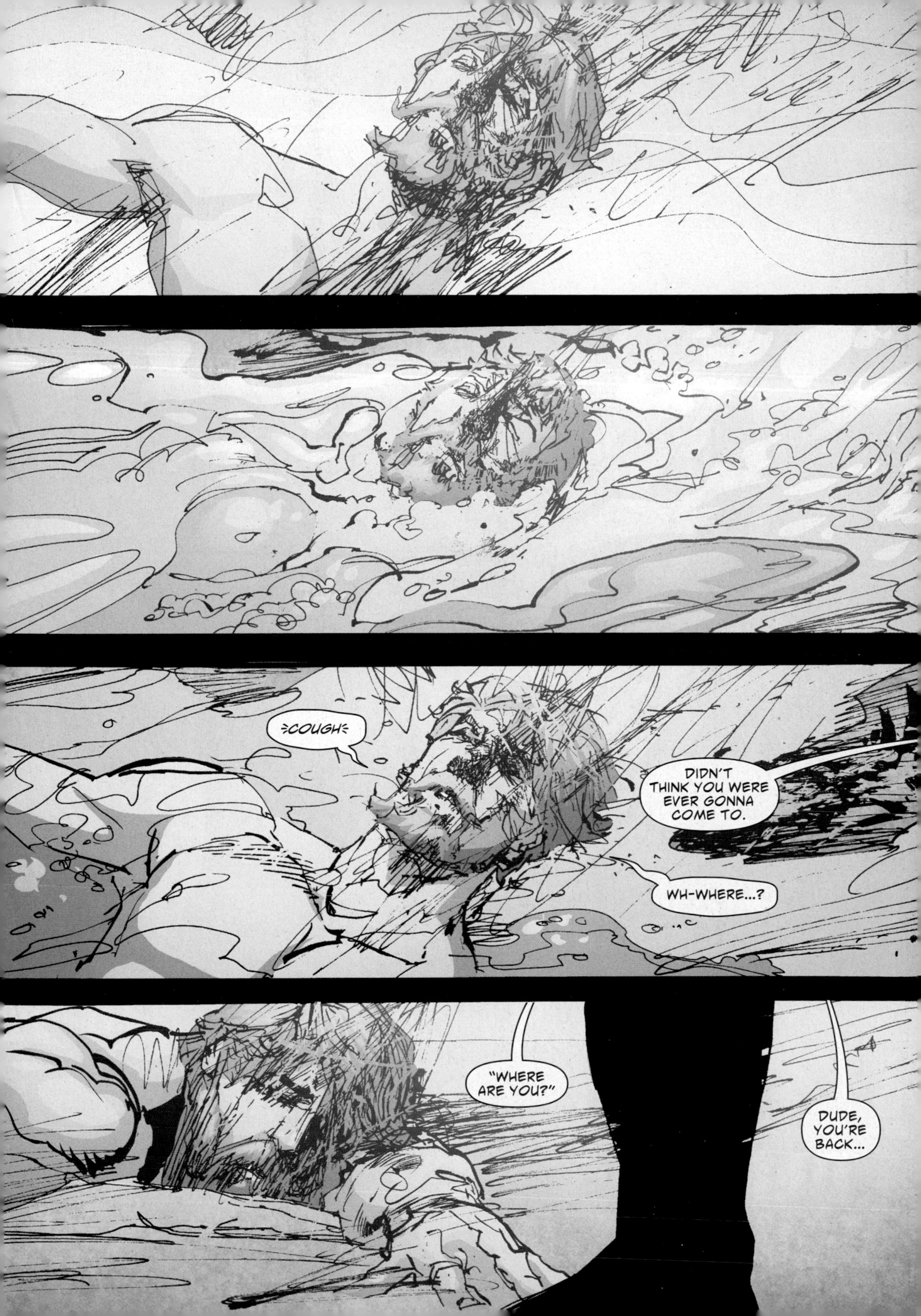

COUGH
DIDN'T THINK YOU WERE EVER GONNA COME TO.
WH-WHERE...?
"WHERE ARE YOU?"
DUDE, YOU'RE BACK...

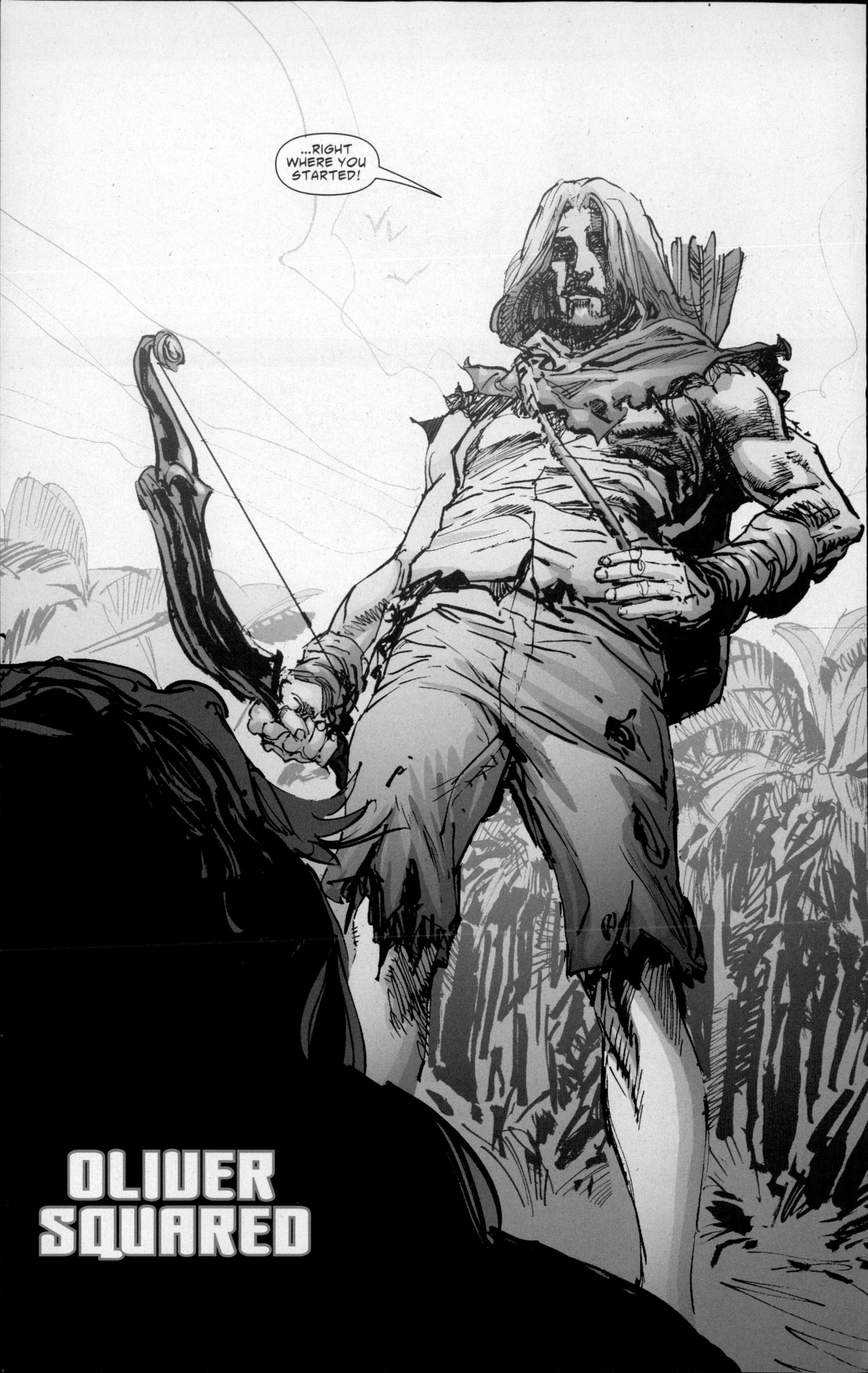
...RIGHT WHERE YOU STARTED!
OLIVER SQUARED

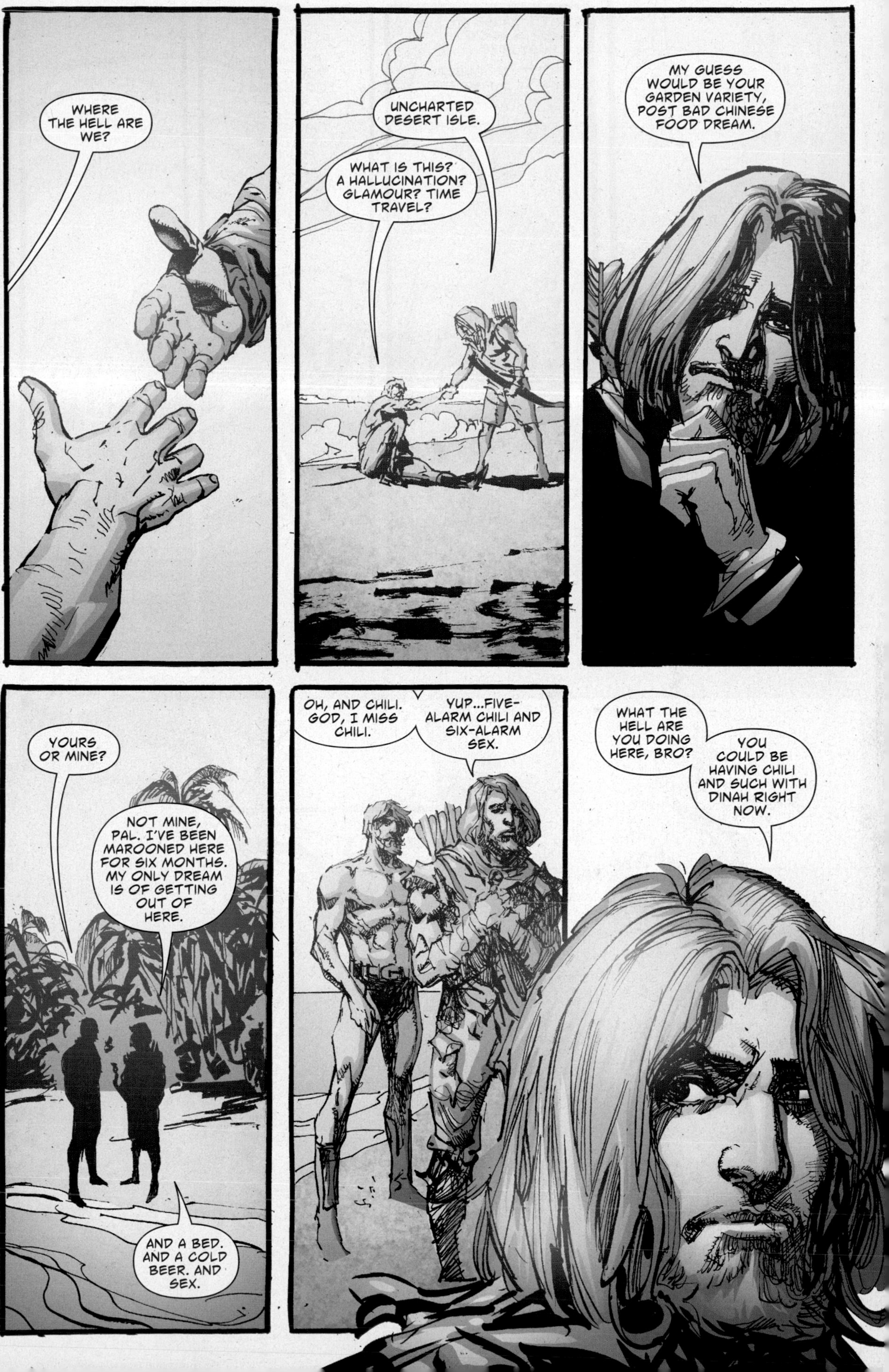
WHERE THE HELL ARE WE?
UNCHARTED DESERT ISLE.
WHAT IS THIS? A HALLUCINATION? GLAMOUR? TIME TRAVEL?
MY GUESS WOULD BE YOUR GARDEN VARIETY, POST BAD CHINESE FOOD DREAM.
YOURS OR MINE?
NOT MINE, PAL. I'VE BEEN MAROONED HERE FOR SIX MONTHS. MY ONLY DREAM IS OF GETTING OUT OF HERE.
AND A BED. AND A COLD BEER. AND SEX.
OH, AND CHILI. GOD, I MISS CHILI.
YUP...FIVE-ALARM CHILI AND SIX-ALARM SEX.
WHAT THE HELL ARE YOU DOING HERE, BRO?
YOU COULD BE HAVING CHILI AND SUCH WITH DINAH RIGHT NOW.

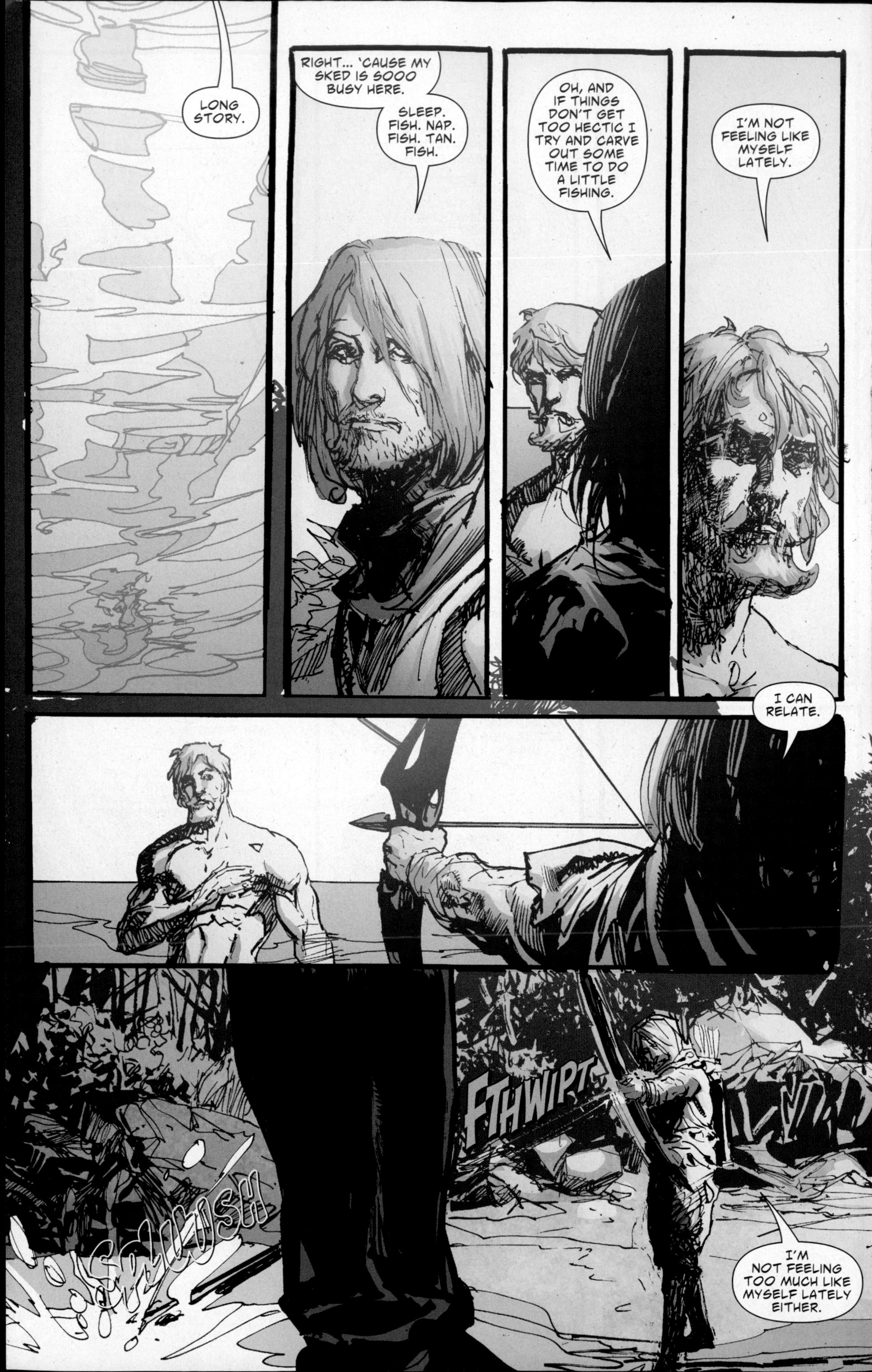
LONG STORY.
RIGHT... 'CAUSE MY SKED IS SOOO BUSY HERE.
SLEEP. FISH. NAP. FISH. TAN. FISH.
OH, AND IF THINGS DON'T GET TOO HECTIC I TRY AND CARVE OUT SOME TIME TO DO A LITTLE FISHING.
I'M NOT FEELING LIKE MYSELF LATELY.
I CAN RELATE.
FTHWIPT
SPLOOSH
I'M NOT FEELING TOO MUCH LIKE MYSELF LATELY EITHER.

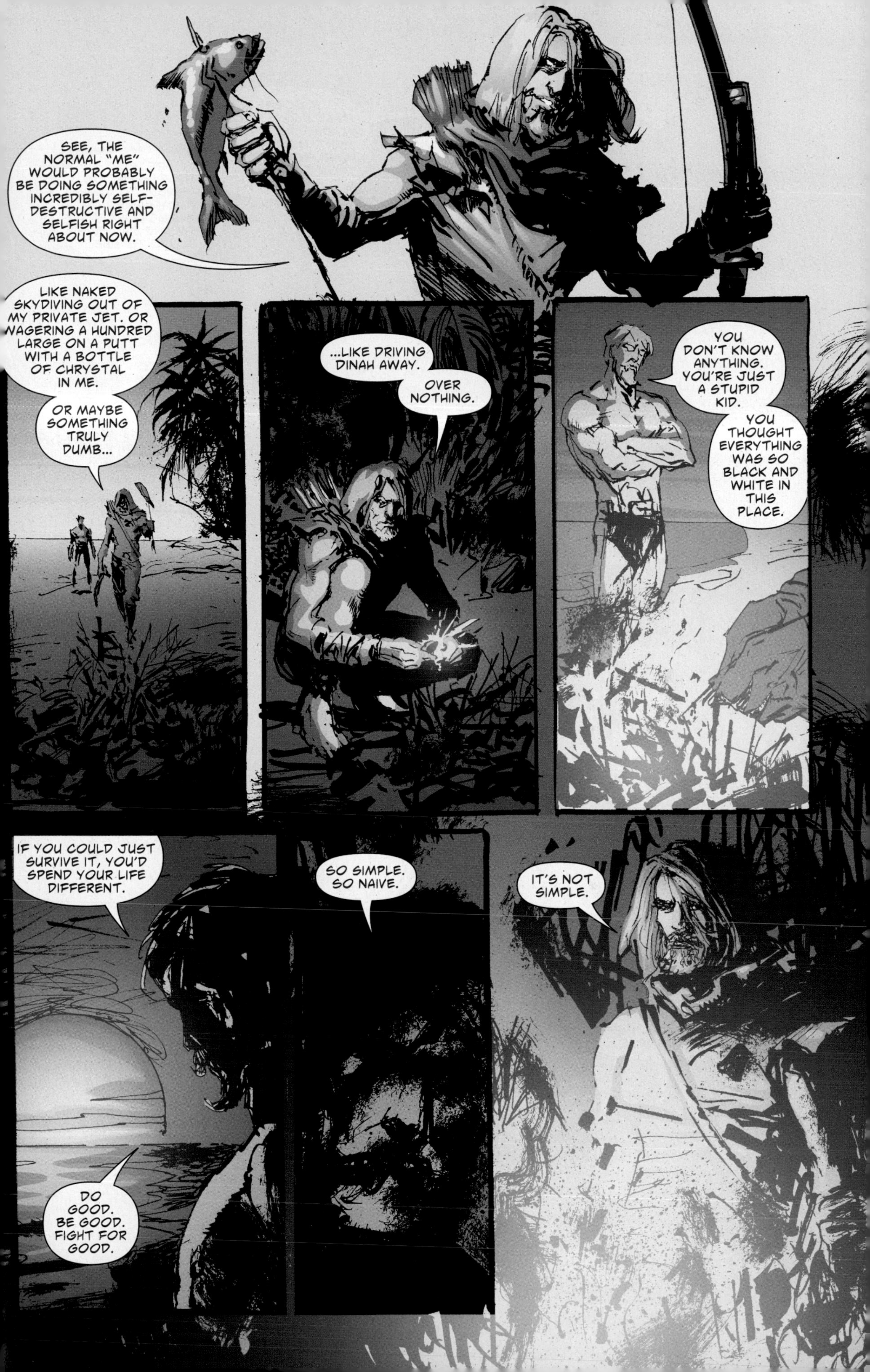
SEE, THE NORMAL "ME" WOULD PROBABLY BE DOING SOMETHING INCREDIBLY SELF-DESTRUCTIVE AND SELFISH RIGHT ABOUT NOW.
LIKE NAKED SKYDIVING OUT OF MY PRIVATE JET. OR WAGERING A HUNDRED LARGE ON A PUTT WITH A BOTTLE OF CHRYSTAL IN ME.
OR MAYBE SOMETHING TRULY DUMB...
...LIKE DRIVING DINAH AWAY.
OVER NOTHING.
YOU DON'T KNOW ANYTHING. YOU'RE JUST A STUPID KID.
YOU THOUGHT EVERYTHING WAS SO BLACK AND WHITE IN THIS PLACE.
IF YOU COULD JUST SURVIVE IT, YOU'D SPEND YOUR LIFE DIFFERENT.
DO GOOD. BE GOOD. FIGHT FOR GOOD.
SO SIMPLE. SO NAIVE.
IT'S NOT SIMPLE.

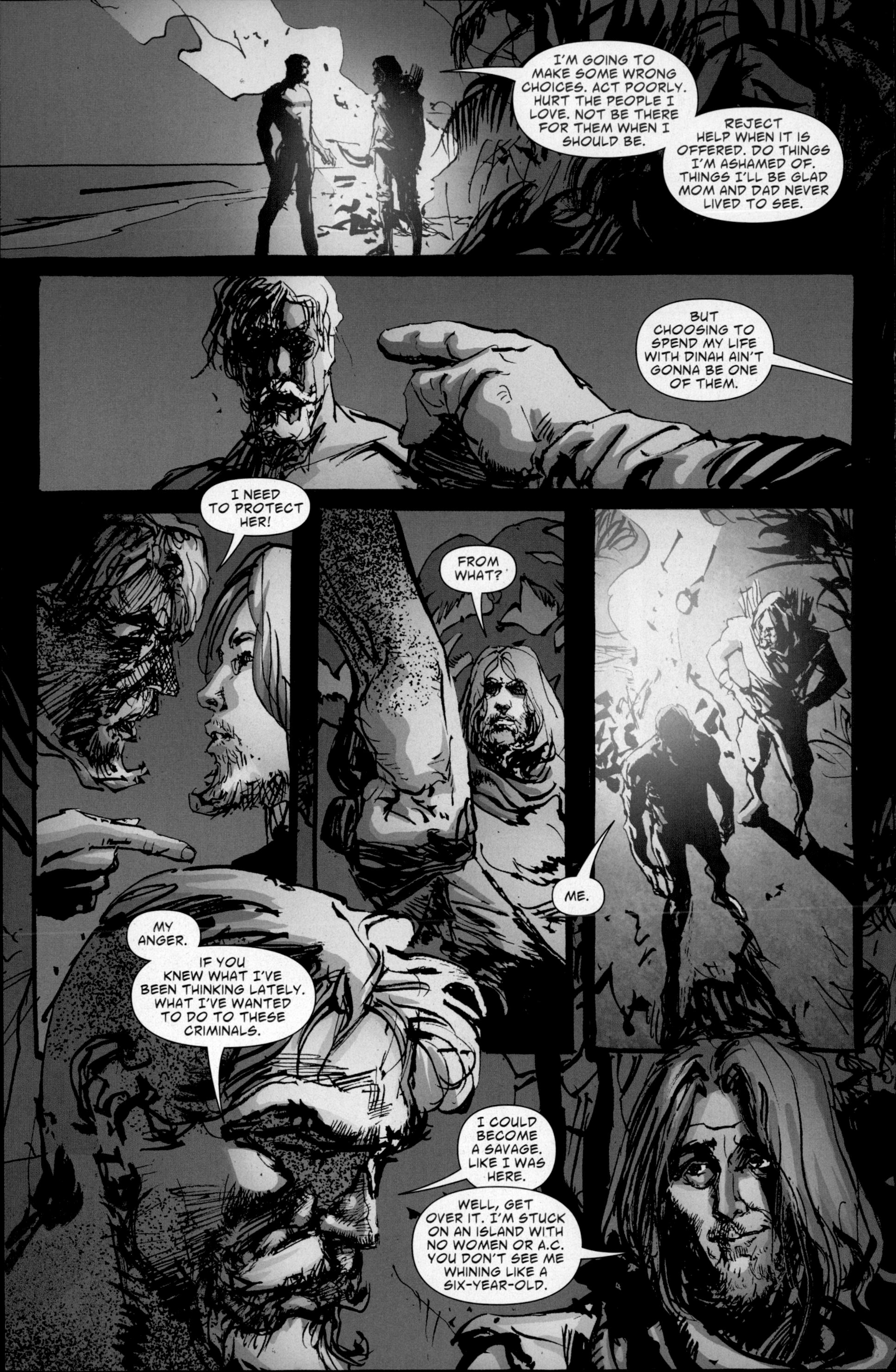
I'M GOING TO MAKE SOME WRONG CHOICES. ACT POORLY. HURT THE PEOPLE I LOVE. NOT BE THERE FOR THEM WHEN I SHOULD BE.
REJECT HELP WHEN IT IS OFFERED. DO THINGS I'M ASHAMED OF. THINGS I'LL BE GLAD MOM AND DAD NEVER LIVED TO SEE.
BUT CHOOSING TO SPEND MY LIFE WITH DINAH AIN'T GONNA BE ONE OF THEM.
I NEED TO PROTECT HER!
FROM WHAT?
ME.
MY ANGER.
IF YOU KNEW WHAT I'VE BEEN THINKING LATELY. WHAT I'VE WANTED TO DO TO THESE CRIMINALS.
I COULD BECOME A SAVAGE. LIKE I WAS HERE.
WELL, GET OVER IT. I'M STUCK ON AN ISLAND WITH NO WOMEN OR A.C. YOU DON'T SEE ME WHINING LIKE A SIX-YEAR-OLD.

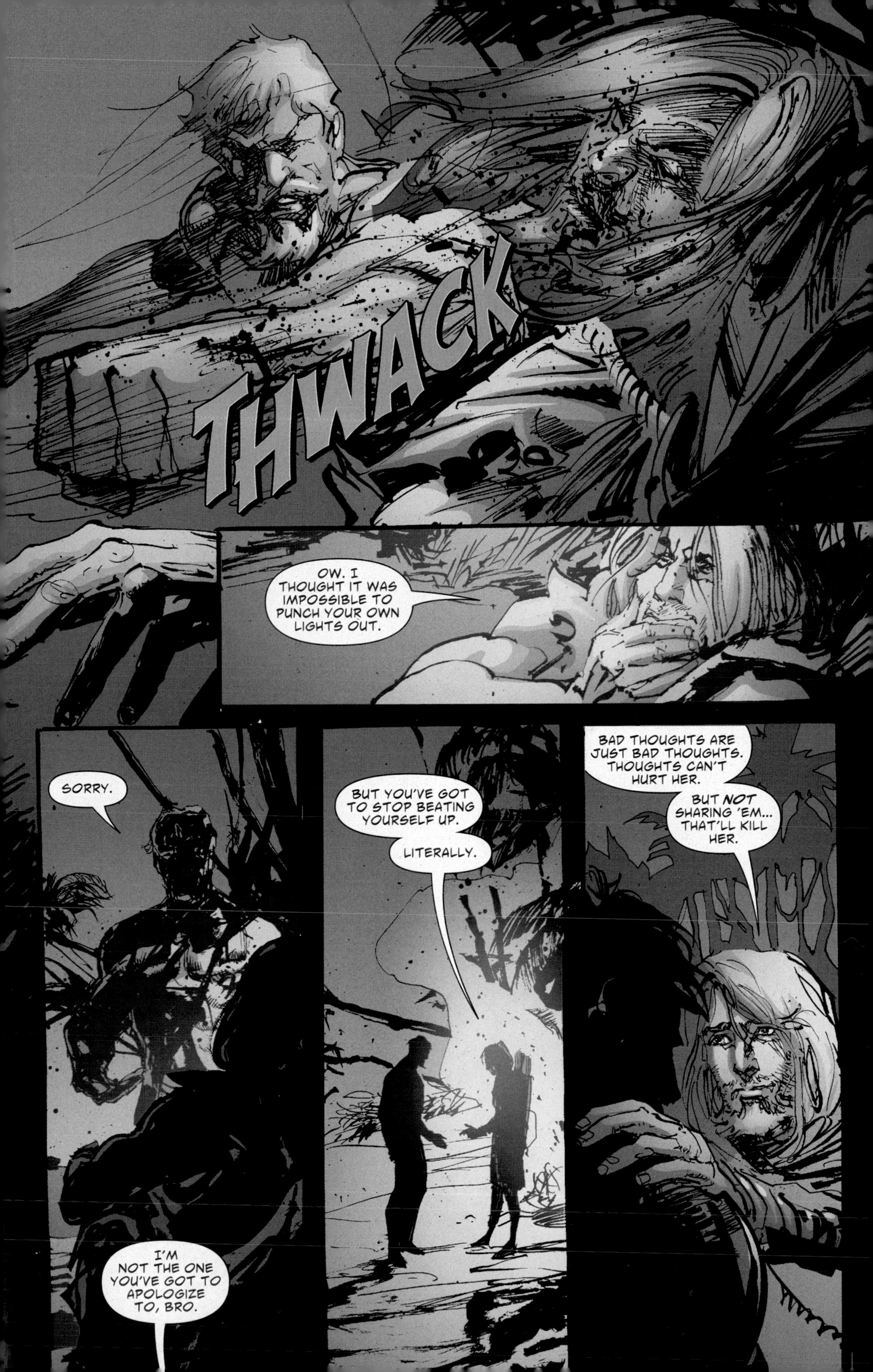
THWACK
OW. I THOUGHT IT WAS IMPOSSIBLE TO PUNCH YOUR OWN LIGHTS OUT.
SORRY.
I'M NOT THE ONE YOU'VE GOT TO APOLOGIZE TO, BRO.
BUT YOU'VE GOT TO STOP BEATING YOURSELF UP.
LITERALLY.
BAD THOUGHTS ARE JUST BAD THOUGHTS. THOUGHTS CAN'T HURT HER.
BUT NOT SHARING 'EM... THAT'LL KILL HER.

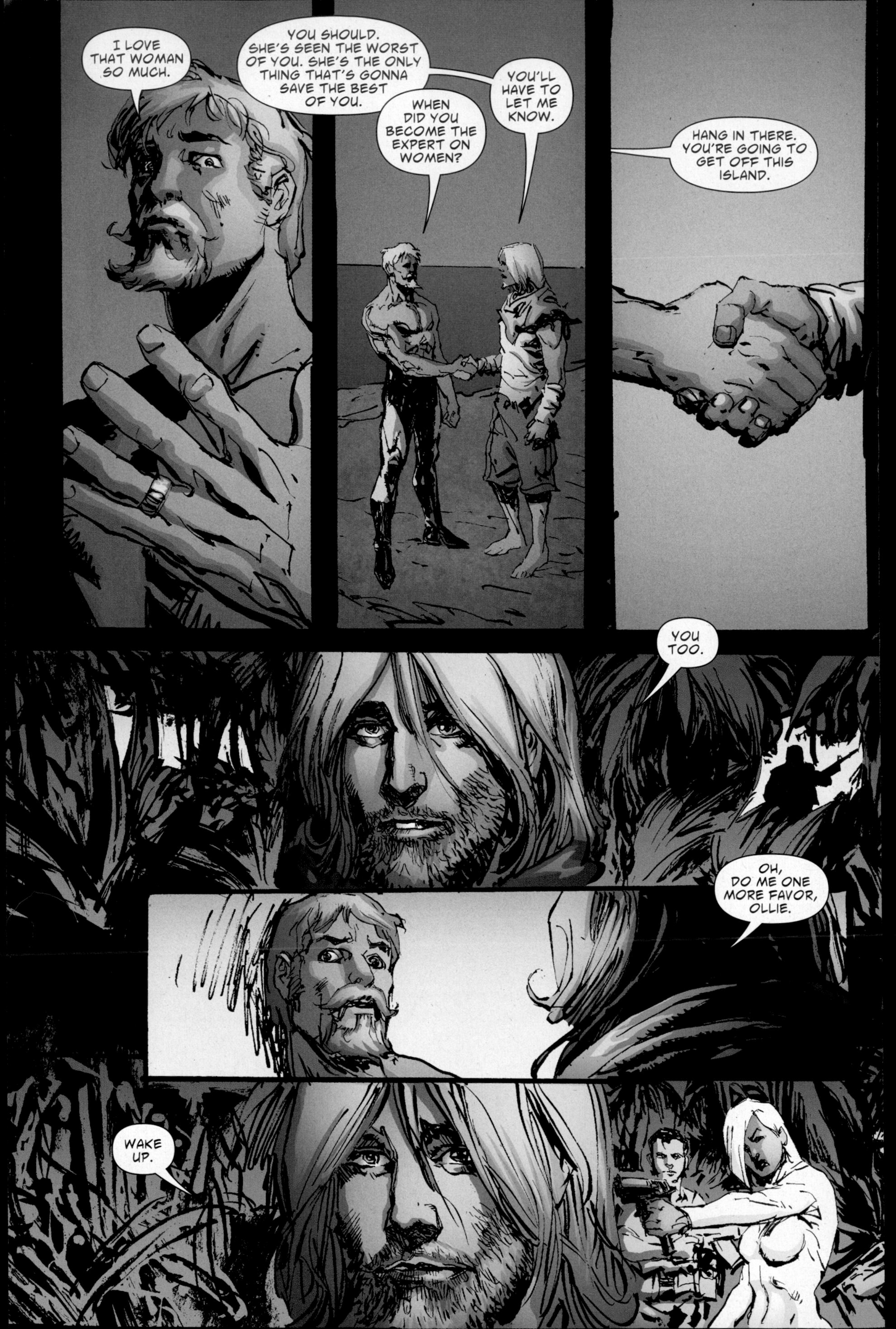
I LOVE THAT WOMAN SO MUCH.
YOU SHOULD. SHE'S SEEN THE WORST OF YOU. SHE'S THE ONLY THING THAT'S GONNA SAVE THE BEST OF YOU.
WHEN DID YOU BECOME THE EXPERT ON WOMEN?
YOU'LL HAVE TO LET ME KNOW.
HANG IN THERE. YOU'RE GOING TO GET OFF THIS ISLAND.
YOU TOO.
OH, DO ME ONE MORE FAVOR, OLLIE.
WAKE UP.

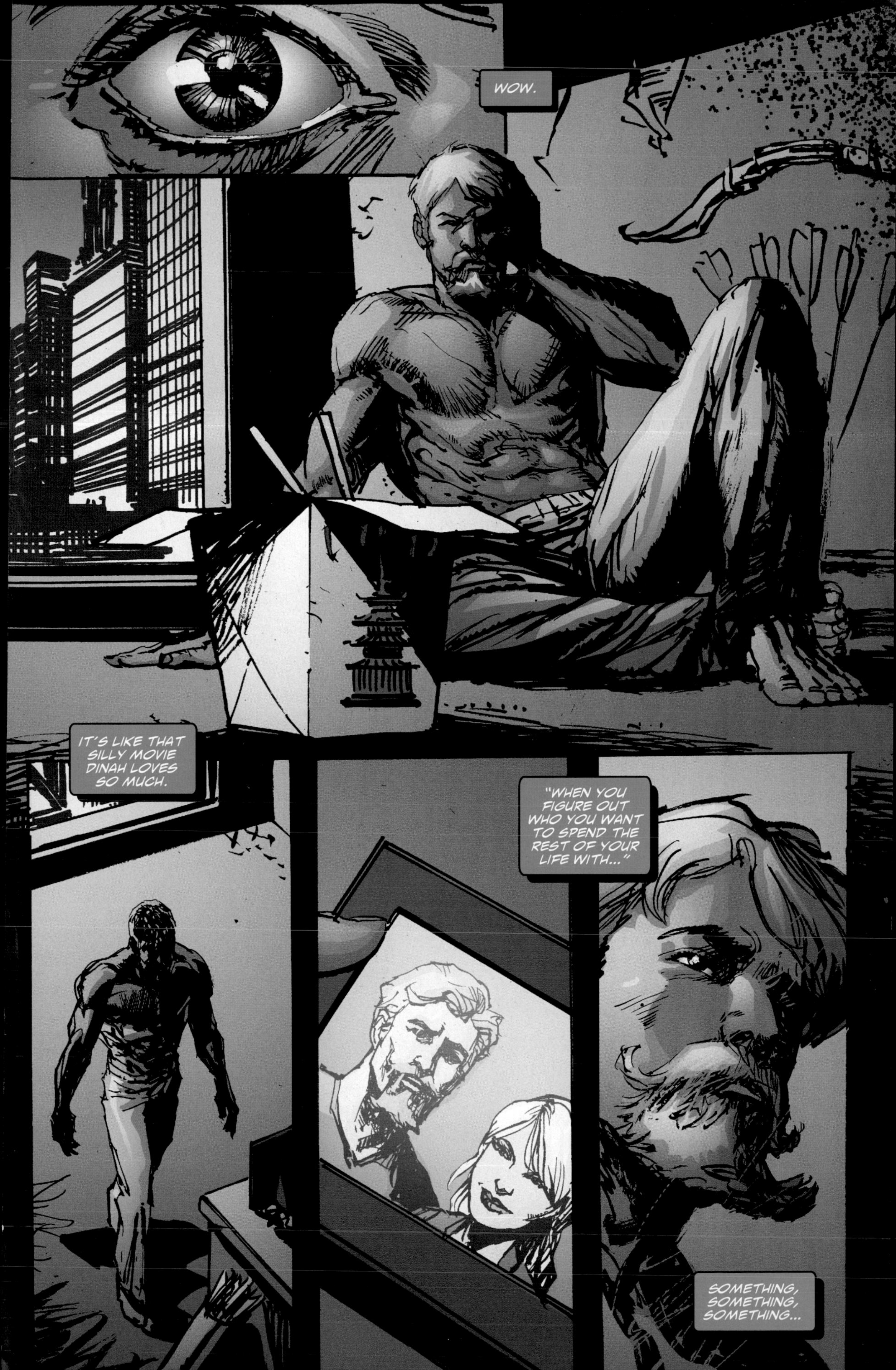
WOW.
IT'S LIKE THAT SILLY MOVIE DINAH LOVES SO MUCH.
"WHEN YOU FIGURE OUT WHO YOU WANT TO SPEND THE REST OF YOUR LIFE WITH..."
SOMETHING, SOMETHING, SOMETHING...

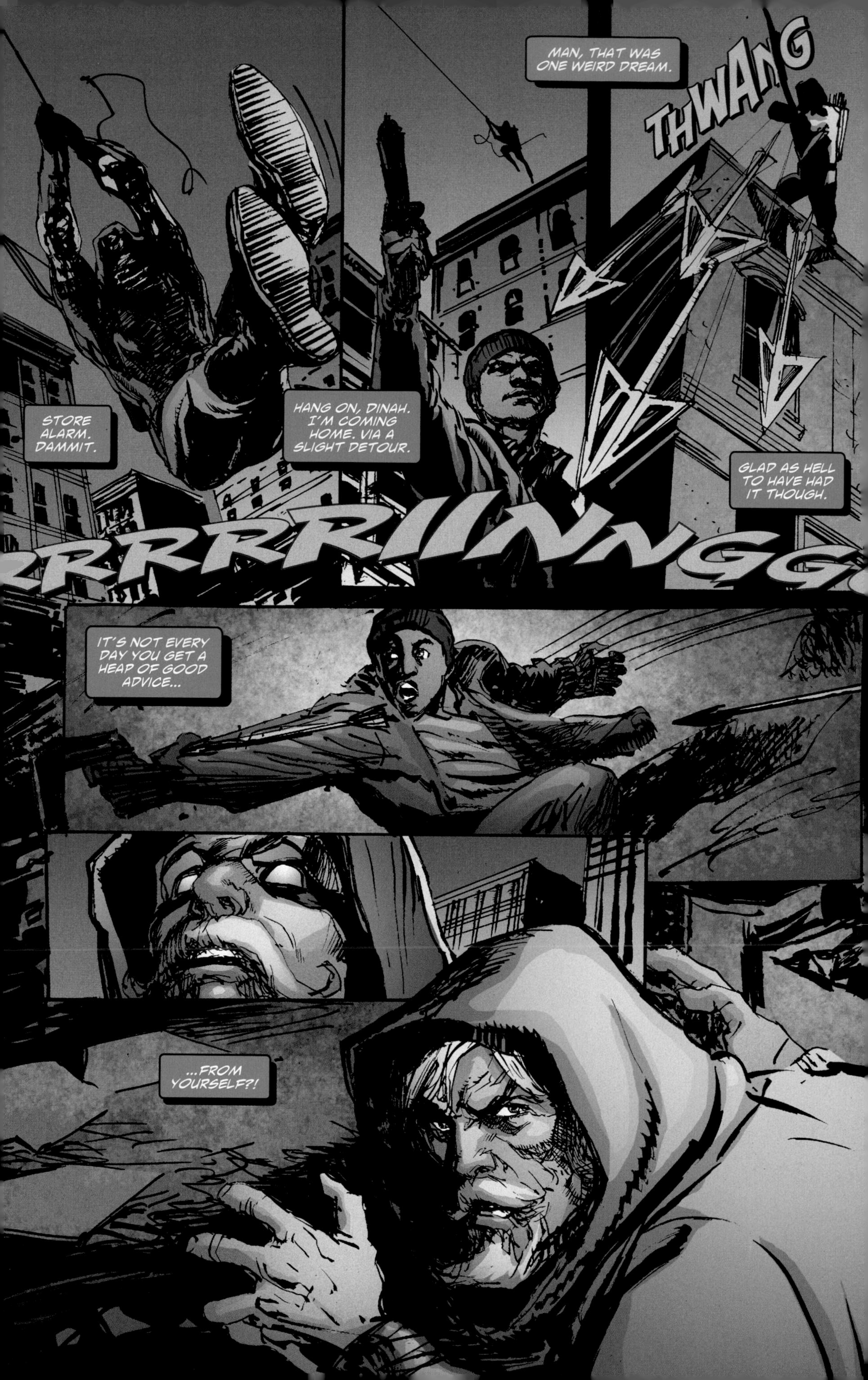
STORE ALARM. DAMMIT.
HANG ON, DINAH. I'M COMING HOME. VIA A SLIGHT DETOUR.
MAN, THAT WAS ONE WEIRD DREAM.
THWANG
GLAD AS HELL TO HAVE HAD IT THOUGH.
RRRRRRIINNGG
IT'S NOT EVERY DAY YOU GET A HEAP OF GOOD ADVICE...
...FROM YOURSELF?!

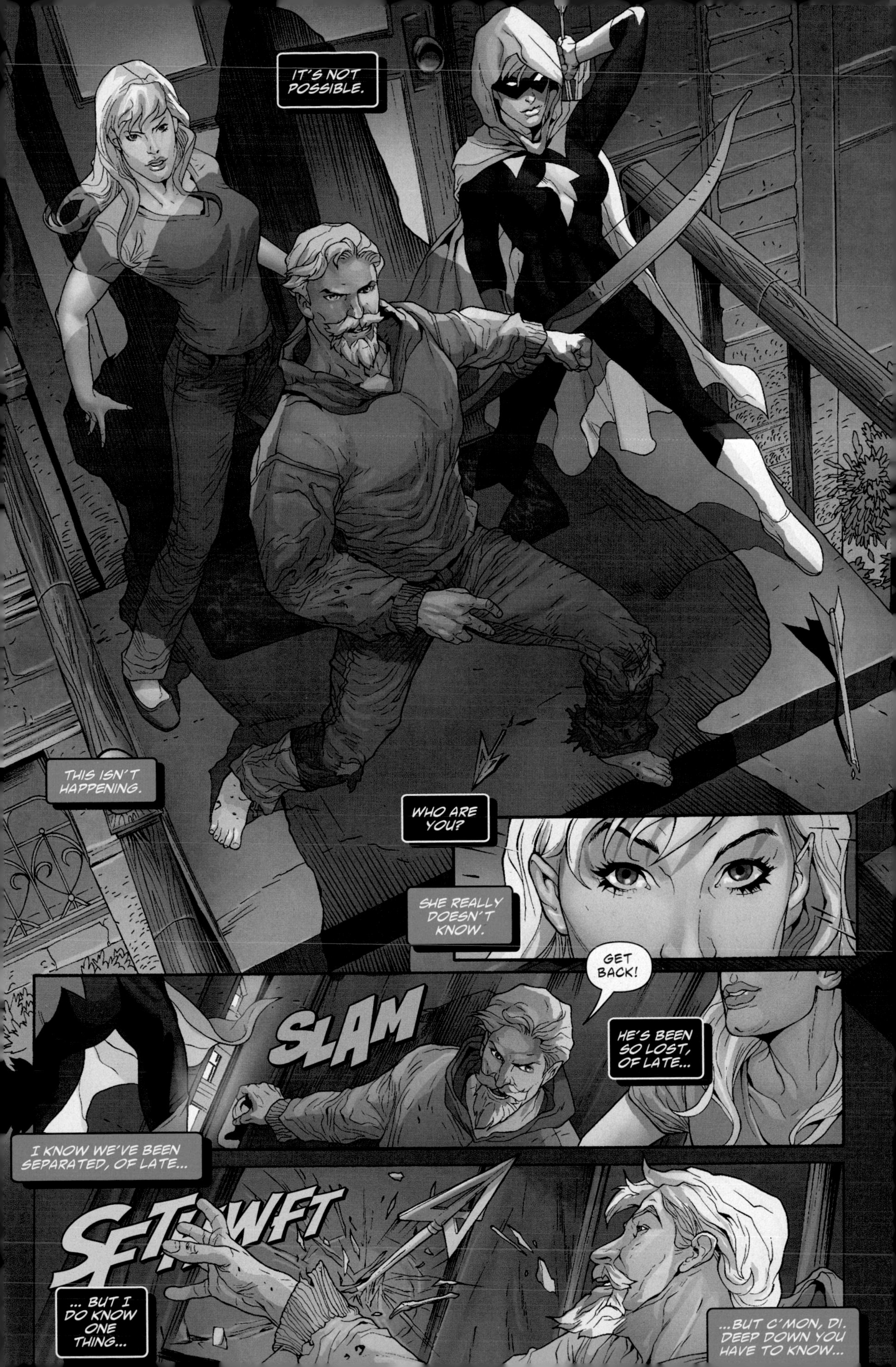
IT'S NOT POSSIBLE.
THIS ISN'T HAPPENING.
WHO ARE YOU?
SHE REALLY DOESN'T KNOW.
GET BACK!
SLAM
HE'S BEEN SO LOST, OF LATE...
I KNOW WE'VE BEEN SEPARATED, OF LATE...
... BUT I DO KNOW ONE THING...
...BUT C'MON, DI. DEEP DOWN YOU HAVE TO KNOW...

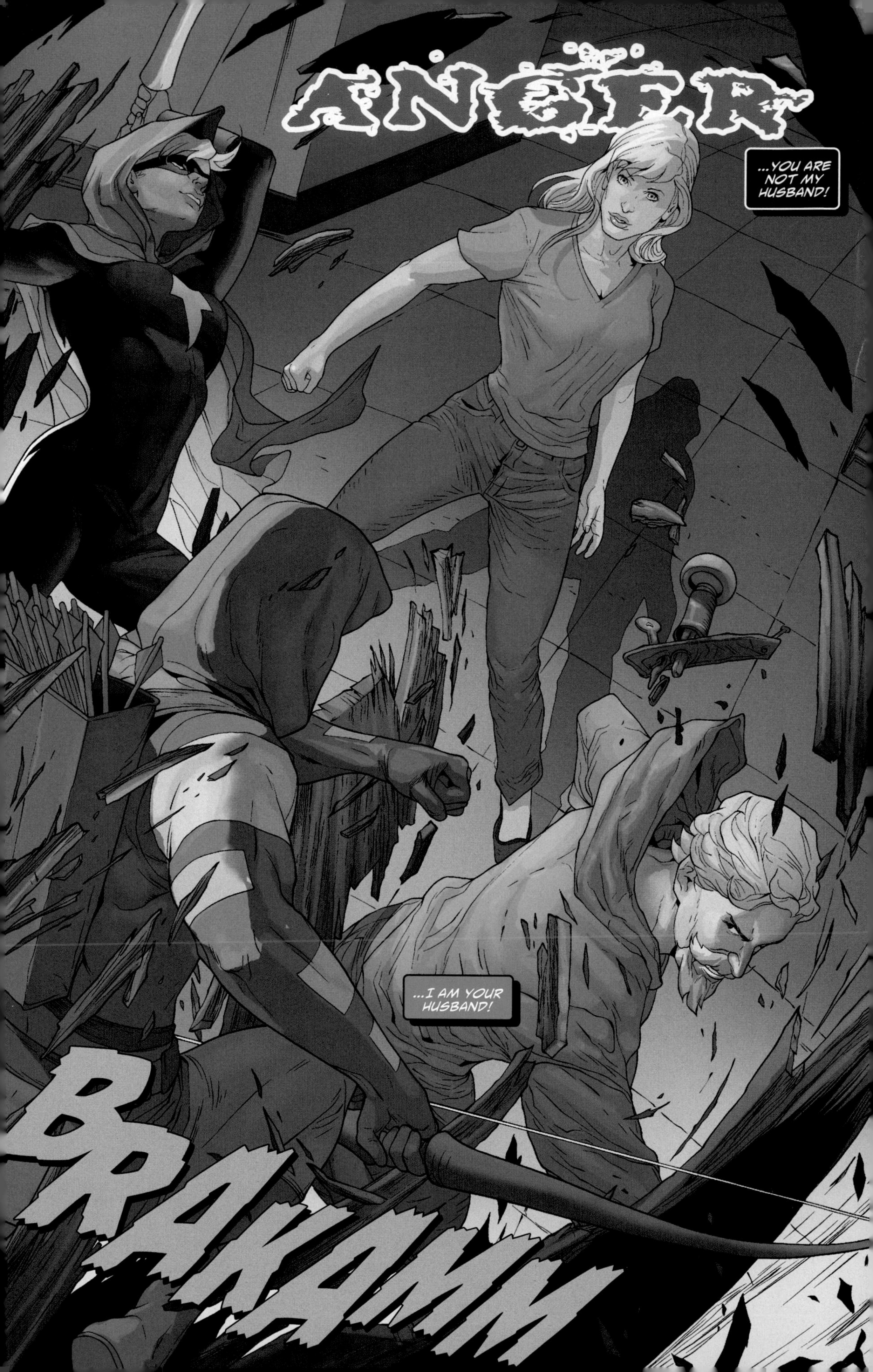
ANGER
...YOU ARE NOT MY HUSBAND!
...I AM YOUR HUSBAND!
BRAKAMM

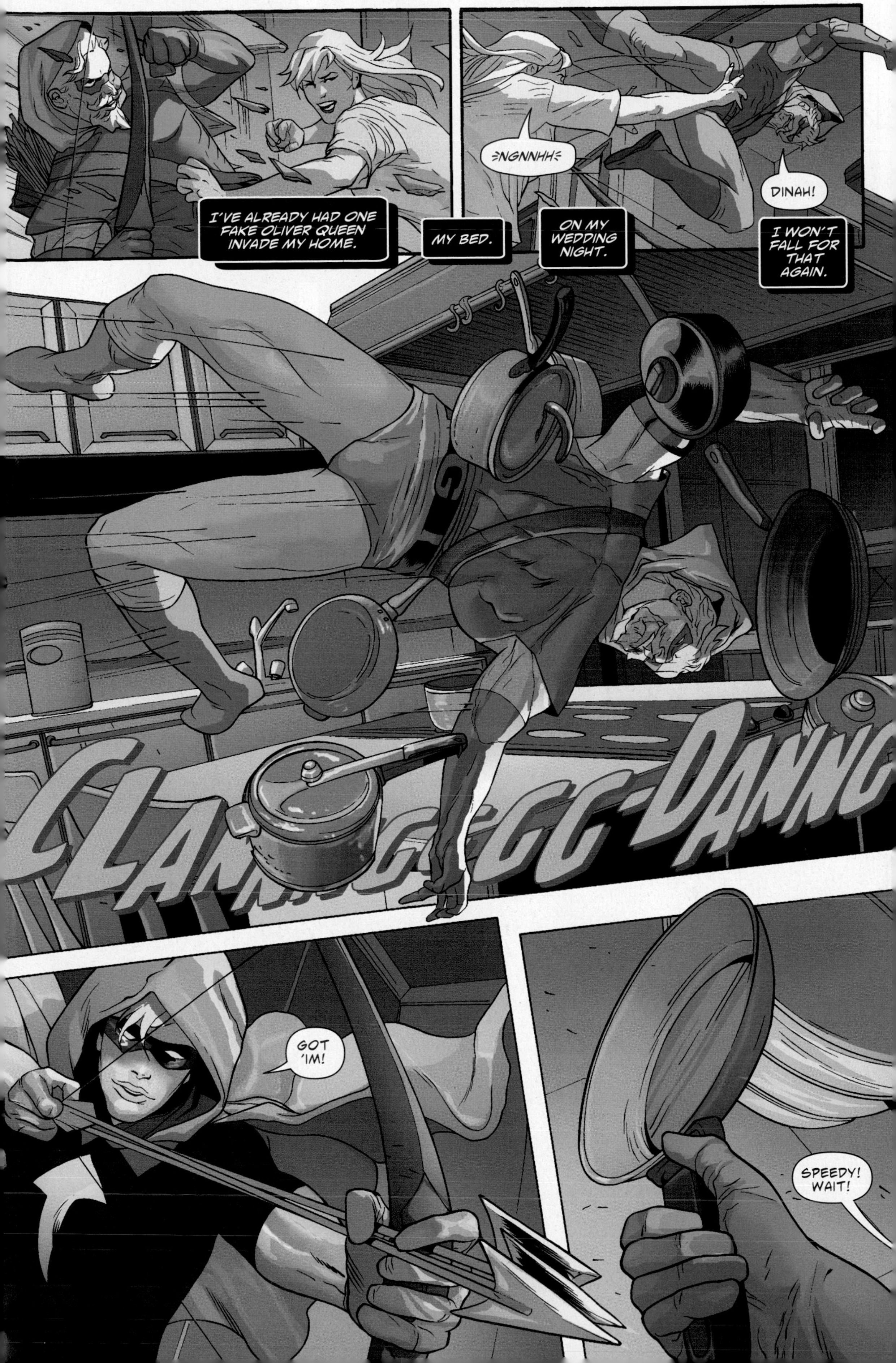

I'VE ALREADY HAD ONE FAKE OLIVER QUEEN INVADE MY HOME.
MY BED.
NGNNHH
ON MY WEDDING NIGHT.
DINAH!
I WON'T FALL FOR THAT AGAIN.
CLANNGGGG-DANNG
GOT 'IM!
SPEEDY! WAIT!

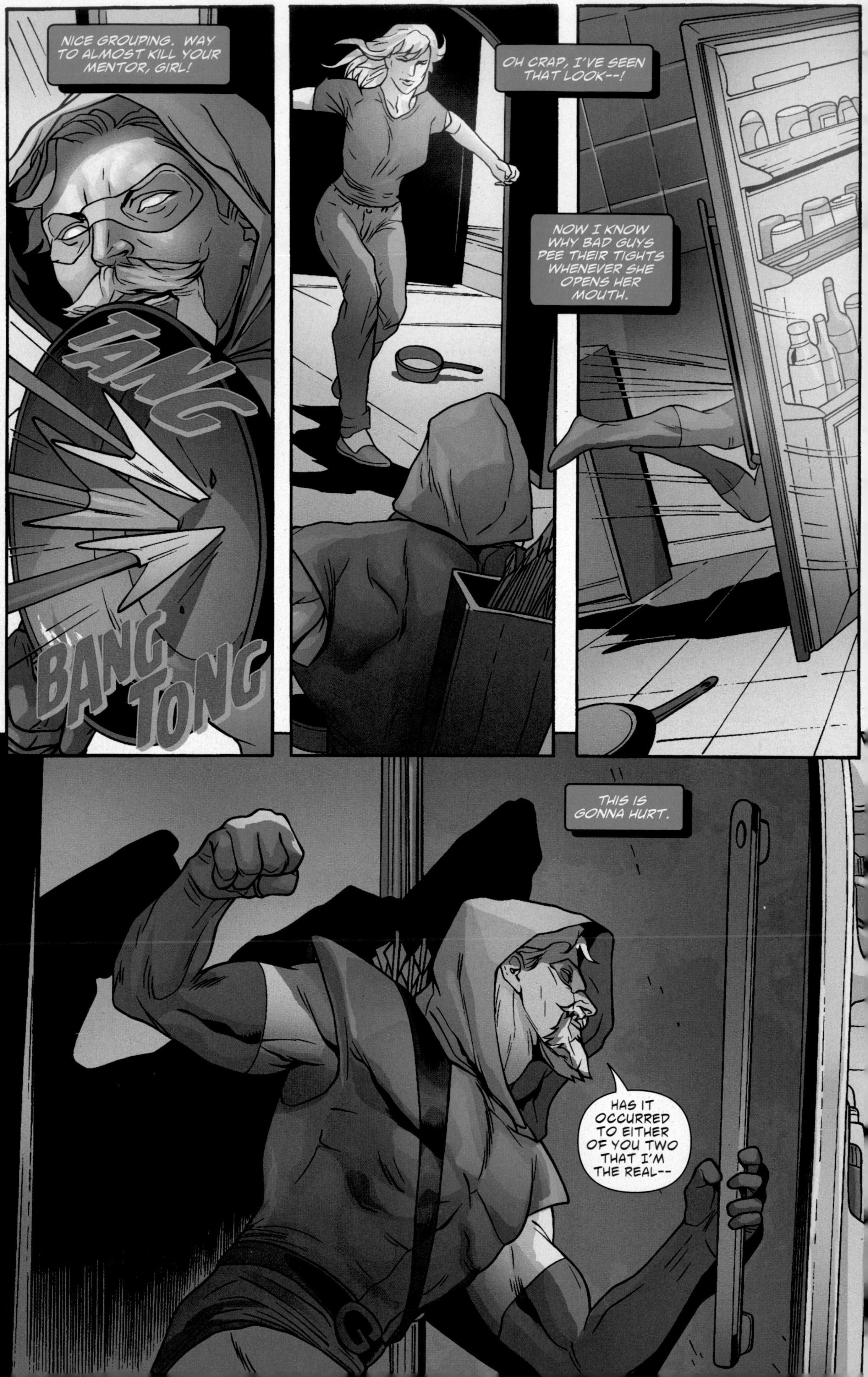
NICE GROUPING. WAY TO ALMOST KILL YOUR MENTOR, GIRL!
TANG
BANG
TONG
OH CRAP, I'VE SEEN THAT LOOK--!
NOW I KNOW WHY BAD GUYS PEE THEIR TIGHTS WHENEVER SHE OPENS HER MOUTH.
THIS IS GONNA HURT.
HAS IT OCCURRED TO EITHER OF YOU TWO THAT I'M THE REAL--

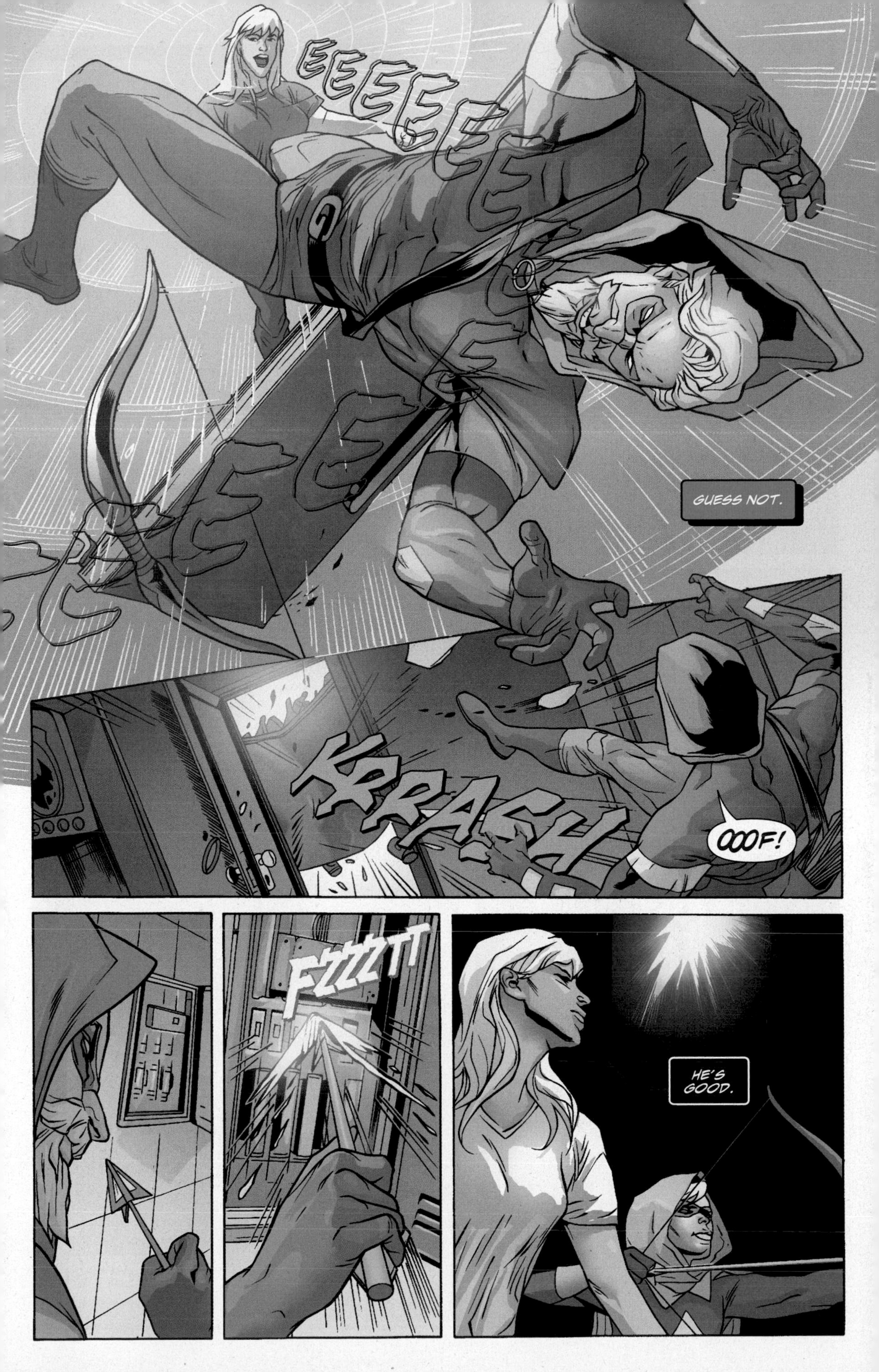
EEEEEEEEEEEEEEEE
GUESS NOT.
KRRACH
OOOF!
FZZZZTT
HE'S GOOD.

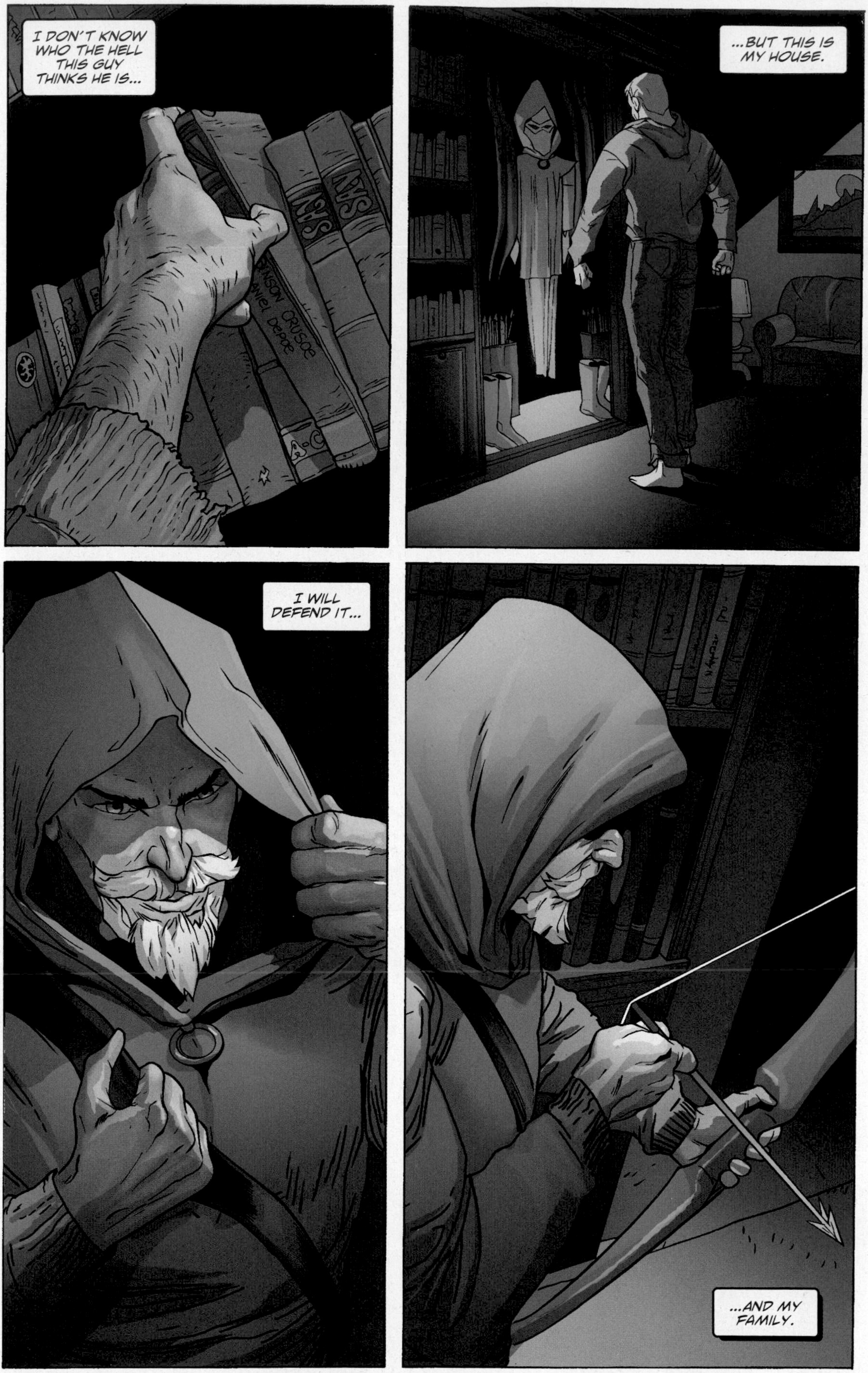

I DON'T KNOW WHO THE HELL THIS GUY THINKS HE IS...
...BUT THIS IS MY HOUSE.
I WILL DEFEND IT...
...AND MY FAMILY.

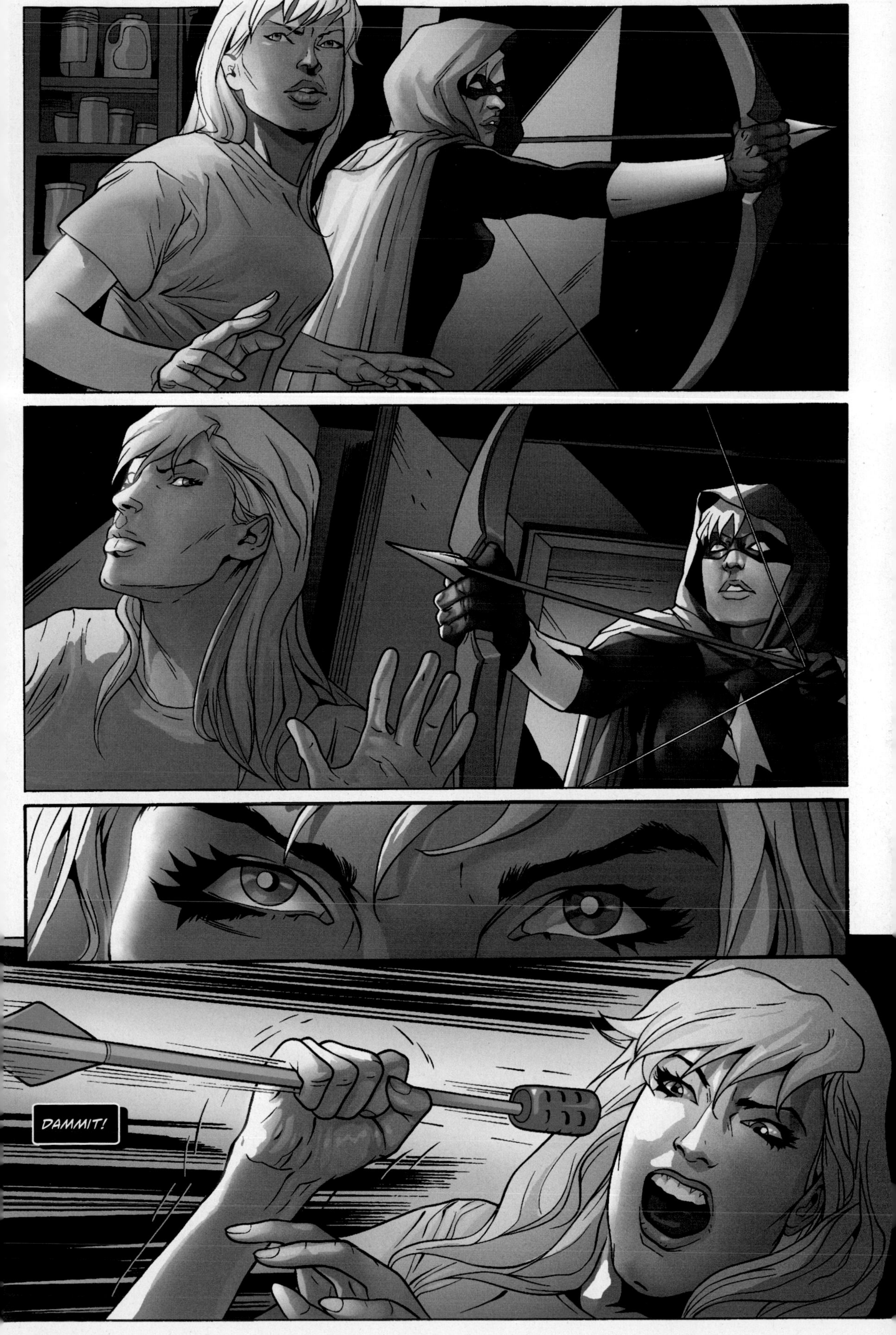
DAMMIT!

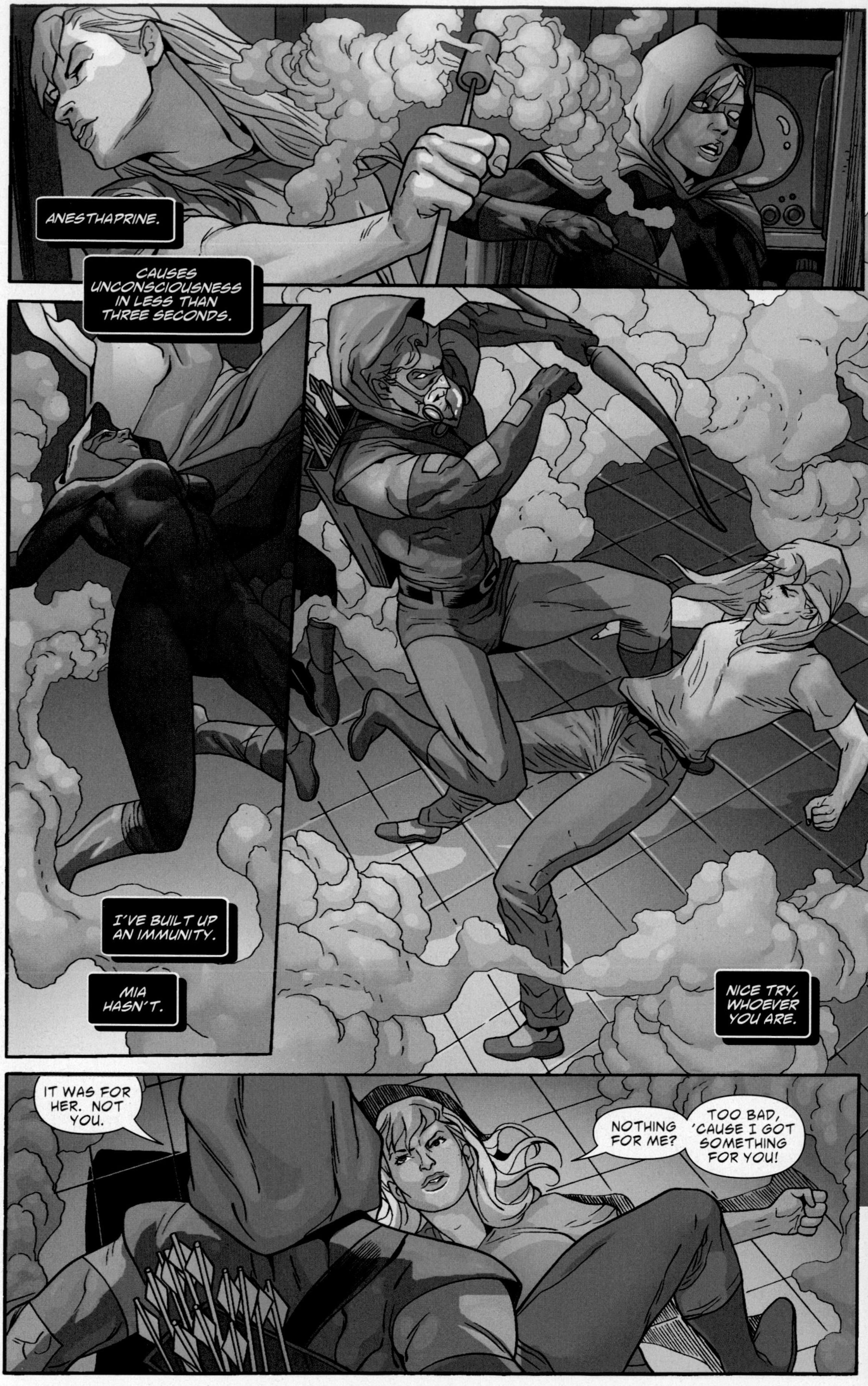
ANESTHAPRINE.
CAUSES UNCONSCIOUSNESS IN LESS THAN THREE SECONDS.
I'VE BUILT UP AN IMMUNITY.
MIA HASN'T.
NICE TRY, WHOEVER YOU ARE.
IT WAS FOR HER. NOT YOU.
NOTHING FOR ME?
TOO BAD, 'CAUSE I GOT SOMETHING FOR YOU!

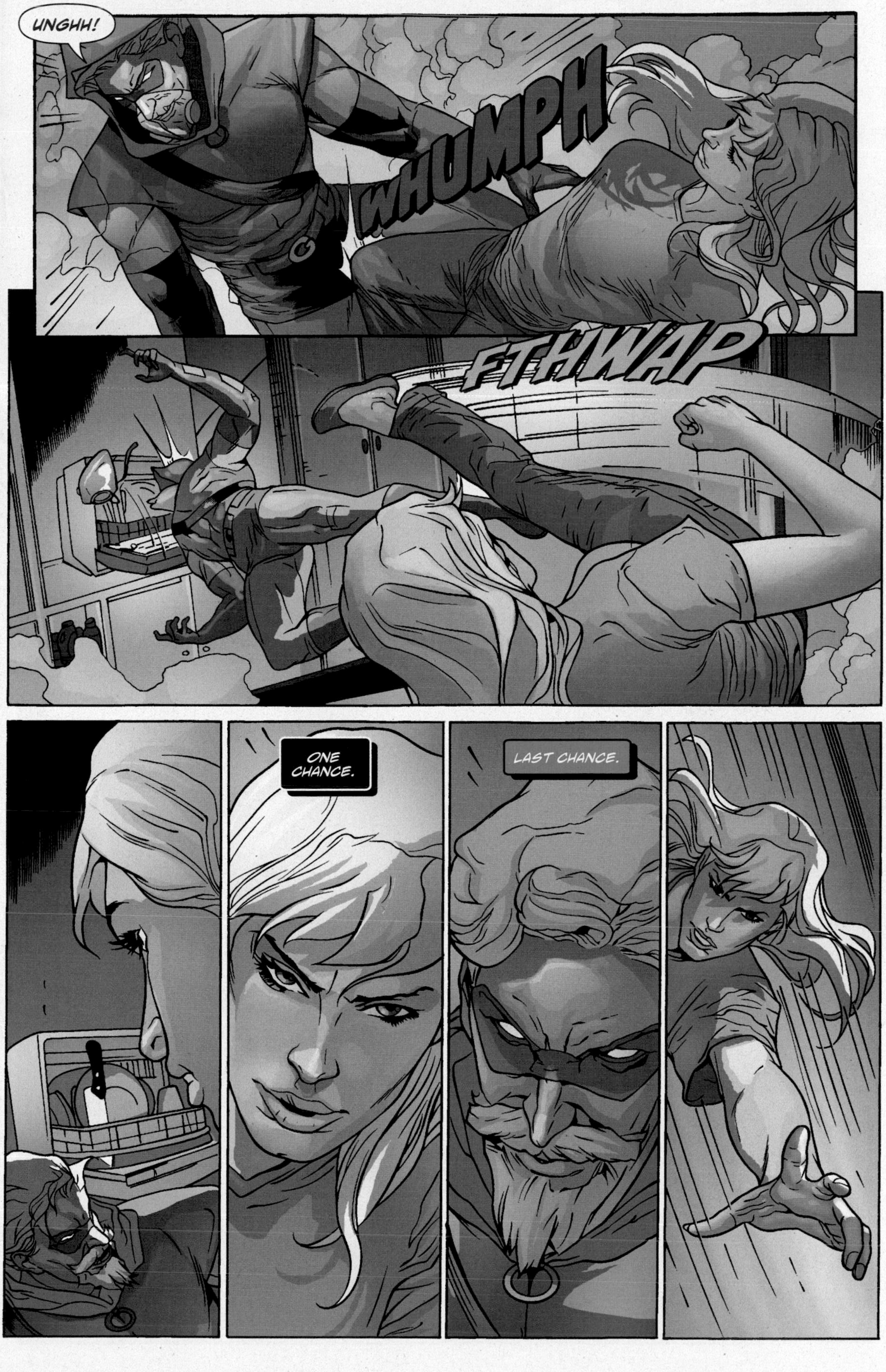
UNGHH!
WHUMPH
FTHWAP
ONE CHANCE.
LAST CHANCE.

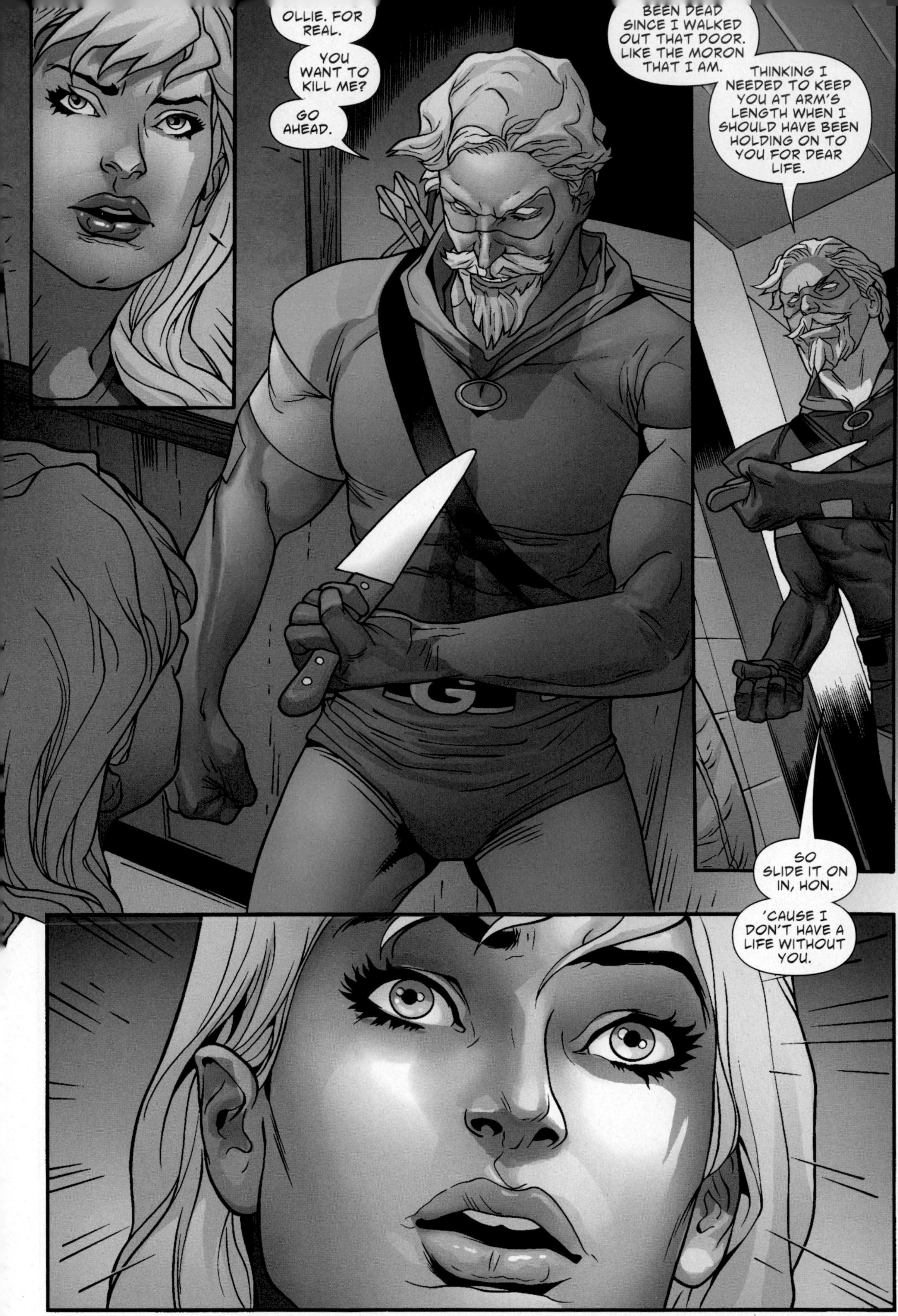
OLLIE. FOR REAL.
YOU WANT TO KILL ME?
GO AHEAD.
BEEN DEAD SINCE I WALKED OUT THAT DOOR. LIKE THE MORON THAT I AM.
THINKING I NEEDED TO KEEP YOU AT ARM'S LENGTH WHEN I SHOULD HAVE BEEN HOLDING ON TO YOU FOR DEAR LIFE.
SO SLIDE IT ON IN, HON.
'CAUSE I DON'T HAVE A LIFE WITHOUT YOU.

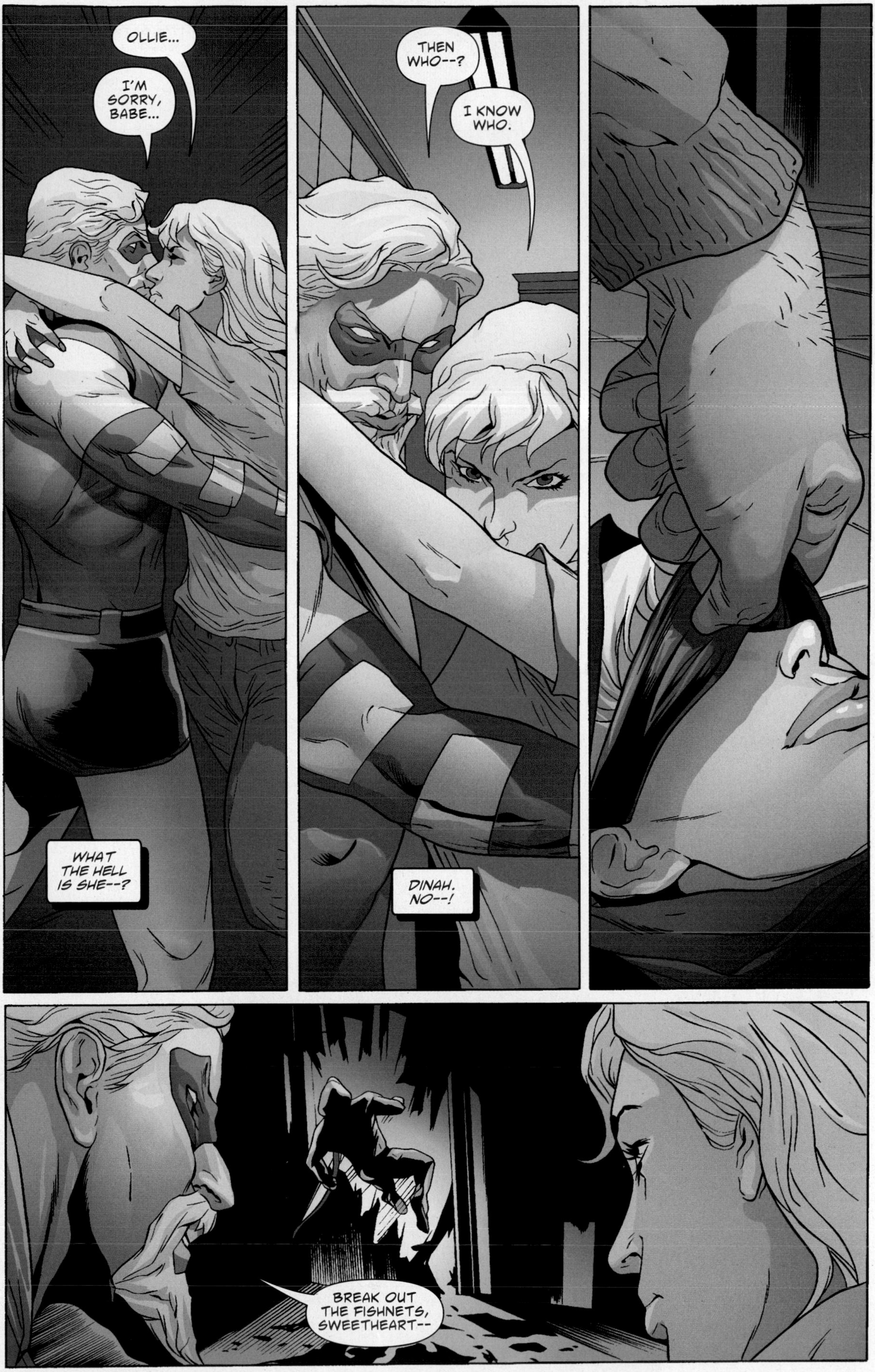
OLLIE...
I'M SORRY, BABE...
WHAT THE HELL IS SHE--?
THEN WHO--?
I KNOW WHO.
DINAH. NO--!
BREAK OUT THE FISHNETS, SWEETHEART--

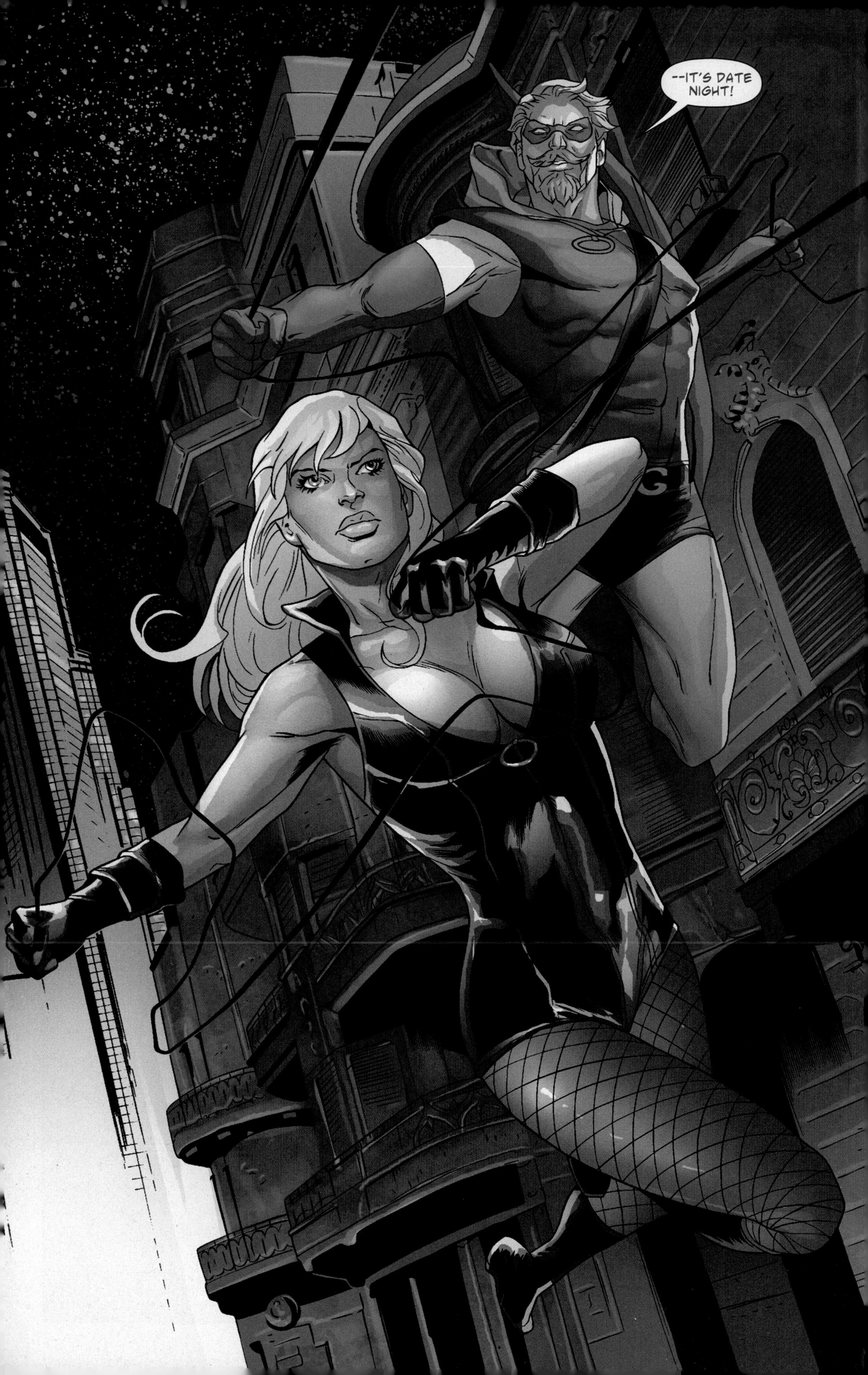
--IT'S DATE NIGHT!

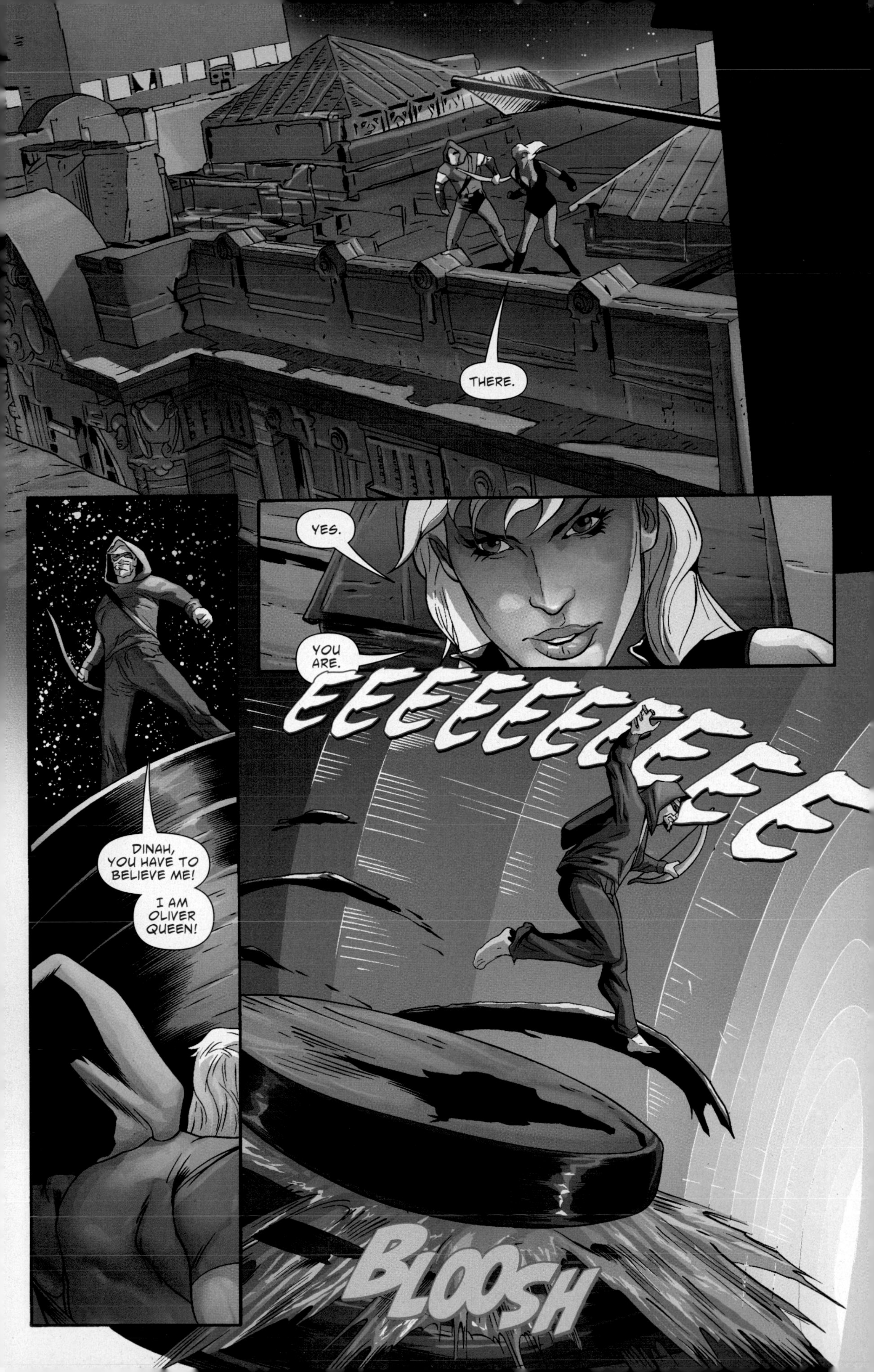
THERE.
YES.
YOU ARE.
DINAH, YOU HAVE TO BELIEVE ME!
I AM OLIVER QUEEN!
EEEEEEEEEEEEE
BLOOSH

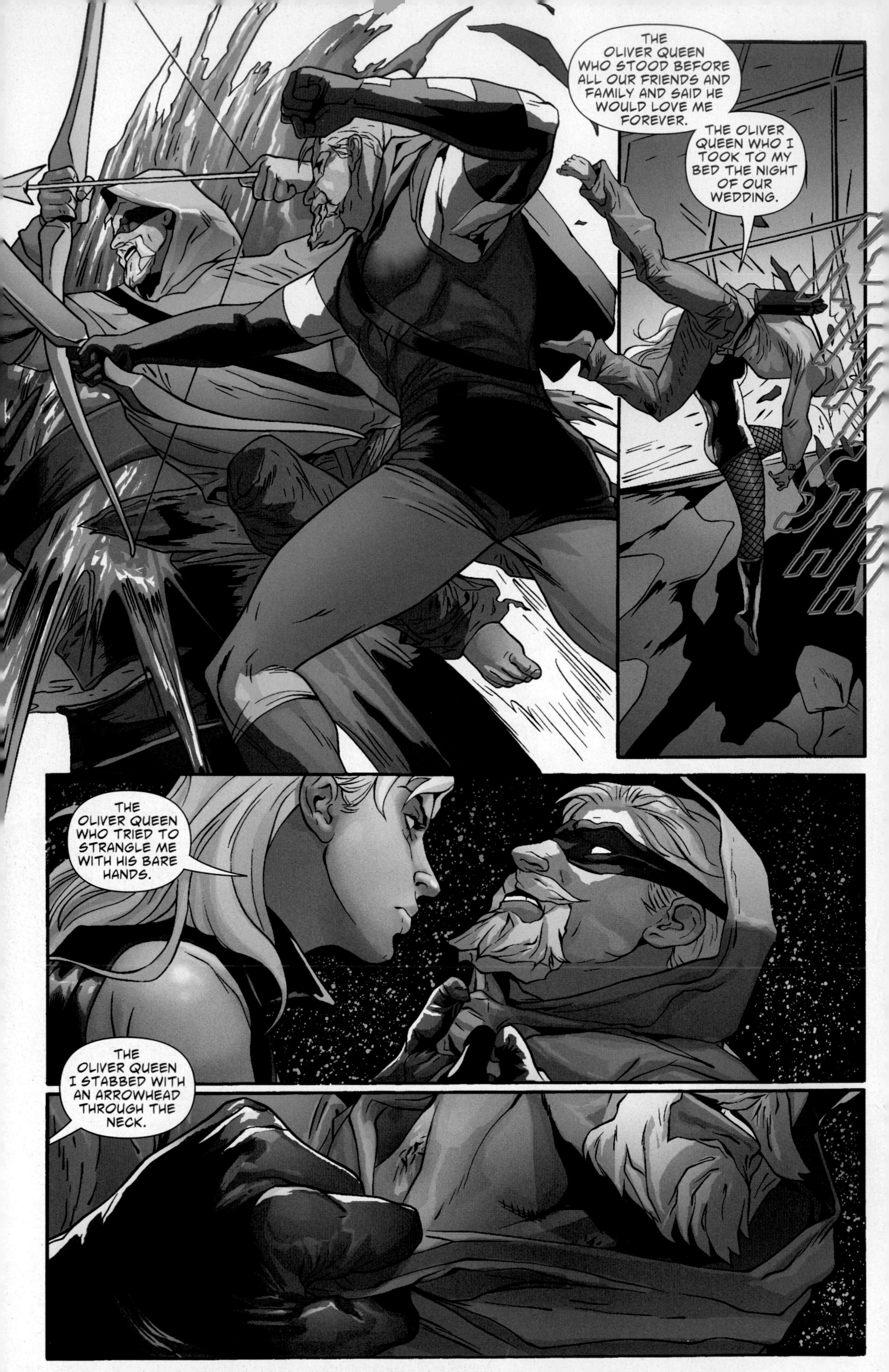
THE OLIVER QUEEN WHO STOOD BEFORE ALL OUR FRIENDS AND FAMILY AND SAID HE WOULD LOVE ME FOREVER.
THE OLIVER QUEEN WHO I TOOK TO MY BED THE NIGHT OF OUR WEDDING.
THE OLIVER QUEEN WHO TRIED TO STRANGLE ME WITH HIS BARE HANDS.
THE OLIVER QUEEN I STABBED WITH AN ARROWHEAD THROUGH THE NECK.

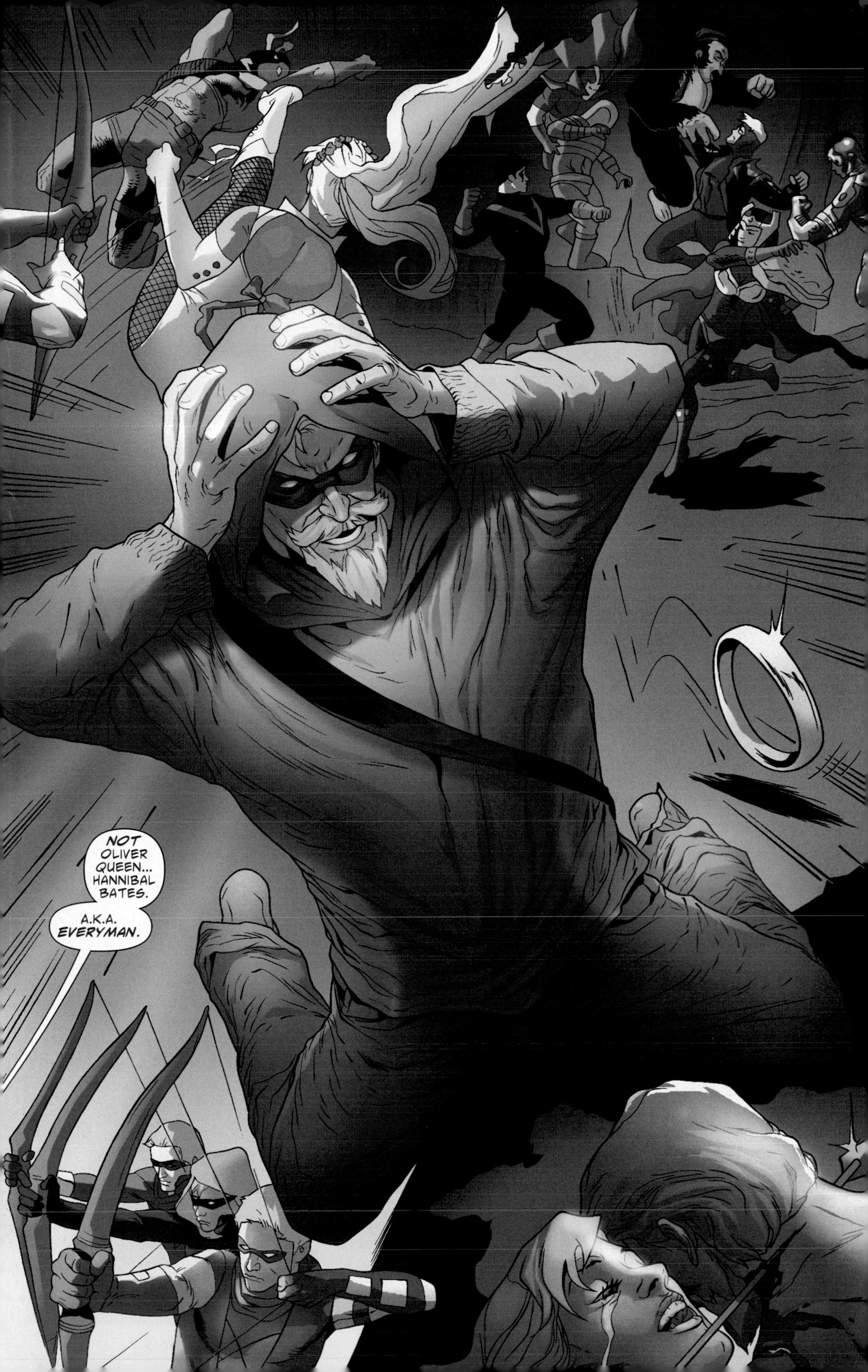
NOT OLIVER QUEEN... HANNIBAL BATES.
A.K.A. EVERYMAN.

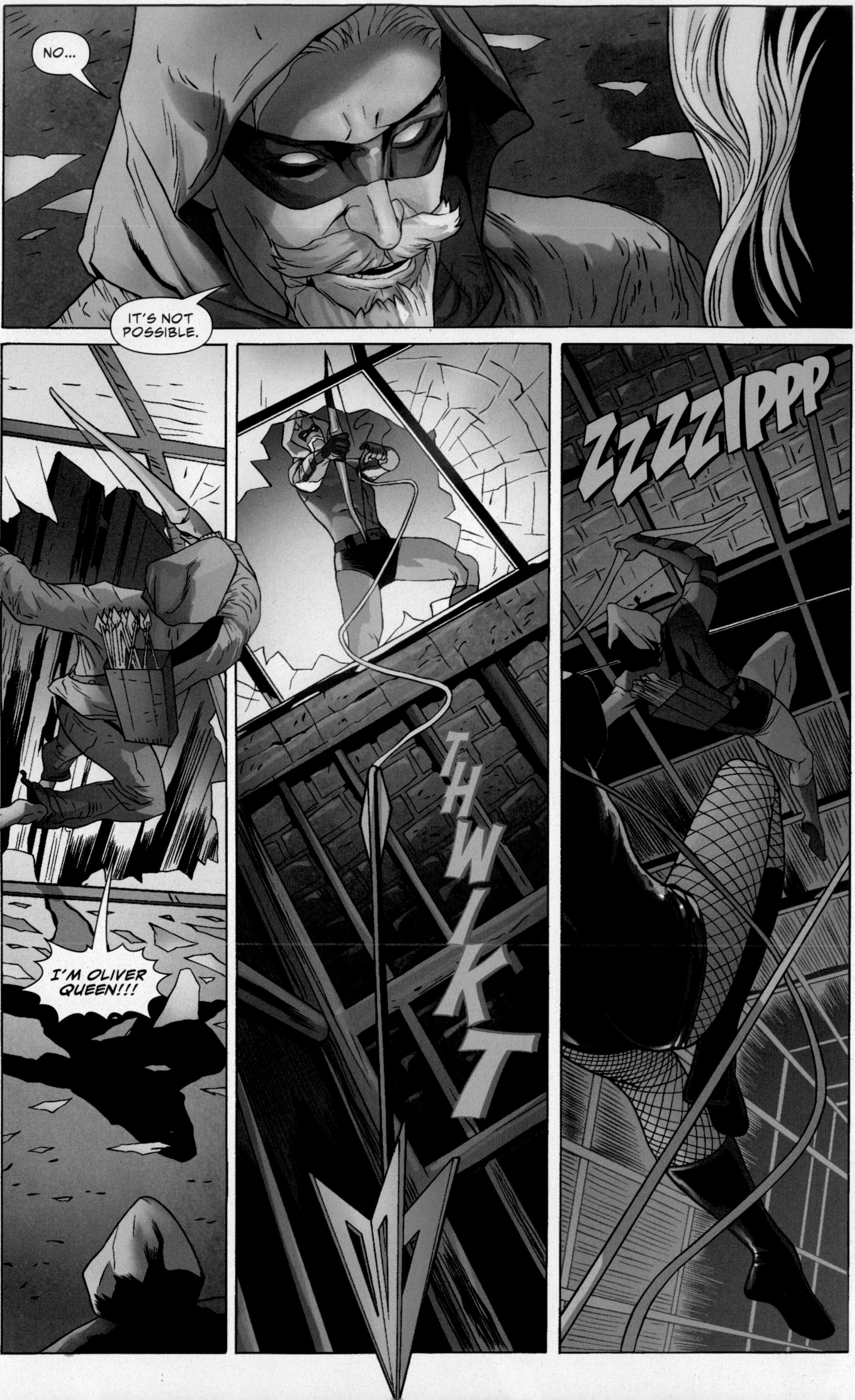
NO...
IT'S NOT POSSIBLE.
I'M OLIVER QUEEN!!!
THWIKT
ZZZZIPPP

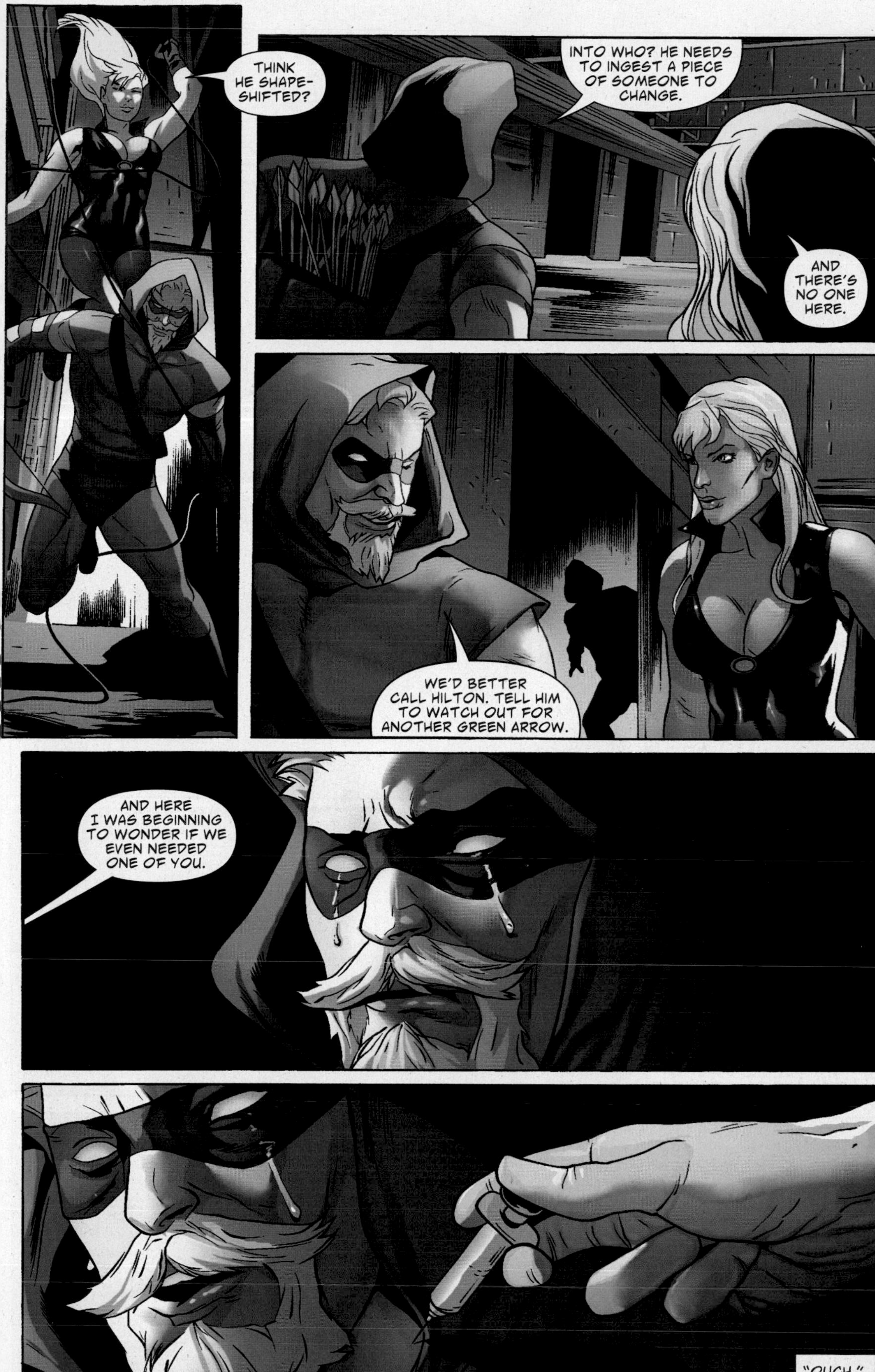
THINK HE SHAPE-SHIFTED?
INTO WHO? HE NEEDS TO INGEST A PIECE OF SOMEONE TO CHANGE.
AND THERE'S NO ONE HERE.
WE'D BETTER CALL HILTON. TELL HIM TO WATCH OUT FOR ANOTHER GREEN ARROW.
AND HERE I WAS BEGINNING TO WONDER IF WE EVEN NEEDED ONE OF YOU.
"OUCH."

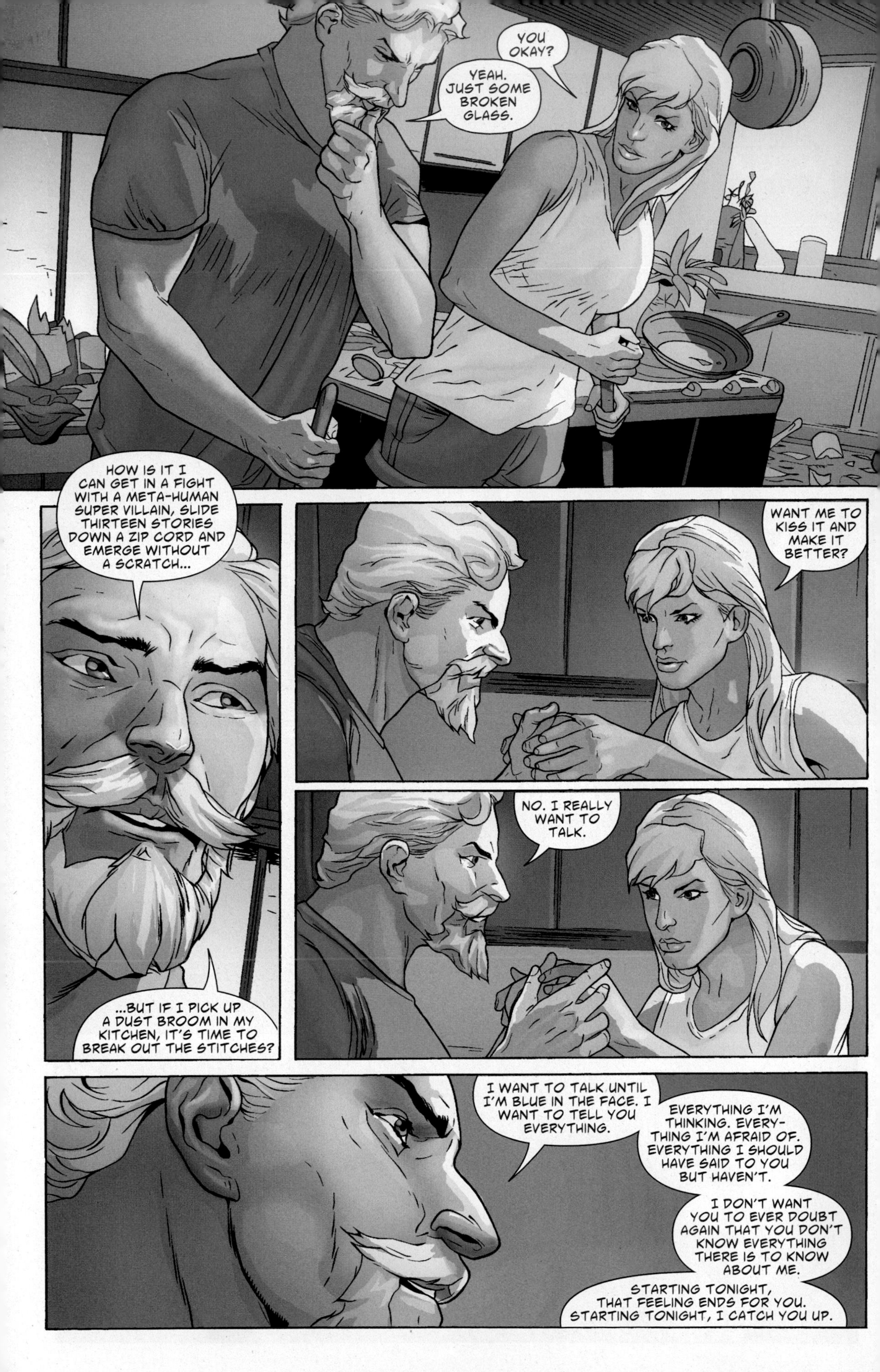
YOU OKAY?
YEAH. JUST SOME BROKEN GLASS.
HOW IS IT I CAN GET IN A FIGHT WITH A META-HUMAN SUPER VILLAIN, SLIDE THIRTEEN STORIES DOWN A ZIP CORD AND EMERGE WITHOUT A SCRATCH...
...BUT IF I PICK UP A DUST BROOM IN MY KITCHEN, IT'S TIME TO BREAK OUT THE STITCHES?
WANT ME TO KISS IT AND MAKE IT BETTER?
NO. I REALLY WANT TO TALK.
I WANT TO TALK UNTIL I'M BLUE IN THE FACE. I WANT TO TELL YOU EVERYTHING.
EVERYTHING I'M THINKING. EVERY-THING I'M AFRAID OF. EVERYTHING I SHOULD HAVE SAID TO YOU BUT HAVEN'T.
I DON'T WANT YOU TO EVER DOUBT AGAIN THAT YOU DON'T KNOW EVERYTHING THERE IS TO KNOW ABOUT ME.
STARTING TONIGHT, THAT FEELING ENDS FOR YOU. STARTING TONIGHT, I CATCH YOU UP.

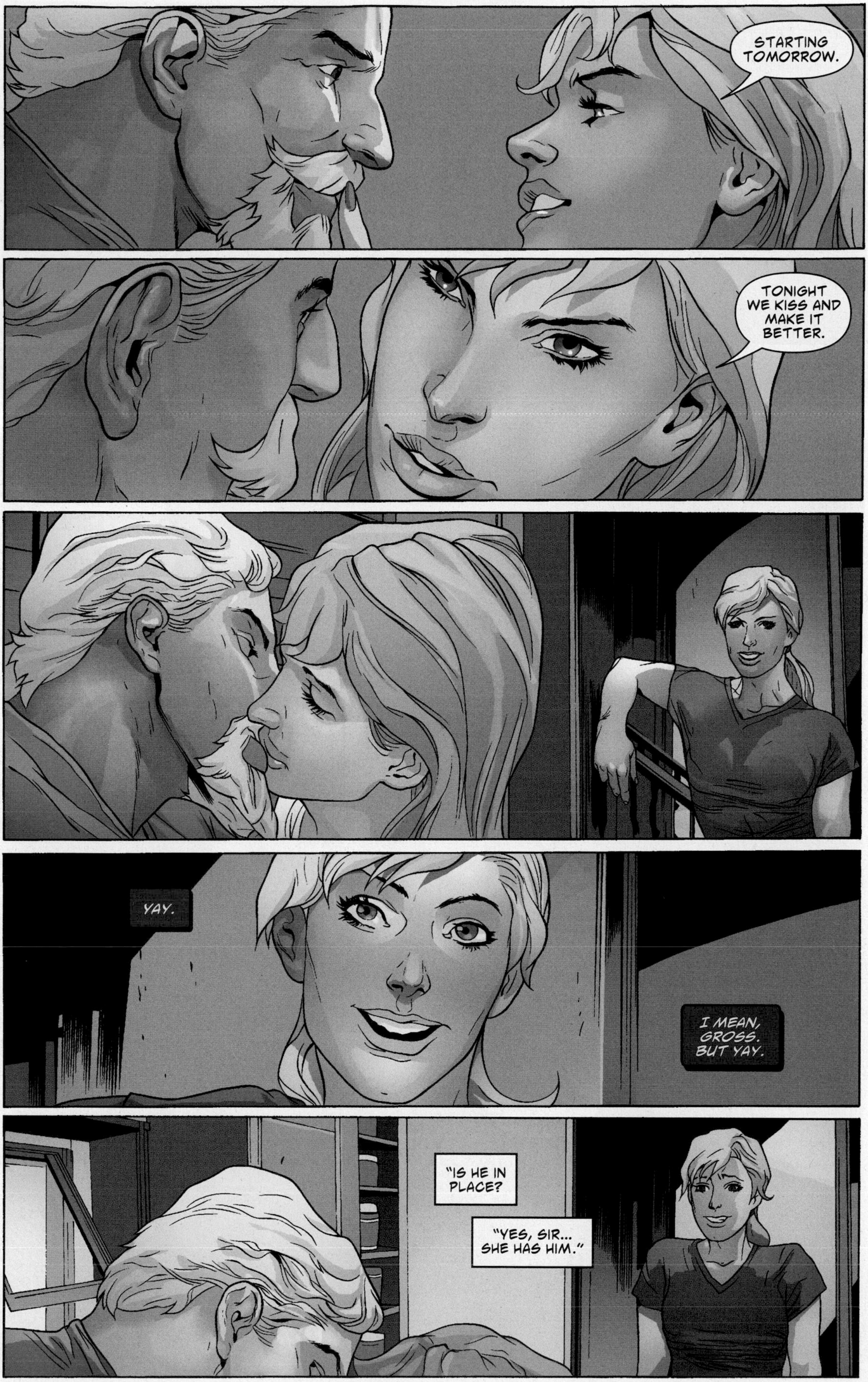
STARTING TOMORROW.
TONIGHT WE KISS AND MAKE IT BETTER.
YAY.
I MEAN, GROSS. BUT YAY.
"IS HE IN PLACE?
"YES, SIR... SHE HAS HIM."

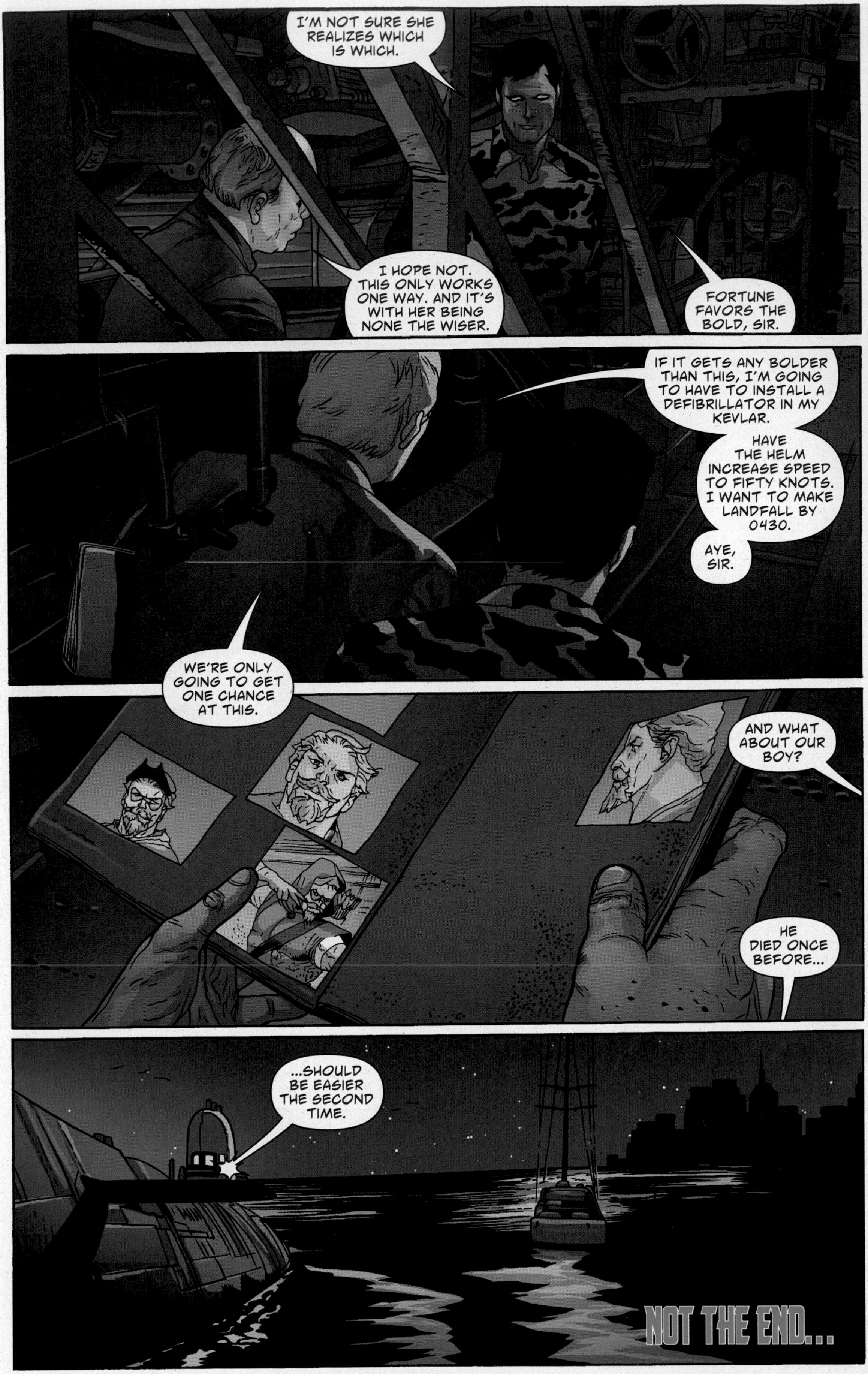
I'M NOT SURE SHE REALIZES WHICH IS WHICH.
I HOPE NOT. THIS ONLY WORKS ONE WAY. AND IT'S WITH HER BEING NONE THE WISER.
FORTUNE FAVORS THE BOLD, SIR.
IF IT GETS ANY BOLDER THAN THIS, I'M GOING TO HAVE TO INSTALL A DEFIBRILLATOR IN MY KEVLAR.
HAVE THE HELM INCREASE SPEED TO FIFTY KNOTS. I WANT TO MAKE LANDFALL BY 0430.
AYE, SIR.
WE'RE ONLY GOING TO GET ONE CHANCE AT THIS.
AND WHAT ABOUT OUR BOY?
HE DIED ONCE BEFORE...
...SHOULD BE EASIER THE SECOND TIME.
NOT THE END...

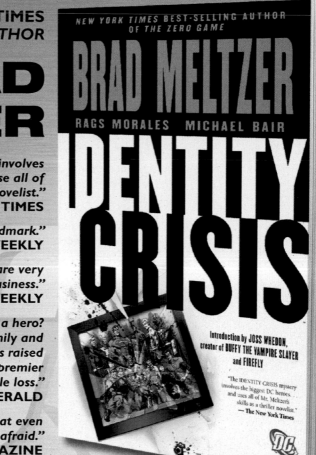